The Reformation in English Towns, 1500–1640

Themes in Focus

Published titles

Jonathan Barry and Christopher Brooks
THE MIDDLING SORT OF PEOPLE:
Culture, Society and Politics in England, 1550–1800

Patrick Collinson and John Craig
THE REFORMATION IN ENGLISH TOWNS, 1500–1640

Christopher Durston and Jacqueline Eales
THE CULTURE OF ENGLISH PURITANISM, 1560–1700

Paul Griffiths, Adam Fox and Steve Hindle
THE EXPERIENCE OF AUTHORITY IN EARLY MODERN
ENGLAND

Tim Harris
POPULAR CULTURE IN ENGLAND, *c.* 1500–1850

R. W. Scribner and Trevor Johnson
POPULAR RELIGION IN GERMANY AND CENTRAL EUROPE,
1400–1800

Themes in Focus
Series Standing Order
ISBN 0–333–71707–4 hardcover
ISBN 0–333–69353–1 paperback

(*outside North America only*)

You can receive future titles in this series as they are published by placing a standing order.
Please contact your bookseller or, in case of difficulty, write to us at the address below with
your name and address, the title of the series and the ISBN quoted above.

Customer Services Department, Macmillan Distribution Ltd
Houndmills, Basingstoke, Hampshire RG21 6XS, England

The Reformation in English Towns, 1500–1640

Edited by

PATRICK COLLINSON and JOHN CRAIG

First published in Great Britain 1998 by
MACMILLAN PRESS LTD
Houndmills, Basingstoke, Hampshire RG21 6XS and London
Companies and representatives throughout the world

A catalogue record for this book is available from the British Library.

ISBN 0–333–63430–6 hardcover
ISBN 0–333–63431–4 paperback

First published in the United States of America 1998 by
ST. MARTIN'S PRESS, INC.,
Scholarly and Reference Division,
175 Fifth Avenue, New York, N.Y. 10010

ISBN 0–312–21425–1

Library of Congress Cataloging-in-Publication Data
The Reformation in English towns, 1500–1640 / edited by Patrick
Collinson and John Craig.
p.   cm. — (Themes in focus)
Includes bibliographical references and index.
ISBN 0–312–21425–1
1. Reformation—England.   2. City and town life—England–
–History—16th century.   3. England—Church history—16th century.
4. City and town life—England—History—17th century.   5. England–
–Church history—17th century.   I. Collinson, Patrick.   II. Craig,
John, 1963– .   III. Series.
BR377.R44 1998
274.2'06'091732—dc21   98–4783
                                                              CIP

10   9   8   7   6   5   4   3   2   1
07   06   05   04   03   02   01   00   99   98

Printed in Hong Kong

Contents

Preface

It was John Craig, at about the time that John Major won his election in 1992, who first suggested to his former PhD supervisor, Patrick Collinson, the generation and production of a collection of essays on the Reformation in the English towns. John's thesis had dealt with the impact of the Protestant Reformation on four East Anglian towns: Bury St Edmunds, Hadleigh, Mildenhall and Thetford (none of them, as it happens, represented in this volume). Patrick's interest in the religious history of towns in the Elizabethan period had begun no later than the summer of 1952 when, freshly down from Cambridge and about to undertake postgraduate research in London, he cut his palaeographical teeth on the Great Court Book, Assembly Books, and Treasurer's and Chamberlain's Accounts of his native Ipswich, sitting in the Ipswich Reference Library under the watchful eye of the town archivist, a certain Mr Collinson (no relation). The material he transcribed in those early days has featured in more than one of the books he was to publish many years later. But in 1976, returning to the English university scene from Australia, he failed to write the essay on the urban Reformation which had been commissioned for an earlier Macmillan collection, *Church and Society in England from Henry VIII to James I* (1977). Fortunately Bill Sheils, another former pupil, stepped into that breach. Patrick would later write what he might have contributed to the Macmillan volume in 'The Protestant Town', the second chapter of his *The Birthpangs of Protestant England*, which Macmillan published in 1988.

Patrick Collinson and John Craig have been fortunate in attracting an excellent team of mostly younger and relatively unpublished historians whose work has centred on the religious history of the early modern town, or which has touched significantly on that subject. They include Mark Byford, whose Oxford DPhil thesis, completed before he was lured into the City of London (which, for the purposes of this volume does not count as an English town), was an early harbinger of the post-revisionist stage into which English reformation studies have now moved; David Lamburn, whose thesis on that jewel of the later English Middle Ages, Beverley, and what happened to its great churches after the Reformation, was supervised in York by Professor Claire Cross; Caroline Litzenberger, whose Cambridge thesis on the impact of religious change on the laity of sixteenth-century Gloucestershire will shortly be published by the Cambridge University Press; Jeanette Martin, for whom the invitation to contribute to this volume was an opportunity to bring to fruition work begun long ago on the Reformation in Reading; Patrick Carter, another Cambridge PhD, who is an expert on Henry VIII's bright idea to place a permanent and differentially punitive tax on the clergy; the late Sir Geoffrey Elton's pupil Peter Cunich, whose doctoral work on the Court of Augmentations has led to postdoctoral research into the dissolution of the chantries; Beat Kümin, a Swiss pupil of Peter Blickle of Berne and of Patrick Collinson in Cambridge, whose book *The Shaping of a Community: The Rise and Reformation of the English Parish c.1400–1560* both inaugurated an important new series, 'St Andrews Studies in Reformation History', and set new standards for the rigorous study of the financial records of the English parishes; and Adam Fox, a Cambridge pupil of Keith Wrightson, whose book on early modern oral culture will appear shortly. The team could only be strengthened by the accession of four relative veterans: Claire Cross and Bill Sheils (reinforced on this occasion by Sarah Sheils) who between them know almost all there is to be known about the Church in the north in the sixteenth and seventeenth centuries; Thomas Cranmer's biographer, Diarmaid MacCulloch; and a leading authority on the public affairs and public architecture of the early modern town, Bob Tittler.

It is not the fault of any of these contributors that it has taken so long to put this collection of essays into the hands of the reader. If there is to be any blame it must be attached, if not to the editors, to their circumstances. We had no sooner set the whole enterprise in motion than John Craig began to teach in Canada, and not just Canada but what Arabs would call the Maghreb al Aqsa of Canada, British Columbia. The eight-hour time difference alone between Collinson in Cambridge and Craig in Simon Fraser University complicated editorial communications, and with John Craig teaching his first courses and Patrick Collinson his last, as he wound up affairs in Cambridge and moved house, matters did not progress as might have been hoped. And then, when everything seemed to be in place, it emerged that we had all written (if our copious endnotes were taken into account) more than Macmillan were able to publish. To extricate ourselves from these difficulties required more generous forbearance from contributors and the difficult decision to jettison John Craig's revisionist essay on the Reformation in Hadleigh and its most famous reformer, Dr Rowland Taylor, which will tell us that, unlike the idealised account of Hadleigh written by John Foxe, the struggle for reformation in this East Anglian cloth town was so fiercely contested that the energies for further reform under Elizabeth were all but dissipated. This essay will now appear in another place. In spite of these difficulties, we are at one with all editors in the series 'Problems in Focus' and 'Themes in Focus' in enjoying and acknowledging the professional help and guidance of the commissioning editors of Macmillan Press and their staff, mentioning particularly Vanessa Graham, Simon Winder and Jonathan Reeve.

Each author makes his own acknowledgement of the help of institutions and individuals which went to the making of his essay. (And, in what follows, for 'his', always read 'his and her'.) What may be said in general is that every historian who attempts to write local, and especially urban, history on the basis of local archives discovers two things. As he jostles for a seat among those hordes of amateur genealogists, always working in pairs (but where would our county record offices be without them?), he invariably finds among the staff not just friendly courtesy but a standard of professional expertise which was rarer when some of us first started. And he is only too liable to find (as Patrick Collinson found in his Shrewsbury study) that usually there is some local historian or antiquarian on the spot who knows far more about the subject than he is ever likely to learn, and who is not over-possessive of his knowledge. We are glad of this opportunity to thank all these helpful people. And, finally, warmest thanks to all our contributors and to our publishers.

PATRICK COLLINSON
JOHN CRAIG

Introduction

PATRICK COLLINSON AND JOHN CRAIG

I

One of the most striking developments of the later twentieth century in the historiography of Tudor and Stuart England has been its localisation. One might, to borrow the title of a notable book on the coming of the English Civil War, speak of a 'revolt of the provinces',[1] a revolt against a history conceptually and archivally anchored in the centre of government in London, or rather Westminster, looking from that centre outwards, and sometimes not very far. Among the causes of this quiet revolution has been the opening up of the rich archives of provincial England in well-organised and accessible county and other local record offices, a post-Second World War development; and the exploitation of these facilities by hundreds of young researchers looking for new subjects for their doctoral theses and monographs. This book is only the latest sheaf of studies in this rich harvest.

We are not talking about the invention of local history, a peripheral pursuit which has a very long and respectable pedigree, but about the writing of national history as the history of the localities of which the nation consisted, interacting with each other and with central authority. Many good books on the Civil War in this or that county were written before our quiet revolution began.[2] But only with the publication of Alan Everitt's *The Community of Kent and the Great Rebellion* (Leicester, 1966) were we confronted with the proposition that these events could only be understood from the standpoint of the county, a place on the map (the maps of coloured counties comprising Saxton's *Atlas* of 1578) many seventeenth-century English gentry considered to be their 'country', first and foremost. This was 'localism', the existential world of the past recovered: and localism ruled, until its worst excesses were revealed, and it gave way to new master narratives of the age, and especially to 'the British Problem'.[3]

If the Civil War was a subject transformed by the new localism, so was the English Reformation. A. G. Dickens's book of that title, first published in 1964,[4] was the consummating achievement of a major

1

scholar whose apprenticeship and early experience as a journeyman historian had taken him, machete in hand, into the dense archives of Yorkshire and of the ecclesiastical province of York, at a time when those fastnesses were hardly more accessible than the African rainforest to its original explorers. These local researches[5] had persuaded Dickens that the Reformation was much more than a political and legislated transaction, contained in acts of Parliament and injunctions imposed, for its own reasons, by an effective royal administration. The secret of its success would be found at the grass-roots, even at a popular level. Protestantism was an idea whose time had come.

The English Reformation was, amongst other things, a call to younger historians to follow the Dickensian example, in the more favourable conditions obtaining in the local record offices in the 1960s and 1970s, and the call was answered in numerous books, articles and essays on the Protestant Reformation in this or that region and county and by the regular conferences now held on the local history of the English Reformation.[6] But, according to Dr Christopher Haigh, the results were not those which Dickens had expected. What came out of these intensified local investigations was that so-called 'revisionism' which has emphasised the religious conservatism of the majority of sixteenth-century Englishmen, the consequential difficulties impeding the progress of the Reformation at a popular level, and even its ultimate failure, or very limited success.[7] This was not, as some suppose, Catholicism taking its posthumous revenge. Many of these revisionists, Haigh included, are not Roman Catholics and appear to have no confessional motivation. They are more or less faithfully reporting what they find in the historical record.[8]

Revisionism in this sense receives support from several essays in this collection, not only from Caroline Litzenberger's story of a reluctant and ambivalent Reformation in Tewkesbury, but from Beat Kümin's account of the ways in which the Reformation as an act of state brought an end to the flourishing and essentially voluntary activities of urban parishioners. However, it is far from our intention in this volume to wade deeper into a debate which threatens to become sterile, an argument about 'fast' versus 'slow' reformation, 'from above' or 'from below'. The intention is less polemical: to suggest the importance of the towns in the story of the English Reformation, and equally the importance of the Reformation for the towns. These essays are so many variegated answers to the double question: What did the towns do for the Reformation, and what did the Reformation do for the towns?

II

A more direct product of the new localism, flourishing alongside the investigation of politics and society in the counties, has been the growth of interest in urban history. This was fostered by an early Open University course on the subject, and by the University of Leicester, with its distinctive commitment to English local history. Peter Clark of Leicester and Paul Slack of Exeter and Linacre Colleges, Oxford, have pioneered the socio-economic history of the English town at what appears to have been a critical moment of transition;[9] while Charles Phythian-Adams of Leicester University's Department of Local History wrote a seminal book on Coventry at the cusp of the later Middle Ages and the early modern period with a title which catches the mood and perspective of much of this literature: *Desolation of a City*.[10] For Coventry as a manufacturing and trading centre was in steep decline as it entered the sixteenth century, and so, apparently, were many other provincial towns. Contraction and crisis were the order of the day: declining industries, receding markets, demographic attrition.[11] A more recent chronological shift towards the eighteenth century, marked especially by Peter Borsay's discovery of an urban renaissance taking off in the later seventeenth century, has tended to deepen the shadows through which the Tudor and early Stuart town has been perceived.[12]

The underlying, and perhaps uncontroversial, assumption of much of this literature, an assumption with debts both to Marxist history and to the methodology of the French *Annales* school, has been that the history of towns, as perhaps of all social forms, is essentially infrastructural, a matter of demography, distributive economics and consequential social arrangements and readjustments. How do the religious and cultural changes we call the Reformation fit into this scenario? It is hard to say. It is not the case that the Clark-Slack school has reduced religion to economics and social relations, although, to cite one example, Professor Clark was inclined to explain the philopuritanism of early seventeenth-century Gloucester in some such terms.[13] It is rather the case that there has been surprisingly little conversation between Reformation historians and urban historians. They belong, as it were, to different clubs and do not conduct their business in the same seminars and conferences. Urban history with the religion left out, or distinctly marginalised, has been the stronger of these suits. In spite of an almost exponential expansion of Reformation Studies, thanks in equal measure to Professor Dickens, his pupils and his critics, the Reformation in the towns is still a strangely neglected topic.

The position has been the opposite to what we find in the historiography of the German cities in the sixteenth century. The history of the German Reformation has always been understood to concern, after the German princes, the great imperial cities, such as Nuremberg, Augsburg, Strasbourg. And if the history of the Reformation has been dominated by the cities, the history of the cities was once equally dominated by the Reformation, as if their conversion to Protestantism, and, in some cases, reconversion in the Counter-Reformation, was all or most of what happened to these places in the course of the sixteenth century.[14] More recent work has put the religious factor firmly in its place. For example the city of Erfurt, where Martin Luther received his education, was Coventry on a larger scale: a city in economic crisis, its internal and external politics in turmoil. Luther's Gospel was a further exacerbating and complicating factor, not the whole story.[15]

If it was necessary to put the politics and the socio-economics back into the story of the Reformation in the German cities, it is no less desirable to recognise religion as occupying a centrally important position in the history of the English towns. For, to quote Debora Shuger and to make a point which has almost universal validity for the period, religion was 'the master-card of pre-capitalist society', 'the cultural matrix for explorations of virtually every topic', 'the discourse through which it interpreted its own existence'.[16]

The institutions of religion, and especially the parishes, and, before the Reformation, guilds and fraternities, provided much of the structural fabric of urban life. Governing elites bore office in their parishes and guilds as well as in their crafts and companies, and we need to know how these different forms of power and responsibility in office interrelated and contributed to the government of the town as a whole.[17] Factional politics, a marked feature of town life in the later sixteenth and early seventeenth centuries, often ran along religious fault-lines. Did religion and religious change make for faction, or did faction, understood materially as a matter of competition for scarce resources and for a limited number of profitable and prestigious offices, draw religion into its magnetic field? Or was it a bit of both? David

Lamburn's essay on Beverley provides an instructive case-study of how these relations worked out in one town after the Reformation.

The urban culture of late medieval England – 'Merry England' – was, in large part, a culture contained and expressed in religious forms. Space and time, the limits and divisions of the city and the rhythm of the civic year, were religious space and time, marked on the one hand by religious perambulations and processions, on the other by a religious calendar.[18] Religion was not invested only in church buildings, although these were the principal monuments to civic pride, prime objects of expenditure, and places used for all kinds of meetings and business before there was very much civic architecture as such. It spilled out on to the streets, in procession, and in the 'mysteries', the street theatre of religious play cycles which, with the richly decorated churches themselves, were the principal creative achievement of the late medieval town. The University of Toronto enterprise, Records of Early English Drama, reflected in some of the essays in this volume, and especially Patrick Collinson's on Shrewsbury and Adam Fox's on religious satire, has supplied us with a wide window on this cultural scene through the opening up of the urban archives.[19]

What one historian of the late medieval drama and its demise called *Mysteries' End* was a major casualty of religious change, the full consequences of which have yet to be explored. The Reformation in the towns, as elsewhere, reduced the numbers of holidays and severely rationalised the festive calendar. Sunday, in the perception of growing numbers of those influential in urban affairs, was now almost the only holy day, and it was to be observed with a strict and redefined religious discipline which limited and even excluded what the sixteenth century called 'pastime'. So did the Reformation in the towns reduce the space and time for leisure and recreation, or did it relocate it in more secular forms?[20]

The urban politics of the period had somewhere near its centre the relations of clergy and laity, the townsmen and their priests and ministers. These relations were radically altered by the Reformation, which drastically reduced the numbers of clergy, from 200 religious and about the same number of secular, parish clergy to a fraction of that number in the case of York;[21] and which rationalised the parochial structure. The number of parish churches in York halved, Lincoln's thirty-eight became nine, Stamford's eleven, six.[22] The frustration of a plan to use an act of parliament to do the same for Exeter became a political sore point in the 1590s.[23]

A great deal of prime urban real estate passed from clerical to lay ownership and management. Peter Cunich's essay deals with one of the most important parts of this process: the confiscation of the chantries and the reallocation of their resources: a mostly negative story. But Robert Tittler explores the resourcefulness and opportunism of many towns in securing some of these assets for the common good and for the future. This was one material precondition for the efflorescence of civic pride which Professor Tittler has celebrated elsewhere in his *Architecture and Power: the Town Hall and the English Urban Community, c.1500–1640* (Oxford, 1991).[24]

Was one of the motive forces behind these changes that 'anticlericalism' which A. G. Dickens put at the centre of his account of the origins of the Reformation?[25] Anticlericalism is a term imported from the politics of another country and another age (late nineteenth-century France)[26] and while it would be foolish to affirm that there was no antagonism or conflict of interest between the clergy, as an occupation and almost a class, and the rest of society, between those who benefited from tithes and those who paid tithes, it is equally a mistake to inflate these differences into a master explanatory principle of anticlericalism. As several of these essays show, the clergy were not, for the most part, interlopers and strangers in their towns, but often well-connected members of provincial society, who had depended upon those connections to get where they were. Patrick Carter observes: 'Urban parish clergy were usually local men, frequently working in the same parish in which their parents and siblings worshipped and were buried.' So far as financial matters were concerned, Dr Carter suggests that it was not in the interest of townsmen that their clergy should find it hard to make ends meet. He leads with the story of the petition made by Coventry in 1548 to relieve the burden of taxation on the vicar of one of its two parish churches. Far from taking pleasure in the financial embarrassment of its clergy, Coventry's leading citizens made the point that a fall in the value of the vicarage had made it hard to fill the living with a pastor capable of feeding his flock with God's word and ministering the sacraments.

Beat Kümin's exploration of what he calls 'voluntary religion' in a sample of eight mostly urban pre-Reformation parishes further emphasises the shared interest and activity of the laity, especially in their role as churchwardens, in the funding of religious life and the sustenance of the parochial community. Inner-city parishes in particular 'distinguished themselves by the sheer size of the resources they were able to invest and by the range of options they could support.'[27] This takes us a long way from Christopher Hill's definition of the parish as a 'compulsory community', and the suggestion that religious voluntarism was a product of the Protestant Reformation and a solvent of the parish.[28] On the contrary, the Reformation, which is to say, the Tudor state, by limiting the available fund-raising religious options and by its vastly enhanced and coercive interest in the parish, not only as a community worshipping in uniformity, but as a unit of social administration, and especially poor relief, limited the discretionary powers of parish officers and robbed the religious life of the parish church of some of its late medieval spontaneity.

But, by contrast, David Lamburn's essay on the interaction of religion and politics in late sixteenth-century and early seventeenth-century Beverley suggests that Christopher Hill was not wrong in all respects. Religious voluntarism could re-enter the scene in critical opposition to political elites, and could provide a crucible of radical conscience and activism. We conclude that voluntarism and compulsion existed in creative if sometimes corrosive mix and tension both before and after the Reformation.

If anticlericalism is a dubious term and tool, 'secularisation' is even more slippery. To what extent was the English town secularised as a consequence of the Protestant Reformation? In the most literal sense, and one which the sixteenth century would have recognised, there was some secularisation. That is to say, the religious orders were dissolved, leaving only 'secular' clergy, which meant the disappearance of the various kinds of friars, Franciscans, Dominicans, Carmelites. There was also secularisation of the urban properties which the friars had occupied. In Ipswich, the priory of the Holy Trinity became the prestigious mansion of Peter Withipoll, Christchurch House: in later years a municipal park and museum where one of the editors of this volume undertook his earliest, involuntary excursions. In Canterbury, the Dominican house, or 'Blackfriars', was converted into a factory, while in Cambridge its sister house, rather more felicitously, became a college: Emmanuel.

To read John Stow's late sixteenth-century *Survey of London*, one would almost think that religion itself was a casualty of the Protestant Reformation, so all-pervasive and persuasive is the tone of nostalgic regret for the old religion and the old ways, and especially for what Stow, remembering his youth, called 'that declining time of charity', the passing of an era of 'charity, hospitality and plenty'. But

Dr Ian Archer has shown that Stow's nostalgia was distorting and misleading.[29] Late Elizabethan London devoted more of its resources to the poor, not less, explored and established new forms and expressions of community, and even spent generously on the fabric of its churches. There was perhaps more rationality, less casual spontaneity, but the motive was no less religious, if differently religious, than it had been in the world John Stow thought he had lost.

III

If the Reformation secularised, it also sacralised. In the words of the historian of early modern Bristol, there was 'sanctification of power'.[30] The Protestant town or city had an enhanced sense of its sacred character, as it aspired to become one of those cities set on a hill of which Jesus had spoken in Matthew chapter 5, verse 14: 'Ye are the light of the world. A city that is set on an hill cannot be hid.' The pattern and exemplum of such a city was Jerusalem, set in the hill country of Judaea: 'Whither the tribes go up, the tribes of the Lord' (Psalm 122:4).

Other words from Psalm 122 have been familiar to generations of English churchgoers: 'Jerusalem is built as a city that is at unity in itself'; or, in the Geneva Bible version, 'that is compact together in itself', commenting in the margin on 'the concord and love that was between the citizens'. Whatever Stow may have thought, the thirst for godly unity and concord seems to have been heightened, not diminished, in the Protestant town. But we are told that the original Hebrew of the 122nd Psalm does not necessarily carry these positive connotations of virtuous solidarity. It may have meant that Jerusalem was a city full of people, and perhaps too full.[31] And even if Jerusalem was a city under God's special and watchful eye, that did not mean that it was pure and spotless. Quite the contrary. Christ had wept over Jerusalem as a city which had killed the prophets, foretelling its utter destruction. Preaching at Paul's Cross in London, Bishop Edwin Sandys applied the moral: 'Our Lord and Saviour Jesus Christ, . . . casting his eyes toward the city of Jerusalem, bewailed the lamentable estate thereof, and that with tears. The like effect . . . I find in myself, beholding this Jerusalem of ours, this famous city.'[32]

As with its attitude to its youth, or to the nation as a whole, the Protestant mind, which dealt instinctively in polarities and dichotomies, regarded the towns with a mixture of equally exaggerated hope and despair, maximising the capacity for both reformation and moral declension. The obverse of Jerusalem in the minds of many was Babel/Babylon (often conflated and associated with Rome), or even Sodom and Gomorrah. Diligent readers of the maps in the Genevan Bible might see for themselves the judgement of God upon those towns represented as they were in the midst of flames, which proved no doubt a sobering thought for the godly when faced with the fires that consumed much of Dorchester in 1613 or Bury St Edmunds in 1608.[33] It was Bishop Hugh Latimer who thought that 'whoring in towns' was replacing the commendable pursuit of archery[34] and one Jacobean writer observed that 'great sins' often had their origin in the city 'from hence derived to the country.'[35] But, by the same token, if London and other 'great towns' could be once reformed, reform would spread to the countryside, along with that precious commodity, 'civility'.

So while London and other towns provided moralists with particularly striking examples of depravity, organised and even commercialised (pubs, gaming houses, brothels, theatres), they paradoxically afforded the best model of the good life. If civility was the product of the town grammar school, an institution especially indicative of these values, godliness was disseminated primarily from the pulpit. To be sure, there were sermons in plenty before the Reformation. But now a higher value was placed on preaching, which was heightened in its tone of moral urgency and outrage, exclusively biblical in its terms of reference, and prophetic in the double sense that it drew liberally on the prophetic texts of the Old Testament and assumed the same prophetic rhetorical voice. From the pulpits erected in or just outside the principal urban churches, with Paul's Cross in London the supreme example, both nation and city were taken to task and apostrophised: 'O England!' 'O London'![36]

Towns without their own preachers demanded them, or, rather, select groups within the towns made their urgent representations. Parliament (probably the parliament of 1584) was told by the 'inhabitants' of Witham in Essex that 'notwithstandinge the cleere light of the Gospell', they lived 'in ignorance of the will of God and the waye of salvation, because the worde of God hathe not been ordinarilie preached and expounded unto us'. The document bears just six signatures.[37]

Readers of these essays will meet with stirring preachers, some of whom made almost as much difference to their adopted towns (and,

unlike the general run of the clergy, they were often imported strangers)
as Calvin did to Geneva; John Pulleyne and Thomas Upcher in
Colchester, John Tomkys in Shrewsbury, John Favour, one of the all-
time greats, in Halifax. Beverley by the later sixteenth century was a
heavily preached-over town.

As Patrick Collinson has shown,[38] the ambition of many a town was
to secure the services, at heavy cost if need be, of a town (or 'common')
preacher of commanding presence and moral authority, the public
conscience of the town and a kind of *de facto* bishop, like the *antistes* of
a German or Swiss Reformation city, on the model of Zwingli in
Zürich, Haller in Berne, or Bucer in Strasbourg. In 1582 in King's
Lynn in Norfolk, the aldermen and common councillors prepared to
appoint a preaching minister for one of the town parishes, such 'as
Mr Saunderson our preacher shall like of'. William Saunderson had
served as town preacher from about 1573 and was a powerful and
controversial figure. In 1577, the corporation 'for the favour and good
will which they bear to Mr Saunderson their preacher', agreed to
repair and improve his house; and in 1586 he was allowed as much
stone as he needed from one of the dissolved friaries for further exten-
sions. When Saunderson got into trouble for nonconformity, the town
rallied to his defence.[39] So it was with a much more famous figure,
Samuel Ward of Ipswich, fifty years later. Bishops of Norwich who
dared to confront this formidable puritan preacher could find themselves literally driven out of town.[40]

But to turn away from East Anglia to Caroline Litzenberger's
account of Tewkesbury, one of our case studies: the absence of a
preacher of this commanding stature was both effect and cause of the
religious mediocrity of a town which as late as the turn of the sixteenth
and seventeenth centuries was still nurturing a religious drama which
had died the death almost everywhere else.

What consolidated the Reformation in many, perhaps most, towns
where it proved a success was the alliance of magistrates and ministers:
the staff and, if need be, sword of severe and righteous justice upheld
and encouraged by godly preachers of the Word. Towns without a
preacher of their own encouraged the clergy of the surrounding country to form a regular preaching rota, with the magistrates entertaining
them to dinner. At Thetford in Norfolk, the preacher 'shall be had to
dinner at one of the burgess's howses, viz, one burgess one day and an
other the other day.[41] William Burton, remembering through rose-
coloured spectacles how it was in Elizabethan Norwich, provides us

with the paradigm: 'the magistrates and ministers imbracing and sec-onding one another, and the common people affording due reverence and obedience to them both.'[42] Such, at least, was the ideal, widely subscribed to. On the other side of England, at Bishops Castle in Shropshire, it was said that its Jacobean minister was 'so grave and discreet, that the grave Aldermen of the Towne would not act any thing of importance without him'; and that the town was 'famoused' from him.[43]

During the long reign of Elizabeth, it was in the urban context that such familiar features of reformation as town preachers, weekly lectures and 'combinations' of preachers,[44] the tightening up of social discipline, the growing influence of Sabbatarianism, and the emphasis on 'godly learning', developed and flourished.[45] Throughout Elizabeth's reign, the forces unleashed by her father's break with Rome and the publica-tion of the English Bible were coming of age, as borough after borough witnessed, and suffered, the ascendancy of godly magistracy and min-istry. Some towns were slower than others (take Tewkesbury, one of our case studies) but in many others, from Beverley to Colchester, godliness was established, enforced and institutionalised by the turn of the cen-tury. The strict bylaws passed by the corporation of Bury St Edmunds in 1607 mirrored developments in other Suffolk boroughs. The bur-gesses of the port of Orford passed an order in October 1589 com-manding attendance at the Friday morning service and lecture on pain of 4*d.* for every default, and, at the same time, enforced stricter Sunday observance. A similar order was passed in 1597 in the borough of Dunwich (now swallowed up by the sea) requiring attendance by at least 'one of every household' at the Wednesday and Friday morning services, a bylaw which followed hard upon the public example made of four fishermen who, in the preceding November, had been sent to gaol for 'going to sea upon the Sabbath day... contrary to the laws of God and of this realm.'[46] In 1575, the burgesses of the town of Sudbury found it worthwhile to ratify and confirm the 'laudable custom', com-mon in many other boroughs, including Mark Byford's account of Colchester, 'for punishing of persons committing adultery or fornica-tion proved by one or two credible witnesses – the parties to be set on a cart and carried about the town with papers set on their heads declar-ing the matter and cause of offence.'[47] What, one is tempted to ask, did 'religious voluntarism' have to do with *this* Reformation in the towns?

Northampton in the early 1570s was already the very model of a little Geneva. Choirs and organs were silenced and common prayer 'brought down into the bodie of the churche amongst the people', with psalm-singing before and after the sermon. Sermons were preached in the principal parish churches every Tuesday and Thursday at nine o'clock, and, on Sundays, morning prayer ended in the parishes in time for the people to attend the main sermon. In sermon time, no one was to sit in the street, or to walk up and down 'vaynly'. There were four 'general' communions a year, preceded and followed by door-to-door visitation by the ministers and churchwardens, acting effectively as elders. Weekly assemblies of the corporation, assisted by the clergy and neighbouring gentry, dealt with such offences as 'notorious blasphemy, whoredom, drunkenness, raylinge agaynst religion or the preachers thereof'. The ministers themselves were regularly 'exercised' under the collective discipline of the whole company. Such was the religious constitution which, it was claimed, the bishop of the diocese had endorsed, although its true author was the town preacher, Percival Wiburn, a veteran of Geneva itself. Bishop Scambler later tore up 'the order of Northampton' and silenced Wiburn, which meant that the godly of Northampton later tended to sectarianism rather than the consensus in godliness to which the order had aspired.[48]

To be sure, these religious disciplines, regarded by many as novel and 'uncharitable', were resisted, and sometimes led to serious conflict. But the focus on friction has obscured the emphasis to be found in so many sermons and so much public discourse on harmony and reconciliation. In King's Lynn, the corporation instituted a formal feast of reconciliation, held on every first Monday in the month, when the mayor, preachers, and a few aldermen and common councilmen met to 'settle Peace and Quietness between Man and Man and to decide all manner of Controversies.'[49] And in Thetford, written entries in the town books and punishments meted out seem to demonstrate a resolve on the part of the urban authorities to settle troublesome matters within the moral language of reconciliation but without enlisting the sanctions of the church courts. So the men caught playing on Christmas Day in 1582, during morning prayer, 'were joyned to knell downe in the church after the end of the Gospell to be sorye for their offence and praye to God to forgive them before the face of the congregation.'[50] Elizabeth Sowenrowe, for 'abusing Mrs Beets with words', was ordered to 'aske her forgivenes openlye in the churche', and only when she refused was she set in the cuckstool.[51] Four men who had broken the Sabbath were released from gaol when they confessed their fault and promised to be of good behaviour.[52] All of these punishments were meted out, within the community, and by the town authorities. Similar examples can be found in the records of Beverley and Colchester, as David Lamburn and Mark Byford have shown. Feasts of reconciliation, public prayers of confession and requests for forgiveness were as much a part of the municipal process of order and discipline as were the more intimidating and utterly shaming ritual punishments of cuckstool, cart and whipping post.

IV

In what we have said about the neglect of the towns in English Reformation Studies there was an element of exaggeration. There are exceptions to prove the rule of relative neglect. Studies of York, Exeter and Rye have all addressed the dimension of religion and reformation.[53] David Harris Sacks and Martha Skeeters have not left future historians of the Reformation in Bristol with much to write about.[54] And how could we forget Susan Brigden's *London and the Reformation* (Oxford, 1989), which provides an almost definitive account of the early chapters of the metropolitan story, up to the early years of Elizabeth? But beyond London and the larger provincial cities of the first rank, much work remains to be done.

We have in mind those hundreds of market towns which peppered the gazetteer and serviced the overwhelmingly rural landscape of pre-industrial England, most of them by our standards ridiculously small and petty. What was especially 'urban' about the little market and port towns of Suffolk – places like Stowmarket, Needham Market, Whickham Market, Lavenham, Long Melford, Orford, Dunwich? or, looking westward and northward, Banbury, Burford, Evesham, Wiveliscombe, Congleton, Barnsley? Almost any place, including most nucleated villages, could and did call itself a 'town'. But towns in something like our sense, and perhaps the presence of a market or the regular occurrence of a fair was a necessary defining feature, may have numbered 600 or 700, and of these no more than a hundred would seem to us to deserve the name. Canterbury had ranked as high as seventh in terms of its tax yield. Yet Canterbury had no more than 4,000 inhabitants, and would have been smaller still, and less prosperous, but for the presence of a substantial immigrant population of Flemish 'Walloons'.

Some of these case-studies are of towns in the second rank in Clark and Slack's pecking order: places of regional importance, but with populations, like Canterbury's, of no more than 5,000, which was the estimated size of Beverley in the sixteenth century. Colchester and Worcester numbered about 4,000 inhabitants, Doncaster and Reading probably somewhat less. Tewkesbury and Halifax were smaller, and representative of a third tier.

Ecclesiastically, these towns reflected the diversity to be found throughout England. Worcester was a cathedral city and was used as a kind of showcase for the religious changes of the Tudor age. But like most cathedrals, Worcester was also a bastion of conservatism, especially as seen through the eyes of the local chronicler whose account of the Reformation in Worcester Diarmaid MacCulloch follows. Beverley had its Minster, which was by far the wealthiest ecclesiastical institution in the East Riding of Yorkshire. Reading Abbey was one of the grandest monasteries in the realm and an important destination for pilgrims, some of them royal. Tewkesbury was dominated by the massive abbey church, its distant tower still a visionary glimpse as one speeds along the M5, a church which its citizens secured for their own use and made the scene for a conservative interpretation of the religious settlement. Colchester may have been the seat of an archdeacon, but it was ecclesiastically so depressed and impoverished that in the mid-sixteenth century it was impossible to find clergy to staff its parishes. As for Halifax, that was something completely different: a town of about 2,600 people (in 1548) but a parish covering 124 square miles and containing 10,000 souls, a whole landscape of scattered townships and substantial farmhouses; a place which valued education as a passport to better things, which produced its share of well-qualified clergy. Among the learned societies of the modern world is a group devoted to the study of something called 'Cartographie Ecclésiastique Comparée'. It is a subject of central importance.

The selection of these towns and not others reflects the interests of those invited to contribute to this volume, and it is not intended to provide a kind of scientific sample of religious townscapes. But, serendipitously, there is some patterning. The essays by Caroline Litzenberger, Diarmaid MacCulloch and Patrick Collinson connect Tewkesbury, Worcester and Shrewsbury, three quite dissimilar towns distributed along the Welsh borders. Halifax, Beverley and Doncaster, in the essays by Bill and Sarah Sheils, David Lamburn and Claire Cross, offer a northern perspective. By contrast, Mark Byford on Colchester and

Jeanette Martin on Reading stand on their own. Complete coverage was not and could not have been our objective. Readers whose interests are confined to the West Country, or to Kent, or to the East Midlands, will need to wait for a sequel to this volume, or are referred respectively to Wallace MacCaffrey on Exeter and David Underdown on Dorchester, Peter Clark on Canterbury, Faversham and Sandwich, and David Marcombe on Retford.[55]

In any event, what these essays suggest is not so much a number of regional regularities as the almost infinite variety of experiences which the Reformation in hundreds of English towns entailed. In the seventeenth century, Lucy Hutchinson, a Nottinghamshire lady, wrote that every county had the Civil War to itself, in effect its own civil war, 'severall stages, where the tragedie of the civill warre was acted.'[56] So it was with the Reformation. Reading, a town for centuries dominated by its great abbey with strong royal connections, had a Reformation which resembled the high political drama of the national Reformation in miniature: the last abbot hanged at his own gates, leading citizens making haste to come to terms with a new world, living as dangerously as Thomas Cromwell. Doncaster, by contrast, seems hardly to have noticed its Reformation, thanks to urban leaders who were no less dedicated than Queen Elizabeth herself to the cause of religious uniformity. Here was local confirmation of that benign myth of continuity, which Anglican historians of the Reformation have loved to dwell upon: Doncaster, Catholic and Reformed. Hadleigh in Suffolk, which we have thought of as having a naturally Protestant soul, something to do with the symbiosis of cloth manufacture and the Gospel, which was a myth first propagated by the martyrologist John Foxe, proves to have owed its precocious Reformation to the fact that, as an ecclesiastical peculiar of the archbishop of Canterbury, who happened to be Thomas Cranmer, it had religious change thrust upon a partly receptive, partly resistant community.[57]

J. J. Scarisbrick has written that the English 'people' did not want the Reformation.[58] A. G. Dickens has proposed a groundswell of popular support for religious change, with only an older generation still strongly addicted to the old ways.[59] The sixteenth century would have found both propositions surprising. Queen Elizabeth's first archbishop of Canterbury, Matthew Parker, wrote that he hoped that England would be spared the kind of Reformation which John Knox had made in Scotland: 'the people to be orderers of things'.[60] These essays do not, on the whole, support the notion that 'the people', in an undifferentiated, proletarian sense, ordered the English Reformation. Or if they did, it was as participants in local politics, for even if we localise the Reformation, we do not depoliticise it, and may still want to endorse the statement of F. M. Powicke, often scouted, that the Reformation was 'a political transaction'.[61] In the hierarchical and socially layered nation which was sixteenth-century England, we should expect the political interests and influence of the middling to higher levels of urban society to count for most, and so, it seems, they did. The puritanism of early seventeenth-century Halifax was not built upon an earlier tradition of evangelical dissent, nor was it a kind of spiritual and ethical by-product of the cloth trade, however central the clothing industry was to the economy of Calderdale. Bill and Sarah Sheils find that Protestantism in Halifax, which matured into John Favour's puritanism, had its roots and beginnings in the parochial establishment, and 'among small networks of the more prosperous families', with their clerical kinsmen.

But Mark Byford's account of the Reformation in Colchester, resembling in some ways what we have learned about such German cities as Strasbourg and Augsburg,[62] warns us against the assumption, not only that the Reformation was an imposed, top-down affair, but that it amounted to a mechanism for 'social control'. What the Reformation was seen to stand for in Colchester, a good moral order which punished and shamed sin but respected the social conventions of Christian and charitable neighbourliness, was not unpopular. The issue of 'popularity' naturally depended upon the constitution and distribution of power within each particular town, corporate or incorporate. These were variable matters, although the period covered by the essays in this volume witnessed a widespread progression/regression from relatively open to closed, oligarchic government.

V

Conventionally, the English Reformation was supposed to have happened between the late 1520s, when Henry VIII's marital problems first began to threaten the ecclesiastical *status quo*, and the Elizabethan religious settlement of the 1560s, which, while from one point of view it settled nothing, since it set the scene for more than a century of further religious instability, from another settled everything, since it established the constitution, doctrine and worship of the Church of England effectively forever.

More recently, the subject has been stretched chronologically far beyond these limits. Christopher Haigh has asked us to substitute for *the* Reformation the notion of a plurality and succession of lower-case reformations, a recurrent feature of English history extending far beyond the sixteenth century;[63] while a recent symposium at University College London which attracted most scholars currently active in the field, retained the definite article but worked with the concept of a 'long Reformation', three or four hundred years long.[64]

Some of the essays in this collection, particularly Martin on Reading, are concerned with the Reformation in the once-accepted sense of a series of events set in motion by Henry VIII and essentially concluded by the Protestant settlement of Edward VI which Elizabeth I renewed in 1559. Claire Cross's account of the Reformation in Doncaster, and the Sheils's on Halifax, on the other hand, pursue the story into the early decades of the seventeenth century. Other essays, among them David Lamburn's on Beverley and Patrick Collinson on Shrewsbury, deal with what would once have been thought of as episodes occurring in the aftermath of the Reformation, the working out of some of its implications.

What is hardly controversial is that the Reformation almost permanently destabilised the religion of England, and with its religion its politics. (Whether the religious scene was wholly stable before Henry VIII threw his spanner in the works is a question which still divides late medievalists.)[65] The religious history of the seventeenth century, in particular, consists of a series of reverberations, not so much ripples as waves, disturbing the surface of a pond broken by the first stone: Laudianism in reaction against an almost dominant Jacobean Calvinism, a politically reactivated puritanism rising up against Laudianism, reactive processes within resurgent puritanism, Independency setting itself up against Presbyterianism, both Presbyterians and Independents taking fright from the sects; and then the Anglican revanche of the Restoration and all that followed from that.

How far the Reformation in the towns, in its longer-term resonances, contributed to that major destabilisation of the English polity which was the Civil War and the so-called Puritan Revolution is a question beyond the scope of these essays. Taking his cue from a chance remark of the great seventeenth-century divine Richard Baxter that 'the war was begun in our streets before the King and the Parliament had any armies', Patrick Collinson has written elsewhere of these 'street wars' as the prolepsis of what John Morrill has called England's wars of religion.[66] Not many lives were lost in these wars, but heads were broken, reputations blasted, and the governing urban oligarchies split by bitter factional disputes which were either provoked by religious antipathy, typically the mutually shared hatred of the godly, 'Puritans', and their enemies; or these religious differences coloured political and economic rivalries.[67] In the little towns of the Kentish Weald, the preachers were said to have brought in division and tumult. 'Hath not Eelie set Tenterden, his parish, together by the ears, which before was quiet? what broile and contention hath Fenner made in Cranbrooke!' The preachers denied these charges, of course, but it was very much a case of the pot calling the kettle black. The minister of Tenterden would have kept the town at peace 'if a few pot companions, disordered and sensuall persons among them, had not sought trouble against him'. In the words of the Psalmist, 'let the lying lippes be made dumbe which cruellye, proudly, and spitefully speake against the right-eous.'[68]

Collinson's essay in this volume is a commentary on the early rounds of a long-running feud in Shrewsbury between the puritans and their opponents, which developed alongside longer-standing rivalries between crafts and companies, mainly the Drapers and the Shearmen. Adam Fox's essay corrects any tendency we may have to idealise the Protestant Reformation as an episode in urban history which made for all sweetness and light. 'The towns were often the greatest centres of mockery in derogation of religion or other forms of authority.' 'For the century following the Reformation of the 1530s witnessed perhaps the highest point of religious satire in England', much of it disseminated through the provincial towns. 'Libels, taunts and jigs were often inspired by the arrival in a provincial town of a new Calvinist preacher who had radical designs...to create a godly commonwealth, a little Geneva in the English provinces.' One of the earliest victims of anti-puritan street theatre was Percival Wiburn of Northampton, 'Maister Wyborne, alias tiburne tyke':

> But I of hym doe well pronounce
> And tyme the truth shall try,
> That he shall trust unto his heeles,
> Or els in Smithfield fry.[69]

In 1581 we hear of 'dissension and discord and almost rebellion' in William Saunderson's King's Lynn, 'slaunderous libels, letters and rhymes' aimed at the preacher, 'sett forth, noysed and published' throughout Norfolk.[70] The politics of the Reformation, especially in the towns, was, at least intermittently, a vicious politics destructive of those very civic values of peace and harmony which the early modern town was meant to embody and that left in the quiet conformity of Doncaster or the radical puritanism of Colchester important legacies to the towns in which they took place.

Part I
Reformation Case Studies

1. The Birth of a Protestant Town: the Process of Reformation in Tudor Colchester, 1530–80

MARK BYFORD

In 1555, the Catholic justice Sir Anthony Browne issued a draconian order to the officers of Colchester, requiring that they make periodic searches 'in every house', and arrest 'all strangers . . . for this town (said he) is a harbourer of all heretics, and ever was'.[1] Tudor Colchester enjoys a similar reputation among modern historians, home as it was to one of Marian England's most persistent Protestant communities. Yet although Colchester is widely cited as an early centre of Protestantism, the process of reformation there, and in other similar towns, has been relatively little explored in print.[2] If Colchester was such a Protestant town, how and when did it become so?

As Browne seems to have implied, Colchester had been associated with heresy even before the official Reformation had started. The town had long been home to a Lollard community. Though relatively small in size, it had been a persistent feature of the town's life since the early fifteenth century. The Lollards' continued presence reflected the fact that Colchester's population was in some respects predisposed to receiving new religious ideas.[3] Colchester traded extensively with London and the Low Countries, both fertile ground for heresy. Its citizens included many itinerant clothworkers, and literate merchants and artisans, noted for their susceptibility to Protestantism. Far from the centre of the diocese in London, Colchester was also free of close supervision by the bishop, and its poorly endowed parishes did not attract many powerful advocates for traditional religion.[4]

Catholicism was clearly vulnerable to attack in such an environment, but even in the 1530s it retained its hold on the affections of the majority of the town. In 1537, most of the parishioners of the wealthy parish of St Peter's were members of the Jesus Guild, organisers of the popular Jesus mass, celebrated in their own chapel on the north side of the church.[5] The guild and its mass were suppressed by statute in 1548, but the instinctive support for Catholic institutions that they represented could not be so easily abolished. Protestantism's success was far from guaranteed. The town's inhabitants may have been susceptible to reform, but it was to be a chain of national and local events which turned that possibility into a fact.

I

One of the earliest of these events, of course, was the decision to pursue the royal divorce from Katherine of Aragon. A subscription list for the citizens of Colchester, declaring their loyalty to King Henry, Queen Anne and their heirs, has survived from 1534. As was true for most of the country, this readiness to subscribe did not indicate a large local Protestant population. Nor is there any evidence that the changes wrought by Henry and Cromwell led to a surge of conversions in Colchester. Even so, the advent of the official Reformation did allow its existing Protestants greater freedom to propagate their views. Thus in 1534 Henry Fasted taunted John Wayne, the rector of St James', with 'certain books of the king's print', probably *The Glass of Truth* and the *Articles devised by the Council*. Wayne was Bishop Stokesley's official, and only three years earlier Stokesley had charged Fasted for opposing images and pilgrimages, and for predicting 'that the day should come that men would say, cursed be they that make these false gods'. Now the boot was on the other foot, Fasted confronted Wayne with Cromwell's books in the presence of some of the aldermen. In response Wayne was said to have shouted, 'Hence, away with them, they be naught.' He was later reported to Cromwell by Fasted for preaching against the books.[6]

Wayne's response to the new religion was not untypical: Colchester's clergy remained largely conservative in the 1530s. The fact that this situation changed only slowly severely limited the potential for Protestant growth. Royal propaganda could achieve little without Protestant ministers planted in the parishes to propagate its messages. Ironically, it was not until after the start of the Henrician reaction that any Protestant clergy were appointed in Colchester. In 1539 Thomas Audley, formerly Colchester's town clerk and now lord chancellor, presented William Wright to the rectory of St Leonard's. This parish, which stretched down to the Hythe (Colchester's port), was later a centre of Protestant activity. Wright was probably its first evangelist. In the parish until 1550, his Protestantism is suggested by bequests for sermons, from Richard Colbronde in 1540, 'to make out a sermon in setting out the glory of God and the honour of our most noble prince', and in 1545 from John Smyth 'for preaching the Holy Gospel'. In 1546 he was questioned concerning the Six Articles.[7] Elsewhere, John Blanke, graduate rector of St James' from 1541, and Thomas Kirkham at St Mary's-at-the-Walls from 1540 may also have been Protestants. By 1548, both churches had sold their plate, reglazed their windows and whitewashed their walls, at least one 'white liming the church and aisle with scriptures'.[8]

In parallel with this gradual emergence of a Protestant presence in Colchester came the first major attacks on its Catholic institutions. Between 1536 and 1538, the town's abbey, priory and two friaries were dissolved, and their monks and friars ceased to be a part of its daily life. Monastic buildings, lands and advowsons soon passed into the hands of local gentry, notably Thomas Audley.[9] These depradations, and the uncertainty about future changes in policy, seriously undermined the financial foundations of Catholic worship in the town. Jennifer Ward has shown that bequests for requiem masses, to be found in almost half Colchester's remaining wills from 1528–37, had all but ceased by 1540, never to recover. Some testators may still have asked their executors verbally for a traditional funeral, but much of this decline must reflect a change in practice. This was no doubt hastened by a sharp reduction in the number of chantry priests in the town. With Audley's help, and anticipating the formal abolition of 1548, two of the town's five chantries were dissolved in 1539, and another in 1543, effectively halving the income of some of Colchester's larger parishes like St Leonard's and St Peter's.[10]

Despite this disruption of traditional religion, Protestants in Henrician Colchester were still subject to frequent prosecution. The force with which some of them expressed their opinions, particularly at a time of uncertainty, meant that they posed a threat to order in the town. The borough courts made sure that those who were too vocal were punished. John Wodcok was charged in 1535 for saying that 'the sacrament of the altar is made of dough, and they would make us believe that it is God in the form of bread, and...that the moon is made of a green cheese'. Four others were prosecuted with him for similar statements in 1539. In 1541, Matthew Estwood was presented for declaring, 'I will do no more reverence to the Cross made in the similitude of the Cross of Christ than I would do to the bathhouse.'[11] Although they tended to be conservative, the aldermen's main concern was to enforce the law rather than support a particular confessional position. Thus, in 1543 and 1545 they charged some of the town's clergy for failing to preach the Gospel and to read the King's statutes in church, while in 1546 they charged at least five people, probably Protestants, in connection with the Act of Six Articles.

Burnings also occurred towards the end of Henry's reign, albeit never on the same scale as under Mary. The aldermen superintended the burning of a Dutch Anabaptist in 1538, and of a heretic Joan Bette, condemned with two other Colchester people by Bonner in 1546 for her views on the sacrament. In the same year, the future owner of St John's, John Lucas, sent a tailor, John Hadlam, up to the Council. He was subsequently burnt at Smithfield, possibly with Anne Askew, 'standing to his own ignorant sense' (denying transubstantiation), a description reminiscent of the unsophisticated steadfastness attributed to some of the later Marian heretics.[12]

It is difficult to be precise about just how large the Protestant community in Colchester was by 1547, although it clearly still represented a relatively small minority. An archidiaconal visitation from 1542 indicates that more than half of St Giles' 320 parishioners failed to turn up for church on Sundays and holy days. Some of these, described as working or going to the alehouse during divine service, would have been Protestants refusing traditional services, but not all. According to the presentment, one simply stayed in bed, not surprisingly, given that the parish was in the suburbs, only served by a curate (at best), and its parishioners widely-dispersed.[13] Fifty per cent would be too generous as an estimate of Colchester's early Protestant population, while the 1–2 per cent represented by the Lollards in the 1520s would be a considerable under-assessment. At a stretch, this lower percentage can be doubled from those named or implied in various presentments, wills and letters to about 3 per cent. But even a generous allowance for the limitations of the sources would mean that no more than 5–10 per cent of Colchester's population of 4,000 was Protestant by the mid-1540s.[14]

II

The years 1547–53 saw the steady, albeit haphazard, destruction of much of the remaining fabric of Catholic religion: guilds, chantries and images in 1548; Latin service books and altars in 1549–50; vestments in 1552, and church plate in 1553. In the diocese of London, the consecration of Nicholas Ridley as bishop in 1550 ensured these requirements were strictly enforced, where necessary with the help of the sheriff of Essex. In common with many of their contemporaries, Colchester's testators responded to this destruction by ending bequests to the parishes. Jennifer Ward has shown that while 60 per cent of testators between 1538 and 1547 had continued to leave money to the high altar for tithes forgotten, and almost 20 per cent made a gift to the Church, under Edward there is no record of any bequests in either category.[15]

Ridley was concerned to do more than simply alter the fabric of the churches, of course. He wanted to ensure that the 1549, and subsequently the 1552, Prayer Book was properly used, and that Protestant sermons and catechising were widely available. Aware of the misuse of the 1549 Prayer Book, his primary visitation demanded an end to ceremonies designed by clergy to make the new service 'counterfeit the popish mass', such as elevation of the host.[16] We do not know whether this sort of crypto-Catholicism was a problem in Colchester, but improving the availability of good sermons clearly was. By 1550, at least five of the town's twelve parishes were vacant, and most of the rest were indifferently served by curates. William Wright had left St Leonard's by this time, and was probably dead.[17]

Colchester's poor livings, compounded by the shortage of clergy which faced all the Edwardian bishops, made the provision of Protestant sermons very difficult. The borough occasionally paid a visiting preacher's expenses, and no doubt one or other of Ridley's St Paul's prebendaries preached in Colchester when they could. But this was no substitute for resident ministers. It was not until 1552 that the bishop was able to place one of his men in a Colchester living, presenting the Protestant Marmaduke Smith to the rectory of St Mary-at-the-Walls.[18] This issue was clearly of concern to the borough as well as the diocese. In the autumn of 1549 one of the bailiffs, Thomas Dibney, was up in London to help draft a parliamentary bill, 'for the uniting of benefices together in the town of Colchester, and the order or rates how the curates may come by a competent or reasonable living'. The bill, however, came to nothing, and like similarly placed towns such as Ipswich and Exeter, no amalgamations took place.[19]

In the absence of beneficed, ordained preachers, Colchester's Protestants resorted to hedge-preachers, committed laymen preaching in the fields or in local houses and inns, outside the largely silent churches. This was not a unique development. Concern about the growth of 'Anabaptist' preachers in Essex and Kent had prompted the Privy Council to send Hooper on a tour of preaching there in the summer of 1550. There are at least two of these local preachers whose names are known to us. Foxe relates that George Eagles, a tailor, 'having little learning or none ... in those most bright and clear days of king Edward the sixth ... had not unfruitfully showed and preached the power and force of the Lord'. Colchester was one of the locations for his peripatetic preaching, so extensive that he was called 'Trudge-over-the-World'.[20]

Another lay preacher was Thomas Putto. He was a tanner who lived at Mile End. This was one of the four parishes within the liberties, the area just outside Colchester subject to its jurisdiction. In mid-1549, he had been brought before the Privy Council, for 'his lewd preaching', and then again before Cranmer, since he had 'continued of his own head' to preach. He was sentenced at that time to bear a heretic's faggot at St Paul's for denying that Christ descended into hell. Entered into a bond in November 1550 not to read or preach until lawfully authorised, almost exactly two years later the forty-year-old Putto was ordained deacon by Ridley. There is no record of Putto's ever having been formally attached to a parish, although he could have served as a curate to William Fiske at Mile End. He was still listed as a tanner in April 1556, when in his absence he was presented for holding heretical conventicles of more than twenty people at Mile End in November 1554. Ridley may thus have been trying to regularise the position of a man who had developed an 'auditory' outside the formal structures of the Church, and was in no hurry to acquire a benefice.[21]

Despite the existence of these groups of committed Protestants, Edward's reign was more notable in Colchester for weakening or destroying Catholic practices than it was for achieving a corresponding increase in Protestant activity. No doubt the repeal of the heresy acts helped, encouraging existing Protestants to proselytise, as did the free circulation of Protestant texts permitted after 1547. Conversions were made: in 1556, the weaver Richard Nichols was to state that, 'he had more plainly learned the truth ... by the doctrine set forth in king

Edward the Sixth's days, and thereupon he had builded his faith'.[22] But without a strong Protestant voice in the pulpits, active Protestants remained in a minority in the town. Paradoxically, although the informal arrangements which some of these Protestants resorted to were symptomatic of the failure of the Edwardian Church, they were an ideal foundation for the rapid creation of an underground ministry after the accession of Mary in July 1553.

III

Under Mary, Catholicism was probably restored in Colchester much as it was in many other parts of the realm. By the time of the 1554 visitation of Mary's bishop of London, Edmund Bonner, the town's Protestant clergy had fled or been removed, and although poverty kept many of the livings empty, one or two Catholic curates were in place to revive the Mass. Much needed to be done if the churches were to be properly equipped, but there is no reason to doubt that Colchester's wealthier vestries proceeded to replace the apparatus of Catholic worship. We know that this happened in neighbouring Harwich, for which (unlike Colchester) we still possess the churchwardens' accounts. This would have meant altars in place by the end of 1554, proper Mass books and vestments provided in 1555, new statues and crucifixes for rood lofts in 1556, and more expensive items like silver chalices only acquired, if at all, towards the end of the reign. In August 1556, Bonner's commissary reported that some of the churches had 'all ornaments with other things in good order', albeit others (probably in the poorer parishes) still lacked certain items.[23]

Meanwhile, Colchester's Protestants continued their extra-parochial worship. On 19 February 1554, the Privy Council ordered the punishment of those (unnamed) persons in and around Colchester who were trying to dissuade people from attending divine service. These included more than just Putto and Eagles. Foxe records a confession to Bishop Bonner, to the effect that 'Master Pulleyne, otherwise called Smith; Simon Harlestone and William, a Scot' were clandestine preachers, based at the King's Head in Colchester. The informant went on to say that Pulleyne and the Scot often travelled to the continent to see the Duchess of Suffolk, 'for they were her chaplains'. Two of these had been incumbents in London: John Pulleyne at St Peter's Cornhill; and 'the Scot', probably either 'the Scot, the curate' mentioned by Machyn working in 1551 at Cornhill with Pulleyne, or William Whitehead, formerly at St Katherine's Coleman Street. Harlestone came from Mendlesham in Suffolk, and was Matthew Parker's brother-in-law.[24]

We do not know whether they supported one congregation or several, but these ministers kept Colchester's Protestants supplied with regular preaching and semi-public acts of worship for at least the first three years of Mary's reign. The character of such services, and the degree to which they conformed to the norms of the 1552 Prayer Book or were more radical, has been the subject of some debate. In this instance, the services probably conformed to the 1552 rite since four of the ministers were ordained, and Pulleyne at least is recorded conducting Easter communions using this rite, at his house in London in both 1555 and 1556.[25] Thomas Tye, a 'false brother' who had infiltrated the congregation early in the reign, and was later sent by Bonner to serve in Colchester as a Catholic priest, described their meetings as an alternative to regular parish worship: 'They assemble together upon the Sabbath day in the time of divine service, sometimes in one house, sometimes in another, and there keep their privy conventicles, and schools of heresy'.[26]

This Protestant activity seems initially to have excited little opposition. By 1555, however, with the revival of the heresy laws and the formal reconciliation with Rome, the mood began to change. Some Protestants were effectively forced out of the town. Margaret Dibney, listed as attending Putto's services in 1554, went into hiding in fear of her life, 'who, being in one of her neighbour's houses secretly, saw when the Papists went into her house and spoiled her goods'.[27] In March 1555, the first of the town's Marian burnings took place. Weakened by imprisonment, the priest John Lawrence was carried to his death in a chair. According to Foxe, young children were allowed to surround the fire and chant, 'Lord, strengthen thy servant and keep thy promise'. Reports of this occasion, and of persistent Protestant meetings in and around the town may explain why, in May 1555, one of the bailiffs, Thomas Dibney, was called before the Privy Council, 'having been complained upon for his evil behaviour in matters of religion'. Forced to perform a humiliating penance in different parish churches on successive days, Dibney was the only Colchester alderman punished for anti-Catholic behaviour under Mary, and even he remained on the bench throughout her reign.[28]

As the persecution gathered momentum, relations between Colchester's Protestants and Catholics appear to have polarised. Writing to

Agnes Silverside, who was in prison in Colchester awaiting execution in 1557, Ralph Allerton talked of 'the old law, where the people of god were most straitly commanded that they should not mingle themselves with the ungodly heathen'. He stated that this included not eating or drinking with them, something which may have been put into practice in Colchester's inns. The King's Head was run by Protestants, the 'goodwoman' of the house being someone 'who had succoured many', and whom Bonner later imprisoned in his 'coalhouse'. Meanwhile its rival around the corner on the High Street, the White Hart, belonged to Richard Cosen, mentioned by Protestants as an informer to the royal commissioners, and later to be a prominent recusant under Elizabeth. It was to his inn that Bonner's agents went when they were in Colchester, and where some heretics were sentenced to be burnt.[29]

The key to increasing hostility between Catholics and Protestants was the impact of the Marian persecution. Colchester had seen periodic burnings before, but the scale of those between 1555 and 1558 set them apart. Foxe records twenty-three people burned in the town in these years, of whom at least fifteen were locals. Two more died in Colchester's prisons, and two people from Colchester were burned at Stratford-le-Bow. No other town outside London suffered more.[30] There is no space here to describe the trials and burnings in detail, but the force of their impact inevitably sprang from just such details: the defiant 'patience of such a reverend old age' of Agnes Silverside, the sixty-year-old widow of a priest; the condemnation of Elizabeth Folkes, a maid twenty years old, whose judge, William Chedsey, tried in vain to save her from the flames, and passed sentence with tears running down his cheeks; the death of Agnes Bongeor, who sent away her child, 'a little young infant sucking on her' to a nurse on the morning of her execution. Indifference to such executions was not an option.[31]

Until the last year or so of Mary's reign, it was intended that the light from these heretics' fires should stand out for all to see. Managed as great spectacles, Colchester's burnings took place either in front of the castle's looming Norman keep, or outside the Roman postern gate, high above the surrounding countryside.[32] The logic for this was clear. Diseased bodies were burned to cleanse communities of infection, whether that infection were physical or spiritual. The burning of heretics, in Bonner's words, 'cutteth away a putrified and festered member' before it infected the rest. It was therefore a matter of policy that the burnings should be made as public as possible. They made an example of those who failed to conform. They were also a public recognition of wrong-doing before God, a corporate penance by the whole community. Lesser offenders against the law of the Church stood in a white robe before the whole town confessing their sins; these heretics were condemned to do the same, but wrapped in a sheet of flames.[33]

Theoretically sound, in practice this policy failed. When the famous preacher Rowland Taylor was burned in nearby Hadleigh, his successor preached the next day that Taylor's perseverance was 'a devilish thing, for it moveth many minds to see an heretic constant and to die'. This movement of minds worked powerfully in Colchester, helped along no doubt by its sometimes vocal Protestant minority. As opinions polarised, most of the town's population appears to have shifted from a law-abiding conformist position to outright hostility to the regime. There is every indication that by the middle of Mary's reign, for the first time, those who remained faithful Catholics in Colchester were in a minority. Thomas Tye, writing to Bonner from Colchester late in 1556, sounds like someone under siege:

> The rebels are stout in the town of Colchester. The ministers of the Church are hemmed at in the open streets, and called knaves. The blessed sacrament of the altar is blasphemed and railed upon in every alehouse and tavern. Prayer and fasting is not regarded. Seditious talk and news are rife, both in town and country....

According to Foxe, at the beginning of August 1557, when ten people were burnt in the town in one day, 'the standers-by, which were by estimation thousands, cried generally almost, "The Lord strengthen them; the Lord comfort them; the Lord pour his mercies upon them"'. Four weeks later, Bonner's commissary asked for armed guards from the bailiffs, and for the town clerk to note down the names of those who abused him, as he tried to escort prisoners 'in great press and danger' through the streets.[34]

By 1558, the 'tumult' occasioned by the trials and subsequent burnings led the authorities to try to conduct them as quietly as possible. To some observers in Colchester, this approach threatened the total eclipse of Catholic order. Asked by the Privy Council to return from Colchester in April 1558, William Chedsey said that if he turned his back he feared the area would be 'in such a roar' that the commissioners there would lose all credit: 'would to God the honourable council saw the face of Essex as we do see. We have such obstinate heretics, anabaptists [and] other unruly persons here as never was heard of.' None the less, the change of policy seems justified. The more diseased limbs the commissioners tried to remove, the more they seemed to spread the infection.[35]

It has been argued by Gina Alexander and others that the Marian persecution could not have happened without help from the local laity. Willing jurors were essential sources of information about heretical activity, and zealous justices necessary to prosecute it.[36] In Colchester, local co-operation was forthcoming, but largely from one group: the aldermen. They would normally have exercised sole jurisdiction in the borough, but in this instance they were strongly directed by royal commissioners drawn from outside, such as the earl of Oxford and Sir Anthony Browne. None the less they acted with what would later appear to be embarrassing efficiency. In 1558 one of Bonner's officers could write, 'the officers of the town be very diligent with us'. Not one of the aldermen resigned during Mary's reign, and several of them are named by Foxe as hostile to the Reformation. Amongst others, the martyrologist included Benjamin Clere, 'sometime a gospeller', in the 1563 edition of his *Acts and Monuments*, as a 'cruel enemy' of the Protestants, and his fellow alderman Robert Browne as 'a hot and hasty justice in persecuting God's people'.[37] Like most of the aldermen, both men were busy becoming good Protestants by the time Foxe's book was published. But while their past deeds were hastily buried, they were not forgotten. This left most of the ruling elite in the first two decades of Elizabeth's reign vulnerable to accusations of hypocrisy, and was to deny them the moral authority to define Colchester's Protestant policy independently of popular opinion in the town.

Willing jurors seem to have been harder to come by. Despite ample opportunity, presentments in the borough courts for non-attendance at church ceased within months of Mary's accession. The one exception was on 28 April 1556, when a special jurors' panel named twenty-one people for non-attendance, heresy, holding unlawful assemblies, and being fugitives. The jurors here were clearly under extraordinary pressure. The sessions had been convened to comply with a royal commission issued days earlier ordering the distraint of the property of those who had fled the realm, and was held the day before six of their fellow townsmen were due to be burned. Significantly, the offences referred to were alleged to have occurred in 1554, and most of those responsible had fled.[38]

Heretics were sought out and punished in Colchester, but almost entirely through the machinery of the royal commission. The workings

of this are obscure. No doubt juries were used, but it may have been
local informers who gave the earl of Oxford the information he
required to indict six people in March 1556, 'because they would not
come to their parish churches'. Thomas Mowntaine, a Protestant who
had sought refuge in Colchester, cited Richard Cosen, Mr [Edmund?]
Tyrrell, and the former town recorder, Jerome Gylberd, as 'counsel' to
commissioner Sir Anthony Browne in 1555, and we know that three
similar informants in neighbouring Ipswich were responsible for presenting almost eighty gospellers to the commission in May 1556.[39]

For the most part, the evidence of those accused suggests that
detections were not obtained without trouble and were biased. It has
been noted by historians how few of the Marian martyrs were of
relatively high social status. Despite the occasional shopkeeper, Colchester's martyrs mostly fitted this pattern, consisting of spinners and
weavers, other craftsmen, servants, labourers and widows. Some of this
was because many of the wealthy, like Colchester's aldermen, conformed. Added to this was a natural reluctance on the part of informants and jurors to present their social peers and betters. The risks for an
informant are illustrated by the case of a servant on nearby Dedham
Heath, who in 1555 reported (correctly) that his master was giving
refuge to heretics, and was put in the stocks by the local officers, 'to
teach him to speak good of his master'. Little wonder that in similar
circumstances jurors, forced to present someone, seem to have played
safe and opted for the least powerful members of the community. As
one of Bonner's officers remarked, they 'most commonly indict the
simple, ignorant, and wretched heretics, and do let the arch-heretics go;
which is one great cause that moveth the rude multitude to murmur,
when they see the simple wretches (not knowing what heresy is) to
burn'.[40]

It was Tyndale who described the Gospel as 'a light that must be fed
with the blood of faith'.[41] Colchester's burnings not only turned most of
the town against Catholicism. They also transformed the profile of its
Protestant community, both within the town, and more widely in East
Anglia, London and the exile communities. In what is perhaps the
most-quoted passage about Tudor Colchester, Henry Orinel, a Protestant husbandman from Willingham in Cambridgeshire, described visiting the town in the summer or early autumn of 1555:

> at that time frequented, because it afforded many godly and zealous
> martyrs, which continually with their blood watered those seeds

which by preaching of the Word had been sown most plentifully in the hearts of Christians in the days of good king Edward. This town for the earnest profession of the Gospel became like unto a city upon a hill and as a candle on a candlestick gave great light to all those who, for the comfort of their conscience, came to confer there from divers places of the realm, and repairing to common inns had by night their Christian exercises, which in other places could not be gotten.

The chronology of Orinel's account is a little confused: by the time of his visit, only two people had actually been burnt in Colchester. It is none the less a powerful evocation of the town's place in the hearts and minds of many Protestants from the middle of Mary's reign. Colchester is on a hill, but this is gospellers' language: the city on the hill and the candle upon a candlestick are metaphors from Matthew's version of the sermon on the mount, and follow a passage describing the blessings awaiting those persecuted for Christ's sake.[42]

The 'Christian exercises' Orinel is describing here seem distinct from the clandestine Protestant services in existence in Colchester since 1553. These latter had been alternatives to church attendance, led by ordained clergy, and catering largely for local people. By contrast, Orinel's exercises included Protestants from the whole region and, being held at night, were presumably less conspicuous and harder to detect. We do not know for sure whether they included services based on the Prayer Book, nor whether they were organised by Protestant clergy. Even so, while Orinel's account leaves this unclear, his own activity in Colchester suggests that Protestant gatherings there did not always conform to the Edwardian Protestant norm. He relates debating the divinity of Christ at an inn (probably the King's Head) with some servants, 'two women Gospellers', and a Dutch member of the heretical Family of Love, Christopher Vitells. Orinel claimed to have been so disturbed by some of Vitells's arguments that he almost went on to Oxford to 'ask counsel of Bishop Ridley and Mr Latimer'. Vitells's extreme views were clearly unusual, but without clergy present such gatherings were probably prone to give expression to unorthodox Protestant opinions.[43]

The twenty-three Protestants, none of them clergy, listed by Foxe as 'apprehended at one clap' in Colchester in August 1556, were probably interrupted at this sort of meeting, since they came from twelve different towns as far as fifteen miles away. Two of those present, Alan

Simpson and Ellen Ewring, were local residents, listed as part of Thomas Putto's congregation in 1554. It would be interesting to know what their presence meant: was this activity in addition to regular local services? Or was it a substitute, either because Putto had fled, or because orthodox services no longer appealed to them? What Foxe records of the group's views on the Mass suggests that they were Edwardian Protestants, but he is sometimes unreliable on such issues.[44]

The period after 1555 was not the first time that Colchester had been a regional centre for non-traditional religious views. In the 1520s, the town was one of the hubs of a Lollard network stretching from Buckinghamshire into East Anglia. What was new was the scale of the reaction against Catholicism, and the degree of national notoriety (or fame) that the town had attracted. For the first time, Colchester's very identity became widely associated both inside the town and out with its status as what one historian has described as 'the provincial capital of heresy'.[45]

IV

When Mary died, John Pulleyne was in Geneva, where he had settled with his family in October 1557. He stayed long enough to sign a letter from Geneva in December 1558, urging the exiles to avoid contention over 'superfluous ceremonies' and instead concentrate on attacking Catholicism. By the spring of 1559, however, he had returned to Colchester, where Catholics were already suffering from the change of regime. On 20 March the Privy Council had ordered the bailiffs to pillory Peter Walker, rector of St Leonard's since 1557, for 'false seditious tales'. Presumably he had been informed against by some of the Protestant parishioners he was originally asked to keep in check.[46]

Pulleyne started preaching in Colchester immediately, and not surprisingly soon found himself in trouble with the Privy Council. We know that Cecil thought highly of Pulleyne, listing him as a potential bishop later that year. But he had no benefice, and a proclamation was still in force 'to forbid all preaching and any innovation of public prayers except the Gospel and the Epistle in English'. More particularly, the content of Pulleyne's sermons was an embarrassment at a time when the Principal Secretary was trying to enlist as much support as possible for the new religious settlement.[47] Fellow-exile William Fuller cited this as the main reason for Pulleyne's arrest in April 1559. He witnessed Pulleyne's arrival at the Court, escorted by the sheriff Thomas Mildmay, and stated that he was 'brought to the court for maintaining in a sermon of his some...disliked points'. These points included criticising temporisers in religion, condemning participation in the Mass and other papist ceremonies, and taking a forceful Calvinist line on swearing, fornication and other moral offences.[48]

Pulleyne could stand up and preach like this in Colchester because he was strongly identified with resistance to Mary's regime, and therefore benefited from the dominant anti-Catholic mood of the town. In April 1559, a local jury presented the first offenders for non-attendance at church 'since the coronation'. Later the same month, the Hocklawday election for lawhundred juries gave all the borough's voters a chance to express their views. Such elections were a significant gauge of public opinion, since the electorate comprised the freemen, which in Colchester's case meant all adult males born within the town. On this occasion, the juries nominated five of their number to represent their requests to the aldermen. Significantly, one of these was John Valey, a veteran member of the Protestant congregation, presented before Stokesley in 1539 for refusing confession and denying the real presence, and who was to be ordained by the new bishop of London, Edmund Grindal, the following year. As part of the restoration of 'good order' in the town, they asked for the appointment of officers in each parish, 'to see men keep their churches and that good order be kept in the time of services, and no unlawful games to be used in service time in vitelling houses or elsewhere'.[49]

This need not have been a purely Protestant move: non-attendance was a traditional concern of the borough courts, though the novel idea of appointing officers for enforcement indicates how great a 'disorder' it had become under Mary.[50] None the less, the fact that Pulleyne was almost the only minister left in the town, and that someone like Valey was voicing this request, strongly suggests a vote for Protestantism. Another sign of popular support came in August 1559, when the electors of north ward voted for Pulleyne to be their 'headman', responsible for representing them in the annual election of the brough's officers. An unusual gesture towards a Yorkshire 'foreigner', this was one of the few formal ways for ordinary townsmen to signal their support for Pulleyne. It was not until the following month that the aldermen retrospectively qualified him for the post, and made him a freeman of the town without fine.[51]

All this confirms the impression that when Grindal advised the Crown to appoint Pulleyne as archdeacon of Colchester in December 1559, he was offering him the legal title to exercise an authority over the town's religious affairs which *de facto* he already possessed.[52] In this way, the bishop obtained a powerful pastor for Colchester, by now a key bastion of English Protestantism, and apparently accepted Pulleyne's indifferent administration of the wider archdeaconry. Like Ridley's ordination of Putto ten years earlier, Grindal's appointment of Pulleyne reflected a determination to draw Colchester's Protestant congregation into the confines of the national Church. Pulleyne's acceptance of the archdeaconry was in turn an action consistent with the contents of his letter from Geneva a year earlier. The Elizabethan Church was not yet a Calvinist's dream, but it was the best place from which to start fighting Catholicism. As archdeacon he had the maximum possible freedom to set about organising Colchester's religious life.

By the beginning of 1560, Pulleyne was the only minister in Colchester with any formal post. The last of the Marian clergy, Peter Walker, had resigned St Leonard's in the presence of the royal visitors in September 1559. The other Marian incumbents had either died in the last year of her reign or left within months of Elizabeth's accession. When Parker's commissioners visited in November 1560, they found all twelve of the town's benefices vacant. Once again the parishes' poverty was remarked upon, the commissioners stating, 'all these will not make three men's livings if they were joined together'. They all remained vacant until 1562, when Grindal managed to fill Holy Trinity and St Mary-at-the-Walls. This was as much as could be done through this route: in the next ten years there were never more than two beneficed men in the town at any one time.[53]

Against this background, Pulleyne improvised. He used curates, readers and preachers to substitute for an orthodox parochial ministry. Their appointment did not depend on lay patrons, and their payment was presumably organised on an ad hoc and voluntary basis. Readers were 'appointed by the order of Mr Pulleyne' from the ranks of the Protestant congregation and attached to at least four parishes. Of these, Peter Hawks was a cobbler, Andrew Brownsmith a courier, and John Watson an alehouse keeper. Their backgrounds evidently belied their abilities: Hawks was later ordained by Grindal, and the other two continued to be licensed as good readers for the next twenty years.[54] At the same time, curates were chosen from the ranks of the bishop's recent ordinands. We know that by the end of 1560 at least two of these were in Colchester: Thomas Harvey was serving St Peter's; and Thomas Upcher was in William Wright's old parish of St Leonard's. Grindal was at pains to do what he could to help Pulleyne, granting the talented exile Upcher, whom he liked 'right well', a dispensation to conduct services without the surplice, which Upcher had argued was offensive to 'their usage where he now serveth' (St Leonard's). For his own part, and exceptionally for an archdeacon, Pulleyne ensured that he was on hand to preach, and to promote Protestant interests, concluding the purchase of a house in All Saints' parish late in 1561.[55]

By providing the basic elements of a parish ministry as quickly as possible, Pulleyne and Grindal sought to achieve two fundamental objectives. On the one hand, they provided worship and preaching for the pre-existing Protestant congregation, drawing them into the churches; on the other, they took advantage of the widespread anti-Catholic feeling in Colchester immediately after Mary's reign to put the necessary elements in place for the conversion of the whole town. None the less, these improvisations were at best short-term measures. To achieve more lasting change, Pulleyne needed to form an alliance with Colchester's governors. This was presumably one of his less palatable tasks. There had been no purge of borough government following Mary's death, and Pulleyne was forced to work with the men who had helped hunt him and his fellow Protestants down only a few years before.[56] For their part, the aldermen themselves had small freedom of manoeuvre, given Pulleyne's ecclesiastical status and his popular support amongst the townsmen. Embarrassment about their role in the Marian persecution must also have been an inducement to avoid confrontation over Pulleyne's demands. Perhaps the more conservative among them refused to volunteer any help, but most did not. The archdeacon secured enough votes from those called by their critics 'Mr Pulleyne's aldermen' to legislate a Protestant Colchester into existence.[57]

The first priority was to provide more resources for a proper preaching ministry. In the autumn of 1561, the town assembly voted to organise the collection of funds 'towards the living and maintenance of a preacher to be had and continued in the same town to the increase of God's glory and the maintenance of his Word'. In the course of 1562, the town chamberlain collected around £40 towards 'the contribution granted to the preacher', of which perhaps half was spent, apparently on occasional sermons. In April 1562, the assembly underlined that the new preacher was not to be parish-based, but would address the whole town as one congregation: 'upon the Friday when the common preacher shall make any sermon, there shall be of every household within the town one person at the least, as well for their edifying as for the good example and comfort of the preacher'. Another vote at the same assembly met the demands of the lawhundred three years earlier, and appointed twenty-five overseers of church attendance. Every Sunday and festival day they were 'to view the streets whether there be any playing or unlawful exercise used, or any idly ranging the streets, or sitting on... stalls, or working'. One of the more poignant of the first volunteers for this office was John Pykas, now in his sixties, who had been one of Colchester's leading Lollards in the 1520s.[58]

The two remaining lists of contributors to the common preachership from this period, from 1564 and 1568, confirm that these policies were widely supported. The 1564 list is incomplete, and only includes the bailiffs, aldermen and common councillors. It was thus probably not, as Patrick Collinson supposed, mostly composed of 'sound gospellers'. Yet the fact that this entire group contributed almost to a man to a 'free and voluntary contribution' was significant. It indicated that the common preachership was not the creation of a faction, but a matter of widespread consensus. Extraordinary local taxes like this inspired fierce resistance when the taxpayers did not agree with them. Moreover, the 1568 list, which is complete, shows the aldermen and common councillors outnumbered by those outside town government who wanted to contribute. These included almost the whole social spectrum from the owner of St John's abbey, Sir Thomas Lucas, contributing 26s. 8d., to Thomas Balle, an alehouse keeper, and the immigrant (Flemish) carpenter Anthony Crowbrooke, contributing 16d. and 12d. respectively.[59]

It was not until late 1564 that the corporation secured its first resident common preacher, but in the interim Pulleyne unofficially took on the role. His sermons provoked strong reactions. Although many in Colchester supported anti-Catholic measures, they were not all prepared for Pulleyne's approach to preaching. When the common preachership was discussed in the house of the apothecary Simon Smyth, in January 1562, his guests all spoke positively about it, and speculated about whether 'Dr Turner might be attained... for that they did hear that he preacheth continually three times in the week at the least against the Pope and all his relics'. But this reminded their host of Pulleyne, and prompted 'marvellous opprobrious and contemptuous words' against the archdeacon for 'he had made his last sermon which he made in St Nicholas' church only of him [Smyth], and against him and none other'.[60]

We can guess at Smyth's offences. Although he evidently consorted with Protestants, he was later to be before the courts for gambling during divine service and for adultery. Yet the reason he 'cared not a fart' for Pulleyne was primarily because of the way in which the archdeacon made his accusations public. Effectively bypassing the normal longwinded process of his own courts, Pulleyne sought to shame offenders directly in the pulpit. This practice of 'personal preaching', a growing tendency amongst godly clergy at this time, was not the only aspect of Pulleyne's sermons that caused complaint. The wife of the butcher John Fowle was presented in August 1563 for speaking 'very disorderly of Mr Pulleyne for his preachings'. Brought before the bailiffs she was unrepentant:

> he did love to make many sermons of beer pots, and ... he was a meet man to be a midwife because of things he spake there touching things that are known but to women only at the birth of children. And also [she] bade a vengeance of them all for they had preached such good sermons that they had preached away all the pavements and gravestones in St Martin's church.

These reactions are hostile, but paradoxically they also show Pulleyne's sermons finding their mark, their messages challenging received ideas. In doing this, the archdeacon provoked opposition, but since he and his followers were the accepted standard-bearers for anti-Catholicism, there was nowhere for opponents to go but the hard-line Catholic camp. While Smyth was to pursue his particular grievance against Pulleyne in the courts, he still subscribed to the common preachership in 1564. So too did John Fowle. Both were members of the Common Council, and neither wanted to be labelled as Catholics.[61]

Others, albeit a minority, were still prepared to stand up for the old religion. Richard Cosen, the keeper of the White Hart, was a leading member of this group. Fined a hefty ten shillings for blasphemy by the lawhundred in 1560, he spoke openly in late 1562 in favour of the Duke of Guise's campaigns against Protestants in the Low Countries, and was finally arrested in December for rumouring the death of Elizabeth, the virgin queen, in childbirth. Examined by the bailiffs, his maid stated:

she hath oftentimes heard her said Master and her Mistress report at home that they are Catholics and that the preachers and other that do profess the Gospel are Genevians. And that they hoped that the Abbeys and Houses of Religion and the Mass should be had in use again before one year came to an end, and talk much against the use of the Church that now is appointed, and that they sit singing together the old Mass in mirth by the fireside.

Here was a household already effectively recusant, long before most religious conservatives in England felt so clearly under threat.[62]

V

By the time of his death in 1565, Pulleyne had effectively taken Colchester for Protestantism. Speed and decisive action had enabled him to channel the anti-Catholic energies of the town into the creation of an explicitly Protestant identity. Like much else in England in the 1560s, the permanence of these arrangements was not guaranteed. But every year that passed without a major challenge helped consolidate the Protestants' gains, and made retreat less likely. A major step was taken with the arrival of William Cole, the town's first full-time common preacher, in November 1564. Effectively Pulleyne's successor, albeit without the same title, Cole was well known to the archdeacon, and was married to a Colchester woman, Jane Agar, whom he had met in exile in Geneva. Former preacher to the Merchant Adventurers in Antwerp, and highly regarded for his learning in Protestant circles, Cole was quite a catch for the town. Later to become president of Corpus Christi College, Oxford, he reinforced Colchester's ties with the Protestant clerical network, and helped ensure that he was only the first in a largely unbroken line of distinguished common preachers stretching into the reign of James I.[63]

This was important, because the common preacher was at the very heart of the effort to win over most of Colchester's population to Protestantism under Elizabeth. He gave a general sermon on Sundays attended by 'the body of the town', including the bailiffs, aldermen and councillors. He also preached on Wednesdays and Fridays, and conducted a public catechising on Sunday afternoons. In addition, as Patrick Collinson has argued, he was more than a lecturer. The common preacher was a pastor to the whole town. His sermons became a natural venue for the public confessions imposed on the town's drunkards and fornicators, for they contained a cross-section of the whole community, giving physical form to what Bishop Aylmer would later describe as 'that great congregation of Colchester'. Deferred to by both governors and the governed for opinions on moral offences, church government, anti-Catholic theology, clerical appointments, and so on, the common preacher was used in public debates against Catholicism, and probably also hosted the seminars, initially called 'prophesyings' and later 'exercises', designed to equip the less well-educated ministers of the region for preaching. All this activity made its mark in the town's affections. In 1583, when the common preacher George Northey was suspended by Aylmer for denying the sufficiency of the Prayer Book and the Articles, a petition on his behalf from the townsmen to the bailiffs reminded them that 'the Galatians so loved Paul, that if it had been possible they would have pulled out their eyes and given them unto him'. The bailiffs got the message, writing in Northey's defence to prominent lawyer and town clerk James Morice, to the earls of Leicester and Warwick, to Sir Francis Walsingham, Sir Thomas Heneage and William Cole, and proved so persistent in his cause that the issue was eventually discussed by the Privy Council.[64]

Over time, a series of ordinances and initiatives embodied the increasing hold of this Protestant teaching on the life of the town. In November 1562, the town assembly voted to ask for the Privy Council's permission to grant asylum to a number of 'Dutch' people, 'banished for God's word', and to allow them to establish their (Presbyterian) church there.[65] In May 1566, a new joint tribunal of the bailiffs and archdeacon threatened fornicators with summary judgement, large fines and whipping on the back of a cart. These harsher punishments were reinforced in the 1570s, and from 1576 juries were sworn in at each sessions specifically to enquire into offences of prostitution and fornication. Drunkenness was another favourite target of Protestant sermons, and by the mid-1580s had appeared as a major category of business in the borough courts for the first time. Ordinances against 'profaning of the Sabbath day, to the dishonour of Almighty God', included the enforcement of church attendance in 1562, and the prohibition of the St Dennis' fair on Sundays from 1578. Presentments for sabbatarian offences, already significant in the borough court in the 1550s, quadrupled over the next thirty years.[66]

It is evident from this that Protestantism retained the political initiative in Colchester throughout the 1560s and 1570s. This was not a foregone conclusion. As early as 1565, George Withers had been employed as a town preacher in Bury St Edmund's, before he took up a similar post in Colchester, yet by the late 1570s his successors in Bury were driven from the town by a conservative group at the heart of town government.[67] Colchester's ruling elite, by contrast, with its past involvement in the Marian persecution on public display in the pages of Foxe, never spawned an overtly anti-Protestant group. By the 1580s, Protestantism's grip on the government of the town was almost unassailable, as the corporation's unwavering support for Northey demonstrated.

Still, there remains the question of how far most of Colchester's inhabitants considered themselves Protestants. The answer was clear for at least one group. The town's burgeoning 'Dutch' community, numbering some 1,300 people by the mid-1580s, constituted a self-governing Presbyterian congregation.[68] The hospitality shown to them was in itself a badge of the borough's Protestantism, albeit shrewd economic policy too, bringing valuable new clothworking skills into the town. But what of the rest of the town's population? How far had the anti-Catholic opinions of the mid-Tudor period been transformed into Protestantism? At one level, the answer was that Protestantism had been very successful indeed. It had driven its advantage home early in Elizabeth's reign and Catholicism had all but disappeared, drowned out by relentless sermons from its talented common preachers, namely William Cole, George Withers, Nicholas Challenor and George Northey, not to mention visitors like Archdeacon James Calfhill, and Bishops Grindal and Sandys. At the same time it is clear that the initial consensus of 1559 had broken down to some extent, to be replaced by persistent religious conflict.

The first major symptom of these divisions was a libelling campaign in 1575–6, prompted by a controversial case of alleged fornication. The more extreme Protestants supported the punishment of the accused couple, and were led by Thomas Upcher, the rector of St Leonard's, and the alderman Benjamin Clere. Here was a striking alliance indeed, between on the one hand a Marian exile, and on the other a man described in Foxe as a former gospeller turned Marian persecutor! Clere's membership of the godly congregation was apparently unquestioned, as witnessed by his daughter's marriage to the common preacher, but his past left him vulnerable. The libels penned by

Upcher's opponents, and sung in alehouses across the town, ridiculed Upcher, addressing him as 'Metropolitan of the Tumbrel' (the cart on which fornicators were punished), and calling his clerical allies 'Mynishers, Common Bull, Man Slayer, Wedlock Breaker, Proud Prelates'. But Clere, who was a bailiff that year, was exposed in further libels as a traitor to Protestantism, responsible in 1557 for the capture and execution of George Eagles, of *Acts and Monuments* fame. After a long and expensive fight, involving special commissions, the Privy Council and Star Chamber, the moderates triumphed. Clere left the bench for good, and a moderate Protestant, John Hunwick, was elected in his place.[69]

This episode was the first of a succession of similar 'contentions' which continued into the seventeenth century. Yet while the divisions ran deep, there was never any question of repudiating the essentials of the town's Protestant identity. Colchester's voters were choosing between two forms of Protestantism, both vehemently opposed to Catholicism. Indeed, even the purging of the more extreme Protestants from the town was apparently not at issue. The corporation and townsmen continued to support Nicholas Challenor, the common preacher chosen in 1575, who was a strict Calvinist. Although Hunwick may not have agreed with all Challenor's views, he still attended the common sermon regularly, and was a keen advocate of the preaching ministry. When Challenor died in 1580, the aldermen elected his chosen candidate, the equally radical George Northey, to succeed him. Even Thomas Upcher remained in his parish, a witness not only to his legal security as an incumbent, but also to the nucleus of local support he had built up over almost two decades of ministry.[70]

VI

These disputes were not a sign of Protestant failure, but of a new phase of change, the troubled adolescence of the Protestant town born in the 1550s. Euan Cameron has recently argued for the European Reformation as a whole that it was a process whose eventual outcome was not obvious to its first participants. The 'coalitions' of reforming ministers and laypeople which characterised the initial wave of Reformation were essentially temporary, the enthusiasm of the laity based more on their acceptance of some of the headline slogans and anti-Catholic policies of the reformers than on any real understanding of Protestant theology. Yet as the Protestant clergy began to build their New Jerusalem(s) on the foundations of that theology, the implications of their ideology for everyday life became clearer to the laity, and prompted many to become rather more discriminating about whom and what they supported.[71]

A similar pattern is discernible in the process of reformation in Colchester. The first step in that process was more of a mass political conversion than a spiritual one, as the deaths of some of Colchester's minority of committed Protestants turned the rest of the town against the Catholics. The beginning of Elizabeth's reign saw what was quite literally a vote for Protestantism by the electorate, with the ruling elite 'playing the weathercock', and moving with the prevailing national and local mood. This political conviction was skilfully nurtured by Pulleyne and his successors until Colchester's Protestantism became central to the town's Elizabethan identity. Magistrates and people publicly committed themselves to the Reformation through new ordinances and institutions. This was as well, for their prosperity was bound up with that commitment, securing as it did the presence of the 'Dutch' congregation and their clothworking skills.

In parallel with this, but much longer in the making and more subtle, was the internalisation of the theology and values of the new religion by the majority of the town. This was a predictable phase in the process of reformation, as the town's Protestantism was brought to maturity. It could be argued that the deference afforded Colchester's Protestant ministers was initially for the power of their sermons, their learning, and their standing in godly circles, and that beyond certain basic anti-Catholic tenets about subjects such as the Mass, their precise theological beliefs had, for the most part, neither been understood nor questioned by the laity. Yet as these ministers strengthened their hold on the government of the town, and began the more profound conversion of Colchester's population, the initial consensus fractured. Translated into tangible policy, the implications of some of their beliefs became clearer to the population at large, and brought at least some of the godly clergy under attack. Moreover, although the moderates appear to have lacked a powerful clerical advocate, differences of opinion almost certainly emerged between the clergy themselves, further weakening their position. The fact that many of the clergy had succeeded in creating a following in the town, whether through careful marriages or convincing arguments, ensured that they were usually able to withstand the attack. This fact, combined with the inability of any one group to capture the hearts and minds of the whole town, resulted in continuing social conflict.[72] By the middle of Elizabeth's reign, consensus on Colchester's Protestant identity remained, but what exactly this demanded of its citizens had become a matter for constant debate.

2. Religion in Doncaster from the Reformation to the Civil War

CLAIRE CROSS

On his visit to Doncaster towards the end of the reign of Henry VIII, in addition to mentioning the two stone bridges which carried the Great North Road over the Cheswold and the Don, John Leland singled out for particular comment 'the fair and large parish church of St George'. He also remarked that 'the soil about Doncaster hath very good meadow, corn and some wood.' All these topographical features have a direct bearing upon the town's religious history in the early modern period and go a long way towards explaining how a Catholic community of the late Middle Ages could be transformed into a Protestant municipality within at the most three generations.[1]

Doncaster, an ancient borough, had become a fully-fledged corporation by the late fifteenth century, its governing body composed of a mayor, twelve aldermen and twenty-four common councillors. The corporation had also acquired manorial rights over a number of rural settlements in its vicinity. Accessible for much of the year by water as well as by road, the town was an important centre for both communications and trade as its wharf on the river Don south-east of the church, large market place and many inns attested. In 1546 the chantry commissioners estimated that the parish contained more than 2,000 housling people.[2]

Although the jurisdiction of the parish church did not extend as far as the town's secular jurisdiction, it also comprised an urban nucleus with a rural hinterland consisting of the hamlets of 'Wheatley, Sandall, Hexthorpe, Balby, Carr House, Tilts, a part of Warmsworth and a part of Stockbridge and Langthwaite'. Since 1100 the rectory, valued in 1536 at a gross £81 19s. 8d., had been appropriated to St Mary's Abbey at York, the abbot and convent allowing the vicar an annual £33 6s. 8d. At the Dissolution the appropriation passed first to the king and then to the see of York, the vicar's stipend remaining unchanged

48

until 1635 when Archbishop Neile augmented the living to £40 a year. More importantly perhaps, certain vicars in the seventeenth century were also able to supplement their income by holding in plurality with the parish church the adjacent corporation-owned rectory of Rossington. The vicars of Doncaster, though scarcely affluent, enjoyed a much higher income than many urban incumbents elsewhere, and consequently the parish could both attract and retain university-educated clergy.[3]

Although St Mary Magdalen may have been the original parish church of Doncaster, by the later Middle Ages local people were concentrating all their energies upon the church of St George within the castle precinct which, with its three large aisles and great central tower, far outclassed every other building in the town. In the early sixteenth century it accommodated at least six chantries of St Catherine, St Nicholas, St Mary, St John the Evangelist and the Holy Trinity together with a 'service' at the Rood. The priests of these chantries lived in common in a college in the parish churchyard. The church in addition contained several religious fraternities. Three lights in the window in the middle choir aisle had been contributed by the guilds of St Mary, St Anne and, possibly, St Erasmus; testators in the 1520s were still making bequests to the guilds of St Christopher and St George, while in 1546 some 50s. annually from the guild of St Thomas went towards the finding of a priest.[4]

Religious provision in the town was in no sense confined to the parish church. Two chantry priests served in the church of St Mary Magdalen in the market place, by this date a chapel of ease, another priest officiated in the chapel of Our Lady on the bridge over the river Don and to the south of the town yet another cleric ministered in the former leper chapel of St James. Two friaries completed the town's ecclesiastical establishment, the Franciscan priory on the land between the rivers Cheswold and Don, the Carmelite convent behind the High Street. At the Dissolution the Carmelite convent housed eight friars, the Franciscan priory ten. It seems likely that earlier in the century there would have been about thirty-five priests in Doncaster, fifteen or so seculars and around twenty friars.[5]

All the evidence suggests that in the 1520s and early 1530s virtually all the Doncaster clergy and laity whole-heartedly supported the purposes for which the town's many religious institutions had been created. At his death in 1528 Simon Robinson, vicar of St George's since 1523, left the residue of his estate to be spent in good works for the health of his soul, and the souls of William Palmer, priest, and William Adam. Robert Denton, chaplain, in 1531 commissioned masses for his soul in both the Franciscan and Carmelite friaries and also established a permanent obit in the parish church, to which he gave a red cope embellished with a rebus. Not to be outdone, in August 1532 John Drynkall, curate of St George's, bequeathed 6s. 8d. to the church works, 12d. to repairing books in the choir, 20d. to the Trinity altar and 4d. to every other altar in the church and to the two altars in St Mary Magdalen's besides six books and 15s. in cash to be shared between the Grey Friars and the White Friars.[6]

If anything, the pious bequests of the richer Doncaster lay people surpassed those of the clergy. Testator after testator committed their souls to 'Almighty God, Our Lady St Mary and all the blessed company of heaven' and most of the more prosperous made elaborate preparations for their funeral. Alderman Richard Marshall's will illustrates the nature of this urban piety. In 1529 he gave the convents of the Grey Friars and the White Friars 6s. 8d. each to 'go the day of my burial afore my body to the church and do their mass and dirige after the custom'. Providing for his burial within St George's church, he also required a 'principal dirige solemnly with the whole suffrage' from the parish clergy and created in perpetuity at the Grey Friars an annual obit for his soul, the souls of his benefactors and all Christian souls. Of the thirty Doncaster wills made between 1520 and 1533 two-thirds mentioned the friars. Many testators asked the two convents to accompany their bodies to the grave, others set aside the standard 10s. fee for a trental of masses, and Oliver Halton and Margaret Firth both established obits in the friary churches. Even more lay people turned for services to their parish church where Alderman William Lynsey, Alderman John Parsonsone and Joan Johnson, widow, all founded obits for themselves and their families. In 1521 Oliver Halton left the reversion of a garth to the service of St George and later in the decade Alderman Richard Marshall also gave 12d. to St George's guild. In 1525 Robert Lyndsay donated 26s. 8d. to the church work at St George's; in 1538 Alderman John Bulloke bestowed a suit of vestments with a crimson velvet cope to the church in return for prayers for the souls of himself and his family.[7]

The will of Thomas Strey reveals the depth of this devotion. In November 1530 he sought burial for his 'carious' [decayed] body 'in the Trinity choir before the image of the blessed Trinity'. After setting aside 10*s*. for his mortuary and 3*s*. 4*d*. for forgotten tithes, he presented the church with suits of vestments to the value of over 100 marks, bequeathed the cantarist, Robert Denton, 100*s*. and instructed his brother, the priest Sir Richard Strey, to maintain a light over his tomb and to augment the chantry he had founded during his lifetime. In addition to payments of 20*s*. to the Doncaster Carmelites and 20 marks to the Franciscans to pray for him and his two wives, Alice and Elizabeth, he granted Sir Robert Hobson, BA, an annual exhibition of 7 marks to study at Cambridge 'until such time as he be promoted to a living'. Four neighbouring monasteries, Nostell, Monk Bretton and Pontefract priories and Roche abbey each received 20*s*., the friars of Tickhill and Pontefract 10*s*. He gave no less than £ 20 for the marriage of poor maidens, 40*s*. for mending the highway and 26*s*. 8*d*. to buy the warden of the Doncaster Grey Friars a coat.[8]

While most of these testators did not look far outside the bounds of their native town, this does not mean that by contemporary standards Doncaster could be dismissed as an intellectual backwater. The town already possessed a grammar school by the early sixteenth century and books were definitely circulating in the area. Besides the Bible Simon Robinson promised Peter Mydleton if he continued his progress at school, the chantry priest, Robert Denton, in 1531 bequeathed Richard Denton and his sister Elizabeth all the books in his chamber, apart from three, St Augustine, *Ad Fratres in Heremo*, Ludulphus, *De Vita Christi*, and the *Decretals* intended for the local priest, Sir Edmund Smyth. In earlier centuries the Doncaster Carmelites had produced several scholars of national stature and both they and the Franciscans retained their libraries until the Dissolution.[9]

The town's links with the universities seem to have been growing in the early Tudor period. Financed by Strey, Robert Hobson took the degree of BA at Cambridge in 1530 and MA in 1533 and became for a short time a fellow of St John's before returning to Doncaster to serve the chantry of St John the Evangelist in the parish church. Anthony Blake, appointed vicar of Doncaster in 1534, had proceeded MA at Cambridge the previous year. During the 1530s in the persons of Thomas Kirkham and John Bale both the Franciscan and Carmelite friaries had graduate theologians as priors, while at least one other graduate, Jeremy Leonard, BD, had migrated to the White Friars by the time of its suppression.[10]

This connection with the universities through its graduate clergy led to the first direct challenge to Catholic orthodoxy in the town. John

Bale had encountered Lutheran beliefs in Cambridge in the 1520s and began spreading the 'new learning' when he arrived at the Carmelite convent in about 1530. In 1535 William Broman confessed that the friar had taught him about four years previously 'that Christ would dwell in no church made of lime and stone by man's hands, but only in heaven above, and in man's heart in earth'. Bale's opinions provoked a counter-attack from the warden of the Franciscans and in 1536 Archbishop Lee thought it necessary to ban all contentious preaching in Doncaster. While it is dangerous to construct an argument from silence, these theological disputes may just possibly have lessened the mendicants' reputation: not a single testator made a bequest to either of the two convents between 1533 and 1538.[11]

The two priories underwent much disruption in their final years. A religious conservative, Lawrence Cooke, replaced Bale as prior of the Carmelites. During the Pilgrimage of Grace in the autumn of 1536 he supported Lord Darcy and acted as an intermediary between the earl of Northumberland and Robert Aske and was condemned to death for treason in 1537, though subsequently pardoned. When Edward Stubbs succeeded him, the convent had shrunk to eight friars. Despite his altercation with Bale, Thomas Kirkham behaved more circumspectly during the rising and remained as warden of the Franciscans until the Dissolution.[12]

After the surrender of the Carmelite and Franciscan convents in November 1538 none of the friars is known to have stayed on in the town. Dr Kirkham obtained a living in Colchester in 1539, subsequently becoming rector of St Martin's, Outwich, London, in 1548, while other former Franciscans found employment as chantry priests, William Hall in Sheffield parish church and John Wilson together with the former Carmelite, William Swanne, in Wakefield parish church. The loss of the two friaries would have reduced the number of clergy in Doncaster by at least a half.[13]

Despite the change of direction at Westminster, the beliefs of the local laity seem to have altered very little. Without exception Doncaster testators, like John Personson in November 1546, continued to consign their souls to 'God Almighty, to Our Lady St Mary and to all the celestial company of heaven'. Alderman Thomas Milnay arranged to have 'a principal dirige with all the suffrages of the church' at his burial 'afore St Sunday' in 1539. After making provision for a very similar funeral John Wirrall in 1543 set aside £4 to be given annually for twenty years to as many priests as his son thought fit to sing for his soul, his wife's soul, his parents' souls and all Christian souls. As late as April 1546 Robert Butterfelde, baker, commissioned a principal dirige and soul mass on the day of his burial 'according to my vocation'.[14]

In the face of this local conservatism, the changes in religion instituted by the Edwardian government, and in particular the abolition of the chantries, must have caused real spiritual deprivation, yet they evoked no public protest. Of the eleven wills made in Doncaster during the reign, only three testators referred to the Virgin Mary, the rest almost overnight adopting a standard preamble in which they entrusted their souls simply to 'God Almighty, my maker and redeemer', some adding 'in whom is all my whole belief and trust for my salvation'. With the exception of Robert Pawmer, who in May 1549 asked to have a principal dirige with a communion for his soul and all Christian souls on the day of his burial in Doncaster churchyard, most made no allusion to funeral ceremonies at all. Specific religious legacies also disappear from the wills, with the majority of beneficiaries being members of the testator's near family, though four left funeral doles or other donations to the poor.[15]

Perhaps the main impetus for this almost instantaneous obedience to central governmental directives came from the vicar, Anthony Blake. Although a considerable pluralist in later life, at this period Blake seems only to have held the rectory of Whiston together with that of Doncaster. In Edward VI's reign he made an open demonstration of his break with Catholicism by marrying Elizabeth Metcalf and setting up house with her in the town. The absence of any concerted local clerical opposition to national religious policies must have greatly eased his task of introducing Protestant changes. On their visitation in 1548 the chantry commissioners found six chantry priests in St George's church, William Howson, Robert Myrfyn, William Palmer, Thomas Roods, John Spink and Robert Hobson; two, John Silvester and Richard Johnson, in St Mary Magdalen's; with Roger Clarkson in the outlying chapel of St James. They noted that six of these priests were aged fifty or over and it therefore seems probable that some died soon after their dispossession. The youngest priest, Roger Clarkson, aged forty in 1548, seems to have moved away from the area. The one graduate, Robert Hobson, in 1551 acquired the living of Rossington. It is just possible that Richard Johnson, the former priest of St John the Baptist's chantry in St Mary Magdalen, eventually secured the living of Cantley. The only two former chantry priests to remain in Doncaster seem to have been John Spink, aged forty-one in 1548, previously priest of the Rood, and the half-blind William Palmer, the former incumbent of Our Lady's chantry in the parish church. Both seem to have followed their vicar's lead.[16]

The accession of Mary in July 1553 brought this growth of Protestantism to an immediate halt. It may be that from the early autumn much of the vicar's parochial work was being carried out by his curate, Robert Dobson, who witnessed as many as seventeen Doncaster wills between 1553 and 1558, virtually all of which once more carried a preamble in which the testator most commonly surrendered his soul to 'God Almighty, to Our Lady St Mary and to all the celestial company of heaven' with a minority trusting 'to be with Our Lady and all the celestial company of heaven'. Of the forty wills which survive for the reign only ten fail to mention the Virgin, and of these half date to within six months of Mary's accession. They do not afford any real evidence of Protestant resistance.[17]

Because of his marriage, the Marian ecclesiastical authorities first turned their attention to the vicar of Doncaster, Anthony Blake. On 24 May 1554 York Court of Audience deprived him from both of his Yorkshire benefices and ordered him to perform a public penance in the parish church, excommunicating him on his failure to comply. The former graduate chantry priest, Robert Hobson, succeeded him as vicar. Blake, however, had contacts in high places, and he exhibited to his judges letters from Cardinal Pole absolving him from all excommunications and interdicts and licensing him to take up another benefice other than in the parish where he had lived with his wife. Yet despite this lenient treatment he continued to behave in a somewhat equivocal way and appeared again in court in May 1556 on the charge that in spite of prohibitions he had suspiciously frequented the company of Elizabeth Metcalf since the preceding Michaelmas 'and lately did light at her house where she inhabiteth in Doncaster and there continued to the evil example of the inhabitants of Doncaster'.[18]

The offence alleged to have been caused locally by Blake's marriage may have been rather more than a legal fiction. Towards the end of Mary's reign the upper echelons of the town were once again displaying a growing commitment to Catholicism. From 1556 testators like Ralph Smithe required 'a principal dirige and mass of requiem' at their burial, and a minority went further and began to re-establish obits. In 1557 John Philippe provided the rent from a house for an annual mass of requiem and in 1558 Sybil Shaw, if her legatee died without issue, wanted an obit to be performed for ten years in the parish church for herself and her husband. Less sanguine about the future, a third Catholic sympathiser, Alderman Richard Alland, desired 'to have mass and dirige sung every year once in the parish church of Doncaster for ever...', but added a proviso that his whole rent charge of 7*s.* should go to the poor, 'if the laws of this realm will not suffer the premises to be so used'. Others besides Alland may have feared that the Catholic restoration would not last. Apart from William Blenkynshopp, a glover, who in 1557 presented a white satin vestment, a mass book and other service books to the parish church, no testators made bequests for the enrichment of the liturgy as they had under Henry VIII and it may be significant that it was an incomer from the south of England, and not a native, who contributed most to the revival of Catholicism. Requesting burial before Our Blessed Lady, Jane Petet left the very large sum of £20 to the church where she should happen to die, giving in addition £6 13*s.* 4*d.* to St Mary Abchurch in London to establish an obit for twenty years for herself and her husband and a further £6 13*s.* 4*d.* to the first house of religion to be refounded in Kent. Whatever their religious inclinations, most Doncaster testators in the Marian period acted with greater circumspection, making their charitable bequests in studiously neutral terms like George Copley, gentleman, who simply instructed his executors to distribute the sizeable sum of £10 as a funeral dole among the poor folks of the town.[19]

On the death of Mary this caution served the people of Doncaster well. By royal commission, Anthony Blake resumed possession of both his Doncaster and Whiston livings, retaining the London rectory of St Dunstan's in the West and that of Ansty in Warwickshire to which in 1562 he added a prebend in York Minster. His extensive pluralism may have prevented him from exercising as much personal influence upon the religious life of the town as he had in Edward's reign, though he compensated for this by supplying an active Protestant as his curate in the person of Christopher Witton. A married minister, Witton recorded the baptism of the first of his seven children in St George's in March 1560. A considerable number of the seventeen wills witnessed by him between then and 1571 bore an explicitly Protestant preamble like that of the husbandman Thomas Dickynson who as early as 1562 affirmed 'my only faith and belief is to be one of the elect and chosen company in heaven.'[20]

Preambles to wills reflect the beliefs of the will-writer and not neces-sarily those of the testator; they certainly cannot be taken to demonstrate that Doncaster became a Protestant community overnight. The first years of Elizabeth in fact saw the late flowering of an example of the type of Catholic piety which had flourished in the town in the early decades of the century. Thomas Ellis, a rich, childless merchant and five times mayor, in 1562 made elaborate plans to dispose of his estate to charitable uses. Having acquired some of the chantry lands formerly belonging to the churches of St George and St Mary Magdalen, he had in his lifetime conveyed the property in trust to support a '*domus orationis pro hospitione pauperum*', vesting the choice of the aged poor men and women in the vicar and his feoffees. When he came to die he made further additions to the foundation. Not attempting to hide his Catholic sympathies he first surrendered his soul to 'Almighty God..., and to Our Blessed Lady, the Virgin, mother of our Saviour Jesu Christ and to all the celestial company in heaven'. He then asked to be buried in the chancel of St George's church in Our Lady's choir on the same side as the altar of his name saint, St Thomas, to whom he had dedicated his hospital. Having bestowed upon friends and relatives a wealth of fine clothes, plate and jewellery, including a gold ring 'having the print of five wounds', he extended his benefactions yet further, giving half an acre of land to maintain a well in St Sepulchre Gate, over £20 for the marriage of poor maidens and a house in Mary Magdalene church yard and cottages in Fisher Gate 'towards the making of one free school in Doncaster... and for the use of virtuous education and bringing up of children in learning in the said school and for the increase and maintenance of the wage and stipend of the said schoolmaster...'. The residue of his estate, which included three closes and gold and silver plate, he left to his executors to bestow 'to the health of his soul as they think good'. They duly erected a stone over his grave calling upon the pious to pray for his salvation.[21]

Of more than 200 Doncaster testators from Elizabeth's reign, Ellis was the last to request the Virgin Mary's intercession or to ask openly for prayers for his soul. Indeed, only three others late in 1558 and early in 1559 referred to the Virgin Mary, while two made a more general mention of 'the celestial company of heaven'. Specific bequests to the church fabric disappeared almost entirely from the wills apart from a nominal few shillings for the 'repairing of the church'. Perhaps, however, for a time at least in the sums put aside for funeral doles conservatives found a substitute for the money they would have spent upon obits under a different religious regime. In return for 13*s.* 4*d.* bestowed upon the poor for six years after her death Isabel Simpkinson might well in 1570 still have expected prayers for her soul. Her husband, Alderman Thomas Simpkinson, who predeceased her, had preferred the less contentious field of education for his charity, in 1559 leaving four acres of meadow 'towards a foundation of a school in Doncaster'.[22]

Whatever reservations individual inhabitants may have had, the town's rapid outward compliance with the national religious settlement can best be explained by the lack of clerical opposition to religious change on the one hand and, perhaps just as importantly, the corporation's co-operation with the new Protestant establishment on the other. Doncaster borough minutes, which begin in the second decade of Elizabeth's reign, contain some hints of the corporation's attitude to the church. Most significantly, the aldermen and councillors looked to administer the town as a unity, auditing year by year not only the civic finances proper but also the accounts of the four churchwardens of St George's and, after about 1600, those of St Thomas's Hospital. In 1570 the corporation approved the expenditure of 29s. upon a Bible, four years later spent 6s. 2d. on whitening the church and in 1577 set down an order concerning seating in the church. The mayor, aldermen and twenty-four common councillors had very probably inherited from Catholic times the custom of formally processing to St George's. In 1586, in an extension of what may have been an earlier ordinance concerning attendance at church on Sundays, the mayor, his brethren and the common council decreed that every householder in Doncaster, either himself, his wife or a member of his household of years of discretion, 'shall repair unto the parish church at Doncaster upon every work day...as often as there shall...happen to be a sermon'.[23]

From an early date after 1558 the corporation had thrown its weight behind Protestant conformity. In marked contrast with York, Doncaster seems to have produced only one persistent Catholic recusant, Jane Fenton, cited at visitation after visitation between 1581 and 1604. The vicar, Anthony Blake, together with his curate Christopher Witton, a licensed preacher, seem to have impressed the principles of Protestantism upon their parishioners from the beginning of the reign. When Blake died in 1570 the archbishop appointed as vicar of Doncaster another graduate, Henry More. A Bachelor of Laws from Cambridge, More had become rector of St Martin's, Micklegate, in York in 1561 and a prebendary of the Minster two years later. Though a pluralist like Blake, he appears to have resided in the town, having six of his children baptised in the parish church between 1571 and 1578. From around 1575 he could rely on the assistance of another very active curate, Witton's successor, Thomas Bell. In 1579 More resigned Doncaster for the vicarage of Rothwell, being replaced at St George's by probably the most influential of all Doncaster's vicars in the early modern period, Arthur Kay.[24]

Kay had studied at Cambridge in the 1550s but, perhaps because of the uncertainties of the Marian period, had not proceeded to a degree. He remained vicar of Doncaster, which from 1591 he held in plurality with the adjacent rectory of Rossington, until his death in January 1614, throughout his long ministry exposing the parish to his own particular version of Protestantism. At the archiepiscopal visitation of 1586 officials accused Kay of having distributed 'the communion to some sitting'. Ten years later they charged his curate, Richard Stainforth, with not observing the Book of Common Prayer and failing to wear the surplice. Kay drew further attention to himself at the 1604 visitation because he also did 'not ordinarily wear the surplice'. In their survey of the deanery the Puritan vicars of Sheffield and Braithwell described Arthur Kay as a nonconformist 'in part', and linked him with thirteen other clergy who seemed 'weary of the ceremonies'. At best a reluctant conformist, he nevertheless avoided deprivation. He married twice, both times into the aldermanic elite. In his will of January 1614 he expressed his assurance that 'I am an inheritor of the kingdom of heaven and shall be partaker of all those good things which God in Jesus Christ hath prepared for his elect against the world to come'. Having provided for his sons in his lifetime, he divided the greater part of his estate equally among his four daughters who included Susan, the wife of Richard Winter, the parson of Sprotbrough, and Elizabeth, the wife of Henry Postlethwaite, parson of Armthorpe, in a codicil granting his clerical sons-in-law part of his books. When Henry Postlethwaite himself died three years later he had among much else in his library *The Book of Acts and Monuments*, *The Book of Calvin's Institutions*, *The Book of the Truths of Christian Religion*, and *The Controversy betwixt Stapleton and Whitaker*.[25]

The Protestant clergy of Doncaster and its neighbourhood seem to have inspired an appreciation of the Bible among some of the laity. In 1585 Marmaduke Lupton, yeoman, left his cousin Robert an English Testament and his uncle an English Bible. In the same year Alderman Nicholas Skargill bequeathed to his son Nicholas, 'whom I pray God to bless, 20s. to buy him a Bible and a book of the Morning Prayer of the largest print'. In 1597 Alice Moore, widow, gave her daughter Jane a Service Book and a Testament, while in the reign of James I Thomas

Bradforth, yeoman, Lee Deareman, mercer, and Robert Trosse, yeoman, all passed on Bibles to their sons.[26]

At the turn of the sixteenth century the town's governors seem to have been placing an increasing emphasis upon sermons. On the reissue of the borough ordinances in 1617 the corporation decreed that the mayor, aldermen and capital burgesses should 'duly every Sabbath day come to the church there to hear divine service and God's word preached both forenoon and after', and every householder, his wife and family, or at the very least one representative of every family should 'repair unto the church at Doncaster every work day so often as there shall be a sermon, and there continue unto the end thereof'.[27]

On the death of Arthur Kay, Christopher Jackson, an Oxford MA who had previously served as rector of Whitfield in Northumberland, succeeded to the cure. Vicar of Doncaster until his death in March 1643, Jackson inspired an appetite for preaching in his auditory. In 1618 the first Doncaster testator solicited from his vicar 'a sermon, which I desire him to make at my funeral'. Between 1618 and 1640 on at least six occasions Jackson received sums of from 6s. 8d. to 20s. to preach funeral sermons.[28]

In 1619, if not before, the corporation had established a lectureship, agreeing to pay Mr Paston £5 a quarter during pleasure 'for his friendly pains in preaching in our church upon the Sabbath day'. Visiting preachers regularly officiated in the church, being rewarded and entertained at the parish's expense. One such cleric, Richard Winter, Kay's son-in-law, who had begun his ministerial career as master of Doncaster grammar school, maintained his connection with the town throughout his thirty years as rector of Sprotbrough, in 1632 remembering the Doncaster poor with a bequest of £1 in his will. Intending that his son Godfrey, another university graduate and Kay's grandson, should become rector of Rossington, he bequeathed him all his books and notebooks written in his own hand. Winter turned to Peter Saxton, rector of Edlington from 1614 to 1640, to witness his will. The husband of another of Kay's grandchildren, Sara Postlethwaite, Saxton spent a year as minister at Scituate in Massachusetts before returning to England just before the outbreak of the Civil War to end his career as vicar of Leeds.[29]

The appointment of Richard Neile as archbishop of York in 1632 temporarily checked the expansion of evangelical Protestantism, being spread by this circle of learned, mildly nonconformist clergy centred upon Doncaster. Under the tolerant regimes of Grindal, Hutton and Matthew godly ministers had flourished so long as, like Kay, they had been willing to make a token compromise. The appointment of an inflexible high churchman to the see of York completely altered the religious climate. In his primary visitation of 1632 Neile concentrated on enforcing outward obedience and improving the physical state of the churches in his diocese, leaving till a later date the railing in of the communion tables and their placement altar-wise at the east end of the chancel. In 1636 Peter Saxton appeared among the clergy resisting Neile's innovations, and Doncaster seems to have been one of the slowest parishes to institute the changes. Reserving the more obstreperous parishes till late in their campaign, the archbishop's officers waited until October 1637 to send the churchwardens of St George's orders to reconstruct the seating in the church so that all the pews faced east.[30]

There can be little doubt that the sympathies of the leading Doncaster parishioners by this stage lay with long-established tradition of constant preaching. At the expanding grammar school, since the early Elizabethan period installed in the former chapel of St Mary Magdalen, the corporation in 1618 agreed to pay for an usher to assist the master; perhaps as a consequence of the accessibility of schools, the literacy of the townspeople seems to have been rising steadily. In the reign of Charles I Doncaster testators continued to dispose of Bibles and service books: in 1644 a grocer, Joseph Fayram, even possessed a Latin Bible in addition to Bishop Hall's *Works* and Rider's *Dictionary*. In the 1630s the corporation was maintaining Edmund Bell as its lecturer, on his departure reluctantly accepting as his replacement the king's nominee, James Hutchinson, though he seems subsequently to have made himself acceptable to his auditory.[31]

With the calling of the Long Parliament and the fall of the Laudians Doncaster reverted to its traditional Protestantism. When she died in 1641 Margaret Carver, widow, made bequests not only to the Doncaster lecturer but to Mr Parson Holmes of Armthorpe and Mr Leadbetter of Thrybergh, preachers whose sermons she had probably also heard in the parish church. Rather than changing the town's religious climate, the king's defeat in the Civil War seems merely to have confirmed developments stretching back to Elizabeth's accession if not beyond. On the death of Christopher Jackson in 1643 the local community welcomed as their vicar another Cambridge graduate, Richard Harvey, who during his short ministry attracted several bequests from parishioners. In 1650

John Jackson the elder, newly graduated from Cambridge, succeeded Harvey. Conforming at the Restoration, Jackson continued his ministry without a break until his death in 1690, when he was followed by his son, John Jackson, junior. Both during the Interregnum and the reign of Charles II there seems to have been a remarkable absence of sectarianism; indeed the town's governors prided themselves on their Protestant conformity.[32]

In comparison with the generosity of many previous Catholic testators, Doncaster Protestants seem to have paid little heed to philanthropy in the latter part of the sixteenth century. The diminution in voluntary giving may, however, have been partly caused by the fact that poor relief had now become a legal obligation and church assessments a compulsory feature of parish life, both closely supervised by the mayor and corporation. In the Elizabethan period about half of all Doncaster testators left money to the poor, but most only contributed tiny amounts of 12*d.* or under; there were thirty bequests of between £1 and £5, four of more than £5, with only two testators, Jane Brokesbanke with a bequest of £13 6*s.* 8*d.* and Alderman Richard Hall with one of £10 equalling George Copley's munificence in the previous reign. In the early Stuart period the token bequests to the poor disappeared almost entirely and the overall number of bequests declined to around a third of all testators, but the sums given were more substantial, twenty-nine being of between £1 and £5 and two of over £5 under James, forty of between £1 and £5 and eight of £5 or over under Charles I with Jane Barwike, widow, leaving £10. By the seventeenth century one or two testators seem once again to have been thinking in terms of more permanent social amelioration, though on a smaller scale than their contemporaries in Hull or Leeds. In 1626 William Fang, yeoman, granted a lease to his wife on condition that she paid 26*s.* 8*d.* annually to the mayor and justices of the peace to place a poor fatherless and motherless boy in a trade. The town, however, did not gain a really substantial benefaction until 1645 when Edward Rennick, a London Merchant Taylor, presented his birthplace with £100 'for the raising and increasing of a stock wherewith to set the poor of the said town on work'.[33]

Doncaster's relatively untroubled transition from late medieval Catholic piety to evangelical Protestantism owed much to its urban leaders who strove throughout the period to maintain uniformity in religion which the virtual concurrence of the boundaries of the parish and borough helped to ensure. After the Dissolution of the monasteries and the chantries the town, unlike York with its myriad small parishes, contained no surplus livings for disposessed clergy. The single, reasonably remunerated living attracted well-educated vicars who, as the sixteenth century progressed, worked valiantly to promote Protestantism in collaboration with the like-minded and similarly educated ministers of the neighbourhood. They did not succeed in making all the inhabitants godly, and the town produced its complement of adulterers, fornicators and breakers of the Sabbath from all ranks of society, but they do appear to have obliterated virtually all traces of Catholic recusancy. With corporation support, constant preaching in the successive reigns of Elizabeth, James I and Charles I seems to have been highly effective and contemporary observers looked upon Doncaster as 'well affected' towards Protestantism decades before the Civil War.[34]

3. Politics and Religion in Early Modern Beverley

DAVID LAMBURN

I

The interaction of politics and religion in early modern English towns has not always received the attention it deserves. In part this is because the English urban Reformation itself has received inadequate study, in spite of the key role towns played in evangelising a reluctant country-side, in advancing the knowledge of primary Protestant doctrines and in implementing more radical religious practices in the early seven-teenth century. A second reason for the failure to undertake the detailed studies required is that recent studies have concentrated on debates over the pace and acceptance of religious change; increasingly, the Reformation has been seen as unwanted and divisive. As a result it has been too easy to accept at face value evidence that conflict in towns was caused by religion. A third cause is also apparent: a reluctance to tackle just what urban 'politics' meant in early modern England. The definition used here sees 'politics as the active expression of a social organism, those dynamic activities which arise from the fact that men create, maintain, transform and destroy the social structures in which they live'.[1] In urban society, politics relates to the community, to objectives and results, to actions and achievements which compel urban governors and the wider political nation to take account of aspirations and opinions which may not be those of the ruling body. Religion could play a vital role in moulding such views.[2]

Studies of the interaction of politics and religion in urban society have followed two broad lines of enquiry. First, internal strife in towns has been ascribed to religion and bitter divisions have been attributed to Protestantism or to the spread of radical religious views. Protestant-ism is seen as a divisive creed. There are more than sufficient examples to justify such an approach; in Maldon, Rochdale, Tenterden, Ashford, Shrewsbury, Lincoln, Banbury and scores of other towns, there were fierce conflicts. Sometimes these were clashes between the godly and papists, provoked by Protestant preachers. Occasionally, the preachers themselves were proud of the division and dissension they brought; in Hull Melchior Smith was willing to endure the divisions within his parish and the reproach this caused since similar controversies had been borne by 'the prophets, the apostles, the disciples, yea and...Christ himself, at whose preaching there was as much dissension as at any mans'. It was natural that clashes between the godly and their enemies would have internal political ramifications.[3]

Secondly, it has been argued that vigorous Protestant magistrates also provoked clashes by demanding and implementing Protestant social discipline, by suppressing traditional celebrations and ceremonies. Laudians were later to allege that puritanism was the root of urban faction and unrest. The presence on the governing bodies of towns of men of differing religious persuasions could have the effect of politicising religious differences and seemingly dividing along lines of formal religious division communities which were previously united.[4]

Contemporaries were not so sure that such an analysis was either cogent or correct. In Lincoln, one of those involved in a struggle which raged in the common council between 1583 and 1587 wrote to Walsingham 'not to be persuaded that their strivings were for a matter of religion, but a matter of faction with religion as a cloak'. In the town of Thetford a recent examination of bitter controversies which came to a head in 1582 has concluded that the contemporary analysis of Suffolk magistrates into the causes of the 'stirs' as being due to two opposing factions divided on matters of religion was innacurate; religious divisions did exist, but personal grievances, office-holding and the wielding of municipal power were more relevant as causes of dissension. Towns were rarely in a state of harmony either before or during the Reformation, but to the increasing political, social, economic and cultural polarisation of urban society was added a religious element.[5]

Religious controversy was but one aspect in urban political unrest. It has been suggested that in towns and cities throughout England it was the urban elite which played a key role in advancing Protestant and later puritan views. The appeal of Protestant and puritan tenets and values was understandable. In a time of rising population and growing numbers of poor, the emphasis of puritanism could serve to reinforce and justify social policy, to cement oligarchic authority and to unify the elite. But often it was only when internal dissension fractured the ruling body that political and religious factions emerged, as each side appealed for support from those they governed. In such circumstances control of town and church was fought over either within or by urban oligarchies, sometimes in the face of opposition from below.[6]

However, such analyses do not fully explain the interaction of politics and religion in all towns. Problems arise in two distinct but related areas. First, Margaret Spufford has made the point that religious belief was not primarily about behaviour and social attitudes but about a man's relationship with God, and that issues of social control and godly discipline were as prevalent in the thirteenth and fourteenth centuries as in the early modern period. Secondly, it will be argued in this paper that the appeal of Protestantism was not confined to the urban elite. Protestantism, and puritan practices and beliefs, could and did have a genuine following among those below the elite. In turn they were perfectly capable of putting pressure on their governors to promote such practices when they felt that the elite was out of step with more popular feeling.[7]

The study of the interaction of politics and religion in Beverley offers an opportunity to examine a continuing and developing division between a body of freemen committed to further reform of the Church and with a tradition of involvement in urban government associated with burgess democracy, and a governing elite which was becoming steadily divorced from freemen expectations and aspirations in both religious and political spheres. In such a situation religion played a critical role. By the 1590s the sympathies of the ruling elite were out of step with the dominant Protestant tendencies within the town. By 1615 puritanism had genuine roots among the laity and some were seeking to propel the corporation towards a more puritan stance; this religious divide stimulated arguments over mayoral elections and increased burgess involvement in town government. The way in which religion influenced politics was not accidental. The Protestant teaching of men such as Cartwright saw the roots of power in church and state as being vested in the people, stressing the necessity for active citizenship in the government of the Church. The arguments between Cartwright and Whitgift, using examples from the election of borough officers, demonstrate the extent to which their respective views were drawn from what was actually happening in urban society. Such disputes reflected a clash between distinct views of society and concepts of order which could affect the political structures of urban society as well as ecclesiastical government, organisation and activity.[8]

II

In order to understand fully the religious and political developments which affected the town from the 1580s to the 1610s some background is necessary.[9] In the mid-sixteenth century Beverley was the largest town in the East Riding of Yorkshire, with a population of around 5,000. On the eve of the Reformation the town had three parishes, sixteen chantries, two friaries and in the Minster, which was also the parish church of St John's, easily the wealthiest ecclesiastical institution in the East Riding with an annual income in excess of £900. Fully staffed, it comprised 74 individuals, not all of whom were resident. In total there may have been around 100 clerics in Beverley at the beginning of the sixteenth century. As a result of the Henrician and Edwardian dissolutions the Minster became merely a parish church and the total number of clergy in the town was reduced to six, of whom four were at St John's; by 1600 St John's had only two clerics.[10]

Protestantism gained a hold in the town quite early. In Mary's reign five cases were brought before the church courts involving Protestants; they show the presence of informed and literate Protestants in positions of authority in the town, for of the nine laymen prosecuted for heretical beliefs, two were serving governors (the equivalent of aldermen in other towns), two were common councillors and one was the son of a governor.[11] In spite of the dramatic changes to the structure and content of religious life, the Reformation and its associated changes were received with relative calm. There was little sign of discontent with the religion established by law. This cannot be explained simply in terms of apathy, for by the early seventeenth century clergy and laity drawn from a wide social spectrum were indulging in puritan practices, such as the repetition of sermons, psalm-singing, deriding one non-preaching assistant curate as a 'dumb dog', private catechising and conventicles. There does not appear to have been any tendency to reform the structure and discipline of the Church along the lines of the best reformed continental Churches, but rather a desire for greater discipline in civic society, sobriety and order in church worship, stress on sabbath observance and the furthering of a godly committed, preaching ministry.[12]

It is clear from the activities of the godly in the town that the faith may have been spread through family connections, friendships, neighbourliness and trading contacts. These would have supplemented the activities of Beverley's clergy. Almost all the town's clergy were graduates from the 1560s onwards and their endeavours bore fruit. The Minster was served by a succession of learned and godly preachers from John Atkinson and William Richardson, to Thomas Wincop, William Crashaw (a noted and prolific puritan polemicist) and later Richard Rhodes. In the 1590s at St Mary's, Thomas Utye held monthly communions, as practised by the best reformed congregations.[13] The necessity of attracting well-educated preaching clergy was recognised by the governing body of the town in 1581, when the death of William Richardson caused the governors to realise the inadequacy of the stipend and the difficulties in attracting a suitable successor; in return for voluntarily augmenting the stipend the governors were granted the right to appoint and discipline the Minster clergy. The stipend was gradually raised to £40 per annum, then to £50 per annum in the early seventeenth century.[14] By the early 1580s magistrates and ministers were working in harmony to build a godly community; strict laws to observe the Sabbath had been introduced into some trade and craft guild ordinances and the governors themselves had dealt with cases involving immorality. The town was also acting as a beacon to the surrounding countryside; Beverley's ministers educated clergy in less well-favoured surrounding villages, and the town was becoming a noted centre of puritan teaching.[15]

Parallel with these religious developments went important administrative and political changes. For much of the sixteenth century the town had a recognised political and administrative structure, being ruled by twelve governors, elected annually by the freemen, from a common council totalling thirty-six; appointments to the common council were made along clearly defined lines. There was close harmony between governors and governed; governors were drawn from the ranks of freemen who were members of the trade and craft guilds and were not always among the wealthiest inhabitants of the town. It was a system which had been refined in the 1530s, to ensure that the redress of grievances was institutionally focused. But in 1573 the town obtained a charter of incorporation which radically affected the established system of government. The new corporation consisted of thirteen men, from whom the mayor was elected annually; governors were appointed for life; replacements were appointed by the remaining governors. The common council was effectively abolished and the role in government of the trade and craft guilds was not recognised by the charter. Incorporation effectively abolished the right of the freeman electorate to have a say in the choice of governing personnel.

In Beverley one by-product of incorporation was internal political unrest; the town attracted gentry interest and saw interference from external authorities. The charter of incorporation altered the structure of urban politics, causing a breakdown of consensus in the freeman body and a divergence of views between governors and governed which, as will be seen, in turn affected the religious life of the town.[16]

However, by the early 1580s there were few signs of the fissures which were to divide the town. Open division was not evident in either religious or political life. The town's governors were firmly in control of the churches; they appointed the clergy at St John's, and some served as churchwardens in all three of the town's parishes. The governors were all members of the town's trade and craft guilds, sometimes combining guild with town office. The town had obtained its charter of incorporation along with liberties and privileges for which it had long argued. With incorporation had come grants of large amounts of lands and tenements which increased corporation income.[17] But by 1615 the lines of political and religious division had become clear for all to see.

III

On 23 July 1615, after the completion of morning prayer, the sermon and communion, a group of around sixty persons remained behind in the chancel of St John's. For the third successive Sunday they sang psalms and but for the intervention of Thomas Brabbes, who was the assistant curate, there would have been a repetition and discussion of the sermon preached that morning. Two things in particular seem to have offended the curate. First, the assembly took place 'without the consent of any save themselves'. Secondly, and more importantly, those assembled showed him contempt rather than respect. When first challenged Alexander Spalding told him 'to make no reckoning'; at the end of the psalm-singing, when he demanded to know the reason for the meeting, the assembly refused to tell him and declined to acknowledge him as their minister; when he offered to join them he was told that his company was not desired; when he attempted to question one man about the sermon he refused to answer; when he informed the gathering that the meeting was unlawful in the eyes of the Church he was rebuffed and advised that they were content to answer to the archbishop; as Brabbes departed John Thornabie informed him that 'there are too many such dumb dogs as you are', something Brabbes considered to be 'most scandalous and most opprobrious...to a minister desirous to do good in the church but that he is outfaced by such peremptory fellows'.[18]

The incident serves to illustrate a number of developments which were taking place in some northern towns early in the seventeenth century. These developments, singing psalms and repeating sermons in private or semi-private assemblies, godly preaching, opposition to 'dumb dogs' and the growth of exercises attended by both clergy and laity, can be found in many towns as clergy and laity, often in close alliance, sought to create the type of Church they wanted within the framework of the established Church. The practice of repetition of sermons had grown under the archiepiscopate of Toby Matthew and was common in some places. In Sheffield, Leeds, Bingley and elsewhere it was usual for the gathering to take place in the parish church after the sermon had been preached, and examples of similar exercises may be found at Wakefield, Bradford and Halifax. Nicholas Ardron asked, 'whether can a true minister of Christ hinder people and not suffer them to repeat sermons, seeing it is so beneficial and profitable for growing by the sincere milk of the word, as the Holy Ghost exhorts'.[19] The advantage of such gatherings for the laity related to their desire to develop voluntary forms of religious edification beyond those permitted by authority; in this way clusters of the godly were able to supplement parochial worship.[20]

In many respects, therefore, the incident at Beverley was unexceptional. Yet within a fortnight twenty-two individuals were identified before the visitation court for their involvement in this affair. On occasions in the past the governors themselves had dealt with matters which would normally have gone to the ecclesiastical courts; not only did they not do so on this occasion, but they may have welcomed the prosecution of those involved in the incident.[21] Undoubtedly those presented were the ringleaders. None of the town's governors were involved, although participants included sons of former governors and some who were related to present governors. This was a rare example of proceedings against the laity for such practices in Matthew's archiepiscopate, for the activities complained of were openly practised elsewhere. In itself this suggests that the incident was regarded as serious. The leader of the gathering was John Garthwaite, the master of the grammar school, and the terms of the admonition issued at the visitation suggest that Richard Rhodes, the puritan curate at St John's, may have been involved. However, the court made it clear that any suggestion that the discipline or government of the Church had been questioned was false. In all probability, it was the lack of deference to the assistant curate which was regarded as the most serious aspect of the affair and Matthew would have been likely to encourage rather than punish a display of scriptural study and piety. Certainly, some of those involved went on to manifest evidences of their faith and to assert confidence in being amongst Christ's elect.[22]

The events of 1615 in Beverley indicate a degree of popular support for godly practices; elsewhere there may have been widespread indifference to and ignorance of matters of religion, but occupational analysis of those involved in the incident shows a deep and widespread support for some aspects of puritanism among a wide social spectrum.[23] However, a closer examination of the participants suggests that there may have been more serious issues at stake than appear from the bare facts of the case. There are grounds for suspecting that there may have been some in authority in Beverley who were only too pleased to see action taken against those involved. After all, criticism of the assistant at St John's amounted to criticism of those responsible for his appointment; Brabbes owed his position to the town's governors who also paid his salary.[24] But more importantly, of the twenty-two named individuals presented at the visitation court seven had been involved in criticism of the governing body of the corporation some five years earlier. According to the town's records, that incident had involved around thirty named townsmen and a large number of others in an attempt to elect as mayor one who was ineligible; assaults on the town's governors, recorder and justices of the peace led to the arrest and imprisonment of Marmaduke Attmar, one of those involved in the demonstration in 1615.[25] In 1607/8 another of those involved in the demonstration in St John's, Richard Levett, offended the town's governors. In 1602 four burgesses were jailed for attempting to secure the election of a candidate who was not a governor, one of whom, John Jackson, was involved in the disturbances in 1610 and earlier incidents questioning the authority and powers of the town's governing body between 1586 and 1597. Jackson, the son of a governor, was not afraid to pursue important and long-lasting legal suits against the town's governing body; it is clear from depositions made by him to the Court of High Commission that he saw himself as the leader of burgess opposition to policies pursued by the governors which he considered to be detrimental to burgess rights, claiming that 'he hath also stood for the defence of the state of the town of Beverley against such others of the town as would have impaired the same and hath moved others to stand for the good estate of the commons of the town against injuries offered him for them'. At least two court cases were commenced before the Council of the North and others were threatened, by townsmen and by the governors. Conventicles held in the town in 1588 were reported to central government. In upheavals which affected the town in the 1590s there were important revisions to the town's constitutional character. Sweeping changes in the composition of the town's ruling body saw the removal, discharge and resignation from office of over half of the governors. In 1595 the Council in the North was forced to intervene to remove two governors, something it would have been reluctant to do had the individuals concerned been of a godly persuasion. One High Commission court case, which lasted over a year and cost over £50, saw burgesses, clergy and two factions of governors arguing about control of St Mary's, the most populous of the town's parishes.[26]

There are two striking features to the political and religious troubles of the 1590s and early 1600s. The first is the continuity of personnel involved in both political and religious radicalism. The same individuals were arguing for radical changes to mayoral elections and to town ordinances, seeking to restore a measure of freeman democracy and of traditional freeman rights, promoting curbs on the control of church lands by the governing body and to limit its interference in appointments of churchwardens, as well as indulging in godly practices of the type in evidence in 1615. Secondly, the type of personnel involved in these activities suggests that increasingly the split was between governors and governed rather than within the governing body. The incident in 1615 involved only one member of the gentry, all the rest being townsmen and women; in social terms there were servants and well-off traders and manufacturers of the 'middling sort'; former receivers of town funds and former churchwardens were present.[27] In the troubles of 1594/5, 1602 and 1610 the same wide social and economic spread was evident. Only in 1594/5 was there clear evidence of factionalism within the governing body, which allowed burgess dissension to surface and which was crucial in securing measures to restore a measure of freeman choice to mayoral elections and the role of trade and craft guilds in the electoral process. But this is not a case of those excluded from the governing elite finding common ground to oppose any policy of their magistrates. More important issues were involved.[28]

IV

What had caused this breakdown of harmony between governors and governed and how far was religion a spur to action? There were three important factors. First, there was a shift in the type and status of personnel appointed to the governing body. This process began around 1578. Until then gentry representation on the governing body in the sixteenth century had been minimal. Thereafter gentry representation increased. By 1590 seven of the twelve governors were members of the gentry. This gentry influx to the governing body had the important consequence of reducing representation of tradesmen and craftsmen. The mayoralty came to be dominated by the gentry; between 1585 and 1595 the office was held by the gentry on seven occasions. The appointment of the town's justices of the peace was manipulated, removing true townsmen and appointing members of the gentry. This situation must be distinguished from similar developments in other towns such as Norwich, Rye and Bristol where gentry involvement in urban politics was insignificant. It is also markedly different to the situation in Suffolk, where towns, for the most part, resisted gentry encroachment. Reasons for gentry intrusion in Beverley are complex. A decline in the town's solvency led to increased dependence on outsiders, just as it did in some Kent towns. But gentry also brought real and practical benefits to the town. They were able to afford the time and expense of service as governors which townsmen found to be increasingly onerous. Gentry were also better placed to take the initiative in seeking and obtaining grants of lands from the Crown to the corporation. The gentry themselves were attracted by the tangible benefits which might flow their way. Common lands and urban property granted to the town by the Crown from the 1550s onwards were vulnerable to gentry predators and in Beverley they swiftly obtained leases of valuable holdings. By the 1590s over a quarter of the tenants of town lands were not persons engaged in specifically urban activities. On occasions there were violent and aggressive confrontations over lands in or near the town. It was not just control over town lands which was threatened; so were freeman rights and privileges in the administration and government of their town. More importantly, so was the type of religion they enjoyed.[29]

For there was a religious dimension to the changes in the type of personnel governing the town. Until 1581 there is every sign that the town's governors were anxious to push forward the Reformation, extending their support for preaching, rejecting elements of popular culture and 'vain' customs and imposing strict discipline. But such evidence is lacking from the mid-1580s onwards. Two of the gentry governors died leaving Catholic wills, in marked contrast to the contents of the townsmen's wills which showed the impact of Protestant preaching. Other evidence indicates at least religious conservatism among the governing body. Michael Wharton was suspected of recusancy along with other members of his family; William Raffles, Thomas Chapman, Ralph Freeman, Richard Marks and Thomas Wilberforce were officers under suspicion of holding conservative religious views. The town was never a Catholic stronghold, and although at the end of the sixteenth century Beverley had a disproportionately high number of known recusants, these were almost all gentry and yeomen from outside the town.[30] Willam Crashaw, the puritan preacher at St John's at the turn of the century, warned against the dangers which could flow from the presence of religious conservatives, a situation which he described as a spiritual poison: 'take heed of one ill town in a whole country, or one ill house in a whole town; and the governors of families and societies of one ill member in a whole body'.[31]

The influx of gentry to the governing body and the existence of conservative religious tendencies on the part of some of those gentry governors goes some way towards explaining an increasing divergence between those brought up and earning a living in the town and outsiders, often of gentry or yeoman origins, not dependent on urban labour and trade. Such a divergence was as marked in political as in religious views for it affected policy in areas of concern to true townsmen.

The choice of clergy at St John's seems to have become a cause for unease, especially after 1604. Appointments of godly and learned preachers such as Thomas Wincop in 1581 and William Crashaw in 1599 were due, in part, to pressure and influence from the Council of the North and to William Gee, the town's recorder and a member of the Council of the North. It was part of the policy of Huntingdon, the President of the Council, to ensure that godly preachers were planted in key towns in the north. The services of such preachers were clearly appreciated by townsmen and much of the commitment of the godly was due to their influence.[32] After 1605 Crashaw's replacement, Thomas Bindes, and the assistant clergy seem to have exercised little influence on the laity and, as has been seen, Brabbes was castigated by some as a 'dumb dog'. As Bindes's predecessor, Crashaw had praised those who entertained good ministers and castigated an 'ignorant and unlearned ministry... which is the source and fountain of all other evils in our church'.[33] The impact of Bindes and Brabbes on the town was insignificant in comparison to that of Wincop, Crashaw and later Rhodes, all of whom vigorously enforced strict moral rules, attacked disorderly behaviour and drunkenness and insisted on sabbath observance and church attendance. Bindes was elected by the governors with no sign of external pressure and seems to have been more amenable to their tastes. During Bindes's incumbency visitation court presentments fell to less than a quarter of the numbers presented when Crashaw came to the town. It was left to Rhodes to recommence in 1615 the campaign begun by Wincop and Crashaw, the number of presentments increasing fivefold. Rhodes's successor, James Burney, was elected formally by the governing body in 1632, probably because his more restrained preaching did not attract hostile attention. Even then, there was an attempt to elect an Arminian candidate to the post.[34]

Financial irregularities also widened the gulf between townsmen and the governing body and again show the interaction of politics and religion. Arguments before High Commission in 1594/5 revealed that surplus funds from church lands belonging to St Mary's were being siphoned off into the town coffers. Later investigation revealed that 'lands, tenements, rents, annuities, profits, hereditaments, goods, chattels, money and stocks of money had been given to charitable and godly use for the common benefit of the parish of St Mary's'. In fact it appears to have been common practice for balances remaining on the churchwarden's account to have been handed over to the Governors. Much the same happened at St John's. The town had received grants of land for the support of the former Minster. In reality the funds were not applied for such a purpose. Only a small proportion of the monies collected were disbursed on the Minster, the remainder being treated as ordinary corporation revenue. The corporation would eventually be ordered to keep town and Minster rents completely separate, but during this period it is noticeable that it was only after townsmen managed to secure the dismissal of conservative gentry governors in 1595 that expenditure on the town's churches increased. Similarly, commitment to poor relief and other urgent town necessities did not increase until after the dramatic changes in the personnel of government which took place in the mid-1590s. John Jackson expressly argued before the High Commission that 'the rents and profits of the said lands...ought to be employed to the use and benefit of the said church....' Townsmen were determined to prevent their governors from profiting from the church lands at the expense of the church and parishoners. Yet that was exactly what did happen. In 1633 a commission of enquiry found that over a long period of time some substantial burgesses, including governors, had obtained leases of lands at favourable rents which had then been sublet at great profit to themselves, with (in some cases) no money whatsoever accruing to the Church, the parishioners or those in need. There were parallel disputes over town lands, issues which were resurrected in political disturbances in 1602, 1604 and 1610. After the troubles of 1610 governors were threatened with discharge for non-payment of money to the town's receivers, one of whom was involved in the protest of 1615. Low-key abuse of this kind was widespread; yet the willingness of some burgesses to take action against their own governors reflects a desire for more upright behaviour in their rulers. This agreed with the preaching of active Protestant ministers such as Crashaw and Wincop, in placing stress on the honesty and integrity required of civic magistrates. Elsewhere, the Suffolk minister Robert Pricke attacked covetousness as an evil to be avoided, 'as a vice most abominable', likely to lead to the punishment of the innocent whilst the wicked escaped.[35]

Gain and covetousness led to civil unrest. But it also extended beyond mere financial and pecuniary gain to the coveting of and control of all offices in the town. The author of the *Mirrour of Policie* wrote that 'the first cause [of disorder] is contempt: and that happeneth when as some citizens are despised, and excluded from offices and public charges, and when as in a city dignities are not bestowed indifferently, for then they which are contemned do mutiny and rise against those that have the politic government'.[36] One reason underlying the unrest in the 1590s and early 1600s was the narrowing of the political framework of the town, concentrating power and excluding tradesmen and craftsmen from even minor office. The High Commission case of 1594/5 arose from an attempt by one faction of governors to interfere with and control the elections of churchwardens.

Paradoxically, at the same time that governors were seeking to gain greater influence over the selection of personnel to office in town and church, they were withdrawing from holding such offices themselves. They ceased serving as churchwardens and guild officials, relying on an increasingly narrow social, economic, political and religious base for support.[37]

In themselves such moves were a cause for concern amongst the godly. But what tipped them into open discontent expressed against the governing body were a number of other actions. Systems of government in church and town had been focused on men with a vested interest in the well-ordering of the community, aware of the mutual rights and obligations which were expected and demanded, and knowing that their authority rested as much on these presumptions and perceptions as on their instruments of power. But the presence of so many outsiders from the 1580s onwards, with no real interest in the town's well-being and with little desire to build upon the town's reputation for preaching and 'true religion', produced adverse results. Between 1578 and 1592 virtually no town ordinances were passed. Even minor revisions to guild ordinances all but came to an end. In 1592 further restrictions were passed on the burgesses' rights in mayoral elections, with penalties for resistance; the role of the guilds in elections was swept aside. The say of burgesses in selecting new governors was effectively removed. And although freemen managed to secure changes to the personnel of government and revisions to some ordinances in 1595 these gains were short-lived. In such circumstances townsmen had to take matters into their own hands to remove governors. Although he was writing in a different context Crashaw might have approved: 'out with him ... let none such bear office in church or state; let no such serpent or viper lurk in your societies'.[38]

V

The disputes which have been referred to were in part about municipal office-holding, but only because the policies pursued by the governing body did not meet the expectations of many in the burgess community; and those expectations had been moulded by the teaching they had received from godly ministers. Crashaw urged strict laws against swearing and profaneness, the observance of the sabbath, public prayers and strict execution of laws. The governors did not punish irreligious behaviour or encourage presentments at visitations in the late 1580s, early 1590s and early 1600s. In spite of this, it was still possible for some of the townsmen to express their vision of a godly town. In particular those holding guild office were able to enforce sabbath observance and ensure that the ordinances of the trade and craft guilds were in accord with their religious views. In comparison, town ordinances introduced by the governors did not reflect such desires for a further eighteen years.[39]

The godly knew what to expect of their magistrates: their preachers told them. In 1594, at York, John King compared the governors of towns to masters of a ship:

> So let masters and governors within this place who sit at the sterns of another kind of shipping and have rudders of a city... in their hands, let them awake themselves, that they may awake and rouse up other sleepers, all careless dissolute indisposed persons who love the thresholds of their private doors upon the Sabbath of the lord and their benches in ale booths better than the courts of the lord's house... how long shall the drunkard sleep within your gates in puddles and sinks of his boozing and lose both honesty and wit without controlment, the adulterer in chambering and wantonness upon his lascivious bed of pleasure... the idolater and superstitious upon the knees and in the bosom of the whore of Babylon?

Earlier in his sermon he had summarised the qualities required of magistrates:

> Let masters and magistrates learn... that when they are put in authority they receive as it were a role from the Lord... wherein their duties are abridged and summarised in this short sentence 'carry them in thy bosom'... pity their miseries, redress their wrongs, relieve their wants, reform their errors, prevent their miseries, procure their welfare and peace by all good means... Neither is the commonwealth theirs to use as they like but they the commonwealth.

To King those who failed to live up to these standards were foolish governors, like apes on the top of houses, 'highly perched, but absurdly conditioned'. In his printed works Crashaw echoed similar sentiments.[40] Yet the qualities demanded of urban governors by the preachers and their audiences were lacking in Beverley during periods when the governing body was dominated by gentry.

It is clear from this examination that Protestant and increasingly puritan views were motivating factors in the determination of townsmen to recapture political influence and preserve and advance the cause of true religion. In stressing the role of the magistracy, Protestantism could actually create distance between governors and governed. But if the governing body became divorced from popular expectations in both religious and political spheres it was more likely that puritanism would reinforce popular criticism of governors. The continuity of personnel engaged in political and religious radicalism in the town at the end of the sixteenth and beginning of the seventeenth centuries may well support views that the 'religious experience born out of puritanism . . . would prove a crucible of radical political consciousness and action'.[41] It was to the magistracy that puritan ministers like William Crashaw looked to further God's work in the Church. A divided magistracy, corrupt, contemptuous of those it ruled, interfering and overbearing, was in no position to advance the cause.

4. The Coming of Protestantism to Elizabethan Tewkesbury

CAROLINE LITZENBERGER

*By indenture then dated made between his majesty of the one part
and the bailis, burgesses and commonalty of the Borough and
town of Tewkesbury in the county of Gloucester of the other part.
It is witnessed that whereas the body or nether part of the late
abbey church of Tewkesbury aforesaid at the time of the
dissolution of the late monastery . . . and continually before the
same dissolution, was the parish church for the inhabitants of
the said town of Tewkesbury and other the parishioners of the
same, the said king for £453 paid to his receiver etc. by the said
bailis, burgesses and commonalty . . . did grant to the said bailis,
burgesses and commonalty and their successors the said abbey
church with the bells etc. and the church yard etc to be used for
ever there after by the bailis, burgesses and commonalty and
other parishioners as their parish church and churchyard.*

(4 June 1543)[1]

With this document the parish and town of Tewkesbury regained
the worship space they had lost three and a half years earlier when
John Wakeman, the abbot of Tewkesbury, surrendered the monastery
to the king's commissioners. Thus the parish was able to keep
its traditional place of worship by the apparently united action of the
town leaders. But while this action may have accurately foreshadowed
the town's resistance to religious change during the next two decades,
the unity among the civic leaders exemplified by this action would not
last. In particular, during the early years of the reign of Elizabeth,
religious divisions among the urban elite would lead them to present
each other to the church courts for acts of religious nonconformity.
Furthermore, by their continued support of religious drama and

79

church ales, and by their ongoing reluctance to divest themselves of the appurtenances of traditional religion, the leaders seem to have done their best to minimise the impact of religious change on the parish and town of Tewkesbury. Protestantism came to Tewkesbury very slowly.

It is helpful to link parish and town together in discussing the effects of official religious change on this locality. As the purchase of the abbey church indicates, the town was fully involved in the life of this parish. It was after all the leaders of the town 'and their successors' who made the purchase. At various times during the next sixty years those leaders would assert their authority over the churchwardens. Furthermore, at the end of the churchwardens' terms it was the bailiffs of the town who received the parish accounts and passed them on to the incoming churchwardens.[2]

Although the residents of Tewkesbury may not have felt the effects of the changes in religious policy until the dissolution of the monastery, they would undoubtedly have been aware of some aspects of the new religion. A short distance to the north lay the parish of Toddington, home of William Tracy, esquire, a former sheriff of Gloucestershire. His very Protestant will of 1531 had been circulated in manuscript form within a year after his death, and it was printed in 1535 with commentaries by two of the leading English promoters of reform. This will caused much concern among the guardians of traditional religion both within Gloucestershire and throughout the kingdom. It was refused probate and Tracy's body was exhumed and burned in 1532. Approximately ten years later the printed version was included on a list of prohibited books.[3] In addition, in 1535 the reformer, Hugh Latimer, became bishop of the diocese of Worcester which then included Tewkesbury, and he and his licensed preachers actively promoted the new religion throughout the diocese. By 1539 some individuals in Gloucestershire were including strongly Protestant statements of belief in their wills, possibly as a result of Latimer's efforts. Furthermore, groups were meeting in private homes not far from Tewkesbury to discuss the new theology.[4]

In fact, Tewkesbury's geographical position makes it quite likely that Latimer and his preachers would have travelled through the town, and given the size of the parish and its prominence in the region Bishop Latimer must surely have preached there at some time during his episcopate.[5] The parish of Tewkesbury had 1,600 communicants in 1547, and was located at the confluence of the Avon and Severn rivers, approximately ten miles north of Gloucester on the road to Worcester. It had been a market town since shortly after the Norman Conquest and by the sixteenth century had gained freedom from all fees and tolls for shipments down the river past Gloucester.[6] However, it was not just a stop along the way between two larger towns. It was also the centre of local commerce and a manufacturing town known for its production of leather goods.

As residents from the surrounding countryside brought their goods to market and perused the gloves and shoes made by local craftspeople, they would surely have been impressed and perhaps inspired by the sight of the abbey church of Tewkesbury rising from the banks of the Severn near the centre of the town. Looking more like a cathedral than a parish church, it was and is a huge structure, cruciform in shape, with an imposing central tower and massive pillars rising to support its high roof in both the nave and the chancel. Possession of such an imposing edifice by the town of Tewkesbury brought with it not only the opportunity for the parish to continue to worship in their accustomed place, but also the burden of huge maintenance costs associated with tending to the structural needs of an ageing edifice. These needs became urgent when the steeple collapsed on Easter Day in 1559, just days before Parliament's approval of the return to Protestantism under Elizabeth.

Each of the changes in official religion introduced between the Dissolution in 1540 and the promulgation of Elizabethan Protestantism in 1559 made new demands on the leadership of the parish and on the parishioners themselves. While the inhabitants of Tewkesbury may have successfully ignored the changes urged on them by Bishop Latimer, and thus hardly noticed the swing back to a more conservative religious policy during the last years of Henry VIII's reign, they could not have ignored the changes introduced under Edward VI. Tewkesbury, like most other parishes, had a number of chantries. These were established in memory of deceased loved ones for the expressed purpose of offering intercessions for the dead through the celebration of the mass, a practice which was anathema to Edwardian Protestants. They were dissolved by statute in 1547; the endowments which funded them were confiscated by the Crown; and the priests who staffed them were left without positions. In addition, those priests were no longer available to assist the vicar of the parish in his duties. This happened in Tewkesbury, and that very large parish was left without adequate clergy.[7] Other changes would follow.

The most significant and unsettling change promulgated by the Crown came with the introduction of the first Book of Common Prayer in June 1549. That book which prescribed the accepted forms of worship for the Church in England stipulated that all worship was to be in

English instead of Latin. Tewkesbury probably responded to this change as did many others, by adopting the new book without changing all the accoutrements of worship. The curate, Robert Erean, was learned and a licensed preacher, and may have supported the move toward Protestantism, as may some of his parishioners.[8] However, later evidence would indicate that many parishioners, including most of the parish leaders, may have clung to the old religion no matter what their priest preferred.

Most of the people and clergy of Tewkesbury probably welcomed the return to Catholicism in mid-1553. During Mary's short reign at least one parishioner even made provisions in his will to support the re-foundation of the monastery 'if thys abbey be sett up agayne'. In that same year, 1557, another parishioner provided that if his son should die without issue the residue of his estate should be used to establish either a grammar school or a chantry, another indication of a preference for traditional religious practices, even though the Marian Restoration did not include the re-establishment of chantries. Bequests in support of Catholicism were not limited to lay people. In April 1557 John Assum, priest, bequeathed to the parish his vestments of blue and yellow silk, albs, amices, stoles, a velvet chasuble, a red and green altar cloth with fringe, a second altar cloth and a cross containing a relic.[9] Also, during Mary's reign Tewkesbury testators generally followed the same pattern as those in the rest of the county and diocese of Gloucester, preferring to bequeath their souls 'to Almighty God, the Blessed Virgin Mary and the Holy Company of Heaven', rather than opting for a bequest of their souls simply 'to Almighty God' as most had done during Edward's reign. The former was the traditional form of soul bequest most commonly found in pre-Reformation wills, while the latter theologically neutral declaration was clearly the religious statement of choice during the years of most radical official Protestantism. The simple bequest found in most Edwardian wills disclosed nothing about the individual's religious preference, and perhaps provided a way for testators to avoid disclosing beliefs which were counter to official policy. In contrast, Marian testators seem to have generally preferred the form of bequest most consistent with the official religion of the day. Testators appear to have been much more comfortable with the old religion than the new during the reigns of Edward and Mary.

Not all testators, however, were espousing traditional beliefs during Mary's reign, and in particular, one of the leaders of the town chose not only to include a more Protestant statement of faith in his will, but also drew attention to the fact by establishing a charity to aid the poor. Giles Geast was a mercer in Tewkesbury, and after the monastery's surrender, he purchased a number of that institution's former holdings. He died in 1557 and in his will, dated 20 August 1557, he bequeathed his soul 'to Almighty God prainge hym throughe his infallyble promyse his moste mercyfull forgivenes of my synnes for the meryttes and deservynge of the passyon of our savyor Jesus Christe my redeamer whereby onely I truste to be saved', a remarkably non-traditional statement especially considering that it was made at the height of the Marian Restoration. He then went on to establish a charity for the poor of Tewkesbury to be funded by rents from his various tenements.[10] During Mary's reign prominent testators' expressions of faith reflected divergent religious beliefs similar to those found among the living civic and parish leaders.

While the town leadership had been united in their desire to purchase the abbey church and churchyard in 1543, by 1563 there were clear divisions within their ranks. In that year the churchwardens presented the bailiffs of the town to the church courts for two offences. The bailiffs, John Butler and Thomas Godwin, along with William Cole, gentleman, were presented for walking 'with their cappes on ther heades at the tyme of the holy communion before the chauncell doore', actions which indicated both their disapproval of the form of worship being practised beyond that door and their refusal to communicate. In addition, since the bailiffs were ultimately responsible for the parish, they were also implicated by the disclosure of a number of 'not defaced relics' in the possession of Tewkesbury parish church. These included a pax, crosses, candlesticks, censers, incense, a Mass book, processionals, and two 'clappers to go about with on Good Friday', all items which should have been destroyed prior to that time because they 'savoured of popery'. But were they being used? Conflicting evidence comes from the curate, who was presented at the same court session for not wearing the requisite square cap, a sign of Protestant nonconformity.[11] Thus, the parish had items which might have been used to celebrate the eucharist according to the traditional Catholic form; however, the presiding cleric was probably not using them. The churchwardens chose to present both the Protestant curate and the more religiously conservative protesting laymen, perhaps an indication that those parish leaders favoured the middle way of the Elizabethan Settlement over either extreme. Evidence from twenty years later tends to further support that assessment. In 1582, members of a number of prominent families, some of whom preferred Catholicism and some known to favour a hotter form of Protestantism than that described in the Settlement, were reported for not having received Easter communion. At the same time, the clerk was presented for administering the cup during the communion service, a clear violation of the provisions of the Book of Common Prayer since he was not ordained or otherwise authorised to perform that function.[12] Thus, a desire for conformity rather than nonconformity may have motivated the individuals who made those presentments as well. And yet, those same parish leaders held on to various, prohibited accoutrements of the old religion even after 1581.

Inventories of church goods held by the parish survive from 1577 and 1584. The archbishop of Canterbury ordered a visitation of the diocese in 1576, and at that time Tewkesbury was found to lack a number of required items. They were still using a chalice rather than the requisite communion cup, and they lacked a Bible in English of the appropriate size. A few items were sold that year, but the inventory made the following year indicates that they also still possessed a number of items specifically prohibited in the visitation articles of 1576, including a vestment or cope and albs. They still had a tall candlestick, 'one riche coape, ... vij albes', and 'a pece of imagerye'. An inventory made eight years later contains a similar though not identical list of items, including 'the best coope of tynsell with redd roses', 'iij awbes of lynnen', and 'one amyce'.[13] Very possibly some of those pieces had been bequeathed to the parish by John Assum in 1557, but the parish should have destroyed them long before 1584. The cope was finally transported to London, presumably in response to an archiepiscopal order, in October 1597.[14] The other offending items may have been destroyed or sold by that time, although the records are silent on this point.

Of course, the fact that Tewkesbury still possessed prohibited items late in Elizabeth's reign is not conclusive evidence of continued traditional religious practices. However, Tewkesbury stands out as the sole recorded parish in Gloucestershire which possessed such a large number of forbidden items so late in the reign. Furthermore, a comparison of Tewkesbury's churchwardens' accounts with those of St Michael's, Gloucester, shows that the former parish spent relatively little preparing and providing for Protestant worship between 1563 (when Tewkesbury's records begin) and 1576. In the first year of Elizabeth's reign St Michael's removed the earth under the altar to lower the chancel to the level of the nave so that the officially preferred communion table would not be elevated above or separated from the worshippers. At the same time they removed the roodloft including the images of Mary and John which had been erected less than a year earlier. They also purchased the new Book of Common Prayer and a psalter, and sold a number of their Catholic vestments, torches, books and a chalice. Receipts from the sales totalled over £10. Four years later (in the first year for which the records survive), Tewkesbury purchased a Book of Homilies and the Book of Common Prayer. These may not have been the first purchases in support of Elizabethan Protestantism; however, the records reveal only very small liturgically related expenditures by Tewkesbury (as compared to St Michael's) prior to 1576, and as noted above Tewkesbury still had a number of Catholic vestments and a chalice at that later time. Before the end of the 1560s, St Michael's and a number of other Gloucestershire parishes had whitewashed the walls of their churches to cover the pre-Reformation wall-paintings in the body of the church. In addition, some had hired carpenters to build pews around the communion table, and painters to inscribe the Ten Commandments, the creed and the Lord's Prayer on the newly white-washed walls.[15] No similar expenses appear for Tewkesbury before the 1570s.

During that same decade Tewkesbury purchased psalters, books of special prayers and a second Book of Homilies, and repaired a Prayer Book.[16] Then in the early 1570s they purchased more psalters and a special prayer for the queen, and acquired a table and frame from the bishop. (This would have been either a table of the ten commandments or of the degrees of consanguinity, probably the latter given the con-servative theological leanings of the bishop, Richard Cheyney.[17]) This was the time when followers of the new religion began to emerge as parish leaders. One was probably responsible for the inclusion of the following two religiously reformist statements between the church-wardens' accounts for 1570–2 and those for 1572–4:

The Lord doth choose no man worthie,
but by chooseing he makes them *worthie*.

He hath chosen us that we should be *holly*.

The first reference to whitewashing then appears in the records as well.[18] Then in apparent response to the metropolitical visitation of 1576, the whitewashed walls were touched up, and whitewash was applied to portions of some windows, perhaps to the faces of the images of saints. Those were the pieces of glass which Protestants believed most clearly violated the prohibition against graven images in the Ten Commandments. Such concealment would have been consistent with practices in other parts of the realm.[19] Other changes were made as a direct result of the visitation. The parish purchased a communion cup 'gilt with a cover and also a nother communion cupp ungilt and without cover' and sold their chalice. They also purchased 'a Bible of the largest volumn' and built a desk for it 'that standes at the pulpett'.[20] Tewkesbury was finally conforming more fully to established religious policy. Two years later, in 1578, the very prominent Cordwainers' Guild of Tewkesbury took a step which indicates there was support for an even more Protestant religious policy, locally. They declared that

> it is ordered and agreed by the full consentes of the holle companie that none of that same companie shale have theire shope windowes or windowe open at any tyme apone the Sonedaye after the tyme it have ronge all in to service under payne of iiij *d.* for everie defaulte.[21]

Such an ordinance would have been consistent with the sabbatarian leanings of many Elizabethan Protestants at the time.

Looking more broadly, civic as well as religious change came to Tewkesbury in the mid-1570s. Just a year before the archiepiscopal visitation, the queen granted the town a royal charter. In this case the change was one which Tewkesbury had sought. The town leaders had approached the earl of Leicester in 1574 to request his support for their cause, and had sent him a silver and gilt cup. A year after receiving their charter the town named him High Steward.[22] The charter brought with it the reorganisation of town government including the creation of a number of new offices in addition to the customary two bailiffs. Thus, after 1575 there would be more opportunities for leadership in the town, and those new positions would be filled predominantly by promoters of Protestantism.

Tewkesbury was not yet ready, however, for a complete rejection of all aspects of the old religion. Practices which were being legislated out of existence in most cities and towns as a result of growing pressure from the hotter sort of Protestants were continuing in Tewkesbury, even though Protestants were beginning to gain the ascendancy among the town's elite. These included church ales, a lucrative source of funds for the parish until at least 1578, and religious drama which continued into the early seventeenth century. Both of these events were typical sources of revenue for rural parishes and single-parish towns. They typically attracted people from the surrounding parishes, who in turn would have expected Tewkesbury parishioners to join in their ales and other revels.

Plays, and in particular religious plays, were frowned upon by many Protestants, but had a long history in Tewkesbury, having been popular there from the fourteenth century. These 'miracle plays' were often organised by the clergy or other parish officials, and there is evidence that they were sometimes presented along with plays mounted by guilds.[23] The parish of Tewkesbury had a set of 'players gere' which they hired out from time to time, usually to parishioners. It was loaned once in the late 1560s, but its recorded use increased in the 1570s just when other towns were beginning to prohibit such diversions. Occasionally performances were even given in the parish church, in one case damaging a newly constructed pew. In 1576 the 'gere' included 'five players gownes, iiij jackets, iiij beardes, [and] two heades'. Over the next eight years it would be refurbished and augmented to include eight 'heades of heare for the apostles', a 'face or vysor for the devyll', and 'Christes garments'.[24] During that time it was used frequently, yet another indication of Tewkesbury's continued support for traditional practices, even those being discouraged or prohibited across most of the rest of England at this time.

According to the parish records, however, the 'players gere' then lay forgotten from the mid-1580s to 1600. In that year the churchwardens turned to that familiar source of revenue to raise the funds necessary to cover the expense of a major parish building project. They 'undertooke to sett a battlement of stone uppon the topp of the tower' where the steeple had been until Easter 1559. Finding the project substantially underfunded after soliciting private donations, they mounted three stage plays to be performed within the church on the first three days after Whitsunday. The festivities included three trumpeters and other musicians playing incidental music, as well as food and ale served by hired waiters. Financially the plays were a disaster, losing over £20. Perhaps most people had lost their taste for such activities. The churchwardens made one further attempt to recoup their losses, by requesting permission from the bailiffs and burgesses of the town for a church ale. However, their request was denied because 'of abuses accustomed to be reformed', another sign of growing Protestantism among the leaders of the town. References to costumes, plays and ales then disappear from the parish records.[25]

Meanwhile, parish worship seems to have become more Protestant after 1585. By May 1589 the churchwardens had taken down the communion rails, although there is no record of them building pews around the communion table as had so many other parishes. Also, in the early 1590s they created a 'preching place' in the churchyard, signifying a new emphasis on the value of sermons typical of late sixteenth century English Protestantism. A short time later they repaired the pulpit in the church and added a desk to it. However, it was not until approximately 1614 that the parish moved the pulpit into the nave of the church, purchased John Foxe's *Book of Martyrs* and built a desk to hold it, all additional indications of growing Protestantism in the parish.[26] Protestantism in Tewkesbury had now clearly moved beyond mere conformity, but this development came some forty years after it had come to many other parishes, even within the diocese of Gloucester. There, copies of Foxe, special communion pews in place of rails and scripture painted on the walls of the nave had been in place since the 1570s.

Why was there such a delay in the acceptance of Protestantism in Tewkesbury? A number of factors probably contributed to the tardiness. The parish lacked the leadership often provided by a strong local noble or upper gentry family, and the Elizabethan bishops of Gloucester were singularly ineffective in promoting Protestantism in their diocese. In addition, the rectory had been impropriated by the king, and the parish had to rely on a string of curates of varying levels of ability to minister to its sacramental and pastoral needs. Finally, and probably most significantly, there seems to have been a distinct division over religion among the leaders of the town and parish.

There was a lack of leadership in the upper echelons of the parish throughout most of Elizabeth's reign. Tewkesbury was a Crown manor during the sixteenth century and the monarch did not give it any significant attention. Further, no other local magnates stepped forward to fill the void. Similarly, the Crown's involvement in the parish contributed to the lack of effective clerical leadership. Since the monarch was in effect the rector of the parish after the dissolution of the monastery and often neglected the parish, it frequently fell to the local lay leaders to procure the services of a curate, and the results of their efforts were mixed at best. Robert Erean, the curate during much of Edward's reign, may have been highly qualified, but such was not always the case. During Mary's reign a number of individuals served as curates in quick succession, the last, William Whitehead, dying in 1560.

Nicholas Crondale then served in that capacity through the first portion of Elizabeth's reign, disappearing from the records after July 1572. Nothing further is known about the qualifications of either Whitehead or Crondale. In 1579 William Mawson became curate, having been transferred to that position from nearby Lassington. However, he does not appear to have been licensed to preach, since shortly after his arrival he was prevented from presiding at a funeral by key lay leaders of the parish. They wanted to replace him with a licensed preacher. While their actions may have been motivated by a desire to hear a sermon at the funeral, it may also indicate that they were not accustomed to deferring to ecclesiastical authority. The Elizabethan bishops of Gloucester certainly did not command broad respect from the inhabitants of their diocese.[27]

As with most Elizabethan towns, Tewkesbury was dominated by a group of powerful families. Church officials were seen as a part of the civic leadership, while town officials in turn helped run the parish, perhaps to a greater extent than was common elsewhere. The latter was undoubtedly a vestige of the way in which the town had gained possession of the abbey. The intermingling of civic and ecclesiastical responsibilities appears to have gone beyond the overseeing of the accounts of the parish. In 1576 for instance, the bailiffs netted £3 from the sale of some church goods, and then three years later used lead from the church for the gutters on the new boothall (probably a combination market place and city hall). Later, in 1595 the bailiffs and burgesses of the town found it necessary to intervene more directly in the affairs of the parish. A year earlier the churchwardens 'without advice taken' had incurred substantial expense when they removed the lead from the roof on the south side of the church in order to replace it with a new roof. Unfortunately, they ran out of money and that side of the church stood uncovered and exposed to the elements until the following summer. It was then that the town leaders intervened, assessing the inhabitants of the town for the cost of reroofing half the body of the church. Revenues were collected and used to fund not only the reroofing project, but also the reglazing of a number of broken windows. Furthermore, a precedent had been established and in 1598 the inhabitants of the town were again assessed by the town to fund the maintenance of the fabric of the parish; in this instance the sum of £22 was collected. Three years later a similar assessment brought in £29.[28]

The overlapping responsibilities of parish and town leaders were further complicated in Elizabethan Tewkesbury by the religious leanings of the members of the leading families. The signs of differences appeared early when protests by the bailiffs against current religious practices were reported by the churchwardens. In this and later instances those expressing strong religious opinions seem to have preferred either Catholicism or official Protestantism. None seem to have wanted a more radical form of the new religion. This contrasted with the conflict occurring within another Gloucestershire parish, Cirencester, at about the same time. There, both Catholics and radical Protestants were refusing to take communion, while the clergy seem to have been conducting worship according to the approved rites.[29]

In Tewkesbury, those who would have preferred a return to the old religion seem to have dominated both the town and parish through the first fifteen years of Elizabeth's reign. They were led by John Butler and Thomas Godwin, the bailiffs who protested in 1563. Butler, in particular, was both powerful and highly respected. He was chosen by a number of other prominent individuals as an overseer of their wills. In addition, he served at least three separate terms as bailiff, was one of the original burgesses in 1575 and held the office of constable in 1580. Others with traditional religious leanings who shared in the leadership during those early-Elizabethan years included four other burgesses: Thomas Downbell, William Wakeman, Edward Alye and William Willis. In 1563 John Downbell, Thomas's father, walked in the church during 'commone prayer' with members of three other leading families, an act of protest similar to that of Butler and Godwin. Then between 1569 and 1571 (just four years before he became a burgess), William Willis disrupted worship services so often that he was described as a 'comen tawker in the churche at the tyme of devine service'.[30] Others in this group were less overt in their support of Catholicism, but were linked through ties of kinship and marriage, sat together in church, or were named in each others' wills.[31]

Those who favoured Catholicism began to fade from prominence in the early 1570s, as they were replaced by supporters of the new religion. First serving as churchwardens and then moving into positions of civic leadership, these individuals gained nearly complete control of both the parish and the town by 1585.

The mid-1570s were the most tumultuous period in the transition from the old order to the new. When the council of burgesses was formed as a result of the charter in 1575 it included not only six supporters of the old religion, but also five who preferred the new. The latter were George Morrey, Roger Malliard, Thomas Perkins,

William Hill and Edward Leight. Hill, Perkins, Malliard and Morrey were part of what appears to have been an inner circle of committed Protestants. All of these men left distinctly Protestant wills.[32] Others in the group were Edward Baston, Humphrey Davis, Richard, John and William Field, Thomas Geast, John Millington, James Phelpes, Richard Rudgedale, Hugh Slicer and Giles Tovey. These individuals were linked to each other and to a second circle of families by ties similar to those which linked the more conservative group, except that the links among the Protestant families seem to have been tighter and more exclusive. Baston, Phelpes and Rudgedale were the men who prevented the curate, William Mawson, from presiding at that funeral in 1579 just after his arrival. The next year Rudgedale and Slicer served as bailiffs together. Meanwhile, marriage linked some of the men together. Giles Tovey's wife, Anne, was a sister of John and Richard Field. John Millington had married Elizabeth Geast, a niece of the noted philanthropist, Giles Geast, and by that marriage he was related to Edward Baston, Thomas Geast and Richard Rudgedale. Similar ties connected other families, as well.[33] In addition, the leaders and their relatives sat together in church, and not just in a special pew for burgesses or bailiffs.

The assignment of seats in Tewkesbury contributes further to the emerging image of a particularly idiosyncratic parish in its customs as well as in its religion. Places in pews there were controlled and dispensed by the churchwardens. This may have occurred in some other parishes, but seating was supposed to be the prerogative of the clergy of the parish.[34] Payment appears to have been made only when the place was first assigned, and there seems to have been an informal custom of inheritance whereby the heir or heirs had first claim to the seat previously held by the surviving parent. By a similar procedure permission was occasionally granted to an individual to construct his own pew. Thus, each year a few people requested seats and paid the fee, often specifying with whom they wished to sit. This piecemeal pattern of pew rentals was disrupted in 1576, however, when large numbers of people relinquished their old seats in favour of seats in new pews constructed just after the town received its charter. At this time members of the Protestant elite claimed the pews in the front of the church, and various combinations of other individuals from the new oligarchy moved into the pews just vacated by the elite.[35]

Seating patterns disclose more about the parish than just its leadership network, however. Some less prominent adherents of Catholicism who none the less attended church may have been among those who requested seats as far as possible from the pulpit and communion table. In Lancashire and Cheshire it was reported that such individuals often withdrew 'to the farthest partes of the churche from the worde'.[36] Thus we might be suspicious of John Rekes and Thomas Mondy who requested seats in St Nicholas Chapel, and Parrys of the Lode who asked for 'a seate at the nether end of the churche'. Similarly, Harry Thompson requested seats for his wife and her mother in the 'hynmust seat in Seynt Gorgys Chappell'.[37]

Furthermore, despite the apparent pattern of separate seating for men and women, the sexes were not always in practice separated, once again demonstrating Tewkesbury's preference for local customs over conventionality. In 1574, for instance, Humphrey and John Davis, and Robert Dryver, all members of prominent families, rented seats for their wives in the pew with Mr Freebanck. Husbands and wives also sometimes requested seats together, as did Roger Tyrret and his wife, and Thomas Malliard and his wife. The latter went further, paying eight pence 'for grounde to builde a seate upon for him and his wyfe nexte beneathe the pulpytt on the southe side'.[38] This absence of strict physical separation by gender is in sharp contrast to the recent findings of Margaret Aston. She asserts that until the early seventeenth century women and men occupied separate areas of the church during worship, typically but not always with the women on the north side and the men on the south. Only then, in the early 1600s, did men and women in the parishes she studied begin to sit together, and then whole families were grouped together.[39] In Tewkesbury gender-segregated seating did not emerge until the 1590s, just before other parishes began moving away from this practice. Then early in the seventeenth century, galleries were built for the young men of the parish so they could be seated separately from adults and young women. Family seating would not come until later, as even in terms of church seating Tewkesbury lagged behind other areas of England.

The Reformation did eventually come to Tewkesbury, but much later than in other towns, even other towns in Gloucestershire. In the early years of religious change the town's leaders seem to have been united in their preference for the old religion, and their control of religious policies within the town and parish appears to have continued through at least the first decade of Elizabeth's reign, except for a brief interruption in 1563. As with much of the rest of the kingdom, the clarification of royal religious policy in the early 1570s may have been a catalyst for changes at the local level. At this time it became clearer to the people that England was neither going to return to Catholicism nor introduce additional Protestant innovations. In Tewkesbury the changes which came at that time coincided with the granting of the new charter to the town, and with the metropolitical visitation of the parish. The result was confusion among the chief inhabitants for the rest of that decade, as Catholics and Protestants alternated in positions of leadership. The Protestants finally gained control of both the town and parish in the early 1580s, but Tewkesbury's acceptance of established religious practices had been and would continue to be marked by its local idiosyncrasies.

5. Worcester: a Cathedral City in the Reformation

DIARMAID MacCULLOCH

This study concentrates on a narrative of religious change in sixteenth-century Worcester, contained in a largely unknown Worcester chronicle; it compares what the chronicle tells us with what we know of religious changes elsewhere, particularly in other cathedral cities, during the English Reformation. The Worcester Chronicle, recently rediscovered by Dr Pat Hughes of Worcester, deals with civic matters as well as the religious changes chiefly under consideration here; it forms five folios in a manuscript volume of miscellaneous collections and memoranda.[1] It is structured as a list of the annually-elected pair of senior and junior bailiffs of the city of Worcester from 1483 to 1578; to this list, annalistic entries have been added, taking the year of the bailiwick from September to September. Internal evidence indicates three levels of compilation in the work. First, entries up to 1547 are fairly laconic; second, from 1547 on, the descriptions of events are clearly those of an eye-witness with decided opinions, particularly about religion. From the tone of their comments, both pre- and post-1547 chroniclers are conservative in religious sympathy. Third, the whole work is now in the hand of an early seventeenth-century copyist, who has added material of a commonplace nature about kings and queens, after he had copied the more interesting original entries.

All these three people can be identified with a reasonable degree of certainty.[2] The earliest (pre-1547) layer can be ascribed to one of the most important men in Tudor Worcester, Robert Yowle. Yowle was four times bailiff (1546, 1548, 1552 and 1559), and four times MP for the city (1547, November 1554, 1555 and 1558).[3] The staunch early Protestant John Davis described him scornfully as 'a jolly Catholic'; Davis was understandably bitter at his boyhood memories of Bailiff Yowle ordering him to be confined in chains in freezing cold for his religious views during 1546-7.[4] Nevertheless, Yowle's conservative religion did not prevent him serving three more terms as bailiff under Edward VI and Elizabeth. Moreover, like so many who deplored the

Reformation, he took full advantage of the financial opportunities offered by the break-up of the existing religious establishment. When the Crown released to the Corporation the lands seized from the two friaries in the city, it was Yowle who acquired the lease of the Grey Friars' land inside the walls, and he made his home in the Grey Friars.[5]

At his death in 1561, however, Yowle affirmed his true religious sympathies once more. He had already done much to secure the refoundation and endowment of Worcester free school, and in his will he made generous provision for it. He was clearly hoping to inoculate the youth of the city against the Protestantism which had inspired John Davis; his will required the master and boys of the school to come yearly to his tomb in the cathedral to pray for his soul and those of his family and of all Christians.[6] Additionally, the poor were left large doles at his burial and his month's and year's mind. The Chronicler notes Yowle's burial in the cathedral, the building which is so central to the entries in the Chronicle.

The second, post-1547 layer which forms the bulk of the Chronicle is the work of Yowle's son-in-law and executor, another prominent Worcester resident, John Rowland alias Steynor (*c.* 1507–80). He married in 1547 Ann, daughter and co- heiress of Yowle, thus consolidating Steynor's already well- established position as a member of the city's governing body, the Twenty-Four.[7] Steynor outwardly espoused the new religion, at least enough to serve as bailiff under Protestant monarchs in 1551 and 1571. He too benefited from the property released on to the market, taking over the chapel of the Trinity Guild and turning it into a house for his large and growing family.[8] He showed no obvious sign of open papist sympathies when Catholicism was proscribed, and the preamble to his will is noncommittal in its religious expressions. However, in the Chronicle his love of the old religion's splendour is clear enough, and his widow Ann was listed as recusant in 1592–3.[9]

The early seventeenth-century copyist of the Chronicle is John Steynor the younger (1560–*c.* 1634), son of John Rowland alias Steynor, and a keen historian of the city: he borrowed the text of the Chronicle out of the city archives, through the agency of his brother Robert.[10] John was a lawyer, in trouble for his Catholic beliefs in 1610.[11] Nevertheless, he was clearly trusted by the city governors; he kept up social contacts with the hierarchy of the established Church, including the early seventeenth-century Bishop Henry Parry, and borrowed books and manuscripts from them.[12] Moreover, his historical interests, his love of the city and his Catholic sympathies combined in a congenial task in 1616; he was chosen as one of the commissioners trying to re-establish the endowment of St Oswald's Hospital, after its lands had been dispersed at the Reformation.[13] From many volumes in the civic and cathedral archives, the younger John Steynor made copious notes and transcripts. He was particularly interested in early charters and customs, and also made out a vast calendar, into which he entered all the events which he considered significant from CE 15 to 1635. It is noteworthy that the year 1588 was left blank, and that the entry for the Armada appears in a later hand: clearly this was a painful and ambiguous memory for a loyal Englishman of Catholic sympathies.[14]

The Chronicle's entries on secular matters reflect Yowle's and Steynor's major part in Worcester's civic life; yet the notes on religious changes more or less exclusively concern the cathedral, with the occasional appended note of changes affecting the city parishes and the county beyond. The relationship between city and cathedral was complex. Many leading citizens, like Robert Yowle himself, were buried in the great church; yet Worcester's modern historian Dr Dyer notes the degree of separation between most inhabitants of the cathedral close and the city round it.[15] The cathedral undoubtedly aroused civic pride, and before the Reformation this was strengthened by devotion to the cults housed there, such as those of Our Lady and Saints Wulfstan and Oswald. Civic worthies attended services there, either to hear sermons at the open-air cross, or in the building itself. However, their attendance could in itself provoke tension: in 1516 there was a careful agreement with the Prior and Convent allowing city officials to bear their maces into the cathedral as long as they claimed no jurisdiction thereby.[16] Ecclesiastical privileges, such as the exempt liberty of Worcester cathedral's close, could also generate friction and jurisdictional disputes, which growing religious differences might exacerbate. Moreover, the cathedral was a potential base for government interference with the privileges of the city. The possibility of such government intervention increased after Worcester Cathedral Priory was remodelled as a secular Chapter by Henry VIII in 1540; the dean and prebendaries were often government nominees, chosen to change the religious flavour of a high-profile religious institution. We know of jurisdictional squabbles in the fifteenth and early sixteenth centuries, and again in the 1620s, when puritan annoyance in the city at the growth of Laudian influence in the cathedral Chapter brought renewed friction.[17] The Chronicle records no clashes between town and cathedral, so we can only speculate about the relationship in the intervening years when the religious views of the civic and cathedral leadership cannot always have been in step.

A cathedral was a showcase in an age of theological and liturgical revolution. To gain local acceptance for changes, central government had to ensure that the devotional life of the mother church in the diocese accurately reflected official policy. Worcester was a key community in which to publicise the government's wishes. Its importance arose not so much because of its size; it was only in the second league among English towns, for the population of its ten intra-mural parishes was about 4,000 in the mid-sixteenth century, experiencing some rapid growth thereafter.[18] Geography and economics gave the city a higher profile than its population size would suggest. Worcester is a city in the lowland zone community, but it is a frontier town, with the hills of the highland zone on its doorstep. It was also then the hinge between two different rural economies: in its market were exchanged the animals and animal products of the pastoral region to the west of the River Severn, and the cereals of the region to the east. Its bridge over the Severn made it the centre of a star-shaped system of roads. The south–north axis included the lines of communication running from Shrewsbury to Oxford and Lichfield to Bristol: the east–west axis included the roads from the headquarters of the Council in the Marches of Wales at Ludlow, and from Coventry. The Severn was navigable well beyond Worcester, and it enjoyed a lively river trade.[19]

Economically, the town had importance far beyond its market function: from the fifteenth century to the eighteenth, it was one of the most active and industrialised cloth-manufacturing towns in England, remarkably in a county which had comparatively little other cloth manufacture. In the 1530s John Leland said, 'noe towne of England, at this present tyme, maketh so many cloathes yearly, as this towne doth,' and modern research bears him out. Half of Worcester's trade and manufacture was to do with cloth, compared with a third in Coventry, or 17 per cent in Elizabethan Norwich, both famous clothing towns.[20] Its greatest early sixteenth-century cloth merchant, William Mucklowe, travelled as far as the Low Countries to pursue his trade.[21] So this was no provincial backwater, as indeed is indicated by John Rowland alias Steynor's alert comments on national political events, particularly under Elizabeth. Another piece of evidence for Worcester's status can be found in the movement and level of building prices in the town: comparable with those in London, and higher than many areas of the home counties and the south-east.[22] The city even boasted its own Protestant printing press briefly during the reign of Edward VI, when John Oswen moved from Ipswich in 1549: he clearly saw it as the best strategic centre from which to begin his campaign of Protestant publication for a new Welsh and Border market. These included editions of the 1549 Prayer Book.[23]

Worcester Cathedral had a particular resonance for Henry VIII as the burial place of his elder brother Arthur, and of King John, whose tomb was refurbished significantly in 1540. But apart from that, a rich and powerful diocese and cathedral would inevitably loom large in the Tudor government's religious priorities. The medieval diocese of Worcester represented the Anglo-Saxon kingdom of the Hwicce, covering the prosperous and fertile valleys of the Severn and the Midlands Avon: Worcestershire, part of Warwickshire, most of Gloucestershire and the city of Bristol. It was not impossibly large by the standards of its neighbours, but Henry VIII saw it as worth subdividing into three, forming two new dioceses out of the southern section, based on Bristol and Gloucester.

The clergy chosen to be bishops of Worcester exactly mirror the varying fortunes of the Reformation, and almost without exception they represent leading figures on either side. On the eve of change, the bishop was the absentee Jerome Ghinucci, watchdog for English interests at the papal court; on his deprivation at the break with Rome, his replacement was Anne Boleyn's protégé, the radical activist Hugh Latimer, previously humiliated in conflicts with conservative churchmen of the Bristol area. After Latimer's more-or-less forced resignation in the wake of the passage of the Act of Six Articles in 1539, his successor was the adaptable careerist John Bell, one of Ghinucci's former officials; Bell mysteriously resigned in 1543 and was replaced by the steadily more conservative Nicholas Heath. Heath was ousted for his opposition to Edwardian changes and replaced by John Hooper, reuniting the diocese with Gloucester. Hooper's arrest and deprivation by Mary brought Heath's restoration, before his move to York, to be replaced by a long-standing Catholic exile, Richard Pate. Pate's Elizabethan replacement was the last Edwardian vice-chancellor of Cambridge and future archbishop of York, Edwin Sandys, and his successor but one was the future archbishop of Canterbury, John Whitgift.

Worcester, then, was an obvious showcase: reasonably accessible from London and Oxford, yet also in constant contact with the difficult territories of Wales and the Marches. The Worcester Chronicle casts sudden shafts of light on the changes in this key diocese: most detailed during the period witnessed by the second Chronicler John Rowland alias Steynor, but also giving some valuable glimpses of what was happening under Henry VIII. The first sign of changing times comes in 1529–30, when the Chronicler records that 'This year the cross before the guild hall door called the high cross and many other crosses were defaced.'[24] This is one of several indications that 1529–30 saw the beginning of serious iconoclasm across lowland England. There were outbreaks beginning in 1529 in Kent, and during 1531–2 in East Anglia: consistently crosses seem to have been a chief target, probably because they were often in deserted open spaces and therefore safer to desecrate. Significantly, the general pardon announced in Parliament in November 1529 for the first time excepted those pulling down crosses on the highways; this must suddenly have become a problem on a noticeable scale.[25] After this, the Chronicler notes in neutral fashion the various key political events of the early 1530s; then in 1535–6 comes the first hint of emotion. Describing the closure of the lesser monasteries in April 1536, he says 'all religious places were suppressed; the monks, friars, canons, were put down, and all the jewels of the said howses as pyxes, chalices, paxes, crosses, censors, cruets with other things of silver, and copes of the best, and other things were taken away from them. And shortly after the body of Christ was taken out of the church.' It is a poignant picture of sacristies being stripped, and then finally the reserved sacrament being taken out from the bare building.

In 1537–8 comes a note of what must have been the most advanced episcopal programme of change in the country: 'all manner of images, crucifixes, and roodlofts were taken out of the churches and destroyed.' This sounds remarkably early, and it is most unlikely that destruction was very thorough in the county at this date, but there are other confirmations of a precocious campaign of attack on traditional religion by Bishop Latimer. As early as summer 1536, in one of his sermons to Convocation in London, he was talking of two Worcester diocesan cults in the past tense: 'I think ye have heard of St Blesis's heart which is at Malvern, and of St Algar's bones, how long they deluded the people.'[26] Latimer worked with the new prior of Worcester, Henry Holbeach, a protégé of Cranmer's, to undermine the chief diocesan cult of Our

Lady in Worcester Cathedral. In August 1537, a year before the national campaign against shrines, they pre-empted the celebration of the feast of the Assumption by stripping bare Our Lady's cult statue. This provoked a bitter outcry and a defiantly ostentatious display of devotion on Assumption Eve from one Worcester man, Thomas Emans, when he saw the statue robbed of its rich trappings; his reward was denunciation to Cromwell by Latimer, Holbeach and the bailiffs of Worcester.[27]

During 1538, when Cromwell had joined in the hunt on a nation-wide basis, Latimer delighted in completing the destruction both of the statue of Our Lady of Worcester and the other star Severn Valley relic, the Blood of Hailes. But this was not the only destruction. In the cathedral, the Chronicler records that 'the shrines of St Wulfstan and St Oswald was taken down also and their bones with the bones of Bishop Constantine were lapped in lead and buried at the north end of the high altar.' The treatment of these historical figures is noticeably different from the complete destruction of cultic objects like images of Mary or the Holy Blood, which did not centre on human bodies. Moreover, Wulfstan, Oswald or the twelfth-century Bishop John of Coutances were not traitors like Becket, so they could be given an honourable, if less ostentatious place of repose beside the high altar: echoing (no doubt unconsciously) the practice of the early Church. Nevertheless, the Chronicler was clear about the attitude of heaven towards these changes: 'And at that time God sent such lightning and thunder that all thereabouts thought the church would fall on them.' And he goes on to say in the same sentence, no doubt with heartfelt relief, 'and this year Mr Doctor Bell was elected bishop of Worcester.' Bell was a familiar face from the diocesan administration in the good old days of Bishop Ghinucci; no doubt he would seem a godsend after Hugh Latimer, who is noticeably never named in any of these entries.

However, change was not at an end. In January 1540, Worcester Cathedral Priory was dissolved, one of the last of England's monasteries, and the Chronicler was aware of its part in a national process. 'In that month all religious men, as the monks, friars, and canons, changed their habits of religion and wore secular mens raiment, *videlicet* gowns, jackets, close hosen etc. And certain were expulsed out of the place [that is, the Cathedral close], and the Priory was then named a College. And the four bells in the leaden steeple were this year taken down, broken in pieces, and carried away.' Even Worcester, now remodelled as a cathedral of the New Foundation, could not escape the general monastic loss of goods. Detached steeples of great churches were to prove particularly vulnerable, only Chichester's and Evesham's surviving intact to this day; Worcester's was demolished during the Interregnum. The term 'college' for the cathedral establishment is interesting: this is technically what the New Foundation cathedrals were, and how they were commonly known at first. The name put them on the same level as Henry's two new foundations of non-cathedral colleges at Burton on Trent and Thornton, or indeed, of his purely academic Oxbridge foundations of Trinity and Christ Church. Revealingly, when John Barlow succeeded Henry Holbeach as dean of Worcester in 1544, the Chronicler referred to the event as Barlow being 'made Master of the College'.

In the seesaw of Henry VIII's last eight years of life, 1541 and 1542 proved years of advance for the reformers. The Chronicler notes two royal proclamations of 1541: the first repeated the Cromwellian order for Bible provision in churches, but for the first time gave the order teeth by stipulating fines for non-compliance. For many previously negligent parishes, this was the turning-point which forced them into buying a Bible, and the Chronicler certainly phrased his note as if the order was new and was only now making its impact.[28] The second proclamation of 1541 abrogated more holy days.[29] Destruction of imagery also continued; this is something of which Henry remained proud throughout his more conservative last years in the 1540s.[30] '6 April 1542 the tombs of St Oswald and Wulfstan were removed and taken away down to the ground.' In other words, the work of destruction begun in 1537 was completed: the tombs were still presumably regarded by many around Worcester as sacred in character despite the removal of their superstructure and their contents, and so they had to go. It was the logical corollary not only of the earlier destruction, but also of the fact that Saints Oswald and Wulfstan had lost their place in the cathedral's dedication; like all Henry VIII's transformed cathedrals of the New Foundation, Worcester was rededicated, in this case as Christchurch. However, Henry Holbeach in his new guise as dean was being strangely dilatory in following the national programme completing the destruction of shrines. In the previous year, 1541, there had been renewed royal orders against shrines and images, on 22 September for the Province of York and in October for the Southern Province. During 1541 shrines were removed at St Paul's Cathedral and at Westminster Abbey.[31] Perhaps Holbeach had to deal with conservative local opinion, which made these tombs among the last major shrines to survive, even in mutilated form.

At Henry VIII's death, the second Chronicler, John Rowland alias Steynor, takes over, and the entries about religious change are recorded with almost as much fullness as in Robert Parkyn's well-known Yorkshire diary.[32] Immediately, the Edwardian changes took effect: Dean Barlow was, after all, the brother of one of the most enthusiastic evangelical bishops, William Barlow. For 1547, Steynor notes that 'In that year was taken away the great brazen candlestick and the beam of timber before the high altar.' This was no doubt as a result of the royal injunctions of 31 July 1547, which extended Henrician restrictions by banning all votive lights apart from two candlesticks on the high altar. Worcester's extravagant altar lights were now drastically pruned.[33] But more was to come. 'And 10 January [1548] was taken down all the images in the highe altar and in all the church were destroyed, and not only there, but also in all other churches, anno Domini 1548.' Evidently a co-ordinated attack was now staged on the cathedrals, and in particular on their ritual focus, the high altar and its reredos. In London, the general attack on churches had been made earlier, in September 1547, but the action at Worcester fits in with action at Canterbury Cathedral: on 16 January 1548, the week after the Worcester destruction, the Privy Council ordered Sir Anthony Aucher to deliver silver ornaments from the high altar of Canterbury Cathedral. As Steynor implies, the definitive general order to take down images came from the Privy Council slightly later, on 21 February 1548.[34]

The transformation of ritual also began in 1548. 'And that year on Candlemas day [2 February] was no candles hallowed nor born. On Ash Wednesday was no ashes hallowed. 25 March was Palm Sunday and the Annunciation of Our Lady, and then was no palm hallowed, nor cross borne, as in former times. On Good Friday was no creeping to the cross.' So far, the cathedral was faithfully carrying out royal orders made from the end of January onwards, which seem to have met with compliance even in places where one would expect resistance. Robert Parkyn noted observation of the prohibition on Candlemas, Ash Wednesday and Palm Sunday celebrations in Yorkshire; likewise the order was observed in Winchester Diocese, the Candlemas ceremony actually being interrupted half-way through at Southampton.[35] This degree of compliance is remarkable, given the short time before Candlemas to spread knowledge of the government's intentions; indeed, the official order in the Northern Province seems to have come after Candlemas, on 20 February. The Laudian historian Peter Heylyn, an early proponent of the theory of 'slow Reformation from above', expressed unwarranted scepticism when he commented about these government orders that they could not have reached 'the remote parts of the kingdom': 'the counsel was as sudden as the warning short... it was not possible that any reformation should be made in the first particular, but in the cities of London and Westminster, and the parts adjoining....'[36] At Worcester at least, Heylyn was wrong. In any case, palms and candles had been among the superstitious ceremonies condemned in the Homily of Good Works, issued in the Book of Homilies during the previous summer, 1547.[37] For those who were listening to the homily, the government's intentions for the next liturgical cycle to start up in Advent would have been clear.

By contrast, the Privy Council had so far made no general orders about the culminating ceremonies in Holy Week, on Easter Eve and Easter Day itself. Perhaps they felt that there were limits to what they could get away with: the ceremonies connected with the Easter Sepulchre were one of the most important foci of traditional devotion. Whatever the reason, a series of local decisions were made about what would happen; most of the lowland England parishes for which church-wardens' accounts survive appear to have abandoned the setting-up of the Sepulchre.[38] However, for once, Worcester Cathedral seems to have hesitated, and worked out a local compromise, possibly along with several parish churches at Worcester. First the rites of Easter Saturday were toned down. 'On Easter Even no fire hallowed, but the pascal taper and the font.' In other words, the cathedral omitted the ceremony of blessing the fire to light the Paschal candle (perhaps the most alarming element to the evangelically inclined), but the lighted candle itself was kept, and also the blessing of the waters in the font. Dr Duffy finds that these Saturday ceremonies which are so dramatic in modern Catholic liturgy had lost their import-ance in late medieval devotion, so perhaps it was felt to be safe to tamper with them. However, the centrepiece of traditionalist lay piety, the Easter Sepulchre, was a tougher nut to crack: the cathedral set up the Sepulchre as of old, but robbed the Easter ceremony of as much dramatic movement as possible. 'On Easter Day at the resurrection was taken out of the sepulchre the pyx with the sacrament, they singing "Christ is risen", without procession.' The surviving accounts of St Michael's in Bedwardine, a peculiar of the Dean and Chapter in the cathedral precinct, also show that parish setting up its Sepulchre for the Easter Vigil; possibly other Worcester churches did as well.[39]

Perhaps in this hesitant destruction, the conservative Bishop Heath was at last making his opinions known, or perhaps conservatives in the Chapter were acting as a brake on Dean Barlow. Heath's more stridently conservative colleague Bishop Stephen Gardiner got into trouble with the Council for allowing the Sepulchre ceremonies at Winchester: in his defence, he argued quite correctly that there had been no national order putting them down, and with his characteristic lawyer's precision, he was careful to distinguish these legally permissible ceremonies from those which had been prohibited.[40] More radical bishops had probably taken their own local initiatives about Easter Saturday and Sunday without government backing. Later in the year Archbishop Cranmer, in his visitation of Canterbury diocese, chased up Kent parishes which in the 1548 Holy Week had erected Easter Sepulchres and 'hallowed the font, fire, or paschal'; he listed these in his articles of enquiry in similar terms to the nationally prohibited ceremonies, suggesting that he had already tried to supplement the national ban by his own initiative to complete the emasculation of Easter Week.[41]

Steynor records the removal of the reserved sacrament from the cathedral high altar on 20 October 1548, 'and in other churches and chapels *anno domini* 1549.' Already the cathedral had done away with the hanging pyx traditional in England, for the reserved sacrament is described as 'the cup with the body of Christ'. In taking this further step of removal, Dean Barlow was here in advance of his reformist colleague Dean May at St Paul's Cathedral, who did not order the sacrament to be removed from his cathedral until 17 March 1549.[42] During 1549 came the greatest break with the past: '19 April: being Good Friday was no sepulchre [set] up, nor service of the sepulchre said or done, nor on Easter Even was the paschal hallowed, nor fire, nor incense, nor font. And 23 April [Easter Tuesday] was mass, matins, evensong and all other divine service said and sung in English, and all other divine service laid down.' Here Dean Barlow was again showing his eagerness for change, anticipating the deadline for the introduction of the English Prayer Book, whose use did not become compulsory until Whit Sunday (9 June) 1549.

After carefully neutral mentions of Kett's Rebellion and the Western Rising, comes further prompt observance of a government order of Christmas Day 1549: 'all books of divine service brought to the bishop of the see: *videlicet* ledgers, mass-books, grails, pies, portases, legends, and all these and many others were burnt.' The only substantial survivor from the cathedral's liturgical books, albeit a spectacular one, is a massive and beautiful antiphoner, probably concealed by someone on the cathedral staff. We need to note here that the man in charge of this destruction was not the enthusiast Dean Barlow, but the conservative Bishop Heath. Robert Parkyn reports the archbishop of York, the evangelical Robert Holgate, implementing destruction in late January 1550, but it is surprising to find Heath toeing the government line on destruction. This may have been the last straw which made Heath determine on resistance to further innovation. By 8 February 1550, he was facing the Privy Council because of his objections to the new Ordinal, and the process was beginning which led to his deprivation the following year.[43]

With Heath a spent force during 1550 and 1551, Dean Barlow seized the initiative, riding out beyond what central government required:

> This year Mr Barlow dean of the College in Worcester pulled down Our Lady's chapel made with white stone and with iron, within and without, and also the altar of Jesus made in white stone, and a chapel of St Edmund wherein was a pair of organs and a chapel of St George made of timber, and grated with iron, and a great pair of organs. And the king commaunded in that year that all altars and the crucifixes and rood sollers [lofts] should be pulled down. And to have a long table of tree, and thereupon to say masse in Englishe and to minister the communion to the people in English and that, to stand for their housel.

The last phrase 'that, to stand for their housel' is obscurely put, but clearly means 'this would have to suffice for their reception of the eucharist'. It is one of the very few signs of emotion which the Chronicler allows himself about the changes which he evidently deplored; in this he contrasts with the frequent comments of pain or distaste to be found in the contemporary account of Robert Parkyn. Moreover, in one detail, he unconsciously reveals Worcester once more anticipating change and exceeding the government's order, if indeed the city was told that the king had ordered the demolition of roodlofts. Privy Council letters were indeed sent to all bishops to demolish all altars on 19 November 1550; we know that St Michael in Bedwardine eventually obeyed in January 1551.[44] However, there does not seem to be any trace of royal orders to demolish 'rood sollers' under Edward VI, and indeed in East Anglia there appears to have been official embarrassment when they were demolished in some parishes.[45] Dr Hutton has found evidence of local Edwardian destruction of roodlofts in only 17 out of the 114 sets of churchwardens' accounts which he has examined across the country.[46] Destruction of roodlofts would have been a local initiative. Perhaps Barlow and the diocesan authorities were already taking their cue from Bishop John Hooper of Gloucester, who would add the diocese of Worcester to his responsibilities in the following year, 20 May 1552. Hooper was a long-standing enemy of screens: preaching before Edward VI in March 1550, he had asked for all chancel screens to be demolished, as a symbol of the destruction of the veil of the Temple with the passing away of the old law.[47] In his diocesan injunctions for Gloucester of 1551, Hooper ordered the destruction of roodlofts and of all screens around side-chapels. One of Dr Hutton's examples of roodloft destruction comes from South Littleton in Worcestershire, in 1552–3, after Hooper had taken over Worcester diocese.[48] The roodloft of St Michael in Bedwardine, next to the cathedral, was taken down in 1553.[49]

Then came the reuniting of the diocese of Worcester with Gloucester: hardly a cause of rejoicing to conservatives, because it brought with it Hooper, eager to spread godliness northwards up the Severn. Steynor has a splendidly dismissive description of the new bishop: 'This year 21 June [1552] Bishop Hooper came to Worcester with his wife and daughter. He had a long beard, and in all his time were no children confirmed.' Hooper was indeed Worcester's first married bishop, and apparently the first bishop to look like a Protestant clergyman.

The reference to the lack of confirmations is doubly interesting. First, it is one indication that we ought to take the late medieval practice of confirmation seriously; often it has been dismissed as a ritual in decay. Not only our Chronicler valued the rite of confirmation; Robert Parkyn was concerned for the effect of Edwardian changes on the ceremony, worrying that the new catechism regulations would mean postponement of confirmation until children were 7, 8 or 9 years old.[50] Admittedly, it is possible that conservatives only started valuing confirmation when they felt that the rite was under threat from the reformers. The second point to consider is why Hooper gave up confirming children. Most of the English reformers felt that the rite needed re-evaluation, and provisions for it to be administered only to candidates mastering the catechism were repeated in the abortive lawcode of 1553, the so-called *Reformatio Legum*.[51] Hooper may well have felt that a renewed rite

of confirmation should wait on his energetic efforts to improve basic
religious instruction in his diocese. However, it is also noticeable that he
never discussed the subject of confirmation in his fairly extensive
theological writings; this was the only sacrament of the medieval
seven not to get some mention in them.[52] At the very least, it was not
a high priority on his reformist programme. After the restoration of
Protestantism in 1558/9, confirmation appears to have become generally much neglected until a drive for its revival by Archbishop
Whitgift in the 1590s.[53]

Still the destruction in the cathedral went on, with Hooper now
present in the city, and enthusiastically backing Dean Barlow. '12
August [1552]: the high altar was taken down to the ground. Also all
the choir with the bishop's stall was taken down to the stalls, and the
great pair of organs were taken down 30 August.' Now the government's increasingly radical programme meant that Worcester was once
more in step with official policy. The destruction of the main organ at
Worcester was part of a co-ordinated national campaign, although
Hooper went further than elsewhere in initiating actual destruction:
at the same time Archbishop Holgate forbade the use of organs in
worship in the Diocese of York, and Dean May made a similar prohibition in St Paul's Cathedral London on 4 September 1552.[54] Parkyn
also records determined efforts by Holgate to order the placing of the
communion table in the centre of the chancel, probably also reflected
in the destruction of the high altar at Worcester. By 'high altar', we
should understand the whole ensemble of altar and the reredos behind
it. Theoretically the altar should already have been dismantled as a
consequence of the 1551 order already recorded by Steynor, but
perhaps it had only been supplanted by a wooden table in front of it.

All this destruction in the cathedral caused an uproar, led by two
conservative canons of the cathedral, Robert Johnson and Henry
Joliffe.[55] Hooper wrote defensively about his destructive efforts to
William Cecil, claiming that despite the outcry 'there is not for a
church to preach God's word in, and to minister his holy sacraments,
more godly within this realm'. Predictably, the bishop won the sympathy of the Privy Council against Johnson and Joliffe, but the dispute
was enough of a national scandal to elicit a reply from the imprisoned
Stephen Gardiner in the Tower of London.[56] The Marian cathedral
canons would remember Hooper's part in the wrecking of their church
when they had their chance to get their revenge on him: in fact they
heaped on Hooper the blame for all the destruction caused by Dean

Barlow, who was presumably by then beyond their reach, and told the government that 'our bells and organs be broken, our altars and chapels are by Hooper violated and overthrown.'[57]

Within a year, the religious situation was abruptly reversed, although Steynor gives the most neutral description of Mary's accession, and ignores entirely the burning of Hooper outside his cathedral at Gloucester. Instead, Steynor concentrates for his Marian entries on the happier subject of the restoration of his beloved cathedral's beauty, after all the damage caused by Barlow and Hooper. This programme of work came during 1556–7, and seems to mark a second phase in the Marian religious agenda; after the initial neutralising or imprisonment of Edwardian clergy, and the provision of absolutely essential religious furniture, four years on, the work of beautifying shattered churches could begin. One finds the same thing happening in the Worcestershire countryside; the Protestant Sir Thomas Hoby disapprovingly and laconically noted Bishop Pate's arrival at Evesham in late May 1556, 'in visitation to set up images, etc.'[58]

In his notes on the restoration of the cathedral, Steynor is at his most valuable: such a detailed and loving description is rare indeed, and it is a striking tribute to a particularly expensive and lavish campaign of making good Edwardian destruction. Queen Mary contributed generously to the work, no doubt mindful of the burial-place of her mother's first husband. The description is worth quoting in full, to get the flavour of a Marian cathedral in all its new glory:

This year [1556–7] the whole choir of the college was removed from the clock house unto the high altar with closure of carved boards round about the choir, double stalls, the high stalls for the canons and petty canons, the lower for the children, and a goodly loft wherein the gospel is read. And on the north side of the choir a pair of organs to serve the choir. And from the choir unto the high altar on both sides closed with stone and grated with iron on both sides with two doors, one on the south side and one on the north side. Also the chapel in the east part of the college was goodly prepared, first the altar, with a picture of Our Lady with her son in her arms. Both sides of the chapel was done with rent boards: on the north side was a fair chapel closed with rent boards, and within two goodly seats. Also on the south side was another fair chapel with two seats, and all thing necessary to the same. And on that side also Mr Philip Hawford then being dean, made a chapel with a gallery therein and all things else thereunto necessary. And the glass windows above were taken down, and new glass was set there, which lighteneth the choir very much.

Once more, Worcester Cathedral was being treated as a showpiece for the religious policy of the new regime, something which was given public expression when Queen Mary and Cardinal Pole visited the building, presumably to admire the progress of the work, in 1557.[59]

Alas, virtually nothing from the Marian restoration survives at Worcester, partly through destruction under Elizabeth and during the Civil Wars, but equally and ironically, because of Victorian pious enthusiasm for the Gothic style: the Victorians pulled down the stone screens and remaining woodwork to replace them with fake medievalism. For the remarkable feature about this Marian work was its Renaissance semi-classical style. Only one small fragment remains in situ: a tomb-chest with Renaissance detail, four semi-classical columns in half-relief, which bears a fourteenth-century bishop's effigy on the exterior screen wall at the north-east of the choir. This is almost certainly part of the reconstruction of the stone choir enclosure mentioned by Steynor. Some of the surviving woodwork, mixed up with work from later refurbishments of Jacobean and Caroline Restoration date, was exiled by the Victorians to Holy Trinity Sutton Coldfield, where it is to be found in several locations, principally in the screen between the chancel and the north chapel. Significantly, the style of this woodwork was exotic enough to defeat the expertise of the *Buildings of England* team, and earn the puzzled description 'mid C17?'[60]

In finding a context for this remarkable Marian restoration in Worcester, one is reminded of Bishop Gardiner's chantry at Winchester, a curious hybrid of Gothic and Renaissance detail. Here were symbols of a work of restoration which looked to the future as much as to the past. The choir at Worcester, with its Renaissance dress and its fashionable clear glass, anticipated the changes of the Counter-Reformation; the Marian restoration was not simply a mindless exercise in nostalgia.

Worcester's new choir survived intact for a mere four years at most. Let Steynor describe the sequence of events, all precisely following on central government orders: 'On St John's Day at Midsummer [24 June 1559] the service altered and all the bishops put from their bishoprics...This year priests were compelled to subscribe, or else lose their livings, the 23 October, 1559.' With this date, Steynor shows us when the royal commissioners touring England in autumn 1559 made their impact at Worcester. The following year he describes the equally traumatic arrival of Edwin Sandys, consecrated for Worcester on 21 December 1559, and soon getting down to renewed destruction. Sandys would reveal his iconoclastic temper in a fiery sermon preached at York, praising Queen Elizabeth because 'she hath caused the vessels that were made for Baal and for the host of heaven to be defaced; she hath broken down the lofts that were builded for idolatry'.[61]

The result at Worcester was predictable. '13 May [1560] the bishop began his visitation in the cathedral church. The 17th day, the cross and the image of Our Lady were burnt in the churchyard after noon.' It is surprising that these had survived the commissioners' visit in the previous autumn; probably the conservatives in the Chapter had proved obstructive, and successfully defended these key symbols of the old ritual. But what exactly was now being burned? It may be that the figure of Our Lady which was being burned was part of the usual pairing with St John flanking the Rood which was also burned, but if so, it seems strange that Steynor did not also mention the figure of St John. Was this statue of Mary in fact a new cult image of Our Lady of Worcester? If so, this is a rare, if oblique, record of a shrine restoration during the Marian years.

Steynor's last entry on religious change is a note of the purge of two Catholic prebendaries two months after the image-burning. 'The 10 July [1560] Mr Arderne and Mr Norfolk prebendaries of the College were discharged of their livings in the chapter house at ten in the morning.' Of these two Catholic stalwarts, Arderne had only been admitted Canon and third Prebendary a fortnight after Mary's death, 30 November 1558.[62] Bishop Sandys took this drastic action of deprivation on his own initiative, and he had to explain himself to Archbishop Parker later in the year; there were various other points unspecified about the visitation in which Parker was 'much offended', at least until Sandys had offered his excuses.[63] Steynor did not have the heart to record the rest of the Elizabethan destruction in the cathedral: instead we can listen to the local Catholic magnate Sir John Bourne, who became locked in feud with Bishop Sandys, and who described what had happened in the course of a long protest to Elizabeth's Privy Council: 'The pipes of a great pair of organs, which cost £200 the making, being one of the most solemn instruments of this realm, are molten into dishes, and divided amongst the prebendaries' wives; the case hath made bedsteads; the like is done and become of certain timber and wainscot which Queen Mary gave for the new making of the choir.'[64]

From now on, with the Elizabethan Settlement increasingly firmly in place, Steynor's record turned to secular civic events, including an enthusiastic description of Queen Elizabeth's visit to Worcester in 1575. Torn between loyalty to the Queen and his love of the past, like so many conservatives, he seems to have embarked on a spiritual interior exile; one could compare that other conservative diarist of the period, Robert Parkyn, still in his parsonage at Adwick-le-Street up to his death. Bishop Sandys did not name John Rowland alias Steynor among the opponents of godly religion in 1564.[65] Steynor could still take an interest in his beloved cathedral, recording the restoration of its rent corn revenues in 1563. His remaining references to the clergy of the established church, such as the 'Lord Bishop', are ranged neutrally alongside the other officers of local government; he does not sound ripe for recusancy, unlike that Suffolk chronicler of a lost liturgical past, Roger Martin of Long Melford, but he can never have felt at ease with the new dispensation.[66]

Around him, the city conformed with a good grace to the new order. This may indicate the final ascendancy of a long-standing radical faction in the city. We have noted the early iconoclasm at Worcester in 1529–30, and Bishop Latimer had already spoken favourably of Worcester in 1538, as a city 'replenished with men of honesty... by reason of their lady they have been given to much idleness; but now that she is gone, they be turned to laboriousness, and so from ladyness to godliness.'[67] Perhaps one should not make too much of this tribute from an evangelical enthusiast who was seeking a favour for the city from Thomas Cromwell; slightly later, the vivid reminiscence of John Davis about his troubles in 1546–7 reveals a city then still dominated by Catholic magistrates including Robert Yowle, working closely with the conservative cathedral and diocesan authorities to harass and imprison Protestant activists in the city.[68] However, the Elizabethan Settlement does not seem to have outraged the city leadership. The small minority of Catholics reported by Bishop Sandys among the town councillors in 1564 contrasted significantly with Catholic majorities at Hereford and Warwick; after 1589, Worcester joined those communities who flaunted their enthusiasm for godliness by financing a town preacher, with steadily increasing generosity.[69] The city remained aloof from the country of Worcestershire which surrounded it: a county where strong gentry Catholicism persisted. Worcester's religious profile remained as distinctive in the area as its heavily industrial clothmaking economy, and at election time, to a degree unusual among parliament- ary boroughs, it jealously preserved its representation in the Commons from interference by outside gentry.[70] The Steynor family remained lonely religious conservatives in a community which had turned its back on the past.[71]

What overall impression do we gain from this new light on the Reformation in Worcester? We see the implementation of an official Reformation conforming closely to and at times outstripping the metro- politan and general lowland zone model: directed by activist clergy handpicked by the government to make an impression in a key centre where many travellers and people coming to market needed to be shown what the latest religious changes were like. It was especially convenient for the Edwardian government that the Easter season, when so many of their liturgical innovations first made their impact, coincided with Worcester's most important and frequented fair, so that the cathedral could show the pattern for other churches to follow.[72] We are also given a rare glimpse of the Marian church at its most splendid: a taste of one of history's might-have-beens. These are certainly a 'quick' Reformation and Counter-Reformation, directed effectively by those in authority: the picture of swift reformation from above is one which Dr Hutton's research, particularly his exhaustive examination of churchwardens' accounts, has indicated for lowland England in gen- eral.[73] Less easy to judge is the wider response which religious change elicited in Worcester; the glimpses of evidence for the city's religious complexion presented here have largely come from other sources. Let us not be ungrateful, however; Robert Yowle and John Rowland alias Steynor bequeathed us a narrative of one cathedral's reformation which no one else thought to provide.

6. Leadership and Priorities in Reading during the Reformation

JEANETTE MARTIN

By the 1520s the ancient borough of Reading – the home of royal servants and ranking ninth among England's thirty most prosperous provincial towns – had already been for four centuries under the domination of one of the realm's wealthiest and most powerful monastic communities, founded there by King Henry I in 1121.[1] Royal visitors, prelates, scholarly priests and pilgrims frequented the abbey and town, their presence adding buoyancy and lustre to the area's social and economic life. Yet apparent local satisfaction with the *status quo* had long been marred by undercurrents of political and religious discontent. In 1539 the enforced religious changes begun by Henry VIII led not only to the dissolution of the great royal abbey but also to the humiliation and public execution in Reading of the abbot, Hugh Cook Faringdon, and with him two priests – one of them a former Reading vicar. They died as traitors, being found guilty of denying the Royal Supremacy over the English Church.

The impact of the dissolution was such that not only did the complexion of local government undergo change but the town itself became impoverished and so, too, as the result of legislated religious changes did the benefices of its three medieval churches. At the same time, the economic position of the parishes was dramatically reversed. What had traditionally been the richest and proudest of the three parishes prior to the Tudors' successive religious changes proved to have resources more vulnerable to doctrinal change than those of the poorest one.[2]

In these turbulent years Reading's leaders in town and parishes found themselves confronted not just by doctrinal questions and the problems posed by religious reform and reaction, but also facing unanticipated political situations and socio-economic reversals particular to their locality. How they reacted to these complex, often interlinked matters, how these issues affected one another, and what means were employed by the urban and parochial leaders to deal with problems as they arose is the theme explored here.

I

First, it is necessary to outline Reading's main characteristics before the abbey's dissolution.

Situated some forty miles from London and twelve from Windsor, one of the Tudor monarchs' favourite residences, Reading lay on the river Kennet close to its junction with the Thames. It thus enjoyed enviable communications by water with the rich agricultural, wool- and textile-producing areas of western Berkshire and with northern areas of the county towards Oxford, as well as with Windsor and London. It was also situated at the crossing-point of important east–west, south–north land routes between London and Bristol, and from Southampton and Winchester through to Oxford and the Midlands. This very favourable geographical position was to prove one reason why Reading could survive both the devastating impact upon it of the Reformation and the coincidental country-wide economic misfortunes of the mid-century.[3]

Until its dissolution, the royal abbey was the source of much local prosperity, the townspeople enjoying the fruits of reflected prestige through trade and through the provision of services and accommodation to throngs of visitors. Over the centuries the abbey had witnessed many great events. Among the most important ecclesiastical occasions were three legatine councils, an assembly to elect an archbishop of Canterbury, and the consecration of a number of English bishops. Yet other events the abbey witnessed proved to be of great political and personal importance to England's rulers; for example, the marriage of John of Gaunt to Blanche of Lancaster in 1359 and the revelation of Edward IV's secret marriage in 1464. The abbey also became the meeting-place for Parliament on three occasions in the fifteenth century. As a royal foundation, the monastery attracted frequent visits by Henry VIII who, like most of England's kings since Henry I, was exercising his special patronal right to enjoy hospitality there. Princess Mary, Queen Catherine of Aragon, Henry's sister known as the 'French Queen', and dignitaries such as Cromwell, the king's chief minister, were among other abbey guests.[4]

This was, however, but the worldly aspect of the prestigious aura attending Reading Abbey. Before the close of the twelfth century the community had become the repository of no less than 242 relics. Foremost among them was the Hand of St James, presented by Henry I, which was greatly revered for miraculous cures.[5]

Pilgrims – including Henry VIII in 1520 – also flocked to nearby Caversham, to a chapel of Notley Abbey there, renowned both for its shrine of the Virgin Mary and certain relics. The king also honoured the Reading Grey Friars whose modest establishment, set up in the thirteenth century, lay at the north-western edge of the borough. The new Supreme Head of the Church in England chose this in 1536 as one of two such communities to celebrate masses for the soul of his illegitimate son, who had recently died.[6]

Continuous throngs of visitors on pilgrimage, attending the abbey's two four-day fairs held in the outer court of its walled grounds, and enjoying the weekly market, were not the only source of Reading's prosperity, but these activities doubtless boosted its principal source of trade, clothmaking, of which the town was one of the main centres in Berkshire.[7]

Yet despite such positive socio-economic advantages benefiting Reading for four centuries, there remained deep local resentment over abbatial lordship of the town. The basis of this ingrained political and economic opposition was that Reading had been a royal possession long before the foundation of the abbey and therefore its inhabitants had certain rights and privileges which successive abbots were held to be eroding or overriding. Spearheading this opposition were the burgesses of the Guild Merchant, an institution of great antiquity, which succeeded in surviving and in retaining some power and independence. By the beginning of the sixteenth century bitter struggles had been waged between abbots and townsmen for at least 250 years, as each generation of burgesses sought to establish and retain an organised and separate legal identity from monastic jurisdiction.[8]

In 1507, after a 19-year bout of such continuing grievance, a settlement resulting from a combination of legal decision and arbitration finally declared the Guild Merchant to be indeed a corporation and its principal officer the mayor. Significantly, this action was initiated by the mayor and burgesses who took their complaint to the highest level. The decree also clarified the respective roles of the abbot and burgesses. The mayor would be chosen and sworn in during Michaelmas week by the abbot or his deputy from three candidates presented by the Guild. The two guardian constables and ten wardmen (two wardmen to each of the borough's five wards) were to be chosen by a combination of the mayor, burgesses and householders.

The burgesses had long formed an exclusive group at the top of borough society. In Henry VIII's reign, prior to 1542, the ranks of this wealthy elite numbered only between 31 and 49 out of a population in Reading and district estimated by contemporaries to consist of about 2,000 communicants, most of whom lived in the borough. It was generally leading members among the burgesses who had represented Reading in Parliament since 1295. In the town the burgesses were responsible for regulation of all the trades, and also supervised and received the revenues issuing from the common wharf and the weighing beams for yarn and wool. With the official recognition granted in 1507 they gained another important step forward politically, but they still had not achieved another of their ambitions, the sole right to appoint all the urban office-holders. Political and economic ascendancy remained with the abbot, who continued to exact dues from each new burgess, take the profits of justice, and had possession of the mills, the fisheries, the fairs, the market and the town's three churches.[9]

The most populous of Reading's three parishes was St Laurence's, whose church was situated adjacent to the pilgrims' and visitors' entrance to the abbey. Principally an urban parish, it was estimated in 1548 to have 1,000 communicants – twice as many as either of the other two larger parishes of St Mary's or St Giles'. Both of these extended beyond the borough and contained rural communities within their boundaries. St Mary's estimated 500 communicants were disposed between the borough and the two hamlets of Coley and Southcote in a parish extending over some 1,263 acres, all of which lands were tithed. St Giles's estimated 500 communicants dwelt both in the borough and in Whitley hamlet in the manor of that name. This parish – covering 2,273 acres of which 1,014 acres (44.6%) were tithe-free abbey lands – was the greatest in area but, being the poorest, was of least social consequence. St Laurence's was the wealthiest and most politically important parish, but again a significant proportion of the land was tithe-free abbey land and its incumbent – as the holder of a corrody vicarage – was far more dependent upon the abbey than the other two incumbents who each held a perpetual vicarage.[10]

As rector and patron of all three churches, the abbot and convent of Reading until the early 1530s attracted highly educated, distinguished priests to these livings, gifted men with considerations beyond the actual income a benefice offered. Association with, and proximity to, an immensely wealthy, powerful patron who was one of the realm's highest-ranking abbots, a spiritual peer of Parliament, and regular host to the royal family, would suggest sparkling prospects. Moreover, as most of these priests were Oxford-educated men it would be very appealing to live within reasonable distance of the university.

Thomas Justice MA, son of one of the abbot's bailiffs who was also a Reading burgess, then stepson of Richard Smyth, a royal servant also a Reading burgess, was instituted vicar of St Laurence's in 1502. He was a Fellow of New College, as were also two incumbents of St Mary's – Richard Herberd, vicar from 1506 until his death in 1508, a graduate in both canon and civil law – and his successor, William Pache MA, vicar from 1508 until his death *c.* 1536.[11] Thomas Justice's successor at St Laurence's in 1518, the Welshman Richard Bedow MA, was a Fellow of All Souls'.[12] Another Welshman, John Eynon, vicar of St Giles' from 1520 to 1533, was a graduate in civil law, and had been admitted principal of St Edward Hall in 1511. He resigned as vicar to become Abbot Hugh's chief counsellor, only to be executed with him in 1539 before the gates of Reading abbey.[13] Eynon's predecessor as vicar of St Giles' from 1494 to 1520 was William Edyngdon, a graduate in civil and canon law.[14]

The priests who succeeded Eynon at St Giles' in October 1533, Bedow at St Laurence's in January 1535 and Pache at St Mary's in March 1536, present a stark contrast. All three lacked scholarly distinction. Clearly, Abbot Hugh and the monks could no longer attract distinguished incumbents, but in view of periodic instances of heresy being detected in the town and, worse still, recently tainting the abbey itself, we may be sure that they proved themselves sound in religion. Of Sir Richard Snow who became vicar of St Giles', we know nothing except that he seems to have been on the expected good terms with very important townsmen and with his predecessor, Master Eynon, who maintained his connection with the parish as an assistant priest.[15] Sir John Mayneforth who became vicar of St Laurence's in 1535 evidently had some connection with Reading nearly fourteen years beforehand when he witnessed a will in this same parish. Described in December 1531 as a notary public and curate, he may well have been assisting Master Bedow for some years.[16] By coincidence, both

Snow and Mayneforth were to die in 1550.[17] Sir John Whetham who became vicar of St Mary's in 1536 also remained in his parish until his death at the age of 72 in 1569, having served there for more than 33 years. He first came to Reading in 1529, aged 32, but the description given of him in 1561 – that he was unmarried, *mediocriter doctus*, and no preacher, but resident and hospitable – would probably serve to describe Snow and Mayneforth, as well.[18]

That priests of lesser account were now appointed vicars in Reading was very likely due to a combination of political, economic and religious factors, a principal feature of which was the aura of uncertainty ominously developing over the question of religious houses and their future from 1529 onwards. This and the king's increasing ascendancy over the English Church from the early 1530s was evidently sufficient to make university dons wary of becoming involved with a royal abbey, especially as they would understand the economic plight the incumbent of a corrody vicarage, such as St Laurence's, might suffer if the abbey were dissolved, or the incumbent of a perpetual vicarage such as St Giles' with a high percentage of tithe-free lands. Not only did the dons' foresight prove accurate but we shall see what other factors seriously affected the status of these Reading priests.

As mentioned earlier, Reading was afflicted by undercurrents of religious discontent. Lollardy had proved particularly strong and persistent in Berkshire, affecting Reading itself at least as early as 1416. In 1499 a group of eight Lollards, including two married couples, from St Laurence's and St Giles' parishes were detected and among other confessions admitted holding conventicles in their homes attended by itinerant Lollard preachers. Furthermore, three confessed to receiving the Holy Sacrament at mass not out of any devotion but 'only for dread of the people and to eschew the jeopardy and danger that we dread to fall in, if we had not done as other Christian people did'.[19]

Having abjured and performed humiliating public penance, these Lollard heretics were absorbed back into the community, successfully recovering their social positions and even authority. The tailor Thomas Scochyn of St Giles' was a burgess but despite being an erstwhile heretic was not expelled from the Guild Merchant and seems to have remained a member until his death. Moreover, a year after his abjuration he was appointed a wardman for London Ward, a peace-keeping office he again filled in 1509. In 1510 he was considered acceptable to stand surety for the entrance fines of three new burgesses.[20] At St Laurence's, the tanner John Bisshopp and his wife Alice similarly recovered their social positions. In 1501 Alice paid for a seat in church, and in 1507 and 1508 received an annual fee from the churchwardens for washing the church ornaments. John Roye, a cooper of St Laurence's who also recanted, was employed between 1506 and 1512 by the churchwardens to repair the church gutters.[21]

Other Lollards were detected in Reading in 1508: Edward Parker, aged eleven; Lewis John who escaped prosecution then, only to abjure in London in 1511; and John Stilman of St Giles' parish. Stilman abjured but later absconded to London where in 1518 he was condemned as a relapsed heretic and burned at Smithfield.[22]

In 1528 Reading's royal abbey was itself found to be infected by heresy at the highest levels. More than sixty Protestant books had been sold to the prior, John Shirbourne, by Thomas Garrett MA, curate of All Hallows, Honey Lane, London, who had formed a Lutheran cell at Oxford University and used an impecunious student as delivery-boy.[23] In 1532 John Frith, a very gifted Cambridge scholar, who like his associate, Garrett, would die for his religious beliefs, surreptitiously visited Reading from his refuge on the Continent, hoping to see Prior Shirbourne. Unsuccessful and forced to hide his identity, Frith was instead arrested and detained as a vagrant. He was rescued by the Welsh humanist Leonard Cox, also a Cambridge graduate and distinguished scholar, who had lectured for some eight years at Cracow university before becoming master of Reading Abbey's free school. Cox, who from July 1547 was actively to serve the Protestant regime of Edward VI as a licensed preacher, may have succumbed to more advanced reformed beliefs as a result of this encounter.[24] A prudent man, he meanwhile succeeded in retaining Abbot Hugh's favour and support while indicating to Cromwell that he was eager to be included among the vanguard of any legitimate advance towards reform. In May 1534 Cox obtained Cromwell's approval before publishing his English translation of Erasmus's paraphrases of St Paul's epistle to Titus, a work which appeared about the time that Henry VIII's Supremacy over the Church was formally acknowledged by statute.[25]

Abbot Hugh himself, despite reassuring evidence of the king's personal good will towards him, and despite the irritation of Cromwell's support first for the erring Prior Shirbourne then for another recalcitrant subordinate, nevertheless found it expedient – like many others – to court Cromwell's favour, and from December 1534 onwards awarded him and his son annuities and stewardships in reversion, together with gifts, and an annuity for a servant.[26]

The pressure now more intensively exerted upon Abbot Hugh, and the nature of Cromwell's principal adherents and sympathisers in Reading, become apparent in 1536, when in late August – just after publication of the Ten Articles and about the time the first royal injunctions were issued – the king and Cromwell visited the abbey. Cromwell had already intervened in London's elections in 1535 to secure a compliant mayor,[27] and one purpose of this visit was to launch a similar policy in Reading, an objective he successfully achieved for three mayoral years from late September 1536 through to 1538–9. The latter year neatly concluded with the dissolution of the abbey, just as the previous mayoral year 1537–8 had neatly concluded in September with the Grey Friars' surrender – an event adroitly used by the government as an early opportunity to confiscate the relics of both the abbey and the Caversham shrine, the latter then being defaced.[28] While royal intervention was an affront to the city fathers of self-governing London, such interference in local affairs was a positive encouragement to Reading's leading townsmen who in 1536 recognised this as the first sign that the resented abbatial authority was beginning to crumble. Prompt compliance with the royal will in order to gain favour was a step towards realising the long-cherished ambition – as good a measure of self-government as could be obtained.

After this visit in 1536 by the king and Cromwell, the abbot's choice of mayor from the Guild Merchant's three candidates was John White, a bellfounder and former churchwarden of St Laurence's already known to Cromwell who had commissioned him to make a great bell in 1529.[29] Significantly, the new churchwarden chosen that same September to serve until September 1538 in Reading's most important and populous parish of St Laurence was the gentleman Stephen Cawood, a secret reformer with London connections. The son-in-law of the recently-deceased and very wealthy, conservative mayor Thomas Everard, Cawood himself never showed interest in pursuing urban office.[30] In this intimidating climate St Laurence's new vicar, Sir John Mayneforth – scrutinised by a Cromwellian mayor who attended church daily[31] and by a powerful, secretly radical churchwarden – had to fulfil with some enthusiasm his obligations under the royal injunctions, extolling the rights, authority and virtue of the Royal Supremacy, while justifying to his flock such matters as the abrogation of certain holy days and discouragement of pilgrimages, from which local families profited. Adding to the misery of the conservative Mayneforth's situation is that, having a corrody vicarage and no glebe, he was directly dependent for nearly two-thirds of his income upon the abbey.[32]

In 1536 another reformer, the zealous William Gray, secured employment within the abbey. An assistant in 1535 to Nicholas Shaxton, the reforming bishop of Salisbury in whose diocese Reading was situated, Gray was a thorn in Abbot Hugh's flesh, who did not want 'his service at a gift' – especially as from about this time he achieved fame as a balladeer who ridiculed the old religion. From October 1545 Gray was to dominate Reading as its major property-holder, a position made even more overpowering locally when in Edward's reign he became an MP and one of Protector Somerset's closest advisers. Out of 46 burgesses, 31 were his tenants, among which were eight mayoral figures. The vicars of St Laurence's and St Giles', both presentees of Abbot Hugh, were also among his tenants.[33] Ironically, in June 1545 the future knight, Francis Englefield, who would become Queen Mary's close confidant and Reading's high steward, was granted the rectories and advowsons of St Mary's and St Giles'. In Edward's reign, he presented a Catholic vicar to St Giles'.[34] By such means did the Henrician regime itself inadvertently affect implementation of the religious policies of future governments, providing channels for reinforcing or disrupting them at the local level.

The mayor chosen by the abbot's deputy in 1537, the wealthy mercer Richard Turner, had already held this office four times, as well as the churchwardenship of St Laurence's twice. Although conservative in religion, Mayor Turner was commended to Cromwell as 'a very honest gentle person' at the time of the Reading Grey Friars' suppression in September 1538 when he very competently assisted the royal commissioner to restore order. The poor had unexpectedly fallen 'to stealing so fast in every corner of the house' they had even taken the bell clappers. At this very time Mayor Turner with other leading townsmen initiated the idea of using the body of the Grey Friars' church as a town hall, prevailing upon the commissioner to broach the matter for them with Cromwell. Mid-way through Turner's sixth term as mayor in 1542 the much-coveted, though limited, charter of incorporation was granted to the burgesses. It included the grant of the body and side aisles of the Grey Friars' church for a new guild hall.[35]

Abbot Hugh's choice of mayor (his last) in 1538 was Thomas Mirth of St Laurence's parish. A merchant and mercer of Reading and London, who became Cromwell's servant, he died in 1541, a year or less before the 1542 charter of incorporation was granted. Unusually for a Reading mayor, Mirth had never first been a churchwarden.[36]

On 13 November 1539 the past mayors Mirth and White and the past churchwarden, the reformer Cawood, were members of the seventeen-strong grand jury which swore to the truth of the accusations that Abbot Hugh, John Eynon and Prebendary John Rugge had denied the Royal Supremacy. Also on the jury was another Reading mercer and future mayor, William Buryton. No specific evidence of connection with Cromwell has been found and he – like his fellow mercer, the conformable mayor Richard Turner – was to remain conservative in religion.[37] The sole named prosecution witness was the burgess, William Pastler, a well-seasoned office-holder who, incidentally, had served as churchwarden of St Laurence's with John White.[38]

By this time Cromwell had already been the king's high steward of the borough and liberty of Reading for two months. The Crown was now also patron of the three churches until the grant of two of them in 1545 to Englefield.[39]

II

From 1536 onwards a small group of Reading burgesses, king's men to the core, were quietly establishing an unshakeable control over their fellows, a process in which the abbot had been obliged to co-operate. These few – all from St Laurence's parish except for a wealthy burgess from St Mary's – were to dominate local affairs for the rest of Henry VIII's reign, their influence extending throughout that of Edward VI. Such was the power and authority of those two of the group surviving longest that it continued undiminished till (natural) death; the Protestant William Edmundes of St Laurence's died late in Queen Mary's reign while mayor, and the Catholic John Bourne of St Mary's died soon after Elizabeth's accession, also while mayor. The group's political control was initially secured by internal action just after the grant of incorporation in 1542. The burgesses, then totalling 49, agreed to establish an inner circle of seven aldermen who alone among them could become mayor. By 1559 the total number of burgesses (aldermen included) had gradually been reduced to 26.[40]

Four men of St Laurence's provided the dynamic force motivating this group. It was their ambitious foresight which had initiated and carried through the desperate push for incorporation, during which they emerged victorious from a power struggle with another of Cromwell's local allies and petitioned the king himself.[41] Two were the Cromwellian mayors Richard Turner and John White who forged an alliance with Richard Justice, a royal servant with good Court connections. Justice, the brother of Thomas Justice MA, sometime vicar of St Laurence's, had been a burgess since 1509, though apparently only entering into the centre of local affairs from 1536 when he became a mayoral candidate of the type acceptable to the king and Cromwell.[42] As rapidly as possible after the Dissolution, the notary William Edmundes – until then under-steward of the abbey's possessions in Berkshire, including the liberty of Reading – was enrolled as a burgess, with Justice as a surety. A man well respected by abbot and townsmen alike, Edmundes had wide-ranging experience of the daily conduct of affairs, having presided over the monastery's views of frankpledge and courts as well as its lands, tenements, rents and services. In addition, in 1523 he had become both a parliamentary representative for Reading and Clerk of the Peace for Berkshire, an office he held until 1541 together with, for one year, that for Oxfordshire. Edmundes had also been a churchwarden of St Laurence's from 1518 to 1520. In 1540 he was restored as under-steward of the liberty of Reading, an office which – in effect – admitted him to royal service, since he now deputised for the king's high steward in both the borough and manor of Reading and in the hundreds of Reading and Theale. Such breadth of administrative and legal experience was an invaluable asset to the burgesses, grimly intent on gaining incorporation. They rewarded Edmundes in 1542 by simultaneously appointing him not only alderman but also recorder of the borough for life, the pivotal office in town government. Of very great importance is the fact that Edmundes at some point became a Protestant, and that he alone of this powerful quartet remained active in local politics until late October 1557, when he died soon after the start of his fourth term as mayor.[43]

The mayoralty circulated among these four alone – Turner, White, Justice and Edmundes, all of St Laurence's parish – for five crucial years, from the abbey's dissolution in September 1539 until September 1544, two years after incorporation, a fact testifying to the confidence they mutually inspired first in the king's officials, then in the burgesses who were responsible for selecting them.[44]

Upon incorporation in 1542 three others were drawn into this powerful group who set the pace for the future. William Buryton of

St Laurence's, the gentleman and mercer who had served on the grand jury which indicted Abbot Hugh and his companions, was simultaneously made burgess and alderman and also began his first two-year term as churchwarden at this time before becoming mayor in 1546–7. As mentioned, he remained conservative in religion, being a witness to the will in 1550 of Sir John Mayneforth, Abbot Hugh's vicar of St Laurence's.[45] Another religious conservative who witnessed Mayneforth's will was the wealthy clothier of St Mary's, John Bourne, who would outlive all of these powerful colleagues. An experienced urban office-holder and a burgess since 1529, he became mayor in 1544–5 and in 1552–3, a Parliamentary burgess in 1553 and 1554, dying in office at the start of his third mayoral term in 1558, soon after Elizabeth's accession. During the 1550s Alderman Bourne's influence was such that he virtually controlled St Mary's parish, his authority being reinforced by the election of his relatives to the churchwardenship there; two were in office together *c.*1550–1 and in 1553, and three others each in turn from Easter 1556 to Easter 1559.[46] In direct contrast to these two colleagues, Nicholas Niclas, son-in-law of the recently-deceased Protestant Stephen Cawood, himself became an adherent of reformed religion. Made burgess and alderman simultaneously in 1542, he was the son and grandson of wealthy burgesses of St Giles' parish who had donated generously to their church. His grandfather was renowned locally while mayor for vigorously opposing abbatial authority at the turn of the century. At some point Niclas, a wealthy beer brewer and royal bailiff, moved to the prestigious parish of St Laurence but survived his father-in-law, Cawood, by only seven years, dying *c.* early autumn 1549 before fulfilling his first term as a churchwarden.[47]

The Henrician charter of incorporation presented Reading with a powerful mayor, now a JP, supported by a governing group of burgesses free to co-opt new members of their choice. It was another important step towards autonomy, but nevertheless remained an *ad hoc* expedient which perhaps inadvertently, but very effectively, exerted considerable political pressure. Responsibility for social control was placed firmly upon the burgesses, who had most at stake in the borough, while the traditional revenues and profits were reserved to the Crown. This left the burgesses continually apprehensive about incurring royal displeasure, since the charter – which made Reading but a form of petty borough – could be rescinded.[48] At the same time there dangled the tantalising prospect that with good performance in the eyes of the monarch the longed-for 'full' charter might be forth-coming. In the event, this did not occur until September 1560, nearly eighteen and a half years later – and then only because Reading was so impoverished by the Crown's neglect that Elizabeth's pragmatic solution was to grant full responsibility to those ready to accept it on virtually any terms.[49]

III

Great stress has been placed upon the mayoralty and indication given of the nature of some of the most significant holders of this office from the mid-1530s. The reason is that the mayor – or whoever was the most recent past mayor in any one of the Reading parishes – by virtue of this top urban office also traditionally wielded great power over affairs within his own parochial community as the head of the 'assist-ance'. This term, in use by 1564, links up with others in vogue locally in the 1520s, such as 'elders' or 'worshipfuls' of the parish. Such terms denote an authoritative group of local dignitaries in each parochial community, an embryonic select vestry, who held sway over their fellows whether dwelling in borough or countryside but who, although oligarchical in tendency, still had an organic connection with the parish members.[50]

For example, the consent of these members – described in Reading churchwardens' accounts as 'the parish' or as 'the inhabitants' – was necessary for all manner of financial outlay. Such generalised terms (in these circumstances, at least) referred to those considered to be the actual 'parishioners', not to the whole population of communicants. The 'parishioners' consisted in the main of the established male house-holders. As the heads of familial groups and the ones, materially, with most at stake in the parochial community, male householders were its economic backbone. It was their resources which provided support for the parish church and habitually cushioned any burden of parochial debt. They therefore had the right to examine bills and the collective power to forgive debts, and so it was to them that the churchwardens had to present their accounts.[51] By contrast, when assessing the size of population in a parish the royal commissioners of 1548 calculated this in terms of numbers of communicants ('housling folk'). The purpose of this was to indicate the burden of spiritual responsibility falling upon local priests.[52] Although every communicant did 'belong' to a parish, not every such person could be considered an 'inhabitant' or as one of 'the parish' when it came to the conduct of public business.

An 'assistance' (apparently a consultative and supervisory body for churchwardens) seems to be a commonplace feature of parishes by 1564 and was supposed by then, properly, to consist of 13 persons who had already been 'churchwardens and constables'.[53] While all or just some of St Giles' past churchwardens may have composed a less formal type of 'assistance' in the 1520s, it is clear that in St Laurence's parish the 'assistance' centred round a core of former mayors under the leadership of the present or most recently-retired mayor.

Although a secular officer whose jurisdiction should, strictly speaking, have been confined to the borough alone, there is no doubt that from the early sixteenth century the mayor was of pre-eminent importance and authority in his particular parish, even though the churchwardens were legally its chief lay officers.[54] The mayor and his wife had special seats in church, the wives of past mayors had first choice of other seats, while those who could afford to pay for one had 'to take [their] place every day as they cometh'.[55] More importantly, the mayor presided over parochial business. In 1507 Thomas Quedynton, who had already received 6s. 8d. from St Laurence's funds for clock repairs, publicly bound himself 'before the mayor and the parish' to maintain its ironwork for 12 years 'at his own cost and charge'.[56] An ordinance of 18 April 1547 sets out the order of precedence among St Laurence's parish dignitaries at a church business meeting. First came the mayor, who presided, then two former mayors, the vicar, the two churchwardens, and seven other named dignitaries of whom two were aldermen and the rest secondary burgesses of the newly-incorporated borough. In addition, there were 'divers others, inhabitants of the said parish'.[57] It seems that whether the vicar was an Oxford don, as earlier in the century,[58] or a less distinguished priest, such as Sir John Mayneforth in 1547, it was customary for the mayor (or the parish's most recent past mayor) – not the vicar – to preside over parochial affairs and to take precedence over elders, clergy and churchwardens.

Furthermore, parish property could be reserved to the mayor or ex-mayor for safe-keeping. Being foremost among the leaders of local society, 'the men of probity', the mayor as the most important parishioner and elder was invested with a particular and ancient obligation to act as custodian of any very valuable church ornament, just as each new mayor of the Guild Merchant was made custodian of its charters, other muniments and silver goblets.[59] In 1533, an order was issued that the gilt bridal cup recently bequeathed to St Laurence's by Mistress Margaret Hyde was 'always to remain in the custody of the mayor, if the mayor dwell in the parish, and if the mayor dwell out of the parish then to remain and be in the custody of him that was last mayor in the same parish'. This order was made by the mayor, with three former mayors (all four having been churchwardens of St Laurence's), two dignitaries and 'divers others of the parish'.[60]

The churchwardens could also take precious ornaments into their safe-keeping. Being officers put in trust for the 'behoof' (benefit) of their parish, their duties not only included provision of various utensils, goods and ornaments necessary for public worship, but they were also regarded in law as having a special property in such moveable items belonging to the church. They could sue and be sued at law in regard to them, therefore it is not, perhaps, surprising to find in St Laurence's inventory of 1523 a note that certain silver and silver-gilt ornaments (including two silver-embossed service books) weighing in total some 463 ounces were in the churchwardens' custody.[61]

Also of paramount importance for the future in respect of church goods were other constraints imposed by common law upon church-wardens and parish dignitaries. No matter whether goods had been donated to the parish church by a man's immediate family or by his ancestors, they could not be retrieved at will. Common law made it extremely easy to donate goods to a church but extremely difficult to withdraw them. A man had only to buy a bell or have it installed in the steeple, or put a pew in the church, and these goods were straightway deemed in law to be parochial property. If any goods or ornaments were once in the possession and custody of the churchwardens, they could 'maintain an appeal of robbery against him that [stole] them, or an action of trespass against him that...wrongfully [took] them away, though it [were] the vicar, or parson himself....' Churchwardens, because of the trust invested in them, could 'neither give away, nor release at their own pleasure, the goods of the church'.[62]

The principle laid down in common law that the only power with which churchwardens were 'enabled... [was] ... the good and profit of the parish'[63] became – together with local custom – the rock to which Reading's dignitaries would cling as the English realm was confronted first by one then yet another of the drastic and, eventually, opposing religious changes of the Tudor monarchy. Already bound by law and custom to safeguard parochial wealth and interest and coming under

ever greater pressure to continue fulfilling such local expectations
satisfactorily, the frightening dilemma unfolding before Reading's top
men and churchwardens was that the monarch and Supreme Head of
the Church – now also lord of the borough[64] – posed the greatest
threat to these very objectives. The future being unknown and therefore the possibility or extent of religious change or reaction also being
uncertain, the safest course was to cleave to that which was known –
common law and local custom. Scrupulous observance of the principles
enshrined in these was therefore to become the method by which the
top townsmen parried the government's doctrinal and economic
designs on parish goods, and at the same time a way of offsetting
possible personal danger to themselves. Some probably feared that
one day they would stand accused in regard to church property,
especially during the minority of Edward VI when many may have
had grave doubts about the legality of religious reforms introduced
then. In addition to these complex considerations, the substantial
men of town and parishes had also to display prompt obedience to
the royal will in order to protect their reputation for loyalty and thus
the charter of incorporation.

IV

Official religious change may have given Reading's leading townsmen
exactly the opportunity they craved to be free of monastic jurisdiction
and to gain incorporation, but such an outcome was not inevitable.
Success in gaining the Henrician charter was entirely due to the
initiative, the driving energy and the ambitious foresight of a small
team with valuable business, legal and administrative experience in
borough, parishes and elsewhere. These qualities, coupled with good
Court connections, meant they shared a considerable amount of
sophisticated knowledge about ways to achieve their goals. Like their
predecessors earlier in the century, these townsmen did not hesitate to
take their cause to the highest levels – in this case, to Cromwell and to
the king himself.

Yet this hard-won charter was not enough. The real goal was full
incorporation. Reading's most powerful aldermen – the Catholic John
Bourne and the Protestant William Edmundes – therefore did not allow
the personal religious differences which eventually emerged to destroy

vital leadership rapport or to threaten the local independence so far achieved. When confronted in Mary's reign by evidence of fellow Protestant Julins Palmer's railing against the Queen and her laws, Edmundes said, 'I am Her Majesty's officer...I may not conceal it, neither will I.' Mayor John Bourne at his will-making a week after Elizabeth became queen stipulated that 'if [God's] service do otherwise alter', all the books and Catholic vestments he bequeathed to St Mary's should be sold and the proceeds given to the parish poor.[65] While bowing before the law, Reading's leaders in borough and parishes found means to work successfully within it for the ultimate benefit of their community.

7. Textiles and Reform: Halifax and its Hinterland

WILLIAM AND SARAH SHEILS

That there was a correlation between textile areas and the progress of the Reformation has become a commonplace of the literature, and studies of later dissent in East Anglia and Gloucestershire have demonstrated the continuing link between radical ideas and the cloth industry, sometimes reaching as far back as Lollardy.[1] It is, however, one thing to establish a correlation and quite another to describe a relationship, especially one which has been characterised by Professor Everitt as 'something of a mystery'. One approach, and that most suited to the surviving sources, is to examine an established dissenting neighbourhood of the seventeenth century and to attempt to trace the origins of that tradition in the earlier history of the Reformation, and this provides the main historiographical focus of this chapter.[2] The geographical focus will be the town of Halifax in the West Riding of Yorkshire, an area of the country with only a modest tradition of pre-Reformation radicalism.[3]

Halifax, unlike the southern clothing town of Cranbrook in Kent, had no known heretical presence in the decades prior to the 1530s, but it was to establish a reputation as a centre of radical Protestant opinions almost as quickly as its Kentish counterpart. By the early decades of the seventeenth century the lengthy ministry of John Favour, vicar from 1594 until 1624, had established a celebrated puritan tradition within the town and its parochial hinterland which was to sustain a reputation for independent action among its artisans and yeomen throughout the Civil Wars.[4] Halifax's reputation for action on behalf of Protestantism had been acknowledged as early as 1576 by Archbishop Edmund Grindal. In a famous letter to Queen Elizabeth he argued that 'continual preaching' had secured a loyal response from the town at the time of the rebellion of the Northern Earls in 1569; he wrote:

> ...one poor parish in Yorkshire, which by continual preaching had been better instructed than the rest, (Halifax, I mean) was ready to

bring three or four thousand able men into the field to serve you against the said rebels.... For obedience proceedeth of conscience: conscience is founded on the word of God, the word of God worketh this effect by preaching.

Grindal's diagnosis as to the source of the town's Protestantism was unsurprising, given the commitment to preaching and the confidence in its efficacy which typified the early generation of reformers. While at York in the early 1570s, he had been active in recruiting evangelical preachers to key positions in the northern province. Given the earlier claim in 1538 by Robert Ferrar, a native of the parish and client of Thomas Cromwell, that Halifax, along with other northern towns, had not one faithful preacher, the diagnosis remains to be tested: both as to the identity of those men who had made such a dramatic impact on the parish and to the local conditions which made Halifax such a receptive community in largely unsympathetic surroundings.[5]

Recent scholarship has suggested that influences other than preachers may have been at work, and that the Reformation may have arrived in the town by less formal ecclesiastical means. Halifax has been identified, along with Hull, as one of only two northern towns where the controversial will formulary first used by William Tracy of Toddington in Gloucestershire, and subsequently published by English Protestants abroad in 1535, was adopted. The will is celebrated for its radical Protestant statement of belief, and its appearance in Halifax in 1548 predated most other provincial occurrences of the form. It no doubt arrived in the town along well-established trade routes which linked the town with the capital and with other clothing communities in which the same will formulary has been recorded.[6] By this criterion, at least, Halifax was already in the forefront of reform by the beginning of the reign of Edward VI. One will formulary, however, does not make a Reformation, any more than the claims of an archbishop establish a preaching tradition. What were the principal characteristics of church life in Halifax in the early sixteenth century?

The town of Halifax, on the banks of the River Calder, had a population of *c.* 2,600 people in 1548 and lay at the heart of an extensive parish of about 10,000 people covering 124 square miles, comprising several townships containing hill-top settlements and a number of substantial houses, occupied by families such as the Waterhouses who lived at Shibden Hall, probably the most extensive and certainly the most famous of these homes of yeoman families of substance. The parish was both well populated and prosperous, and had a dispersed pattern of local government exercised by the chief inhabitants through a number of sub manors of the two great manors of Wakefield and Pontefract which occupied most of the parochial land.[7] The ecclesiastical structures were also dispersed; the parish church of St John the Baptist had been completely rebuilt by the parishioners between 1450 and 1482, and in the following half century chapels were added to house the chantries of William Rokeby and of the Haldesworth family. In addition to the parish church there were two ancient chapels, at Elland and Heptonstall, the latter being described in the chantry surveys as 'distant from the parish church of Halifax aforesaid four or five miles, in a moorish country, having the ministration of sacrament and sacramentals there, and houseling people to the number of 1,600'. With a population of *c*. 2,000, Heptonstall was itself as large as many towns, and in addition to the curate there were four other priests serving the chapelry.[8] Alongside these two ancient chapelries a number of others were established in the half century before the Reformation, reflecting both the prosperity and the piety of the growing population, most eloquently expressed in the petition of the inhabitants of Luddenden to have their chapel consecrated in 1535. It reads as follows:

> forasmuch as part of this parish of Halifax, being a very large parish, is above five miles off the said parish church, and that the number of inhabitants (being in former ages but few) are now much increased, and by reason of foul weather, craggy ways and floods, the feeble old men, and women with child are hindered to come to divine service and sacraments, to their great discouragement, and that also often-times some (especially of the poorer sort) in those remote places so far from the parish church, lie most lamentably three or four days unburied. The petitioners therefore, do most humbly beseech (in regard there is already a fair chapel, antient churchyard, font and books and other necessaries with ornaments fit for a parochial church, and that they will maintain both service and preaching upon their own costs) that your Majesty would be pleased...to consecrate and sanctify the said desolate church or chapel of St Mary, in as large and ample a manner as Heptonstall and Elland.[9]

The local lay initiative expressed in this petition, and the dispersed nature of ecclesiastical and secular authority in a populous but scattered community led by prosperous local farmers and clothiers linked to the wider world through their involvement in the wool trade provided fertile ground for the reception of Protestantism. The more so as the spiritual leader of this community in the crucial years between 1525 and 1556, when he was murdered, was Robert Haldesworth, a member of a prosperous local family, whose ministry was characterised by mistrust and dissension, based on his alleged misappropriation of charitable funds designed for the benefit of the parish. Certainly his bitter feud with the bailiff of Halifax, John Lacy, sustained a long lawsuit which eventually led the supporters of Lacy to side with the rebels during the Pilgrimage of Grace, whilst Haldesworth sided with the Crown. His character was not one to command the undivided loyalty of his congregation.[10]

It would be unfair, however, to take the career of Haldesworth as typical of parochial clergy in the area. Haldesworth had studied in Oxford and Rome, and William Aikeroide, founder of a scholarship tenable at the universities, at Oxford, but the intellectual horizons of most of the clergy working in the parish were grounded in the immediate locality, from which many of them came. Surnames such as Stansfield, Grenewood, Firth, Waterhouse, and Farebancke figure regularly among the curates and chaplains in the parish and represent a roll call of the Halifax yeomanry. The strength of their local connections and the esteem in which they were held is reflected in the frequency with which they appear as beneficiaries in local wills.[11] The two generations between 1480 and 1550 demonstrate strong support for the local clergy by the parishioners of Halifax, not only with money but also with candidates for the ministry. The weight of the surviving evidence suggests that these strong familial links were more likely to produce harmony than discord between pastor and people and, as we shall see, that harmony was not grounded in a narrow-minded localism but was capable of being receptive to new ideas.

The rectory estate was owned by the distant Lewes Priory in Sussex, and though the collection of tithes had been a matter of some dispute for most of the early sixteenth century local dissatisfaction was directed against the farmer of those tithes, Robert Waterhouse, rather than against the priory. There were no religious houses in the parish, which seems to have been untouched by the extensive monastic presence in Yorkshire. Apart from a few small bequests to nearby houses of friars, there is only one reference to a monk or monastery in the wills between 1480 and the Dissolution.[12] For most of the population religious life centred around the parish church or the local chapel, and each figured regularly in the wills of testators between 1480 and 1550, though after 1530 the numbers of such bequests declined as a proportion of the wills made. This probably reflected the uncertainties inherent in a period of rapid change rather than a change itself, for there was no corresponding increase in other forms of pious or charitable bequest and, as table 1 below shows, the latter also declined proportionately.

The substantial investment which the parishioners made in the parish church between 1450 and 1530 can still be seen in the fabric today, and the same is true of Elland, where an early sixteenth-century stained-glass window survives, but the ancient chapel of Heptonstall is now ruinous. This endeavour was, of course, entirely conventional and can be mirrored in most of the prosperous towns in the country, such as Norwich and Bristol.[13] What is more interesting about Halifax is the degree to which the laity were determined to ensure that, as population grew and settlements became more established, the 'moorish country' of these clothing and farming communities should not prevent the regular administration of the sacraments. From the late fifteenth century the inhabitants of these settlements invested heavily in their local chapels, over which they also gained a considerable degree of control. An early seventeenth-century source gives a list of thirteen chapels in addition to the three main churches in the parish, of which five were described as being decayed at that date.[14] Most of these chapels were either established or enlarged in the years following 1450, and many of them were threatened with disruption and disendowment by the Chantries Act. Ripponden chapel had been founded in 1464 with the assistance of the Crown, and that at Luddenden was licensed in 1496. In the early sixteenth century the latter attracted a number of bequests, including vestments in 1518, a gift of 10 shillings in 1521, an annual rent in 1526, and 5 marks towards the expenses involved in the abortive attempt at consecration in the 1530s. A group of inhabitants at Illingworth formed themselves into feoffees to establish a chapel on some land granted to them for that purpose in 1526, and continued to support the new building in their wills.[15] In addition to these new chapels, others were formed from long-standing private chapels attached to houses such as Coley Hall. As population in that part of the parish increased, so a new chapel was required to replace the one in the house, and in 1513 land was granted to 13 feoffees for a chapel. These represented the principal farming and clothing families of the area and they continued to bestow gifts on the chapel until its revenues were confiscated in 1546 and the chapel fell into disuse for a while. A similar fate also befell the chapel at Cross Stone, which served the townships of Stansfield and Langfield, where members of the Stansfield family both endowed the building and served the cure in the early sixteenth century.[16] There is no doubt that in the early years of the Reformation period conventional piety among the inhabitants of Halifax had funded significant improvements in pastoral provision within the community.

Such provision was not confined to the chapels, and a number of chantry and guild foundations were also established at this time. To those already mentioned must be added the Brigg Chantry in the parish church, served at its dissolution by a member of the Hoppay family, one of whom, Edward, was responsible for the radical Protestant preamble of 1548. Unlike his namesake, the chantry priest remained orthodox, producing a strongly conservative will on his death bed in 1556. Other chantries were established at Heptonstall, and at Sowerby and Sowerby Bridge it appears that the chapels were combined with chantry foundations to support their clergy.[17] In all, during the years following 1480 there were 13 bequests to chantries, of which eight were augmentations to existing foundations. Most had clergy attached at their dissolution in 1546 so that Halifax, despite being without a major institutional presence through the religious orders or a collegiate foundation, was a well-priested community with strong kinship links between priests and people. This set the rapidly urbanising community apart from cathedral cities like York or county towns such as Colchester with their more institutionally based clerical establishments.[18] Can the effect of this pattern on local religious life be measured?

The absence of any large religious institution did not deprive the inhabitants of contact with the wider world of the Church. A grammar school was proposed in 1497 but evidence for its existence before 1548 remains elusive. Nevertheless, there was sufficient schooling available for some Halifax youth to gain entrance to the universities. Haldesworth and Aikeroide have already been mentioned, and to these can be added the names of William Rokeby, archbishop of Dublin from 1511, who left money for an annual sermon in Halifax, Kirkby and Beverley in 1521; Robert Ferrar, last prior of Nostell and later bishop of St David's, who was martyred in the reign of Mary for his beliefs; and Edward Maude, a graduate and vicar of Darfield in the reign of Edward VI.[19] Informality in educational provision did not necessarily lead to provincialism, and there were clearly opportunities for advancement which men like William Aikeroide sought to increase through the provision of scholarships. Such men were the exception, however, and for the majority their experience of the Church revolved around their own community.

Some of the more substantial bequests to the chapels have already been noted but, as table 1 indicates, these represent only a part of a wider pattern of support.

This is not the place to quote these wills at length, but one or two will serve to establish the character of local piety. In 1512 Nicholas Wodehede of Elland left 6s. for a trental of St Gregory, 4s. to Ripponden chapel, and 8d. to the bell at Elland; in 1514 Thomas Crabtree left 3s. 4d. to Heptonstall chapel, 12d. to the chaplain Gilbert Stansfield, 13s. 4d. to the poor and 3s. 4d. to the repair of Coldenstock Bridge. All of these were modest members of the community, whose wealth was tied up in stock and goods rather than in land and money. A rather more substantial figure was John Smyth of Lightcliff who left 6s. 8d. to the parish church, where he asked to be buried, the same sum to the needs of Eastfield chapel, and £5 to be distributed to the poor on his day of burial in 1542.[20] These bequests did not exhibit the level of discrimination and sophistication evident in the wills made by the citizens of Bristol, who had a much wider range of devotional possibilities before them, or even the opportunities available to the townsfolk of more established urban communities such as Ludlow. Nor do they suggest the spiritual variety uncovered by Eamon Duffy in the clothing villages and towns of East Anglia.[21] Rather they reflect a concern with the everyday needs of the Church and the community. This is equally true of the charitable bequests, three-quarters of which were directly

Table 1 Pious Bequests

	Chantries	Prayers for souls	Church or Chapel	Charities	Total
1480–90	1	2	2	–	7
1491–1500	3(2)	1	7	–	9
1501–10	2(1)	1	10	4	18
1511–20	–	12	23	12	41
1521–30	2(1)	13	27	10	47
1531–40	5(4)	6	27	5	88
1541–47	–	3	26	9	102

concerned with the maintenance of roads and bridges, further testimony to the importance of trade in this 'morishe contrye'.[22]

The evidence presented so far has suggested a vigorous if conventional concern for the sacramental life of the church, rooted in the quotidian and with a high level of local influence exercised through the feoffees of the chapels. The extent to which this tradition was open to influences from outside remains to be tested. To begin this we must turn to the complex evidence provided in the will preambles. These remain a much-debated source, but recent work has refined approaches to this material and permitted a more sensitive understanding of their value, at least at the level of particular communities.[23]

The traditional will formulary, bequeathing the soul to God, the Virgin and all the saints, was universal at Halifax until 1526, and the dominant role which the clergy played in the writing of these wills can be gauged by the proportion which were written in Latin. In 1526 the first appearance of wills omitting mention of the Virgin and saints was recorded. Three wills of this sort were recorded in that year, but it is unlikely that the testators were making a conscious statement about traditional piety, the more so as one of them, Richard Ambler, left money for 'the maintaining of the service of Almighty God in the parish church before Our Lady, Saint George, and to the morn priest' and another, John Milner, left a mass book to the Lady altar and sixteen pence to Saint Anthony's light. That said, however, some significance might lie in the fact that all these wills were witnessed by John Birkhede, a priest from a local family who was probably serving the chapel at Sowerby. Nothing is known of Birkhede's views, but another member of the family, Richard, made a positive statement of Protestant belief in his will of 1543 as follows: 'I bequeath my soul to God, verily believing myself to be one of the chosen number that shall be saved through Christ, and my body to be buried in the churchyard of Halifax among the chosen brethren of Christ's holy church.'[24]

By the time Richard made his will, such preambles had become quite common in the parish, but the timing of their appearance is instructive. Isolated wills of a non-traditional sort were registered in the early 1530s, but it was not until 1538, after the Royal Injunctions and when the direction of government policy was clear, that another flurry of non-traditional preambles was recorded. The earliest of these, that of Robert Thompson made on 3 July 1538, made explicit reference to the changes of the 1530s and, in particular to the Royal Supremacy, addressing Henry as 'fidei defensoris ac in terris supremis capitis ecclesie anglicane'. The Latin, of course, suggests clerical influence in the drafting of the will, but Thompson went on to bequeath his soul to 'Christ Jesus, my maker and redeemer, in whom and by the merits of whose blessed passion is all my trust of clean remission of all my sins'.[25]

Between April 1538 and October 1540 forty-one wills were written in the parish. Nineteen of these omitted traditional references to the Virgin and saints, most of them going further and referring to the saving power of Christ's passion in the preamble. The greatest concentration of these, thirteen in all, emanated from Heptonstall chapelry, and responsibility for the formulation may rest with the curate there, John Grenewood, who witnessed ten of the wills. Grenewood had been witnessing traditional formularies as late as 1537, and even at this late date one of the testators, William Acroide, combined a non-traditional formulation with bequests for prayers for his soul and for a priest to sing for him. The evidence of the Heptonstall wills is indicative of the trust and influence which Grenewood had amongst his congregation, and of his responsiveness to a lead from central or diocesan authority. Whether this marked the beginnings of a sustained Protestant tradition is more difficult to establish; preambles from the chapelry revert to more conventional formulations in the later years of Henry VIII, with Protestant statements reappearing under Edward. By this time, of course, many of the objects of traditional piety had been officially removed, and the Protestantism of the wills from this period may do little more than reflect these institutional changes, as was the case in the nearby town of Otley, where the curate also had a significant influence on the drafting of wills.[26]

If such formulations can be traced directly to the clergy in Heptonstall, that was not so in the rest of the parish. In Halifax township itself there were five non-traditional preambles recorded in 1538 and 1539, all of them involving members of the Maude family. Richard Maude was a witness to all of these wills, two of which were made by Wiliam and John Maude. It is with this small group that we can see the beginnings of an enduring tradition, for members of the family were later to appear as Protestants under Mary, possibly even as exiles, and some entered the ranks of the clergy.[27] Another family resident in Halifax township, the Bests, may also have been at the centre of early Protestant activity in the parish. One of their number, John, was a priest and both the scribe and overseer of the will of Richard Birkhede which has been mentioned earlier; another family member, Richard, was overseer of the Protestant will of Lawrence Hargreaves; and finally Janet Best was the only female to use a non-traditional formulary before 1548. Like the Maudes, the Bests seem to have established a firm commitment to Protestantism which saw them in trouble under Mary. In July 1554 a Richard Best was accused of the removal of the Blessed Sacrament from Halifax church under cover of darkness, and though the original charge was dropped he was convicted of the lesser offence of receiving communion without going to confession and ordered to stand before the pulpit in Halifax church and 'affirm the contents of a schedule, which the curate shall then read, to be true, and that he believeth them from the bottom of his heart'. Best's penance was required to be performed alongside those of two accomplices who also challenged the sacrament.[28]

That some inhabitants of Halifax were responsive to the Henrician changes of the 1530s is clear, but can we know more about them? Those from Heptonstall identified around the person of John Grenewood included members of the landholding Mitchell and Fletcher families and seem to represent the more substantial, if not the wealthiest, sectors of the community; only one of them, Robert Sutcliffe, makes any mention of the cloth industry in his will. The cloth trade played a greater part in the lives of the Maude and Best families, however. Richard Maude mentioned both shears and looms in his will of 1540, and another member of the family, John, left cloth in his will of 1546, whilst another, Gilbert, was among the first to describe himself as a clothier when making his will in 1547. Janet Best had both shears and a shearboard at the time of her death in 1544, whilst the Hargreaves family, with whom the Bests were connected, also owned looms and tenters. Neither the Maudes nor the Bests were humble weavers, however, but were well established in the community, possessing lands and producing clerical sons, one at least of whom attended university.[29] Though the numbers are small it would appear that the early Protestants in Halifax came from fairly prosperous families who were engaged in both farming and the cloth trade and were well integrated into local church life.

The evidence for Protestant belief in Halifax before the end of Henry's reign is modest, whilst that indicating a demand for the sacramental life extensive. This may reflect the nature of the sources as much as anything; will-making at this level of society took place in an essentially domestic and parochial environment which must have coloured the intentions of the testators.[30] Certainly the regular bequests to clergy and to chapels owed more to the institutional shortcomings of the church in this rapidly urbanising area than to a heightened devotional awareness born of familiarity with its established institutions. In this respect, the conventional piety of the Halifax laity can be characterised as the expression of a demand for the basic amenities of the Christian life. As such both conventional piety and Protestantism can be said to have shared evangelical roots. The dissolution of the chantries, which also disendowed the proprietary chapels in the parish, posed considerable problems for the inhabitants of Halifax, as it did in other places. Not only did it diminish the pastoral provision that had been built up over the previous century, largely by the lay members of the community, but, by rendering the role of the feoffees of the chapelries obsolete, it also removed those corporate expressions of communal life which had grown up around the church and reflected the confidence of this prosperous, urbanising parish. The churchwardens' accounts do not survive, so we are unable to quantify the impact of the Act in the way that has been done for parishes in London, Bristol and the extensive Lancashire parish of Prescot, but the financial implications may have been less important than the institutional ones. As in the parishes studied by Burgess and Kümin, carefully developed regimes were disrupted and the principal inhabitants of Halifax were deprived of an important outlet for their individual and corporate social energies.[31] The evidence from wills in the decade following 1548 indicates that the parishioners had not found an alternative object for those energies.[32] Furthermore, in chapelries such as Lightcliffe and Cross Stone, the legislation had deprived the community of their clergy and, thereby, made regular access to the sacraments more difficult.

It would be wrong, however, to characterise the early legislation of Edward's reign solely in terms of loss. The dramatic statement in the preamble of Edward Hoppay was not repeated, but the wills in general do show an increasing awareness of the Reformation changes among some sectors of the community. This must have owed something to the switch to English in the liturgy, which took place swiftly and was considered sufficiently momentous to be recorded in the baptismal register on 18 April 1549.[33] Protestantism seems to have continued to grow among families associated with the Maudes and the Bests, whose wills reveal a fairly close-knit pattern of contacts within the parish, and their learning was sufficient for one local gentleman to record studying Latin with tutors in the parish and reading Ovid, Horace, Virgil and Cicero under Richard Best at Halifax. There was learning as well as piety among these Protestants, one of whom, the merchant 'Master Farrar', made contact with the Scots preacher and heretic John Rough during a visit to London.[34] Despite these glimpses, however, the fragmentary nature of the evidence from the 1550s testifies more to the general uncertainty over the direction of religious policy, a situation not eased by the fact that the controversial figure of Robert Haldesworth continued as vicar until 1556. To these uncertainties must be added those more material ones which the parish felt as a result of recession in the wool and cloth trades and periodic demographic crises, as in August 1551 when 42 people died of the sweating sickness.[35] These were not the circumstances in which confident expressions of support for the Church could be expected.

The evidence from the early years of Elizabeth's reign is equally inconclusive, and it is important to note that Grindal's letter commending the Protestant loyalty of Halifax in 1569–70 was written retrospectively in 1576 in the immediate context of the Queen's determination to suppress the prophesyings and the archbishop's determination to point out the error of her ways. As such, Grindal's remarks may record his own policy, as archbishop of York from 1570, to secure good preachers in key locations in the diocese, as much as any earlier tradition of consistent preaching in the area.[36] If there were such preachers, and no doubt there were some, their impact has gone unrecorded in the surviving records. Given the importance of the parish, and the fact that the living was a well-endowed one in an area of the country desperately short of able Protestant clergy, the silence from the records makes it unlikely that earlier Protestant support had made dramatic advances in the parish during the first half of Elizabeth's reign.

Although there were isolated instances of nonconformist practice reported in the 1580s, it may have been a perceived lack of Protestant commitment, or the need to provide Protestants in the parish with strong leadership, which attracted the attention of Henry, earl of Huntingdon. As president of the Council of the North, Henry used his access to Crown patronage to secure a committed preacher, John Favour, as vicar in 1594. Favour was also a friend of the archbishop Tobie Matthew, who used him in controversy with Catholic recusants, for which Favour received cathedral preferments. This activity did not detract from his influence in the parish, which was immediate. A comprehensive, and never to be repeated, presentment was made against the vicar at the visitation of 1596, when it was reported that no surplices were worn in any of the churches or chapels of the parish. Thereafter, however, Favour seems to have won over the principal inhabitants of the parish to his reforming policy, and consistent and thorough presentments against sexual offenders, drunkards and profaners of the sabbath were made by churchwardens at successive visitations throughout the thirty years of his ministry.[37]

Favour's ministry was not solely confined to combating Catholicism and ungodliness, and it is in other aspects of his work that we see a revival of parochial life. The foundation of a new grammar school in the parish, at Heath, was a particular object of support. Prior to Favour's arrival the governors, who had been established in 1585, had achieved little, but thereafter the vicar involved himself in all aspects of the work, securing donations from all the principal office-holders in the parish and from those Halifax men who had moved on elsewhere, such as Sir Richard Saltonstall, Lord Mayor of London, Sir Henry Savile, provost of Eton, and Joseph Lister, an alderman of Hull. By 1623 the school had received grants in excess of £700 from the parish or those connected with it. In addition Favour revived the charitable impulses of the community which had lain dormant since the end of Henry VIII's reign, so much so that, the cities of York and Hull excepted, Halifax gave more money for charitable purposes than any other place in Yorkshire between 1480 and 1640, the great bulk of that money being given in the years following Favour's arrival. In addition to the school, charities for the poor, and bequests to clergy and for sermons increased fourfold, and a number of those chapelries decayed after 1548 were revived and re-endowed by the parishioners: Raistrick was restored in 1602, Ripponden rebuilt in 1610, Cross Stone in 1616, Sowerby enlarged in 1622, Luddenden consecrated in 1624, and Sowerby Bridge rebuilt in 1632.[38] Clergy were supported and sermons established in these chapels, and when puritans fell foul of the diocesan authorities they were offered the protection of the vicar.[39] The achievement of Favour in Halifax in touching the charitable wellsprings of his congregations compares with that of John White in early seventeenth-century Dorchester, though the objects of Halifax charity appear more parochial.[40] It was also in these years that the reputation of the town as a noted puritan centre serving a wider area through the sermons preached at the exercise was established. Favour's ministry was clearly a watershed in the history of the Reformation in this textile community, but in considering its success we can form some conclusions about the process of reform in the upland, urbanising regions of the country.

That the puritanism of seventeenth-century Halifax was built upon a tradition of evangelical dissent was clearly not the case, however much contemporaries would have wished it thus. Nor is it clear that the cloth trade had any more than a marginal influence on religion; the town was in touch with other centres and ideas as well as goods passed along those routes, but the impact of those ideas, never mind the specific character of them, is hard to establish at a communal level, notwithstanding the influence which they may have had on one or two individuals. When Protestantism made its beginnings in the parish it did so among small networks of the more prosperous families, which had clerics among their kinsmen. That is to say, it rooted itself, rather precariously before 1548, within the parochial establishment. The surviving records do not tell us precisely how productive this growth was to prove in the generation between 1550 and 1580, but they suggest that it remained low-key. What the records do tell us, however, is that no alternative focus for communal evangelical endeavour was found to replace that which had been removed in 1548. That focus was to come with the demand for a preaching ministry in the years after 1590.

The Reformation in Halifax was characterised by the inability of the Church's institutions alone to provide the basic requirements of the Christian life and by a long tradition of lay support for the provision of those requirements. To this must be added periods of relative prosperity among the farming and clothing communities and, from the late sixteenth century, strong clerical leadership. The activities of the puritan churchwardens and sidesmen of seventeenth-century Halifax in support of a preaching ministry had more in common with the activities of their grandparents and great-grandparents who were feoffees of chapels in the early sixteenth century than with early Protestants like the Bests, though they too played their part in the story. The paradox was that, in recently settled and growing textile towns and parishes like Halifax, the official Reformation in its early stages cut off the very institutions which sought to overcome the deficiencies of the late medieval Church and, two generations later, it took puritanism and a preaching ministry to revive them. In Halifax and its hinterland the Reformation years were disruptive ones. If continuity can be demonstrated it was expressed not through dissent, but through lay integration into the life of the local worshipping communities.

Part II
The Resources of Urban Reformation

8. Economic Problems of Provincial Urban Clergy during the Reformation

PATRICK CARTER

In the summer of 1546 the leading citizens of Coventry petitioned the Crown to reduce the tax assessment of the vicarage of Holy Trinity.[1] One year had elapsed since the death of the last incumbent, and all efforts to secure a suitable replacement had failed. The immediate cause of their difficulties was the reluctance of any prospective incumbent to pay the tax of first fruits due to the Crown, which owing to a decrease in income now exceeded the current value of the living. The parishioners could find no one who 'laboryth or regardyth to be owre pastor to feede us gostly with gods worde and to minister unto us the holy sacraments as to Christ's flocke behovyth'. In response the Crown appointed local commissioners to inquire into the decay of the vicarage; they convened a public hearing in the church at which more than a dozen witnesses testified to the impoverishment of the benefice. They ascribed the decline chiefly to the collapse of the cloth trade at Coventry, which had indirectly reduced the net annual revenues of the vicarage from over £26 to only £15 6s. 4d. While the resulting reassessment helped to solve the immediate problem of finding a fresh incumbent for Holy Trinity, Coventry's woes continued; during the later 1550s both Holy Trinity and its sister parish of St Michael's again fell vacant. At the root of the town's troubles lay a general decline in population and prosperity owing to the collapse of the cloth trade, which was summarised by the traveller and commentator John Leland: 'the towne [Coventry] rose by makynge of clothe and capps, that now decayenge the glory of the city decayethe'.[2]

The extent of urban decline in late medieval England and its consequences for religious life remain controversial.[3] While petitions pleading for reductions in tax assessments and fee farms provide graphic descriptions of decay and depopulation, some allowance must clearly be made for the framers' employment of rhetoric. Such laments were echoed in the early Henrician statute designed to reverse decline by promoting rebuilding and the revival of provincial urban economies, which bewailed how 'the husbondry whych ys the gretest comodyte of thys realme for sustenance of man ys greatly decayed, churchys destroyed, the servyce of God wythdrawen, Christen people there buryed not prayed for, the patrons and curats wronged...'.[4] Yet if perhaps exaggerated, the frequency of such complaints strongly suggests that they reflected the true situation in many provincial towns in the early sixteenth century, and thus should not be dismissed lightly by historians. Notably, the above statute drew a close connection between economic decline and the deterioration of religious life, although here again the evidence admits of various interpretations. In some towns (most famously at Louth in Lincolnshire) the early sixteenth century witnessed the erection of grand new churches and towers, while even at Coventry John Leland praised the town's twin parish churches (St Michael's and Holy Trinity) for their fine construction and good state of repair. Elsewhere, however, as at Lincoln and Northampton, churches lay abandoned and in ruins.[5] It is within this context of perceived decline and decay that the economic consequences of the Reformation for urban clergy must be considered.

Provincial urban clergy were not immune from the economic problems which beset the broader community. By the early sixteenth century towns from Stamford to Southampton shared a common problem: shrinking populations could no longer adequately support the numerous small urban parishes which had evolved by the later Middle Ages. As the number of parishioners decreased, incumbents' incomes from personal tithes and offerings fell sharply. At the same time the casual employment of clergy as private chaplains or temporary chantry priests proved less lucrative, as corporations and wealthy merchant families encountered growing economic difficulties. Historians are probably correct to attribute the decline in fresh urban chantry endowments during the early decades of the sixteenth century to an economic rather than spiritual crisis.[6]

Care is required, however, not to exaggerate the impact of late medieval urban decline upon parochial clergy, for despite economic difficulties provincial towns continued to offer employment to large numbers of priests. Even at Stamford, which had been sacked in 1461 and had then seen the European market for its celebrated scarlet cloth collapse, the town's eleven parishes employed at least two dozen clergy in 1526. The largest parish, St Mary's, had a staff of five priests:

a rector, chantry priest, and three stipendiary clergy. In addition to the parish clergy proper, the town's almshouse provided employment for a warden and two other stipendiaries, while to these secular clergy should be added the friars residing in the town.[7] At Boston in Lincolnshire, which suffered a steady decline in trade owing to the silting up of the river Witham, the single parish church still employed 33 priests, and similar hosts served in Northampton, Lincoln, Leicester and other towns.[8]

Yet this continuing demand for clergy obscured a serious structural weakness of clerical finances, for many urban benefices barely afforded their incumbents a living wage. A brief examination of the 1535 *Valor Ecclesiasticus*, the comprehensive survey of ecclesiastical incomes undertaken in preparation for increased taxation of the church, clearly illustrates the extent of the problem. In a sample of fifteen larger provincial towns, barely one-fifth of the benefices assessed (rectories, vicarages, and perpetual chantries and free chapels) were reported to be worth £10 or more per annum, while a similar number fell between £6 13s. 4d. and £10.[9] The majority of benefices were worth less than £6 13s. 4d. per annum, and at Stamford and Norwich the median annual income was considerably less (£3 17s. 8d. and £4 13s. 9d. respectively). By comparison, almost one-half of all parochial benefices in the county of Kent as a whole were worth £10 or more per annum, and fewer than one-quarter fell below the ten marks threshold (£6 13s. 4d.). While in some cases the crisis confronting urban incumbents was not as severe as the *Valor* data might suggest (as casual income from fees and offerings often went under-reported, and many of the poorest benefices were held *in commendam* with others to provide a living wage), at the same time this analysis excludes many decayed benefices which could no longer support an incumbent and were omitted entirely from the returns (for example at Ipswich and Lincoln).

The root cause of this impoverishment of urban benefices was a reliance upon personal tithes, rents, and offerings and other casual income, rather than agricultural tithes and the profits of glebe land. Personal tithes were payable on all net rental income and profits of trade (less legitimate business expenses). At Worcester in 1535, for example, personal tithes alone accounted for 68.2 per cent of incomes, as compared with only 17.8 per cent from greater and lesser tithes combined. More significantly, two of the most valuable livings in the town enjoyed substantial tithes of agricultural produce.[10] After personal tithes, offerings and oblations supplied most of the remainder of urban clerical incomes: in Exeter tithes (chiefly personal) made up 60.2 per cent of rectorial incomes, and offerings supplied most of the rest (35.9 per cent).[11] Personal tithes had long been a source of controversy and dispute, even when tied to rental values of properties, as at Canterbury and Bristol. Evasion was common, and the decay of rents during the early sixteenth century compounded the problem. Full and just payment of personal tithes became a perennial demand of clergy in the lower house of convocation, and in 1531 the issue sparked a clerical revolt in London.[12] The dependence of urban clergy in Worcester and Exeter upon personal tithes and offerings revealed by the 1535 survey points to the vulnerability of clergy both to the fall of rents brought about by urban depopulation, and to the loss of lucrative sources of casual income through attacks upon pilgrimages, images and other elements of popular piety.

The 1535 returns also demonstrate the degree to which any division between urban and rural clergy is necessarily arbitrary, for some urban clergy supplemented their incomes by leasing a second, rural benefice. Three Stamford incumbents occupied other benefices within a few miles of the town, as did at least two at Exeter and two at Southampton.[13] Not all subsisted entirely on the meagre revenues of their urban benefice. As well, in some cases a portion of the revenues of an urban benefice actually came from the surrounding countryside: the incumbent of Philip's chantry in St Mary's church, Stamford, received £9 from lands in neighbouring Rutland, while the emoluments of the rectory of St Swithin's, Worcester, included 50s. from tithes in the Worcestershire parish of Cleymor. When rural clergy obtained an urban living, they sometimes augmented their new income with a pension drawn from their previous parish. Thus George Polley, formerly incumbent of Great Hardes in Kent, continued to enjoy an annual pension of £6 13s. 4d. from his previous benefice after he became rector of St Mildred's, Canterbury (worth £7 19s. 8d. per annum).[14] While urban clergy faced peculiar problems not encountered by their rural counterparts, one must avoid isolating the two groups completely from one another. Rural and urban benefices were not infrequently held by the same clergy. Indeed, securing a rural source of income (whether tithes or a pension) offered one option for minimising the economic difficulties which plagued provincial urban clergy.

Despite these links to the surrounding countryside, urban parish clergy were usually local men, frequently working in the same parish in which their parents and siblings worshipped and were buried. John Carlyn, a native of Bristol, was successively curate at St Leonard's and rector of St Mary le Porte; his colleague John White, rector of St Peter's, was described by an opponent in a lawsuit as 'a man of great substance having one alderman to hys father inhabytyng within the sayd towne of Brystoll and many other frends there'.[15] At York the parish clergy were overwhelmingly local, like the chantry priest who asked in his will to be interred next to his father in a neighbouring church, or William Coker, chantrist of Holy Trinity Micklegate, who requested burial 'besydes my fader and my moder within thaforesaid kyrke'.[16] The prevalence of local men in urban parishes is attributable, at least in part, to the active role of laymen in hiring clergy in many parishes, offering indirect evidence of the importance of family connections in furthering clerical careers. Local roots strengthened the ties between lay and clerical culture in towns, preserving the 'symbiosis' which had existed between urban clergy and laity during the later Middle Ages.[17]

Sharing a common background, urban parish clergy formed a close-knit community. They lent each other money, stood surety for one another when compounding for first fruits, and witnessed their colleagues' wills, which frequently contain bequests by the testator to his clerical brethren. The will of John Hilton, a stipendiary priest at All Saints', Northampton, was witnessed by two of the town's incumbents. When Oliver Sutton compounded for the first fruits of the vicarage of St Martin, Lincoln, in May 1544, his sureties included his neighbour Robert Arnold, rector of St Mary Magdalene.[18] Nowhere is this clerical community more clearly visible than through a series of Southampton wills and inventories. In 1549 John Newton, rector of St John's, Southampton, left all his books to Lawrence Sutton, vicar of St Michael's. Sutton in turn left the residue of his estate (including 'certen olde bookes') to the rector of St Lawrence parish, William Morrell, upon his own death in 1557. Seven years later Morrell bequeathed to Sutton's successor at St Michael's 'a black gown that I had of his predecessor'. Included in the inventory of Morrell's goods were 'vj olde bookes': probably those which had originally been the property of John Newton.[19]

As active participants in the urban economy, parish clergy were vulnerable to changing economic fortunes. Many were landlords and moneylenders, and a few even supplemented their income through farming or the practice of a trade (motivated by economic necessity rather than a desire to emulate the example of St Paul). Most chantry priests and some incumbents relied upon rental income for their survival, making them important urban landlords. The incumbent of the free chapel of St Thomas in Stamford received his entire annual income of £7 15s. 6d. from rents of shops and tenements within the town; at Lincoln the rector of St Mary Magdalene depended upon the lease of a single house for one-third of his annual income. Properties were sometimes administered by churchwardens, as in the parish of St Alban's, Worcester, where rental income accounted for two-thirds of the rector's gross annual stipend of £5, but in other places the clergy were directly involved in managing the properties. They encountered difficulties similar to those of lay landlords, in both maintaining properties and securing tenants in a time of economic decline.

Some wealthier urban clergy were also active as moneylenders. Probate inventories, with their lists of debts owing to the deceased, can provide evidence for these activities. While some of the recorded debts are for unpaid tithes, others clearly represent outstanding loans. Liquid capital was essential to engage in moneylending, and in this regard it is striking how many parish clergy held considerable sums in specie. For example William Morrell, rector of St Lawrence Southampton, left £14 in ready money, and Lawrence Harryson, vicar of St George's Fishergate in York had £13 6s. 8d. in his purse at his death. John Watson, a York chantry priest, had £4 11s. 4d. in coin, but over £25 in desperate debts due to him 'as doithe appere by his one booke off parcelles maid there off': the majority probably represented unpaid rents, although some loans may also have been included. Richard Rundall, rector of St Saviour's in York, specified tithe debts from his two benefices, as well as £6 due from Robert Barker (most probably a loan). Rundall possessed considerable capital, including £18 in coin and a further £11 in plate. Several Boston chantry priests were owed substantial sums at their death.[20] Some clerical loans were motivated by pastoral concerns, as when the rector of All Saints Southampton lent 20s. to one merchant's widow to help discharge her late husband's debts. Another Southampton incumbent, John Newton, was a creditor of two Genoese merchants in the town, although it is unclear whether Newton was a business partner or simply provided a loan (the exact sums due are not specified).[21] Loans to merchants and other parishioners by urban clergy from their accumulated capital represent a further aspect of their involvement in the economic life of their communities, increasing their vulnerability to the vagaries of trade.

For beneficed clergy who already faced serious economic difficulties as a result of the decline in trade and urban depopulation, the early stages of the Reformation brought further threats. The first of these was the Crown's demand for increased taxation. Beginning in 1535 all new incumbents were obliged to pay first fruits (a sum equal to one entire year's income) upon collation or institution to a benefice.[22] While Mary's reign brought a brief respite from this harsh tax regime, and from 1559 poorer incumbents were released from payment, first fruits none the less remained an unwelcome burden upon clerical finances. In some ways royal demands for annual clerical tenths and subsidies presented even greater problems. They were payable by all beneficed clergy (and subsidies extended to curates and stipendiary clergy as well), whereas first fruits were confined to new incumbents. As well, arrears of tenths and subsidies were chargeable upon the benefice, rather than the individual incumbent and his sureties (as with first fruits). This was a crucial difference, for such accumulated arrears discouraged prospective incumbents from accepting some vacant livings, lest they be held liable in turn for the debts of their predecessors. In May 1561 Bishop Bentham of Coventry and Lichfield alerted the Crown to the predicament of the recently restored vicar of St Michael's in Coventry. A learned and godly minister, he none the less 'cannot be able nor wyll contynue and take upon hym the charge of so great a cure and ministerye and payment of suche arrerages beynge daylye required'.[23] Finally, while rural parish clergy with glebe land to farm or extensive income from agricultural tithes found that the relative burden of taxation upon their benefices fell as their incomes rose in line with prices (while the 1535 assessment remained fixed), few urban clergy benefited from this indirect tax relief.

Increased taxation was followed by further attacks upon clerical incomes. In 1538 the second set of royal injunctions ordered the removal from churches of images which attracted pilgrims and their offerings, and thus promoted idolatry.[24] In some cases the consequences of this order for urban clerical finances were catastrophic. In the church of St Gregory, Northampton, the removal of the celebrated image of 'the rood in the wall' reduced the rector's annual income by more than two-thirds, from £10 to little more than £3.[25] Formerly 'frequentide and usede with great resort of people' (including Henry VIII himself in 1511), the end of the pilgrimage associated with the image proved fatal for the parish, which found it impossible to secure a suitable incumbent after 1538. By the mid-sixteenth century the church building had been converted into a school.[26] Given the importance of offerings and other casual income, the removal of images and discouragement of pilgrimages could only spell disaster for many urban clergy.

Worse, however, was to follow, with the dissolution of monasteries and then chantries and guilds. The latter development was especially grave, since guilds supported large numbers of chaplains, many of whom assisted parish incumbents. At Boston the three town guilds employed fourteen clergy in 1535; similar arrangements existed at Stamford, Coventry, Leicester and elsewhere.[27] The effects of the monastic dissolution varied from town to town, depending upon the level of urban appropriations. Some urban vicars found themselves much worse off, when they lost the support provided by the appropriator. At Totnes in Devon the vicar had relied upon the local priory for food and fuel to supplement his benefice; after the dissolution all that remained was an annual stipend of £8.[28] It must be acknowledged, however, that the dissolutions did not represent an entirely unmitigated disaster for urban clergy. Some former monks and chantry priests were able to secure a decent living by combining their royal pension with a poor benefice. Of course, this offered little comfort to parishes and incumbents who lacked the pastoral assistance previously provided by chaplains and chantrists, nor did it alleviate the insufficiency of many urban livings.

Having examined the economic plight of urban clergy during the early stages of the Reformation, and their close involvement in an ailing urban economy, it remains to be seen how urban laymen responded to the crisis confronting their clerical neighbours. Martha Skeeters's recent suggestion that, far from being alarmed at the decline in clerical incomes, lay leaders were either indifferent to their plight or even welcomed the opportunity to replace beneficed incumbents possessing a freehold with stipendiary clergy entirely dependent upon parishioners and corporations for employment, cannot be sustained.[29] Such a view fails to accord sufficient weight to the concerns voiced by townsmen about the improverishment of livings and their efforts to address the problems confronting provincial urban clergy. It also neglects the continuing significance of laymen in providing employment for (and exerting control over) large numbers of clergy as guild chaplains and chantry priests throughout the late medieval period. It is true that the efforts of civic leaders to reform clerical finances and thereby ensure an adequate level of pastoral services in parishes, in the absence of urban guilds and fraternities, may ultimately have strengthened their control over ecclesiastical affairs. However, this change represented less a net increase in lay control than a shifting of responsibility for provision of services from one local elite group to another (often dominated by the same leading citizens).

Laymen pursued several strategies in an attempt to alleviate the growing financial crisis facing urban clergy. Sometimes assistance took the form of direct financial support, as at St Ewan's in Bristol, where the rector's income was supplemented from parish coffers; in many other instances the clergy clearly could not have survived without additional private support from parishioners.[30] In a revealing admission, the parishioners of St Gregory's in Northampton acknowledged that it would fall to them to make good any significant shortfall in income; loss of a lucrative pilgrimage had made it impossible to secure a suitable incumbent 'without the further charges of the saide parishioners to be contributories to the salarie and here [hire] of the saide priste'.[31] Elsewhere parishes took complete financial control of the benefice, which they proceeded to farm from the incumbent. St Aldate's in Gloucester went even further, simply paying a stipendiary priest to officiate at services, without any incumbent. In 1556 the civic authorities of Totnes in Devon promoted a plan to recover the town's impropriate rectory from the Crown. Having lost the services of at least three chantry priests after 1547, the town fathers proposed to remedy the shortage of manpower by assigning the rectorial income to the incumbent while using that currently allotted to the vicar (£8 per annum) to hire an assistant priest.[32] Similar difficulties existed at Boston in Lincolnshire, where the corporation secured a grant of the properties of three town guilds, in part to pay the stipends of two priests to serve in the sole parish church. They also purchased an impropriated Lincolnshire rectory to help support the town's remaining clergy.[33]

Some town corporations sought to remedy the fundamental economic weakness of small unviable parishes by uniting poorer benefices in order to provide a sufficient income for the remaining incumbents. Such schemes for reorganisation and rationalisation were not easily implemented, however, for they required the consent of bishops and patrons, as well as the co-operation of parishioners. As a first step, civic authorities secured powers under an act of Parliament to unite churches. A statute of 1545 allowing the union of adjoining parishes where one benefice was worth no more than £6 per annum did not refer specifically to urban cases.[34] Accordingly, in 1547 the corporation of York led the way in obtaining statutory powers to unite parishes, and to devote the materials of the redundant church buildings to various public works including the repair of bridges and the restoration of remaining churches. The preamble, which eloquently expounded the plight of urban parishes and clergy (and the consequences of these economic problems for the progress of Protestantism), deserves to be cited in full:

> Where in the auncyent Citie of Yorcke and Suburbes of the same there is many parishe Churches which heretofore, the same being well inhabited and replenished with people, was good and honnest Livings for learned Incumbents, by reasone of the Privye Tythes of the rich marchaunts and of the Offeryngs of a greate multitude which lyvings, is now so muche decayed by the ruyne and decaye of the saide Citie and of the trade of marchaundise there that the Revenues and proffits of divers of the same benefices ar at this present not above the clere yerelie vallewe of xxvjs viij d. So that a greate sorte of them ar not competent and honnest Livinge for a good Curate, yea and no persone will take the cure but that of necessitie there is some Chauntrie preist or ells some late religious parsone being a stipendarye taken and appointed to the saide cure and benefice, which for the moste parte ar unlearned and verie ignoraunte parsons, not hable to doo anny parte of their dewties; By reasone whereof the saide Citie is not onelie replenished with blynde guydes and pastors but allso the people moche kepte in ignoraunce as well of their dewties towarde God as allso towardes the Kings Majestie and the common wealthe of this Realme, and to the greate daunger of their soules.... [35]

The following year the authorities in Lincoln and Stamford each secured similar powers by means of statutes copied almost verbatim from that of York.[36] Devising and implementing such schemes proved a long and difficult process, however. At York the first proposals were presented to Archbishop Holgate in 1549, but he was slow to respond. Despite this delay fifteen churches had been closed by 1551, but the final agreement was not signed until 1586, when the suppressions were at last confirmed by all the parties involved. Plans progressed more smoothly at Lincoln. As early as the 1520s the civic authorities there were demolishing disused churches, and with the new powers granted by the statute of 1548 a sweeping reorganisation was undertaken. Whereas John Leland claimed to have been shown an old roll listing 38 parish churches in the town, by 1550 only nine remained. Stamford also witnessed a drastic reduction following its 1548 statute: from eleven to six parishes.[37] Such schemes did not meet with universal approval, of course. Two civic attempts at Exeter were both blocked by the bishop during the later sixteenth century, while episcopal interventions delayed the consummation of plans in Lincoln and York. Parishioners directly affected often resented any attempt to close their church and incorporate them into neighbouring parishes. At Winchester the bishop reported in 1562 that he had agreed with the corporation a plan for reorganising the town's parishes but that 'the comon sort be against it' (an attitude which he ascribed to their conservative religious views, and an unwillingness to support preachers). Similar sentiments surfaced at York, where parishioners in one instance successfully petitioned for the reconstitution of their dissolved parish.[38]

As well as reorganising parishes in an effort to create viable economic units capable of attracting clergy of a suitable educational and moral standard, corporations also turned their attention to the appointment and financial support of preachers. The rise of town or corporation lecturers from the 1560s onwards is a subject deserving separate study. In the context of this discussion, however, one point must be stressed. While an important vehicle for the active promotion of Protestantism, these lectureships may equally be seen as an attempt to improve the remuneration of local ministers capable of preaching, and thereby address the damaging economic consequences of the Reformation. For example, at Lincoln a local incumbent received a £5 annual stipend as town preacher, which was intended to supplement the income of his urban benefice. Only later was a full-time corporation preacher appointed. Elsewhere (most notably at Ipswich) a generous financial incentive was offered in order to attract educated clergy of the highest quality. While encouraged by the zealous example of their godly continental cousins, such efforts by urban authorities to establish civic lectureships were also a response to the crisis in clerical finances brought about by economic decline and religious reform. They aimed to augment incomes. From the perspective of urban corporations, the creation of stipendiary lectureships possessed several advantages as a solution to economic problems. Unlike the reorganisation of parishes it did not require agreement from a host of interested parties, and it strengthened civic control over the activities of preachers within towns.[39]

In 1546 the citizens of Coventry had lamented that the impoverishment of the town and its parishes meant that they could find no one 'to be owre pastor to feede us gostly with gods word'. By the following year the number of clergy serving in the parish had dwindled from at least fourteen in 1522 to only two; furthermore, the incumbent whom they eventually secured for the vacant vicarage was obliged in 1550 to lease the benefice in order to be able to employ an assistant. When this lease expired, the civic authorities in Coventry sought parliamentary approval for a new tithe rate to be levied upon rents, in a further effort to place clerical finances upon a more secure footing. Despite these trials, by the beginning of Elizabeth's reign it must have seemed that Coventry's prayers for a suitable pastor had been answered, when Thomas Lever, recently returned from exile on the continent, accepted an invitation to become a resident preacher in the town. In a letter to his friend Bullinger at Zürich, Lever related how he came to Coventry:

> After I had discovered, by the experience of some weeks, that vast numbers in this place were in the habit of frequenting the public preaching of the gospel, I consented to their request, that I should settle my wife and family among them; and thus, now for nearly a whole year, I have preached to them without any hindrance, and they have liberally maintained me and my family in this city. For we are not bound to each other, neither I to the townsmen, nor they to me, by any law or engagement, but only by free kindness and love.[40]

The 'liberal maintenance' furnished for Lever by the citizens of Coventry represents further evidence of efforts of urban parishes to counteract the damaging effects of depopulation and religious reforms upon the economic welfare of parish clergy within their communities. Amalgamation of impoverished parishes, appointment of civic lecturers, and active parish management of benefices were all strategies designed to preserve pastoral services in provincial towns. The late medieval economic crisis and the Reformation which followed hard on its heels strained and loosened, but did not sever, the close ties which bound urban clergy to their colleagues and their lay neighbours.

9. The Dissolution of the Chantries

PETER CUNICH

The dissolution of the chantries in 1548 has long been recognised as a momentous event in the development of English parish life but, compared with its more famous antecedent, the dissolution of the monasteries in the late 1530s, it has received a disproportionately less thorough treatment by historians of the Tudor Reformation. In one respect this is not surprising. The monasteries were much larger institutions whose extensive ruins have left enduring monuments to the iconoclasm of the Henrician regime. All but the wealthiest of the chantries, however, were on a much smaller scale, and the majority of them had incomes which were only a small fraction of the resources of a medium-sized monastery. Yet it is generally agreed that, at least in the towns of England, the group of intercessory institutions which are known collectively as 'chantries', probably played a more important role in the lives of the common people than the monasteries ever had. In any town of reasonable size there was likely to have been at least one chantry or some other intercessory institution such as fraternity or guild with which the local people would have been familiar. The larger market towns and the cathedral towns boasted dozens of these institutions and in London they were to be found in their hundreds. It was not just the towns that could boast of these types of institutions. In the smallest rural villages obits were celebrated and lights burned before the reserved sacrament of the altar, and even in the most out-of-the-way places, free chapels provided mass centres for local populations. But nowhere in England were the chantries more visible or the religious and social services which they provided more valued than in the towns. They were a significant urban resource to both church and state and their abolition in 1548 was attended by major structural changes in urban communities throughout the kingdom.

It was their value as a resource which attracted the interest of Edward VI's fledgling administration towards the end of the first year of his reign. In financial terms the chantries, like the monasteries before them, were thought to be a major source of revenue for the church. This was a resource which the government felt could be better used for the defence of the realm during the protracted difficulties with France and Scotland. The Act dissolving the chantries seems to have been treated as a subsidy bill as it made its way through Parliament, and the first commission for the sale of chantry lands makes it quite clear that the Act was passed for 'the relief of the King's Majesty's charges and expenses which do daily grow and increase by reason of divers and sundry fortifications, garrisons, levying of men and soldiers which at this present is so chargeable and costly unto his Majesty...' and so that the commons '...might thereby be relieved of the continual charge of taxes, contributions, loans and subsidies... which by reason of the wars they were constrained... to abide'.[1] On the other hand, and perhaps more significantly, the chantries represented one of the most potent spiritual resources of the traditional English Church. The Catholic doctrines concerning purgatory and the remission of sin through the sacrament of the mass, persistent prayer, and the intercession of the saints gave the Church enormous power over the laity as they struggled from their mortal coil towards eternal life. The chantries were at the intersection of this world and the next. They provided a means by which the living and the dead could be united as one community under the vault of heaven. They empowered the living, through prayer and the intercession of the saints, to assist the dead in gaining a quicker passage through purgatory and into heaven. Such beliefs were, of course, completely at odds with Protestant teachings and it is not surprising that intercessory institutions should have been singled out by Edward's reformers as the first of the old beliefs to be cast aside. The dissolution of the chantries, therefore, enabled the Crown to confiscate a valuable financial resource of the Church for its own use, and further weakened the traditional structures of the Church by removing one of its most important spiritual supports.

Very little is known about the passage of the Chantries Act through Edward's first parliament of 1547, but two things are clear – its progress was stormy and it was substantially amended before receiving the king's assent. A chantries bill was first introduced into the Lords by the Privy Council on 6 December, but two private bills relating to the chantries had already been heard in the Commons on 30 November and 1 December.[2] The Lords bill encountered fierce opposition from some of the bishops before being dropped altogether after it was introduced into the Commons, probably because it included a proposal to confiscate the endowments of the trade and craft guilds as well as those of the intercessory foundations. A new bill was introduced into the Commons on 21 December, only days before the prorogation of Parliament. Once again, this bill produced intense opposition, especially from the burgesses of King's Lynn and Coventry who felt that the legislation would cause 'the utter desolation' of their towns. Deals were struck, however, and several saving clauses were annexed to the bill before it could be pushed through both houses in time to receive the king's assent on Christmas Eve. The passage of the Chantries Act gives every indication that it was unpopular with both the spirituality and the commonalty of the realm.[3] Yet, when the dissolution process began on Easter Day in 1548, there seems to have been little commotion and virtually no opposition. The change over of ownership was handled by the commissioners and Augmentations officials with their usual efficiency, chantry goods were sold, former incumbents were granted pensions or were reappointed as crown employees, and the unseemly scramble for ex- chantry lands began in much the same way that it had when the monasteries were dissolved ten years earlier. By the summer of 1548 it was already clear, of course, that these measures were only the beginning of religious change. Worse was still to come.

While the dissolution of the chantries should be considered as a distinct stage in the ongoing English Reformation, its impact upon the lives and the religious beliefs of townspeople can only be properly understood in the context of the longer-term changes which took place in the reigns of both Henry VIII and Edward VI. In the late 1530s, it was the suppression of the monasteries, which were themselves little more than very large chantry foundations, and the attack on relics, shrines, pilgrimages and holy days which marked the first stage of this revolution in religious belief. Henry VIII later authorised the dissolution of selected college foundations, all of which were first and foremost chantry institutions. This was a prelude for the wholesale dissolution of all intercessory institutions in 1548 and ushered in the many other changes to the traditional religious institutions and beliefs of England as Edward's reign progressed. While the ultimate aim of this programme was to turn England into a Protestant nation, these particular changes in 1548 were directed at overturning three of the central beliefs of the traditional Church – the existence of purgatory and the need to do penance for one's sins, the sacrificial efficacy of the Mass in securing remission for the sins of souls in purgatory, and the role of saints as intercessors between humans and God.[4] These beliefs lay at the centre of a complex system of relationships between the church militant and the church triumphant and produced a Christian community encompassing both the living and dead which Eamon Duffy considers to be the most distinctive feature of parish life in England before the Reformation.[5] The lives of individuals in urban communities and the nature of community life itself were therefore heavily influenced by both the inward and outward manifestations of doctrinal belief at all levels of society. The dissolution of the chantries, like the numerous other changes which took place during the English Reformation, had a major impact upon the corresponding inward and outward manifestations of communal identity in the towns. This impact was felt at many levels, but before it can be properly assessed it will first be necessary to examine in a little more detail exactly what the chantries were and to discuss why they played such an important role in the religious and social life of the English towns.

The Act dissolving the chantries specified a number of intercessory institutions as falling within its purview. 'All manner of colleges, free chapels and chantries' together with 'fraternities, brotherhoods and guilds' were the main targets of the legislation, but the Act also confiscated all endowments which had been given for the finding of perpetual or stipendiary priests, or toward the maintenance of any 'anniversary or obit, or other like thing, intent or purpose, or of any light or lamp'. All of these foundations were to be confiscated by the Crown on Easter Sunday 1548. The chantries proper which gave their name to the legislation were therefore only one of the classes of intercessory institutions which were confiscated by the Crown. The chantries varied in size and importance, but they all performed the same basic role of providing a daily stream of masses and prayers for the soul of the deceased benefactor and his or her family. Depending on the size of the original endowment and the nature of the trust created to administer it, the chantry could be established either in perpetuity or for a term of years. A priest would be employed, either with tenure of his benefice or as a stipendiary, and frequently had a specially endowed chapel or altar in the parish church in which to perform his duties.[6] Some chantry chapels such as those of bishops Wykeham (1404), Wayneflete (1486), Langton (1500) and Fox (1528) in Winchester Cathedral were architectural and artistic masterpieces which still impress today, and wealthy merchants such as the Springs of Lavenham were determined to endow chantries which reflected their status in the local community.[7] The majority of England's chantries were on a much smaller scale, did not have specially constructed chapels, and probably shared busy altars where obits, dirges and trentals were also being celebrated on a daily basis. The priests who served in the chantries were normally expected to assist the vicar in his ministrations, and a chantry priest might also conduct the local grammar school as part of his duties. Sometimes the cantarists serving in a large number of chantries within one church were organised into a college of priests who were given the cure of souls in that parish. This was the case at Hemingbrough, Howden and Lowthorpe in Yorkshire, but more often the collegiate churches were much earlier foundations such as the minsters at Beverley and Southwell. These colleges were on a similar scale to the larger monasteries and played an important role in the economies of the towns in which they were situated. Beverley Minster had fifty-six in its community while Southwell, with its sixty-three priests and clerks and an income exceeding £1,000 per annum, was a boon to local commerce and considered to be the 'head mother church of the town and county of Nottingham'. Other colleges had been founded for special purposes, such as the Jesus College at Rotherham, which provided chantry priests to teach in its three schools of writing, grammar and singing.[8] So the chantry institutions, far from being purely religious foundations, often performed important social and economic functions in the towns.

Chantries and colleges were usually the best endowed of the urban intercessory institutions, but perhaps the most visible and certainly the most active were the guilds, lay fraternities or brotherhoods which existed in nearly every parish. It has been estimated that there were as many as 30,000 lay confraternities in England in the later Middle Ages, or an average of approximately three in each parish.[9] These associations of lay people were mainly concerned with providing proper funerals and regular prayers for their deceased brethren. Most owned some urban property such as a guildhall or 'brotherhood house' and many employed priests to sing the masses for the dead. The Holy Trinity guild in Coventry was one of the best endowed in the country, with hundreds of members, a splendid guildhall, a whole church of its own, and thirteen full-time priests in its employ.[10] The Holy Trinity guild at King's Lynn was not nearly so well endowed, but still it supported thirteen chantry chaplains and was involved in a range of public works in the town beyond its purely religious functions.[11] These large urban corporations were among the largest landowners in Coventry and King's Lynn and wielded considerable patronage in their own districts. At the other end of the scale, the Jesus brotherhood of Holy Cross parish in Canterbury was a much smaller association which, with an income of little more than £11 per annum, needed the 'help and devotion of the parishioners there' to support its priest, bell-ringer, two annual obits and enough wax to maintain the 'cross light' in the parish church.[12] Another small fraternity in Langport, Somerset, assisted in the repair and maintenance of the great stone bridge of thirty arches, and in Wisbech the local fraternities looked after the river banks and sluices.[13] Numerous guilds, such as those in Wisbech and Stratford-upon-Avon, supported schoolmasters, others kept substantial almshouses, and some provided an even wider range of social, civic and medical services. The Birmingham guild, for example, kept an alms-house, two 'great stone bridges', repaired several highways, supplied wine, wax, oil and other necessities for the church, paid salaries to three chaplains, an organ player and a clock-keeper, and even employed a 'common midwife' for the benefit of the local community.[14] Such examples could be multiplied at great length, but what is already quite clear is that the fraternities based in the towns of England were much more than just religious institutions. They were an integral part of the fabric of urban life in pre-Reformation England and, together with the chantries, the colleges, and the thousands of endowments for obits, lamps and lights, must have given urban dwellers a feeling of pride and security. They were vitally important in establishing local identity and civic values, especially in towns which had not yet been incorporated as boroughs.

While these various intercessory institutions have long been recog-nised as having impinged directly upon the lives of individual towns-people in the later Middle Ages, there has been some debate in the past as to whether they were playing as important a role on the eve of the Reformation as they had done in the late fifteenth century. While it is clear from parish records that the chantries and fraternities were still being endowed right up to their dissolution and that testators were still leaving money for obits and trentals, it must also be noted that bequests and donations appear to have been slowing down after the mid-1530s.[15] Whether this represents a decline in belief or was simply an indication that canny townspeople, suspicious that further religious changes would follow the dissolution of the monasteries and the dismantling of the shrines, decided to hold on to their cash, is a moot point which still needs to be investigated more thoroughly. Some writers have also raised questions as to the efficacy of the educational system or the poor relief provided by these institutions, and it is probably true to say that their disappearance was not nearly so harmful to the educational opportunities of urban dwellers as has been suggested in the past. But one thing which is not in doubt is the very substantial influence which these foundations were able to exert by virtue of the sheer number of institutions involved.[16] The number of intercessory institutions in England at the time of the dissolution has long been seriously underestimated. The traditional figure of 2,374 chantries at the dissolution is well short of the true total because it only takes account of perpetual chantries and not the others which were endowed only for a term of years. Likewise, Professor Scarisbrick and Dr Rosser have demonstrated that there were thousands more fraternities and guilds than those which appear in the records of the Court of Augmentations.[17] We must therefore acknowledge that the influence of these institutions on the lives of individual townspeople on the eve of the Reformation was probably far greater than we have previously allowed.

The majority of the intercessory institutions, and certainly the most generously endowed of them, were located within urban parishes. These town parishes also boasted thousands of smaller and more transient foundations which had been endowed through bequests by deceased parishioners. The churchwardens and the governors of the intercessory institutions administered trust funds established through such bequests which provided for obits, trentals, lights, lamps and the various other expressions of lay piety to which testators turned in preparing for death. They nearly always appear in conjunction with the larger foundations and together these extraordinarily varied manifestations of grassroots piety represent the hopes and beliefs of a wide range of men and women, both living and dead, within the urban community. They were, in fact, at the centre of the urban parish's sense of identity, but they also provided links to the more nebulous concept of a universal Church.

The greatest concentration of this vast array of urban foundations was in London, the commercial and political centre of the kingdom. There were approximately 370 priests serving chantries within the London churches, with 48 in St Paul's Cathedral alone. A further 368 individual obits were kept by the parishes and the city companies, over forty fraternities existed alongside the wealthier livery companies, and hundreds of smaller endowments for lamps and lights were to be found scattered across the city.[18] York was another city in which there was a particularly high concentration of chantries, as were other cities such as Exeter, Wells, Lincoln, Salisbury and Hereford whose cathedrals had not been disendowed during the suppression of the monasteries. County towns such as Huntingdon, Colchester and Shrewsbury all boasted large numbers of chantries and fraternities in each of their numerous parishes, as did the larger market towns. Towns which had collegiate churches such as Beverley and Southwell were particularly well-supplied with priests. Even much smaller towns were often substantially endowed with intercessory institutions. Week St Mary in Cornwall, a village with a population of not much more than 200, had received a school building together with a master and manciple through the generosity of Lady Thomasine Percival in 1508, while the nearby market town of Bodmin was without any educational facilities.[19] The chantries in pre-Reformation England must therefore be counted as an extraordinarily important urban resource for both the traditional church and the lay communities of the towns.

What, then, was the effect of the dissolution of the chantries on the English towns? This is a question which has produced many and varied answers in the past, but most historians of the period would agree that the dissolution should be considered in terms of both its religious impact and also the wider social effects which it had on urban communities. A. G. Dickens believes that it 'impinged far more obviously and directly upon the spiritual and social life of the English people' than did the suppression of the monasteries, and Eamon Duffy considers it to have been nothing short of a disaster for lay religious life.[20] There can be no doubt that the destruction of the whole structure of intercessory prayer uniting the living and the dead in urban parishes did much to create a spiritual void which the Protestant reformers were able to begin filling with their own Calvinist beliefs concerning justification, predestination and salvation. Duffy would argue that most people in the parishes of England held on to their traditional beliefs at least until the accession of Elizabeth, but even if this is so, the lack of formal structures of intercessory prayer between 1548 and 1553 must have done much to weaken and dilute those traditional beliefs which had held parish communities together right up to the eve of the dissolution and made the revival of Catholic devotion during the reign of Mary Tudor less effective than it might otherwise have been. The weakening of a sense of religious community inevitably had an impact on social and civic values, and Dickens is quite right in concluding that, in the long term, the suppression of intercessory institutions in the reign of Edward VI did much to lower the cohesion and morale of the whole nation.[21] These psychological effects were felt most acutely in the towns because it was there that the chantries had played such a vital role in both the religious and social lives of urban dwellers.

While it is true that parishes whose churches did not have full-scale chantries probably had just as deep a feeling of community as parishes which did have endowed chantries, it is also true that chantries tended to provide a natural and especially potent focus for the validation of ideas about purgatory and salvation through intercessory prayer. What was achieved through the reading of the parish bede-roll and the masses for the dead at All Hallowtide and the feast of All Souls in other parishes was similarly accomplished through the daily masses and prayers in the chantry foundations of urban parish churches. Even in parishes which did not have chantries, however, there were the endowed obits, diriges and trentals which would have performed the same role but on a smaller scale. The dissolution of the chantries brought all of these foci of intercessory prayer to an end in 1548 and even the bede-rolls were abolished in the next year. The effect on the urban laity must have been both immediate and shattering. In each of the parishes of St Peter Cornhill and St Dunstan in the East in London, nine perpetual chantries were dissolved, while many other parishes lost three, four or five such foundations. In Coventry, twelve chantries were suppressed and another fourteen guild priests lost their chantry jobs.[22] These are extreme cases, but even in the majority of parish churches with no more than two or three chantries, the sudden abolition of intercessory prayer and purgatory, the consequent downgrading of the patron saints of the chantries, and the effective casting out forever of deceased loved ones from the living parish community into a 'collective anonymity' must have had a disturbing impact upon both individual parishioners and the whole fabric of parish life.[23]

The case of the lay fraternities also gives us some indication of the enormous impact of the dissolution in local areas and especially in the towns which had higher concentrations of guilds. As well as providing the particular religious and social services which have been outlined already, these associations played a vital role as the social 'cement' which helped to bind together in a complex amalgam of intersecting relationships many different and divergent groups within the towns. Gervase Rosser has argued that the annual festal mass and fraternity feast were in many ways at the centre of this bonding role which these associations had in the pre-Reformation English towns.[24] The mass was a collective affirmation of shared identity in a sacramental setting and, like the control exercised over chantries by lay people, it was a potent symbol which reflected the empowering of lay people in an otherwise clerically-controlled church. At a deeper spiritual and emotional level, the mass and its prayers for the souls of deceased members reinforced the idea of the guild as an association of both the living and the dead. The symbolic power of the festal mass was amplified in the commens-ality of the fraternity feast which followed, and both of these ritualised occasions gave the lay person an enhanced feeling of spiritual worth. The fraternity feast also had a more practical political purpose, and Rosser argues convincingly that 'in economic and broadly political terms, going to feasts contributed significantly to the peaceful evolution of the internally diverse communities of late medieval England'.[25] Individual guild members were able to negotiate new and valuable political and personal relationships while at the same time strengthen-ing older bonds of friendship which very often bridged traditional economic and social boundaries. In this way the lay fraternities con-tributed significantly to the solidarity of urban communities. While it must be admitted that such associations also had the potential to cause as much division as unity within a large town, there can be no denying the fact that a guild with a local hero-saint such as St Wilfrid of Ripon or St Helen of Beverley as its patron was a powerful catalyst for corporate unity within the urban community.[26]

When the fraternities were disbanded in 1548, England lost thou-sands of institutions which were of more than just religious importance, for the guilds had for centuries been active in promoting a high degree of civic pride and unity within towns. The impact of the change on local communities is difficult to assess and no doubt depended very much on the prevailing conditions in individual towns, but overall the effect must have been extremely disheartening for most people and rather worrying for civic leaders. The several hundred members of the Holy Trinity and Corpus Christi guilds in Coventry lost yet another symbol of their city's former prosperity, deepening their depression over the future. The burgesses of York and Boston, who had also fallen on hard times in the early sixteenth century, were now denied the dozens of fraternities which had in the past enabled them, on at least one day of every year, to drown their collective sorrows and gain reassurance from each other that better days were not far off. It is impossible to assess the impact on Northampton's civic pride of the closure of its fourteen guilds and fraternities, but we are surely not too far short of the truth in saying that such an event in a relatively small county town must have seriously undermined the self-confidence of the local community.[27] Across the country, in towns both large and small, fraternity houses, guildhalls, alms houses and chapels, all of which were a source of enormous pride for urban dwellers, were suddenly divested of their treasures and closed to the public. There would be no more fraternity feasts, no more urban bonding encouraged by the guilds. In some towns the dissolution of guilds and fraternities may even have exacerbated age-old problems of keeping the peace. The disappearance of the Saint Thomas Becket fraternity in Oxford removed one of the few opportunities enjoyed by 'town' and 'gown' of coming together peacefully in a symbolic expression of common civic goals.[28] In other towns it was feared that vital public services supervised by the fraternities on behalf of the commonalty would no longer be performed. In King's Lynn, the Trinity Guild had long assisted in 'every public enterprise' which the borough assembly had initiated.[29] Who would now maintain the bridges, sluices and seabanks which were so necessary for the town's continued prosperity? Likewise, who would repair the bridge at Abingdon after the Holy Cross guild was disbanded? Who would maintain the chiming clock and the community midwife in Birmingham? Would Ashburton's water supply be maintained after the dissolution of St Lawrence's guild? In every town of any size across the kingdom, these were the sorts of questions which must have exercised local authorities in the months following Easter 1548.[30]

While these changes did much to undermine the foundations of community life in the English towns, it was probably the physical changes which the dissolution of the chantries brought about which were the most noticeable for the person in the street. How can we assess the psychological impact of the disappearance of an entire genre of church decoration and the worship which it encouraged? The removal of chantries and their furnishings was the first great change to the interiors of cathedrals and parish churches since the dismantling of the shrines in 1538 and it heralded the more general clampdown on Catholic practices later in the reign. Eamon Duffy has described in great detail the effect which the stripping of the altars had on local communities. We should remember, however, that in many of the urban parish churches, the chantries were the first of the trappings of traditional religion to go and therefore the impact was perhaps even greater than the later wholesale desolation.[31] The structural damage done to the hundreds of perpendicular chantry chapels which had been the glory of cathedrals and large urban churches since the early 1400s was probably not great at first, but the removal of the plate and fittings from these chantries robbed local communities of cherished corporate possessions of which they were justifiably proud. At Ilminster in Somerset, to give just one example, the parish's chantry contained three chalices, a large silver gilt cross, candlesticks of parcel gilt, crystal cruets, an incense boat, and an assortment of twenty vestments, most of which were made of velvet, and even included a cope of cloth of gold. There were also satin altar frontals, various altar cloths, corporals and curtains of white sarsenet.[32] All these visual stimulants were replaced by bare stone. Even the sacring bells and the larger bells which called the faithful to services were confiscated, leaving the towns of England considerably quieter than they had been in the past. In Somerset alone, the commissioners sold more than three thousand pounds of lead and bell metal from the chantries for a profit of £128 10s. 0d.[33] The confiscation of endowments used to maintain candles and lamps within the chantry chapels completed the demystification of the whole institution of intercessory prayer. One might well say that the lights went out all over England after Easter 1548, and that the parish churches were far duller places because of it. The sense of loss experienced by the common people must have been acute, especially for the families of those who had donated personal items to decorate their favourite chantries. What was the reaction of the heirs of the woman who gave her wedding ring to provide shoes for the statue of St Sidwell at Morebath? What of the other donors who had presented gifts as humble as their own clothing or as lavish as precious gems and silver plate to chantry chapels across the country?[34] It is not surprising that many of these items were purchased by parishioners from the chantry commissioners and preserved for posterity in the hope that one day they would be returned to their altars.[35] One of the outcomes of this stripping of the chantry altars was that iconoclasm, spoliation of church property for profit, and the destruction of things of intrinsic beauty became a common occurrence in England. This may help to account for the apparent ease with which the later changes in religion were enforced by Edward's reformers.

One of the major resources which the chantries had provided for the towns was a large supply of non-beneficed clergy to assist with the running of urban parishes. These supernumerary priests did not usually have cure of souls, but in some towns, such as Crediton, Beverley, Southwell and Newark, the colleges of chantry priests provided the only clergy in the local parishes. The number of chantry priests serving in English parish churches at the time of the dissolution has never been established with any accuracy. The records of the Court of Augmentations reveal that nearly 2,800 chantry priests were awarded pensions while around 250 were appointed to continue as vicars, curates and schoolmasters.[36] This number includes only the perpetual chantry priests, however, and takes no account of the many other priests who worked as itinerant mass-sayers or who were on short-term contracts to sing masses for a certain number of years. These priests do not appear in the records and we have no way of knowing how many of them there were. Even without taking them into consideration, however, the 3,000 or so chantry priests who did receive pensions or new jobs as crown appointees constitute a very large group. They slightly outnumbered the monastic pensioners still living in 1548, although the total value of the chantry pensions (at £13,265 per annum) was little more than half that of the surviving ex-religious.[37] The individual pensions were calculated on a sliding scale based on their original chantry salary and this gave most ex-cantarists annual incomes of between £4 and £6 for life. The heads of the collegiate foundations fared much better than the rank and file, of course, and someone such as John Lybbe, master of Penryn College, was granted a pension of £18 7s. 1d. per annum, while Robert Silvester, master of Rotherham College and suffragan bishop of Hull, received £14 4s. 8d. per annum, and John Chamber, dean of St Stephen's College at Westminster, had compensation of £52 10s. 0d. per annum. At the other end of the scale, much less generous provision was made for men like Robert Bentley of Greenwood's Chantry in Halifax (18s. per annum) and Roger Wheler, a prebendary of St Burian's College (£2 per annum).[38] It should also be remembered that the majority of part-time and stipendiary priests received nothing at all.

What happened to these men? Did they stay on in the towns and become part of the restless underclass of impoverished urban unemployed as rampant inflation began to eat into their meagre pensions? Or did they continue to perform their priestly duties in their old parishes for whatever fees they could command? How many of them were able to gain preferment to better livings and more secure lifestyles? We shall probably never know the answers to these questions for the records do not have a great deal to say about the later careers of these men. Many were already quite elderly (perhaps even retired from full-time parish duties), and it is likely that the remainder of them were already members of the clerical underclass who had neither degrees nor social distinction to help them find better jobs after the dissolution.[39] One thing, however, is certain. Parishes throughout the country suddenly found that they had to make do with a seriously diminished complement of clergy. Some villages lost their only priest as free chapels were closed, but in towns where a chantry or college priest had previously held the cure, the chantry commissioners nearly always appointed a new vicar or curate who was invariably the former incumbent. A large number of schools also lost their endowments and schoolmasters, but here again the commissioners were diligent in reappointing men to continue instructing the young. Nevertheless, even though the urban education system probably continued to function in a relatively satisfactory manner until the eventual re-endowment of many educational foundations later in Edward's reign, there must have been much uncertainty about the future and, in the short term at least, no money to carry out repairs or maintenance to school buildings and furnishings.[40] Likewise, the provision of alms to paupers certainly suffered even though payments continued to be made throughout Edward's reign. These payments only represented the perpetual endowments for that purpose, however, and must have been only a fraction of the total doles which had previously been made by chantries and fraternities, and in connection with obits. The urban communities of England therefore suffered to a greater or lesser extent through the termination or scaling down of social services which had previously been provided by the intercessory institutions.

Perhaps the most obvious resource of the chantries and fraternities, and certainly the one which interested the Crown the most, was their wealth which had accumulated through centuries of bequests and donations. The size of the ex-chantry estate has often been exaggerated in the past through a misunderstanding of the true value of the various possessions of the intercessory institutions. Jordan's figure of £636,535 for the capital value of all these possessions gives an annual income of nearly £32,000, but an examination of the Augmentations accounts reveals that the lands of the chantries were probably worth no more than £17,000 per annum and that by the end of 1553 these lands had been reduced in value to £9,640 per annum through alienations to land-hungry buyers.[41] Compared with the monastic estate confiscated by Henry VIII (worth approximately £120,000 per annum) this is a rather insignificant figure. Even in 1547, despite the massive sales of ex-monastic land, this source of income was still generating more than £61,000 per annum. What is even more surprising is the fact that little more than 40 per cent of the chantry lands had been sold by the time Mary came to the throne. These sales had produced less than £250,000 in capital during the whole of Edward's reign compared to profits well in excess of one million pounds from the ex-monastic estate. The chantry lands do not therefore represent the massive boost to the crown's finances which it has always been suggested was their chief contribution to the Edwardian government. Moreover, it seems that the chantries ultimately became a serious drain on the finances of the state as the expenses associated with them (and especially the pensions for the ex-chantry priests) began to exceed the income which they generated. By the end of 1553, the chantry lands' current account with the Augmentations was showing a deficit in excess of £12,000.

This is not to say that the confiscated chantry lands were not an important financial asset for the crown – they clearly were. It is also apparent that the town corporations considered them to be valuable resources which were well worth the effort and expense of acquiring when they were put up for sale. Numerous boroughs bought back from the crown the recently-confiscated endowments of their intercessory foundations. The aldermen and livery companies of London, for example, spent more than £18,700 in regaining control of the city's chantry endowments. The inhabitants of Coventry and King's Lynn eventually recovered the chantry lands which they had fought to protect in the parliament of 1547, and other towns such as York, Chichester, Colchester, Derby, Leominster and many others were also able to regain chantry endowments in their towns.[42] Other towns were able to acquire former chantry, fraternity and obit endowments upon resale by the initial purchasers and thus it was possible for town corporations to regain valuable possessions which were then put back into use for the support of local services.

The dissolution of the chantries in 1548 therefore had a significant impact upon the towns of England. By confiscating the economic resources of the traditional church, the state was initially concerned with lining its own pockets, but more importantly it was able to ensure that the new religion would be preached in a parish environment stripped of its old certainties and therefore more open to change. The upheaval in the towns which these changes brought about must have produced an increasing sense of uncertainty and fear after the summer of 1548. Without their old supports, both spiritual and social, the urban communities of England must inevitably have been further weakened and less able to resist the more sweeping religious changes which began to be imposed from 1549. Professor Scarisbrick has suggested that the suppression of the fraternities and guilds and the consequent lessening of lay participation and control in the parishes eventually allowed for a strengthening of clerical control in England as the Reformation became more established.[43] The case of the chantries seems to support this conclusion, but it is virtually impossible to find evidence to support such assertions. The dissolution of the chantries was ultimately carried through with such efficiency and so little opposition that we are left with a lack of firm evidence as to what people thought about the changes, how they reacted to them, and the impact which the dissolution had on them personally. There are still, therefore, many unanswered questions about the dissolution of the chantries which may never be answered conclusively.

10. Voluntary Religion and Reformation Change in Eight Urban Parishes

BEAT KÜMIN

Terminological concerns are at the heart of most recent accounts of the English Reformation(s). Some would like to see the momentous events referred to by a plural rather than a singular, many more endeavour to dissociate terms such as 'decline' or 'discontent' from the late medieval Church and to discredit any attempts to explain the changes as a result of pressures 'from below'. The establishment of a new vocabulary, however, has proved rather more elusive. Prevented from labelling late medieval Catholicism as a 'popular' religion by a whole series of inappropriate connotations, some have now suggested that historians speak of the 'vigour, richness and creativity' of 'traditional' religious practices. The search, no doubt, will continue.[1]

This essay proposes to contribute to the review of another important notion. The rise of 'voluntary religion', 'the outstanding feature' of Elizabethan ecclesiastical life, has conventionally been related to the apparent 'breakdown' of the parish and the resulting 'triumph of the laity' in the post-Reformation period.[2] The Middle Ages, in contrast, have been characterized as an era of religious compulsion, tight clerical supervision and parochial uniformity, with nothing but Lollardy to cater for those longing 'to be free of hierarchical control and canon law'.[3] Such a simple dichotomy, however, is no longer tenable. Recent scholarship has pointed to chantries and fraternities as sub- and extra-parochial institutions offering ample scope for voluntary activities before the mid-sixteenth century, with kinship commitments (attendance at baptisms, churchings, weddings and other rites of passage), mystery plays, local shrines and – for a small minority – heretical movements increasing the options further.[4] The parish community, however, is still often seen as an essentially compulsory organisation which subjected its members to a strict regime of financial contributions and communal rituals. Medieval feasts, pageantry and specialised religious cults are not normally associated with churchwardens and parochial resources. A recent collection of essays on 'voluntary religion', to substantiate the point, included only studies of sects, fraternities and heretical movements among its pre-Reformation contributions.[5] But the picture is changing: a closer analysis of the relationship between parish churches and chapels, for instance, yields strong indications of how much variety and diversity parishes could offer in the late Middle Ages.[6] The following argument will attempt to anchor the concept more firmly and broadly in this period and to replace the crude Reformation divide with a more balanced assessment of the mid-Tudor changes. For this purpose, the present volume's focus on urban evidence seems especially appropriate. Towns, after all, offer the densest concentration of heterogeneous social groups and interests and thus a particularly strong potential for a broad range of religious expressions.

In what follows, 'voluntary religion' shall be defined as 'collective spiritual activities pursued in addition to or instead of those prescribed by the Church'.[7] It must be readily admitted that any attempt at classification in this field leads into a methodological minefield, for 'in the near chaos of actual religious and social experience, the relation of voluntary to involuntary religion has always been complex'.[8] While it is true, for example, that membership of the local parish was the result of birth or settlement rather than individual choice, it did not follow that *all* communal activities were necessarily 'compulsory'. Similarly, while membership in a religious sect might be freely undertaken, such groups almost always confronted their new recruits with serious and far from voluntary commitments. And how are we to interpret the fact that many parochial incumbents were involved in the presentation of clerics to 'voluntary' chantry and fraternity institutions?[9] Quite clearly, drawing distinctions in this field can only be relative and conclusions must be treated with a great deal of caution.

The first important observation to be made is the fact that a certain amount of compulsion characterised both the pre- and post-Reformation periods. From the thirteenth century, parishioners were required to attend and maintain their local church and to absorb a modest catechetical programme. Much of this canonical framework was preserved by the reformed Church, which continued to expect knowledge of fundamentals such as the Creed and the Ten Commandments and reinforced the emphasis on regular attendance by statutory authority.

There is little evidence to doubt that the large majority of early as well as late Tudor parishioners resorted to their parish church on Sunday and that separatism did not pose a serious challenge until well into the seventeenth century.[10]

But continuity can also be detected in the sphere of voluntary religion. Our definition excludes any attempt to assess or measure individual devotion, partly due to methodological difficulties, but also because of a common-sense acknowledgement that large numbers of English men and women engaged in additional religious activities on both sides of the Reformation divide. Leaving heretical affiliations to one side, medieval parishioners might opt to join the many voluntary institutions within or without their community, to endow anniversaries, to enter their name on the bede- or prayer-roll, to go on pilgrimage, to support monastic houses, or to secure indulgences for the health of their souls, all of which produced valuable extra income for the clergy. Apart from tithes and customary dues, rectors and vicars, for instance, received bequests, payments for extra services (particularly masses for the dead) or other contributions which 'were more voluntary in character, and could...reflect fluctuations in patterns of religious practice, and even personal relationships between the parishioners and their clergy'.[11] The vicar of Hornsea in East Yorkshire, whose reckonings are among the few surviving clerical accounts of the fifteenth century, regularly records donations (among many others 'ex dono Ricardi Wetherby 12*d*.' in 1484) and he could count on additional revenue from indulgence collectors paying fees for the right to raise funds in his parish ('de questore sancti Thome de Urba Rome 4*d*.', 'de questore beate Marie de Southwell 3*d*.' and similar other entries made up a total of 3*s*. 5*d*. in 1481).[12] As for the post-Reformation period, additional religious activities were pursued as a matter of course by puritan or sectarian groups and a quick reminder of the importance of 'gadding to sermons' may suffice in illustrating such practices here. The parish did not disintegrate in the face of such activities, indeed there was now little in an average church to distract from the importance of incumbent and pulpit, but – as in previous centuries – it held no monopoly.[13]

The attempt to establish voluntary religion as an integral part of the medieval parochial community, however, requires more detailed analysis. What kind of evidence can be adduced? The empirical basis of the argument consists of a database of all financial transactions in the churchwardens' accounts of eight urban parishes, from the earliest

Table 1 The sample (with year of earliest surviving evidence)

Andrew Hubbard (1454) and Botolph Aldersgate (1468), London
All Saints (1406) and St Ewen's (1454), Bristol
Ashburton, Devon (1479)
Halesowen, Worcestershire (1487)
Peterborough (1467)
Prescot, Lancashire (1523)

surviving years (normally in the fifteenth century) to the accession of Elizabeth I.[14] The quantitative analysis thus covers the last pre-Reformation decades and the impact of religious change under Henry VIII, Edward VI and Mary. Table 1 lists the case-studies, which include parishes from England's two largest cities as well as a number of smaller market towns.[15]

Given the idiosyncratic nature of source survival, no selection can claim to produce a mathematically exact random sample for the country as a whole. This (as any other possible) choice is biased towards the south of England, and the conclusions, of course, primarily reflect the circumstances of the particular case-studies. However, an attempt has been made to include a large variety of demographic and territorial size (between 56 and 1,100 communicants in 1547, and from a few houses in the case of St Ewen's to no less than 50 square miles at Prescot), as well as a fair mixture of ecclesiastical status, geographical location, economic prosperity and social milieu. Comparison with other, structurally similar communities suggests that the trends emerging from this sample are by no means unrepresentative.[16]

The long lists of individual items have been grouped into a series of categories to facilitate comparison. These include costs for church building and repair, for ornaments, additional clergymen, parish employees and the churchyard, to name but the most important purposes. But is there a way to determine which transactions can be classed as 'voluntary spending'? The information in the accounts is limited and rarely explicit enough to judge whether, for instance, a particular ornament was purchased freely by the parish or as a result of an order from their ecclesiastical superiors. Still, an attempt can be made to group expenditure into items with an established basis in canon law or secular legislation and those made without such encouragement. Hence, any vestment, book or roof repair would fall under the former category, since the upkeep of nave and churchyard, as well as the provision of bells and ornaments were undisputed duties under canon law. Furthermore, payment of subsidies and military expenses resulted from demands made by the crown. On the other hand, lights and candles, additional clergy, parish employees or local ceremonial life can be subsumed under the voluntary heading, because there was no legal or canonical requirement for the support of side-altars, images or stipendiary clergymen. Similarly, public works, alms-giving and the costs connected to the administration of pious bequests were not yet the result of statutory incentives: compulsion in the fields of highway maintenance and poor relief dates from the Marian and Elizabethan periods only.[17]

The line between voluntary and compulsory spending, however, could be a fine one. Given the force of custom in contemporary society, there was always a risk that spontaneous initiatives turned into more permanent (quasi-compulsory) engagements, and many a parish may have found it difficult to stop supporting causes after a certain amount of time. And yet, changing circumstances could be taken into account. The wardens of All Saints, for instance, were able to cut their payments for a well-established anniversary in 1519–20, because 'we be unpaid of the Tailors'. The dangers of setting precedents were certainly recognised, for officers carefully recorded the specific purpose of all their financial transactions: when those of Botolph Aldersgate received £6 13s. 4d. from the Trinity fraternity in 1489, they noted that this was a single payment 'for performing and making of a new crosse of sylver gylt with Mary and John in the sayd chyrche' and not a general subsidy. All Saints parishioners stressed in 1510–11 that a new rent agreement would remain valid 'as long as hit shall please the parishe to the churche avantage', and those of Andrew Hubbard were even more explicit when they recorded in January 1547 that the parish 'of char- yte . . . ys moved to gyve unto Robart Lynsey [the sexton] forte shyl- lynges by the yere . . . soo longe as they shall thynk he dothe hys dyllygennt . . . servys yn neydfoll thynges & busones yn the churche. Allways provyded [that the parish is] at ther lybarte to wythdrawe ytt.'[18] It is therefore not unreasonable to assume that any longer-term commitments were the result of a free parish decision and that the respective payments can safely be assigned to our 'voluntary' category.

Other problems remain. Whilst the sources yield a fairly full account of the ordinary day-to-day activities of an early Tudor parish, there are some awkward inconsistencies. The stipend of the parish clerk, for instance, a well-established duty under canon law, was sometimes raised and paid by the churchwardens, but sometimes by a rota of parish households or special collectors who have left no written traces. For practical purposes, there is no alternative to defining communal activities as those listed in the wardens' accounts. We may therefore underestimate the 'compulsory' quota of those parishes which farmed out certain administrative duties, but this is more than compensated for by the fact that *all* spending on ornaments has been subsumed under the same heading; surely, many books, images and vestments were purchased freely by the parishioners, even if there is no explicit proof. As for the 'grey' area of unrecorded activities, *ad hoc* communal initiatives were certainly more easily omitted from the accounts than canonical or official secular duties. Thus, it is the 'voluntary' category which is more likely to be underestimated in this analysis.

Given these reservations, would it be easier to switch the analysis from the expenditure to the income side? In other words, could we determine which resources accrued to the parish voluntarily and which did not? Unfortunately, this approach offers no real alternative. While, at first sight, payments at church ales, collections and gifts appear to be spontaneous enough, there were many subtle and less subtle pressures at work: Ashburton, for instance, issued an ordinance which specified fixed payments for its waxsilver fund,[19] and many a merry church ale resulted from the fact that the parishioners had no other way to meet their canonical responsibilities. On closer inspection, even 'bequests' can turn out to be debt repayments or compensation for 'tithes forgotten'. In spite of its inadequacies, an analysis based on established ecclesiastical or secular duties still yields the more reliable impressions.

What sort of voluntary religion can be found in pre-Reformation parish accounts? There is, for a start, plenty of evidence for the close relationship between one of the foremost expressions of late medieval piety, the maintenance of candles in front of saints' images, and parish institutions. Many Essex lights, for instance, contributed part of their income to the upkeep of the fabric of their churches, while wardens like those of Prescot supervised the purchase and making of candles themselves.[20] It is often difficult to tell where parish responsibility ended and particular groups took over, for the boundaries are blurred. Some testators like the Rutland farmer William Gybbyns in 1535 made bequests to lights explicitly to relieve the parish funds which supported them normally.[21] In the Halesowen accounts, for instance, there are regular collections for the lights of St Catherine, St Stephen and St Nicholas.

Wherever churchwardens helped an image of a local or helper saint (such as St Apollonia with her pair of pincers and particular appeal to those suffering from toothache) to become the subject of particular veneration,[22] it is clear that parish funds supported specialised voluntary cults. This did not mean that every parishioner was now expected to participate in it (it did not even mean that all members of the community agreed with the financial support, for parish decisions were not always unanimous[23]), but it shows the community's positive attitude towards choice and variety. While most churchwardens assisted a limited number of lights on a regular basis, there was scope for changing needs and fashions: the accounts of Botolph Aldersgate, for instance, include collections for Our Lady, St George, St Katherine and St Christopher in 1485–6, for St George, St Margaret and St Bartholomew in 1506–7, and there are many other combinations, each yielding somewhat different totals.

At All Saints, Bristol – to move to another area – parish funds repeatedly covered the deficits of the Halleway chantry. The churchwardens were the managers of the institution, and in order to boost its revenues, repeated initiatives were taken to preserve a business on the chantry's Lewensmead property. In 1530–1, churchwarden John Hewys received an award of 19s. from the parish 'for the grete paynes and labors that he hath taken abowte owr brewhouse in lewensmed'. It was repaired at the enormous cost of over £30 (largely paid for by the parish), and John Winter, 'berebruar', received a loan of £20 to encourage him to start a business.[24] In 1536–7, the chantry was said to be 'in dette to the paryshe' and one would be hard-pressed to find evidence here for the claim that the structural differences between voluntary chantries and compulsory parishes necessarily led to incompatibility or mutual resentment.

Much the same can be said about the relationship between parishes and guilds. The extra efforts made by fraternities and their priests were often appreciated by the local community: the Ashburton churchwardens, for instance, paid £3 to the fraternity priest John Vyne in 1519–20, and 'voluntary' stocks or stores in the church contributed nearly £3 10s. per annum to the parish in the pre-Reformation accounts. At Andrew Hubbard, as late as January 1547, it was agreed 'that the churchwardenns of the paryshe shall paye or delyver unto the wardenns of the brotherhod of the trynnyt[y] iiis iiiid every quarter of the yere', while the Peterborough parishioners apparently made appointments on the fraternities' behalf: a memorandum of 1544 records that Robert Merchant had been chosen 'by ther hole assent...to syng within the seyd Churche for the brethren and systers of all the Gyldes'.[25] The inhabitants of Botolph Aldersgate enjoyed an equally close relationship with their Holy Trinity and SS Fabian and Sebastian fraternity: testators entrusted property to both church- and guildwardens for joint administration, and the personnel of the two institutions was recruited from the same pool of parishioners: 37 of the Botolph wardens who served the parish before 1560 joined the guild at some stage in their lives, and no less than 17, for instance the goldsmith John Frende (as fraternity warden 1482–4), or the brewer Thomas Smith (master 1432 and 1436), took office there too.[26] It thus comes as no surprise that the parishioners decided to support the Trinity chaplain for some time after the dissolution and that they invested considerable resources to take over the guildhall situated across the street from the church: William Harvey acquired it from Edward VI by a grant of alienation dated 4 July 1548, and the churchwardens' accounts of that year record £7 13s. 4d. paid to him 'for the waynscott & other Implemente belongyng to trynytye hall' and 13s. 4d. in quit rent.[27] Many London or Bristol parishes also introduced 'general minds' or collective anniversaries, which adopted features of fraternity feasts. All parishioners assembled to commemorate their benefactors and their dead, monetary rewards encouraged priests and clerks to attend the ceremony, and food and drink were served to mark the occasion. This was an important part of the social calendar, and parishes such as All Saints struggled to keep the cost in check.[28]

Tithes, customary dues and individual bequests were by no means the sole financial contributions made to the late medieval clergy. Churchwardens' accounts yield examples of communal support for vicars and rectors, curates, auxiliary clergy, morrow mass-priests, clerks or extra confessors, particularly during the busy Easter period. The size of investment varied according to the wealth and needs of individual communities, but it could reach as much as 53 per cent of total expenditure (or over £30) in the enormously prosperous parish of St Mary-at-Hill in London in the late fifteenth century. Here, the wardens administered no less than six chantries, and this typified the tendency of most parishes to support 'traditional' (intercession- related) rather than 'advanced' (evangelical) religious options.[29]

It should be noted that voluntary religion was more than just a spiritual phenomenon. As parishioners entrusted more and more responsibility and resources to their churchwardens, they gradually arrived at a point where religious initiatives started to develop distinctly secular consequences. It would, however, be anachronistic to try to distinguish between the two in an age which associated otherworldly benefits with 'good works' such as poor relief or bridge repair.[30] The accumulation of lands and tenements by the parishes can help to illustrate the complexity of the relationship. The lion's share of this property derived from benefactions by individual parishioners. Evidence dates back to the first surviving set of sources from St Michael's, Bath. As early as 1349, churchwardens Thomas the tanner and Thomas the mason spent over 11s. for the support of seven anniversaries celebrated within the church.[31] The blend between religious and secular aspects cannot be overlooked: the benefactors' endowments for prayers, masses and ceremonies forced the wardens to develop considerable administrative and legal proficiency. A combination of informal arrangements and enfeoffments to use, for instance, was devised to allow the parish to circumvent its lack of corporate status.[32]

As a result, property might also be purchased using the community's own resources. This inevitably involved a great many secular considerations, including the search for potential sites, the collection of rents, the maintenance of the holdings and the prosecution of negligent tenants, but the additional income from rents was normally channelled into better religious or ceremonial provisions. At Peterborough, the wardens and eight other parishioners bought three acres of land near Sexton Barns in 1482 for 33s. 4d. out of parish funds, which resulted in an extra 9s. of annual income. In 1517, the wardens of Botolph Aldersgate, London, borrowed £10 from the Holy Trinity fraternity and paid £23 2s. 8d. for the tenement next adjoining the south side of Blackhorse Alley (an area where the parish already held property). Thereafter an annual rent of 24s. represented roughly a 5 per cent return on the investment.[33] The decision to spend over £1 'pro scriptione unius libri de seruicio beate marie' at Peterborough in 1484–5 and the increase in payments to clerks and organ players at Botolph in the wake of the purchase might well have been impossible without these initiatives.

The same overlaps can be observed in the field of culture and in particular in the staging of religious plays. At Ashburton in this sample, the pre-Reformation wardens paid on average 3s. per year for musical and dramatic performances which served the dual purpose of communal entertainment and religious education. The events took place on Corpus Christi day, one of the high points of the liturgical year, and the accounts record the existence of costumes, wigs, gloves and even devils' heads.[34] A cursory glance at the evidence collected for the *Records of Early English Drama* will confirm that contemporary theatre was indeed strongly parish-based and that it made a considerable contribution to the support of local ecclesiastical provision.[35]

Finally, there is substantial evidence for the performance of public works in parochial accounts. In 1437, the churchwardens of Tintinhull were authorised by their fellow parishioners to spend 3*s*. 5*d*. for stones to mend the village road. At Appledore in 1511, the conditions attached to a benefaction make it clear that the parish was about to start major works on its highway, while a memorandum at Halesowen records contributions to the same purpose in 1500.[36] A similar picture emerges for the upkeep of bridges. As early as 1250, visitation records of St Paul's Cathedral reveal that a body of six parishioners administered the profits of a small flock of sheep to deal with the problem at Heybridge,[37] while the Peterborough wardens repeatedly used communal resources for the repair of bridges in their parish: the first payment of this kind was made in 1475 and amounted to £1. In 1514, church funds, Corpus Christi money and the profits from the sepulchre light, in total over £7, were combined to finance the necessary repairs, and another £1 was needed in 1533–4. All these activities had secular benefits for all members of the community, but their spiritual dimension should not be ignored. It is clearly no coincidence that public works were such an important feature of wills: in London, for instance, 15 per cent of early fifteenth-century merchant benefactors thought that their chances of salvation would be increased by generous support of civic duties, while the amounts of labour, material and money bequeathed to London Bridge suggest that it must have been considered as some kind of 'civic chantry'.[38] Similar gifts are known from Norwich and other towns, while it was common for many public utilities to be maintained by revenues generated by papal and episcopal indulgences or the foundation of a hermitage.[39]

The impression left by this survey is clear: while membership of the parish remained compulsory throughout the medieval period (and indeed much beyond), the scope for voluntary activities supported by the parish wardens always existed, and it increased over time. This can be illustrated by a comparison of four crucial phases in parochial development. Figure 1 depicts the average of the respective percentages

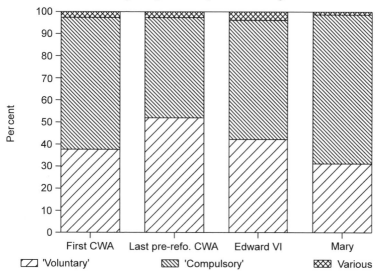

Figure 1 Voluntary and compulsory spending: eight urban parishes (to 1558)

scored by voluntary and compulsory spending in our eight parishes during the following periods: (i) the first surviving accounts, (ii) the last records before the Chantries Act and the reforming injunctions of 1547, (iii) the reckonings compiled under Edward VI, and (iv) those from Mary's reign.[40]

Of all communal expenditure in this sample, on average 38 per cent can be classified as 'voluntary spending' in the first surviving accounts (the lowest section of the left-hand column), but no less than 51 per cent on the eve of the Reformation.[41] Parishes, just like fraternities and chantries, do not fit the traditional image of compulsion for the later Middle Ages. In fact, close regulation and tight supervision should be associated with the post-Reformation parish, for the religious changes reversed the trend: the share of voluntary spending fell from 51 to 42 per cent under Edward VI and to 31 per cent under Mary. Given the 'grey areas' and methodological problems, it is not the actual percentage figures we should note, but the general trend towards a more restrictive religious atmosphere, confirming impressions gained from studies with an emphasis on subparochial institutions.[42] The various interventions by both Protestant and Catholic reformers in the 1550s contained an astonishing amount of regulation about all aspects of communal worship. Crown and bishops took an unprecedented interest in the details of parochial administration, commissioners confiscated a great deal of property associated with pious bequests, lights before images disappeared, intercession was no longer acceptable, poor relief was stripped of its spiritual benefits, and the room for manoeuvre became very tight indeed: during the vestiarian controversy, for instance, both bishops and radical puritans sought guidance from Protestant authorities overseas.[43] Payments instigated by Crown and Parliament absorbed more than 10 per cent of parish expenditure in the reign of Edward VI, most of which related less to the traditional areas of subsidy collections and military duties, and primarily to the costly implementation of various Reformation measures such as the whitewashing of walls, removing of altars and the provision of Bibles. The dismantling of elaborate and heavy ornamentation often required paid labour, and the painting of scriptural texts, the acquisition of a communion table or the purchase of new service books did not come cheaply.[44] In accordance with the definitions adopted for this study, all parish measures included in acts of Parliament, visitation articles or royal injunctions have been classified as 'compulsory' spending. This is admittedly a matter of interpretation, and potentially an underestimation of spontaneous local initiatives. However, churchwardens never elaborate on their community's attitude, and expenditure motives have to be reconstructed from indirect evidence. Every community was of course a special case; some responded early and exceeded their brief, others dragged their feet like the conservative vicar of Morebath who had to be summoned to Exeter no less than four times, but in the end few found a viable alternative to conformity.[45] The changes were enforced too quickly, too uniformly, too comprehensively, and also reversed too frequently to reflect genuine grass-roots developments. In fact, any divergent parochial initiative would have been stifled by the flood of meticulous guidelines and the intensive supervision.[46] From the late 1530s, parishes incurred an ever-increasing proportion of their legal costs explicitly at visitations and ecclesiastical courts.[47] The catch-phrases for the post-Reformation period, in both Catholic and Protestant countries, were discipline, coercion and order. As a potentially destabilising factor, religious deviation could not be tolerated. With various degrees of success, princes used the Church as a means to increase their domestic power, and this was not the time for spontaneous parish initiatives, quite apart from the fact that the Reformation had created and reinforced divisions all over the country, leaving many

communities visibly 'scarred' by the years of controversy.[48] An extension of the quantitative analysis into the reign of Elizabeth would most
probably confirm this impression, for voluntary religious activities were
bound to be given a rather lower priority by parochial officers who had
more than enough to do with all their new local government duties.[49]

But how representative is this aggregate trend of individual case-
studies? Space allows little more than a quick survey: five out of the
eight parishes, from metropolitan as well as market-town backgrounds,
display exactly the same chronological development, and all of them
record considerable voluntary expenses in their pre-Reformation
accounts. Some diverge marginally by scoring the highest voluntary
quota in the earliest accounts, and two manage to preserve or increase
it under Edward. Both of these, however, are special cases. Botolph
Aldersgate continues to support some priests from the dissolved subparochial institutions, and the Andrew Hubbard accounts start to
include tithe revenues. Given that the wardens collect something they
are not canonically supposed to, the payments inflate the parish's
voluntary quota, even though they represent nothing but a transfer of
compulsory individual responsibilities under communal administration.

The trend in this sample is clearly more than an optical illusion, but
are we dealing with a specifically urban phenomenon? The surviving
evidence for rural parishes is not very extensive, but glimpses can be
caught in various parts of the country. Yatton in Somerset fully conforms to the pattern in figure 1, and Boxford in Suffolk displays an
equally impressive growth in voluntary activities over the pre-Reformation period.[50] This seems to provide another indication that – whatever
their peculiarities – town and country did not necessarily differ in their
religious experiences.[51] And yet, prosperous city-centre parishes in
particular displayed three very distinctive features. First, they were
normally able to divert more spare resources into voluntary religion:
All Saints, Bristol, raised over £50 per annum from around 240
inhabitants (1530–42), but Boxford a mere £13 from 370 (1540–6).
Second, money in rural communities tended to come from more
'secular' sources such as church ales rather than intercession-related
pious bequests,[52] and third, the higher turnovers of urban communities
enabled them to support a wider and more sophisticated range of
voluntary religious activities. Rural parishes, to take but one example,
organised the occasional play and communal entertainment, but would
have found it impossible to match the quality and quantity of musical
services provided at some of the prosperous metropolitan churches,

where churchwardens' accounts testify to the purchase of expensive service books and the presence of choirs, conductors and distinguished composers.[53] It is hard to avoid the conclusion that the impact of religious change in urban parishes must have been particularly acute.

In spite of the rather paradoxical Reformation-related decrease in voluntary religion emerging from this sample, continuities should not be ignored. There are obvious structural similarities between, say, organisational patterns of Lollardy, recusancy or the Family of Love,[54] the importance of the household unit in both pre- and post-Reformation worship, between late medieval and puritan fasts, between market-town preaching by friars and 'lectures by combination', between Catholic books of hours and Protestant primers. The Reformation caused not so much a sudden rise or fall in the sum total of voluntary religion, but an increase in doctrinal variety and readjustments in the range of its main sponsors. Social elites, urban corporations and pious individuals continued to play a prominent role amongst the latter. The nobles and gentlemen who used to found chantries and monasteries in the Middle Ages now invested in clerical education and the provision of sermons. The Stour Valley clothiers, who had 'made their parish churches one of the last glories of pre-Reformation England' were now bringing 'preaching and education into the same townships'.[55] Towns, accustomed to the supervision of chantry endowments and clerical discipline, now established municipal lectureships. Individual pilgrimages, vows of chastity and *devotio moderna*-inspired spiritual introspection found post-Reformation equivalents in 'gadding to sermons', puritan asceticism and the incessant soul-searching of the would-be elect. The fragmentation of the religious spectrum, however, multiplied the doctrinal options for such individual, sub- and extra-parochial efforts. From the 1520s, voluntary religion could not just take place within or without *the* Church, but within or without a Catholic, Lutheran, Zwinglian, Calvinist, Anglican or Anabaptist framework. Not all of these gained equal prominence in England, of course, but each became a more rigidly defined 'confession' than any of the religious challenges of the late Middle Ages. Small wonder that the parish and its officers, absorbed by mounting secular concerns and faced with heterogeneous congregations of Church Papists, Prayer Book Protestants and semi-separatist puritans, found it more difficult to make the same efforts in the field of voluntary religion.[56] Most parishioners seem to have conformed to the (modest) demands of the *ecclesia anglicana*, but additional emotional satisfaction was found elsewhere. There were, however, exceptions. Fairly homogeneous conservative as well as radical communities would still find the energy and resources to launch collective initiatives, and London vestries in particular continued to promote voluntary religion in their parishes.[57] Here, perhaps, the fairly select ruling bodies had the necessary political power, social cohesion and monetary resources to do so. And to underline the importance of continuities, there was in fact a striking correspondence between those parishes with a flourishing late medieval fraternity life and those which established puritan lectureships.[58]

The empirical basis of this essay allows no more than speculation about later developments, but there may have been a partial recovery of voluntary communal expenditure after the first Reformation generation. Historians have pointed to the emergence of a new doctrinal consensus once England had overcome the years of uncertainty. The concerted resistance to the Laudian initiatives certainly suggests reinforced parochial identities as does the revival of building and embellishment activities from the 1590s.[59]

Voluntary religion, to conclude this preliminary survey, should no longer be seen as the preserve of pre-Reformation heretics and post-Reformation radicals, but deserves to be recognised as an equally important feature of mainstream ecclesiastical life, particularly before the mid-Tudor changes. The various activities supported by late medieval churchwardens developed a considerable innovative potential (the administration of pious bequests paved the way to the parishes' secular future) and foreshadowed many forms of early modern spirituality. The phenomenon affected both town and country, but prosperous city-centre parishes distinguished themselves by the sheer size of resources they were able to invest and by the range of options they could support. These, perhaps, were the communities that had most to lose. More detailed insights into the readjustments in emphasis and intensity will have to await further microhistoric analysis, yet the general tendency seems clear enough: the various Tudor Reformations provided an enormous impetus for some aspects of voluntary religion, but they also destroyed many of its earlier incarnations and – at least temporarily – dissociated the phenomenon from its links with the parish institutions. Godly magistrates rather than churchwardens co-ordinated communal initiatives in the Elizabethan period. The religious life of the nation, however, continued to be characterised by 'compulsory' as well as 'voluntary' components.

11. Reformation, Resources and Authority in English Towns: an Overview

ROBERT TITTLER

In light of the importance attached by Reformation historians to the urban context, and the keen attention directed to English towns of this era by the work of urban historians like Peter Clark and Paul Slack,[1] it is perhaps a little surprising that the connection between the two concerns has taken so long to develop. Nevertheless, that connection is now at hand, a good bit of it coming in response to Patrick Collinson's public lecture of 1986 on 'The Protestant Town', published as the second chapter in *The Birthpangs of Protestant England* two years later.[2] It is here that we find the central question, 'What did the Reformation do for the towns?'[3]

The signal contribution of that essay (as well as some other distinguished work on the same theme[4]) to what we know of urban life has been to flesh out the Protestant notion of 'godly rule'. Reformed theology provided an ideology for civic governance, inspiring lay officials ever onward with visions of the 'city on the hill'. An underlying assumption to that consideration, reasonably enough, is that the English Reformation was an essentially religious phenomenon, culminating in the triumph of Protestantism from about the 1570s.

This effort to link religious and ideological concerns with political themes, whether in the general terms adopted in Collinson's essay or in the specific application drawn, for example, by Professor Underdown, seems extremely important. Collinson's question must indeed be asked. Yet depending on one's perspective, there are a number of alternative responses which might be offered. To an urbanist, an earlier and equally important aspect of this relationship is that episode known as 'the dissolutions' and its aftermath: that is, the dissolution and redistribution of ecclesiastical resources, and the effects which those activities seem to have had especially on urban politics, finance and government. Here the Reformation appears as something more than a shift, however substantial, in doctrine and belief. In this wider sense it may be taken as deriving from the parliamentary legislation of the 1530s rather than from the change in popular religious attitudes brought about in a subsequent generation.

Dissolution, both of the religious houses in the 1530s and of the chantries, guilds, fraternities and associated funds and institutions in the 1540s, proved profoundly important for a great many individual towns. Though it affected different types of urban communities in different ways and some towns more than others, it frequently accelerated changes in urban economics and finance, politics and government, even in society and culture, to a degree which is at the least noteworthy and at best dramatic.

As wary as one must be of 'watersheds in history', this even suggests to the urbanist a new label in the periodisation of English Urban History. Succinctly stated, what might be called 'The Age of the Reformation in English Urban History', may be dated to the dissolutions of 1536 and after. It appears to be characterised by a vast sorting out of urban communities, in which some plunged from the ranks of the urban almost completely, and others moved toward economic restructuring, greater local autonomy and legal authority. For those numerous, small towns whose *raison d'être* had been bound up with the very ecclesiastical establishments gobbled up in the 1530s, the Reformation meant sudden and often prolonged crisis. The fate of these towns, the Ramsays and Cerne Abbases of the realm, has long dominated our common impressions of the social and economic impact of the Reformation on the towns. Having economies which remained one-dimensional and political structures largely dominated by a monastery or abbey, they too often had nothing upon which to fall back when dissolution struck. Within the century many slumped from the status of urban communities altogether, and/or exchanged an ecclesiastical lord for a lay seigneur upon whom their economy and governance continued to depend.

For other, more substantial towns, however, the dissolutions proved a watershed in ways which were much more complex and, in the long run, often constructive. This is the less familiar story, and the one upon which the following pages will dwell. Leaving aside for lack of space both the national context of political and economic change on the one hand and questions of doctrine and belief on the other, we turn to that great number of towns which experienced very significant changes in the patterns of land holding and attendant political authority. In this narrow vein, the impact of the Reformation may often be characterised by five themes which appear in rough chronological sequence. Taken together, and seen in the context of substantial social and economic changes of the same years, they paved the way for the onset of 'godly rule'.

First we have the unprecedented and rather sudden availability on the open market of a great deal of urban property and other resources for the better part of the century following that date. Second came the ardent effort of local officials to obtain these resources for their towns, and in a manner which was as legally secure as possible. This in turn prompted a quest for greater legal authority over those resources which, especially in the middle decades of the century, often came in the form of incorporation.[5] Fourth, and in the Elizabethan years especially, that enhanced authority accelerated the tendency toward urban oligarchy: the form of rule which Clark and Slack saw as most characteristic of the era.[6] And finally, by the century's end appeared the enhanced allure for many ruling elites of progressive Protestant or puritan views as an ideology emphatically supportive of the new order.

No doubt the central position accorded here to the redistribution of property, and to its attendant political authority, bears some familiar resonances for weary veterans of the 'rising gentry/declining aristocracy' wars. Nevertheless, the reality of the dissolutions, and their implications for other aspects of urban society, demands emphatic attention. Though the wider thesis so crudely sketched out here will be treated at more appropriate length elsewhere,[7] let us turn now to the first steps of this proposed sequence, and to the central question of urban resources.

Clearly, our prevailing impressions about the impact of the dissolutions on the disposition of urban property have not been encouraging for those who would see the experience working to strengthen the local community. Whether we follow the extremes of pessimism laid out by the modern chroniclers of iconoclasm and destruction,[8] or the gentler verdicts of those who have written more dispassionately,[9] the overall assumption has been one of loss rather than gain. A general disruption in the operation of schools, hospitals and other formerly Church-run institutions has long been obvious.[10] In addition, though modern and scholarly documentation of such things is surprisingly rare on the ground, it is not difficult at least to imagine the havoc wreaked in the lives of lay employees of such institutions, to livelihoods sustained by the needs of supply, or to the flow of business brought by pilgrims to many towns.[11]

On the other side of the ledger there has been very little recognition of any more constructive effects of such dramatic changes, especially for those towns which met this challenge from a position of greater economic diversity and strength. Yet we tend not to discover what we do not seek to begin with, and almost none of the extensive corpus of scholarship on the issue of post-dissolution lands and resources has derived from an interest in urban communities as such. Most of it emerged from the interminable debate on the rise or fall of the landed gentry prior to the Civil War, often in the form of theses or monographs on the politics of a particular county. Such work considered property which was rural and politics which were shire-based. Seldom did it dwell on things urban. Scholars have taken little interest in the role of individual townsmen or towns in the corporate sense as purchasers of dissolved lands, nor have they much noted important acquisitions by such urban interests.[12] Very few political historians have considered the town or city as a subject of its own, or related it to national politics, as has been done so often with shires. Some of this neglect may be excused by the small size of all English towns outside of London, and by the small proportion of the total population which lived therein. English towns were simply not as important as, for example, Dutch, Italian or Imperial cities at this time. Yet excuse it as one may, this neglect has done little for the study of English urban society as a subject of its own.

In addition, most studies of dissolved lands have dwelt upon the first wave of dissolutions, those of the 1530s, which took in the monasteries, priories, abbeys and other religious houses, at the expense of the lands of the second wave. This latter round, in the 1540s, took in the fraternities, guilds and most of the chantries, as well as the lights, obits, anniversaries and other endowments which went with them.[13] The resources of this second group were more densely distributed in urban areas. Their dissolution and redistribution had a much greater impact on urban society.

To be fair, this is not an easy subject to investigate. For a variety of reasons, urban property in general proves more difficult to trace than agrarian. Aside from the large urban estates developed by some of the wealthier monastic institutions, it tended to lie in small and scattered units. Much of it consisted of chantries or similar charitable bequests held by lay foundations, such as fraternities and guilds, by parishes or by town governments – mayors and aldermanic councils – themselves. Few of these lands were likely to have been counted in the *Valor*

Ecclesiasticus (1535) which was designed to assist in the dissolution of the religious houses, or to be listed in the accounts of such houses.[14]

Purchase of such urban properties, whatever their provenance, was more likely to have been made in socage tenure which, not requiring a licence of alienation, went without record of transfer in the central archives.[15] In any event, the statute requiring the enrolment in the central or county courts of purchases of lands in freehold, or which were in any other manner heritable, specifically exempted the 'cities, boroughs and towns corporate'. In those jurisdictions, sales were supposed to be recorded locally, but can only rarely be traced through local archives.[16] In addition, as has often been noted, urban lands were probably more likely to have been purchased by agents acting on behalf of groups of townsmen rather than by townsmen themselves, effectively concealing the identity of the true holders.

Factors of timing and location further hide urban property acquisitions from our view. While most of our studies of dissolved property deal only with initial purchases or those made but a decade or so after dissolution, it appears that neither towns nor individual townsmen tended to be the *first* purchasers of dissolved lands from the Crown. Most made their acquisitions as the century wore on. For individual townsmen, investment in urban property had not been as strong a tradition as it had amongst their country cousins, nor were townsmen known to be as quick to respond to economic changes as some other investors.[17] Acting either as individuals or as corporate officials, they may well have taken longer to come round to the idea even in a period of rising rents such as ensued especially after *c.* 1540. Towns themselves often lacked the funds to make purchases at the immediate point of first sale. Their cumbersome fiscal mechanisms made it more difficult for them to raise such funds than for the private purchaser. They more often waited until lands came on to the market a second or even a third time before they could step forth with ready cash.[18]

In addition, whether acting in their own right or as corporate officers, townsmen knew their own community better than most of the landed or court interests which made most of the early acquisitions; they often drew caution from that knowledge. They knew of the longer leases which had, in the preceding period of stagnant rents, often been granted to tenants, especially of the more marginal buildings, in return for the obligation of maintenance. Indeed, some such leases extended three or four lifetimes, proving extremely uneconomical to their landlords in an inflationary era.[19] They knew, too, about the physical condition. While applying the sanctions of the Henrician rebuilding statutes to local properties requiring renovation on the one hand,[20] borough officials often sat on their hands until leases came close to term and rental values increased sufficiently to make purchase of marginal tenements worthwhile. Perhaps of greatest importance, towns often lacked the legal authority either to purchase lands in mortmain to begin with or to hold them securely thereafter.

These factors suggest that we may well reach different conclusions about the redistribution of urban property if we look specifically at towns as opposed to counties, at properties dissolved in the 1540s as well as those of the 1530s, and, perhaps especially, at acquisitions undertaken not only in the immediate aftermath of dissolution, but on even to the end of the century. These strategies fly in the face of almost all the research we have before us on the redistribution of dissolved lands. It should not surprise us if they yield a different story.

In one additional respect does a prime interest in urban property demand a different approach. While virtually the entire literature on the subject from whatever perspective takes up the story at the literal point of dissolution itself, the urban historian must look at two alternative forms of obtaining lands prompted by fear of that event: pre-emptive acquisitions just prior to dissolution (many of them between 1536 or 1539 and 1545) and concealments.

To begin with pre-emptions, a number of examples may be found of towns sufficiently empowered, wealthy and prescient to acquire control of church or guild property before the Crown demanded its surrender.[21] Most often prompted by rumour and fear for the loss of local resources, the lion's share of these pre-emptions came between the first and second waves of dissolution. In this manner the officials of both Hull and Southampton confiscated church plate and ornaments before they could fall into the hands of the King's commissioners, using the proceeds for public works.[22] York officials successfully carried out in 1536 a municipal dissolution of some local chantries and obits, absorbing those properties into the city's holdings.[23] The unincorporated borough of Richmond similarly seized in 1544 six chantries, two chapels and ten obits.[24] Both Plymouth and Dartmouth seized plate to finance purchase of military ordnance during the French War of the early 1540s,[25] and the Cornish borough of Looe confiscated lands set aside for obits to finance repair of its bridge in 1544.[26] Even before 1540 the precociously Protestant officials of Canterbury replenished civic coffers with proceeds from the sale of goods and property from

chantry, fraternity and chapel. In addition, they invited a textile man-
ufacturer to set up shop in the Blackfriars, and they used rents from
former monastic properties to help the poor.[27] And in one of the most
substantial of all pre-dissolution acquisitions, the declining port of
Boston, after securing a charter of incorporation in 1545 expressly for
that purpose, purchased for £1,646, to be paid out over twelve years,
extensive guild and other resources worth £525 a year: a relative
bargain at the time.[28]

Failing successful confiscation prior to dissolution, many towns
turned to concealment: the intentional neglect to 'tell all' to the royal
commissioners who came to catalogue church property eligible for
dissolution, followed by the absorption of those properties into borough
control. Though by their very nature concealments are difficult to trace
unless they were uncovered by the Crown itself, they seem to have been
easy enough to carry out.[29] Concealment bore two advantages. It kept
the coveted resources under local control, and it divested the town
government of the financial obligations, e.g. to chantry priests, for
altars, candles and the like, for which those resources had usually
been bequeathed.[30] The corporation of Hull, for example, had been
taking an annual loss because obligatory payments for the requisite
chantries, anniversaries and obits had come to exceed the rental
income attached for their support. In the event, the corporation concealed the bulk of the chantry endowments from the King's Commissioners, keeping the revenues for the borough's coffers without
incurring the expenses for which they had been earmarked.[31] When
and if concealments were discovered, the conventional response seems
to have been an offer to compound rather than confiscation by the
Crown: most concealments remained in the hands of the concealers.

Larger institutions eligible for dissolution were obviously more difficult to conceal than the small, scattered holdings which probably
comprised the majority. Yet it is surprising how many substantial
properties were successfully hidden from the Crown and absorbed
into local resources. The mayor and corporation of Walsall, for example, retained the chantry lands and hall of the Guild of St John.[32] The
leading citizens of the still-unincorporated Bury St Edmunds, acting as
feoffees, did the same with their guildhall.[33] The borough of Andover
concealed and appropriated lands of the Hospital of St John the
Baptist, which had been financed partly by the Merchant Guild of
the town.[34] Bedford concealed St Leonard's Hospital whose lands, at
£20 a year, constituted a large proportion of this small town's annual

revenue.[35] Winchester officials managed to appropriate over fifty tenements of the Hospital of St John, along with the hospital itself and some
additional properties.[36] The corporation of Beverley concealed rental
units whose value had reached £195 per annum by the time they were
discovered late in the century.[37]

Moving on from pre-emptions and concealments to actual purchases
made in the years after the dissolutions, those made directly from the
Crown and recorded in the Augmentations until its abolition in 1554[38]
are obviously the easiest to trace and have thus received most notice.
Some of these purchases were for very modest sums;[39] most would
seem scant in contrast to some of the great outlays of some members of
the aristocracy or court circle. Yet in the context of individual towns
themselves, inevitably burdened by fragile and limited fiscal resources,
they counted for much more than we might expect. In towns like
Bristol, Coventry, Ludlow, Norwich and Warwick, where a substantial
proportion of the local housing stock thus came into civic hands, they
were extremely significant.[40]

In addition to acquisitions through the Augmentations, many towns
legitimately purchased former ecclesiastical lands after the abolition of
that court, and often from third parties rather than from the Crown.[41]
These are particularly difficult to trace, a difficulty compounded by the
fact that many such purchases were carried out by agents, in whose
name, rather than in the corporation's, the purchase was then
recorded.[42] And, as urban corporations found it difficult to move
quickly, as noted above, a great many such purchases came later in
the century.

Although only £24 worth of lands are recorded in the Augmentations as being purchased by the corporation of Gloucester, we know
from local records that resources acquired even in the early 1540s were
worth nearly £500 a year. Though some of these initial lands were later
resold, additional and very lucrative acquisitions of former ecclesiastical
lands followed later in the century.[43] In Winchester (as, presumably,
elsewhere) most dissolved lands went to private individuals: townsmen
and especially regional gentry. Yet despite this, total purchases by the
town by 1604 included over fifty rents of the former St John's Hospital
and over 70 properties in all, comprising more than half of the city's
corporate income at that time.[44] Worcester's purchases are also unlisted
in the Augmentations, nevertheless it added dissolved religious properties which brought in nearly two-thirds of its corporate income by the
end of the century.[45] Exeter, listed in the Court of Augmentations as

receiving only the farm of a small, local manor,[46] actually bought (at *third* hand) virtually all the monastic lands within its bounds in 1549 for the sum of £1,460 2*s.* 3*d.* The purchases were made, and the lands subsequently managed, by five feoffees acting on behalf of, but not in the name of, the city.[47] And in Bristol purchases of properties formerly held of the Grey Friars, White Friars and Gaunt's Hospital together amounted to £315 per annum by the 1580s.[48] In almost all these cases, and in many more like them, we have to turn to the records of the local corporations rather than the central archives to learn the full story: a cumbersome business.

Of these last three examples, Exeter and Bristol represent two of the largest cities of the age outside of London, while Worcester was a cathedral city of considerable size, ancient reputation and still-considerable importance. Of course, not all towns by any means could contemplate such steps. The Ramsays and Cerne Abbases were too small, insufficiently wealthy or politically developed to do so. Many other small, lay seigneurial towns had neither the resources nor the opportunity: their status often remained unchanged and unchallenged throughout this era. Yet in a great number of the middling and larger sort of towns throughout the realm such common acquisitions followed within at least a few decades of dissolution, usually with substantial consequences for the life of the community. Amongst them, in addition to those noted above, we would find the likes of, e.g. Abingdon, Bridg-water, Chichester, Chipping Sodbury, High Wycombe, Ipswich, Leominster, Ludlow, Maidstone, Marlborough, Romsey, Stratford-upon-Avon, Totnes, Wisbech and Woodstock.[49]

In addition, a great many towns, small and large alike, benefited substantially from personal bequests of lands which had initially been bought up privately. This common activity may well be a post-Reformation version of an old pattern, whereby a very large propor-tion of urban properties in ecclesiastical estates had derived from charitable bequests. Instead of being left to a monastery, chantry, fraternity, guild or parish for intercessionary purposes, they now went to local governments out of a concern, for example, for local poverty relief, the commemoration of the donor, or that combination of grati-tude and loyalty which increasingly accrued to local communities in this era. Sometimes, ironically, such bequests thereby completed a curious circle, deriving from dissolved ecclesiastical holdings which had once before been given by laymen, albeit for somewhat different reasons.

Typical of such benefactors was Richard Pate (1516–1588), born in Cheltenham and active both there and in Gloucester despite his career at Westminster. Before his death Pate conveyed some £100 of the former ecclesiastical lands he himself had purchased to the city of Gloucester. At his death he made an additional bequest to Gloucester, and also money for the school and foundation which still bear his name in Cheltenham.[50] Even a little research into local communities assures us that the Richard Pates of the realm were, happily, a thriving breed in this era: there can be few towns of any substance which did not have a local benefactor endowing it with post-dissolutions gains. Yet a great deal of research remains to be done on this source of civic resources after the Reformation.

Where do these observations leave us? It goes without saying that the flow of former ecclesiastical properties to towns themselves is a mere trickle compared with the amount which went elsewhere. It also remains difficult to measure that trickle with any precision. Yet this flow seems virtually certain to be much more substantial than one has previously assumed. If we look at these acquisitions from the local perspective, they seem often to have been extremely important to particular communities. Indeed, for that less than 10 per cent of the nation's population which lived in towns and cities, a little went a long way.

In the most direct sense, these newly acquired resources brought new and badly needed income into civic coffers. Acquired property ensured for many a borough treasury a steady source of rental income from year to year, income enhanced by the population increase and subsequent steady rise in rental values throughout the period. This served some communities as an increasing proportion of all revenues, especially as the marketing or manufacture of traditional products in some towns fluctuated or declined in these years of rapid economic change or as towns sought to replace tolls in the effort to encourage more trade.[51] Acquired funds which had accured, for example, in chantries, guilds or fraternities, or for such practices as anniversaries and obits, often went far in replacing traditional forms of charity which had been swept away. And local control of schools, hospitals and other institutions which were often re-established, albeit after some disruption, under local, civic auspices in their former buildings, ensured a civic replacement for what had been church-run institutions. In addition, the placing of these resources in the hands of local officials further empowered the governing authority of many boroughs. Sometimes this worked well; sometimes not. In Ludlow, for example, the acquisition of rental properties by the corporation augmented the civic coffers and permitted as well the discretionary power to let tenements to freemen at advantageous terms, thus cushioning the impact of hard times. But in Ludlow and elsewhere, allegations of favouritism in awarding leases, a powerful weapon in the frequent factional rivalries which typified the age, also became common.[52] The example serves to remind us that greater empowerment also opened the door to greater official abuse: it, too, may have increased in these years.

More important than these direct applications of newly gained resources were the legal steps necessitated by their quest, and the powers which thus accrued to offices of local government. These climactic elements of the overall thesis remain to be substantiated more fully elsewhere.[53] Yet some additional and much broader conclusions seem possible even on the basis of what has been discussed above.

On the one hand it seems incontrovertible that for the very small, ecclesiastically-dominated towns which had failed to diversify economically or develop politically – what have been called here the Cerne Abbases and Ramsays of the realm – dissolution often brought stagnation or even catastrophe. Yet for many other towns the dissolution and the restructuring of resources was often far from calamitous. At its best, especially in the middling and larger boroughs of the realm, such restructuring often established the foundations for solvent, autonomous and stable governments during the several decades after the event.

There are, of course, other factors to consider in accounting for the strong foundations for civic government thus established in these towns. The outpouring of social and economic regulatory legislation of the time, which empowered mayors and aldermen as never before to be agents of regulation and enforcement; the remarkable increase in borough incorporation and re-incorporation beginning about 1540; and the development of a civic political culture which enhanced the authority of oligarchic rule, all played their role in these years. But of at least equal importance to these factors, and intimately linked to them as well, lay the bedrock of material resources acquired by civic authorities following the Reformation legislation of the 1530s and 1540s.

In sum, the economic and, especially, the political impact of the Reformation on the towns seems much more complex than has often been recognised. Against the more familiar picture of catastrophe which has been drawn from some examples, we must begin to hold up the substantially more beneficial results which accrued in those communities better able to cope. The emerging picture draws sharp distinctions amongst urban types, and indicates a point of dramatic change, in one direction or another, for most of those types.

Part III
The Changing Culture of Urban Reformation

12. The Shearmen's Tree and the Preacher: the Strange Death of Merry England in Shrewsbury and Beyond

PATRICK COLLINSON

The first Friday after Michaelmas, 4 October 1594, was election night in Shrewsbury. This was not a parliamentary election but the election which mattered most in this partly self-contained urban commonwealth, the choice of next year's ruling bailiffs.[1] This was an annual occasion for licensed misrule,[2] and it found some apparently aimless young men milling about the streets. We catch a fragment of conversation: 'Where was he upon Sondaye that he came not to shoote?' But there was purpose in this drifting. Towards ten o'clock there happened an affray, apparently premeditated, and a certain Thomas Lacon, the servant of a leading citizen and draper of the town, Richard Chirwell, received blows with a great cudgel from which, later that night, he died.

It was not clear whether the fatal blow had been struck by one William Morris junior, a shearman and the son of a shearman, or by William ap Rees, the servant of another shearman, Robert Taylor. (The occupation of a shearman was to process or 'finish' woollen cloth, raising the nap with teasels and trimming it with their great shears.) With both young men in goal, the matter was closely investigated. In his dying hours, Lacon had repeatedly identified Morris as his fatal assailant. But everyone knew of a quarrel, 'great malice', between Lacon and ap Rees, and of a series of angry encounters between them. On Tuesday 29 October, both Morris and ap Rees were hanged before a large and appreciative crowd, making, according to the local chronicler, a good end, 'to the exsample of all youthes and people present.'[3] In the terrible 1590s, executions in Shrewsbury were routine.

A year later, with the town gaol full to overflowing, no less than twelve felons were strung up at a single sessions, with six more 'put away' eight months later at a 'very busy' assizes. The chronicler does not trouble to name any of these victims. At the 1597 assizes, six died, and in 1598 five, 'very stubbornly and desperately', saying 'they came not thyder to preache.'[4] So why does the Lacon affair make the front page, for our local chronicler and for us?

To begin an essay on religion in early modern Shropshire with a murder is becoming an almost operatic convention.[5] The Lacon murder will serve to take us under the skin of the culture of a major provincial town undergoing, among other pressures, a kind of reformation. Having gone so far, we shall be in a position to compare Shrewsbury with what might be called the ideal-typical model of the cultural impact of urban reformation in Elizabethan and Jacobean England.

First, we return to the circumstances of the crime, to pick up a few significant details. The two young men who were hanged were both apprentice shearmen, their victim the servant of a draper. Some said that the coroner's jury had been partial, the trial politically biased.[6] That was to be expected where these two trades were involved. Shearmen were the under class, and here are indications of craft war if not class war. Lacon was brought into the elder Morris's house to die at ten o'clock, yet one of Morris's apprentices was still at work, on election night.[7] Such was life for a shearman. Lacon's master, the draper Chirwell, had been told of the quarrel between his servant and Robert Taylor's man, whose name it was beneath his dignity to know. (The name on everyone's lips! the name of the man awaiting the hangman's noose!) He had said, with the *hauteur* of a draper: 'I hope to have that amended, for I will have no fighting nor quarrelinge.' (Taylor said of his own man, with the voice of frustrated middle management: 'A vengeance on him for I cannot rule him.') Chirwell's efforts to deal directly with ap Rees were not productive, 'by reason that he garbled': which is to say that ap Rees, besides being an apprentice in an inferior trade, had the misfortune to be Welsh.[8] Lacon, by contrast, bore a local name and was, says our chronicler, 'a proper youthe, and com of good friends' – which is to say, family.[9] His quarrel with ap Rees had taken its course in aggressive cudgel play, at the fencing school and in the Cornmarket, where the young men of the town regularly played at 'wastrels' on Sundays and holidays. It had been necessary to intervene to part the enemies, to prevent foul play. An assignation to duel with swords and knives came to nothing when both masters came to hear of it.[10] And so to the final act.

The first act of this tragedy, all agreed, was set in the previous summer, when the draper Chirwell, on his way to a Welsh cloth market with Humphrey Hughes, one of the bailiffs and, as it happens, a leading shearman, spotted a tree lying on a waggon in a suburban street. This was no ordinary tree but the 'Shearmen's Tree', brought into town as the centrepiece of an annual midsummer ritual, to be set up outside Shearmen's Hall. By 1594, as we shall see, the Shearmen's Tree had become the symbol of a customary culture under threat, and of a seriously divided community. Chirwell at once sent his servant, Lacon, to fetch a saw to 'cut' the tree. When ap Rees encountered Lacon with his saw and heard what it was for, he called Chirwell 'a woodcock and a whifeler', and it was this insult which Lacon set out to avenge. (A whiffler was a kind of clown. In the twentieth century, ap Rees might have called Chirwell a 'prat'.) By the time Lacon returned, the tree had already been chopped up with an axe borrowed from the constable.[11] At the time of the trial, David ap Thomas, another apprentice shearman, said that it would have been better to have left the tree alone. 'Whye should we not have hit when we have won hit by lawe?' David thought that the perpetrators, great men though they might be, had more need to be 'knocked' than poor Lacon. He was warned 'to take heed of knocking while you see how these speed that be in warde for the like.'[12] If all these circumstances were unknown, the Shearmen's Tree might be regarded as a charming and harmless little relic of Merry England. Relic it was, charming and harmless it was not.

What did the Welsh boy mean by winning it by law, and what was 'it'? It was a sapling oak, cut in the woods and erected outside Shearmen's Hall as the crowning glory of their annual feast, held on the Sunday next after Corpus Christi (modified by this time to 'after Trinity Sunday'). In the old days there would have been a religious procession, with music and fireworks, a little triumph. Our chronicler first alerts us to the gathering drama. In the summer of 1589 'was soome contraversie' about such summer festivals as maypoles, bonfires and, in particular, the Shearmen's Tree, 'whiche one mr tomkys publicke preachar ther did preche against'. Tomkys (to whom we shall shortly be properly introduced) put his person where his mouth was, for he was 'thretenid and pushed at by certen lewde persones'. 'But in the ennde it was reformid by the baylyffs.'[13] Although the Assembly Minutes which might have contained it no longer exist, the bailiffs no doubt made some sort of order and conveyed it through the master and wardens of the Shearman.

According to the bailiffs, defending their actions, the Shearmen were themselves divided over the issue: 'the one partie wold have the tree upp and thother parte wold have the tree cast down.' (As we have seen, Hughes, a shearman bailiff, was anti-Tree.) The leading shearmen spoke of 'contencions and uprores': disturbances which were made a reason, or excuse, for suppression, the bailiffs extrapolating from the particular issue of the Tree to an allegedly countryside scenario of 'unlawfull and riotous assemblyes', 'unlawfull pastymes necessary neyther for body nor mynde'.[14] But some shearmen, especially the young men, journeymen and apprentices, were passionately addicted to their Tree. It was said that in 1590, 500 persons (in a town of perhaps 800 householders) gathered around the Tree, 'refusing by any persuasion to disperse themselves'.[15]

The result was that in 1591 the bailiffs, working through the management of the Shearmen, who were officially anti-Tree, moved to prevent a repetition of these scenes, forbidding the setting up of the Tree 'in superstycyus order'.[16] They reckoned without some of the young hotheads of the Company, who setting out in the twilight of Sunday evening, 5 June, and travelling by back ways, returned to town at 2 a.m. with a stolen sapling worth two shillings, which was duly erected.[17] The government of the town was bound to take a grave view of such insubordination: 'the Common sort of people are greatly incoraged to all disobedyence'. It was not only the junior shearmen but the journeymen shoemakers, another numerous and proletarian guild, who were out of control.[18] But on first examination, the culprits insisted that what they had done had not been contrary to the laws and statutes of the realm.[19]

And here was the rub. Provincial magistrates, practising 'severe' government, introducing draconian bylaws in respect of popular pastimes, petty disorders and 'sin', were prone to exceed their legal powers. This had happened in Bury St Edmunds, and in the Oxfordshire town of Banbury was a matter so notorious that Ben Jonson's *Bartholomew Fair* would parody these issues before a metropolitan audience in the characters of the Banbury man, Zeal-of-the-Land Busy, and Justice Overdo, a Londoner but spiritually a Banbury man. A real-life Banbury householder who said that he hoped that the queen would allow him to entertain some friends to supper was told by an over-zealous officer: 'If the queen do allow it, yet I will not allow it.'[20] So it was, in effect, with the

Shearmen's Tree. In 1589 the Privy Council had advised the Oxfordshire magistrates that there should be no interference with pastimes and recreations, provided they were not used at unlawful times, or with 'disorder, riotts and unlawfull actes'.[21] Hence, perhaps, the stories told by the Shrewsbury bailiffs of riots and disorders, even alleging that what happened on the night of 5 June was an 'insurrection'.[22]

Some of the rebellious shearmen immediately capitulated, but four (I suppose we must call them the Shrewsbury Four) held out and were imprisoned, after indictment by a jury which included the draper Richard Chirwell.[23] Their leader, an apprentice called Richard Fernes, told the bailiff: 'Well Master Bailiff, I trust within these twelve years that I shall see the Tree brought into this Towne of Salop in as solemne Order as ever it was, And that nether Bailiff nor any other person within the said Towne shall gainsay the same.' Now Fernes was not your average apprentice shearman, no 'garbling' Welshman. He was literate, the son of a London haberdasher, and had purchased his burgess-ship for cash, while still an apprentice.[24] The Four now pulled the rug out from under the local magistrates by securing from London (with extraordinary speed) a writ of *habeas corpus* which transferred their case to the assizes at Warwick.[25]

The considerable legal intricacies of the case need not detain us. Suffice it to say that the *habeas corpus* ace played by the Four forced a compromise. Local figures of substance who had always been dubious about the legality of the bailiffs' proceedings were now able to intervene. While the ringleaders made a formal submission, qualified by the proviso that 'all lawfull custome of our company may be saved and reserved', Thomas Owen, a lawyer of rank and recorder of the town, ruled that 'the usuall tree' might be used 'as heretofore', but 'in loving order', without contention.[26] Hence the insistence in 1594 of the apprentice shearman: 'wee have won it by law.'

If the definition of a storm in a teacup is that nothing much happens, then that is what this was. Fernes, the young radical, progressed according to type. There was more trouble over the Tree in 1598, and Fernes was again at the heart of it, 'speaking indecent words' and defying magisterial authority. But by the early seventeenth century, he had been twice warden of the Shearmen, by then no doubt a respectable and substantial householder.[27] As for the Tree, in 1619 the Shearmen would not hear of holding their annual feast without it.[28]

And yet these events were not meaningless, and we now need to widen the frame to discover some of their meanings. There was a past history of bad blood between the two most prominent of Shrewsbury's companies, the Drapers and the Shearmen: prominent because the keystone to the town's economy was the trade in coarse Welsh cloth, bought up at Oswestry and other places by the Drapers, finished ('raised' and 'shorn') in Shrewsbury by the Shearmen, and sold on to London and Rouen.[29] The Shearmen were the more numerous of these two companies, indeed too numerous for their own good and the amount of work available, and for the most part consisting of recent Welsh migrants. One draper wrote of 'those poor brothers and sisters that did usually work to me at my shop',[30] and for piece-rate wages. Shearmen worked from four in the morning until nine at night, and for even longer at peak times. The less numerous and increasingly entre-preneurial Drapers (an unusual and in terms of the economic future proleptic class) did not 'work' in that sense at all, and were dominant in town government. In 1587 there were but sixty-nine master drapers, yet between 1550 and 1600 forty-seven drapers held the office of bailiff, against only two shearmen.

This is but the bare bones of the politics of cloth in early modern Shrewsbury, for while there were internal difficulties within each of the companies, with narrow self-interest often motivating individuals, there was a third company, the Mercers, against whom the Drapers and Shearmen had been known to join forces. But after the 1570s, all three companies were partially reconciled, and Shrewsbury as a combined interest made common cause, in the courts and in Parlia-ment, against threats to its livelihood from other places, most notably Chester.

Against this background, the meaning of the Shearmen's Tree affair may seem transparent. In the late medieval celebration of Corpus Christi, by this time replaced by a more secular kind of summer show, the Shearmen had always played a noisier, more exuberant part: a form of self-assertion perhaps, typical of insecure migrant groups in late medieval towns. The response of the Drapers was restrained and repressive.[31] To call the Shearmen's Tree 'superstitious' was for them a convenient excuse for a piece of social control. The responses from the Shearmen, where not everyone was singing the same tune, were indicative of complex relations across a group led by 'masters', but having some of the attributes of a proletariat. However, few things are that straightforward. After all, Hughes, the bailiff in 1594, was a shearman. And if he was of recent Welsh origin, so were a significant proportion of drapers.[32]

In any case, to describe the turbulent Shrewsbury scene in terms only of distributive economics and race relations would be not only reductionist. It would leave out of account the preacher, Mr Tomkys. It was Tomkys who had first complained about the Tree, and the climax of the 1591 affair, so far as the streets of Shrewsbury were concerned, was a kind of charivari or shaming ritual arranged for Tomkys's benefit. On Sunday 6 June, with the Shrewsbury Four in gaol, some forty apprentice shearmen followed Tomkys through the streets, as he returned from a pastoral visit, 'having a blynd mynstrel playing upon a harpe led before them'. When the preacher stopped, the procession stopped. When he proceeded, they proceeded, so bringing him 'in mocking and flowting manner' to his door, after which they went around the churchyard in a parody of 'the old order of procession'.[33] Tomkys was not the most popular figure in town. A letter survives from a woman in prison, 'justly punysshed for spekyng certen ydell wordes of Mr Tonks the publyke precher.[34] But was Tomkys a 'puritan', and do we need to invoke 'puritanism' to explain what happened in June 1591? Was this an episode in the advance of the Reformation in Shrewsbury? Was the meaning of these events 'religious'?

John Tomkys, who arrived on the scene in the summer of 1582, did not introduce the Reformation to Shrewsbury, not by a long chalk. Nor was he the first of Shrewsbury's civic preachers, employees of a magistracy mainly, if not uniformly, committed to the new ways in religion. The early Elizabethan minister of the largest parish, St Chad's, Christopher Hawkhurst, was described at his death in 1576 as 'late precher of Gods word in Salop'.[35] The most celebrated of these early preachers was Thomas Ashton, the real founder of Shrewsbury's famous school and for many years a fellow of St John's College, Cambridge, where he was a few years ahead of William Cecil, John Cheke and other famous 'Grecians'. He was a presence throughout the 1560s.[36] In 1573, with Ashton departed, an exercise of prophesying (often a substitute for a town lectureship) began in St Chad's church, which had the backing of the bishop and was always attended by the Council in the Marches when it coincided with their meetings in Shrewsbury.[37] Surplices and square caps were not worn in the town, intermittent attempts to enforce conformity proving ineffectual.[38] In 1581, still ahead of Tomkys's arrival, there was illegal iconoclasm, when the cross in St Mary's churchyard was pulled down at night, and the body of an executed criminal buried where the cross had stood.[39]

So this was already a Protestant town, with touches of puritanism. Catholics and crypto-Catholics, numerous as they must have been in this marcher region, will have kept a low profile. The grammar school, its pupils including Philip Sidney and Fulke Greville, was a bastion of robust public Protestantism. Roughly half the pupils were outsiders to Shrewsbury, which meant that the influence of the school must have been felt in the scores of households which entertained student boarders, 'tablers'.[40] When Philip's father Sir Henry Sidney, lord president of the Marches, made a notable visit to the town in 1581, 360 boys 'marched bravely', 'in battel order with their generalls, captens, droomes, trumpettes and ensigns', declaring in their orations 'howe valiantly they would feight and defende the countrey.'[41] Five years later, the scholars 'made a triumphe' in the town fields, 'against the popes army and other rebells whom they triumphantly vanquished'; returning through the town with drums and trumpets, bonfires, and 'thankfull psalmes most joyfully soonge to God.'[42] When Mary Queen of Scots was proclaimed a traitor three months later, there were more bonfires, and bells, the bailiffs and aldermen 'praysinge God with triumph and sownde of trumpet'.[43]

But were these Protestant values more than public and political, and were they fully internalised? Ashton's ordinances for the school made inadequate provision for the religious instruction and spiritual welfare of the pupils (by fully reformed standards), and his successors were not clergymen. 'Tabling' in the households of the town was more certain to push up rents than to accumulate spiritual profit. 'There were plenty of distractions.'[44] It is not likely that Shrewsbury grew, so to say, its own Reformation, without some outside assistance. Part of the story must be that the new religion was imported from London, in part exchange for all that cloth. There is concrete evidence of this in the 1585 stock-list of a Shrewsbury bookseller, which contains plenty of godly items.[45]

Nor should we discount the influence of the magnates who were the patrons of the town and influential in its affairs. These included Thomas Bentham, the first Elizabethan bishop of Coventry and Lichfield, an evangelical veteran of the English congregation at Geneva;[46] and the social taproot of Protestant godliness in the north-west Midlands, the Corbet family of Moreton Corbet. 'Sutche a Juell to all Shropshire' was our chronicler's obituary when Sir Andrew Corbet died in 1578; while Ashton, who was thick with the Corbets, described him as 'the only staid man ... I know in all these parts of the realm'. His son and heir Robert Corbet (whom Sir Philip Sidney called 'cousin') was no less a jewel.[47] The Corbets, with other west Midland families, the Leightons of Wartleborough and the Bromleys of Hallon, bring us within the penumbra and clientage of the most potent and most robustly Protestant political nexus in Elizabethan England: Robert Dudley, earl of Leicester, his Sidney kindred, and Leicester's stepson, the earl of Essex, whose father, Walter Devereux, had been Ashton's employer and patron in his last years.[48] The visits to Shrewsbury of these magnates, always in early summer, Sidney in 1581, Leicester and Essex in 1584, Essex again in 1585, with their attendant celebrations and patriotic and martial demonstrations, literally took the place of the catholic festivities which had marked midsummer in the old days.[49]

Yet the arrival of Tomkys was a sort of landmark, for Tomkys's impact was about the internalisation of Protestant values, in various senses. To be sure, he was not the first 'public preacher' of the town. Ashton was effectively the first, while Edward Bulkeley (1579–82) was the first holder of the title. Bulkeley, as a doctor of Divinity, like Ashton a sometime fellow of St John's, and a clerical pluralist, may have enjoyed more clout than Tomkys ever did. Yet the appointment of Tomkys in September 1582 evidently marked what historians of revolutions call a 'moment' in the history of the town; and it coincided with an attempt to put the office of preacher on a firmer footing.[50] As in some other towns, and Colchester and Ipswich come to mind,[51] we should not see the public or 'common' preacher as some kind of supernumerary luxury, a mere 'lecturer', but as a quasi-episcopal figure, the town's conscience who was looked to for a lead in all religious and moral aspects of its affairs.[52] (How that squared with the rights and interests of the incumbents of urban parishes was another question.) Tomkys's predecessor, Bulkeley, once interceded for a condemned thief, 'a mayde', guilty of a 'tryfull'. Her life was saved.[53] Bulkeley had been paid the enormous salary of £72, £52 of which had been raised from voluntary contributions, £20 from the revenues of the school, to which the tithes of the two principal parish churches had been appropriated. But now the Assembly took steps to lay this burden on the entire rateable community. Tomkys arrived with the commendation of Sir George Bromley, elder brother of Sir Thomas Bromley, lord chancellor, and currently Shrewsbury's recorder. If Tomkys was Bromley's nominee, he seems to have been Bulkeley's choice. Tomkys, Bulkeley and the Bromleys were all Shropshire-Staffordshire men.[54] Tomkys now began to style himself 'Her Majesties Stipendiarie Minister', St Mary's, where he was also incumbent, being a royal

peculiar.[55] Evidently he expected, and was expected, to be a commanding religious presence in the town.

It would be good to know more about Tomkys. On his appointment
he was credited with an MA,[56] but no record of a university education
seems to have survived, although a dedicatory epistle addressed to Sir
Richard Pipe, lord mayor of London and like himself a Staffordshire
man, speaks of Pipe maintaining him in his studies.[57] Tomkys was a
native of Bilston, hard by Wolverhampton, from which address he
published learned translations of works by the Swiss reformer Bullinger,
one of them from the French and dedicated to Bishop Bentham, which
may suggest a connection with the French Protestant world, perhaps
even with Geneva.[58] A high point in Tomkys's career was the sermon
preached before Leicester on the occasion of his visit to Shrewsbury in
May 1584 (and the published version of the sermon helped to make the
visit famous), which hints at an earlier connection with the earl.[59] This
was published, significantly, by the puritan printer Robert Waldegrave,
as was another, catechetical work dedicated to the 'Christian parents
and godly householders' of Shrewsbury, phrases with semi-sectarian
resonances. Such a publication, and pastoral strategy, was indicative of
a radical 'new broom' puritan ministry.[60]

Tomkys was to preside over a godly commonwealth in Shrewsbury.
Such, at least, was his intention, and perhaps the expectation of his
employers. If the inhabitants were to be taxed to pay his stipend, they
were also to be subjected to a weekly poor rate, following a survey of all
poor inhabitants, to be undertaken by the 'best parishioners'. That was
a decision taken in December 1581.[61] Like those other puritan com-
monwealths, John White's Dorchester and Ignatius Jordan's Exeter,
Shrewsbury was also prepared to relieve in times of necessity their
'poore neighbours and brethren in Christ'. This happened in 1593–4,
when the town of Bishop's Castle was devastated by plague.[62] At
another level of policy, an order was made in St Mary's church in
May 1584 (a fortnight before Leicester would sit in the church) to
eradicate certain superstitious images and inscriptions from the north
window (shades of Henry Sherfield's Salisbury), and to remove the
stone altar 'sometimes used to Idolatry', which (surprisingly) still
remained. (A year later, the churchwardens, perhaps not reconciled
to the Tomkys regime, had failed to remove 'a fained miracle' of the
Virgin, to whom the church was dedicated.)[63] St Mary's, where Tomkys was minister, had its own peculiar consistory court, over which he
legally presided. Did this provide effective immunity from episcopal

visitation? It looks like an opportunity to erect a Geneva-style 'discipline' within the parish. The Shrewsbury counterpart to the Ecclesiastical Ordinances of Geneva (or the 'order of Northampton') consisted of seventy-nine visitation articles of Tomkys's making, forty-nine of which apply to the religious duties and behaviour of the parishioners. They laid down stringent requirements in respect of church attendance and sabbath observance, and forbade such 'notorious sins' as scoffing at God's word and indulging in precisely the kind of irreverent excesses in churchyards to which Tomkys would be exposed in the shaming charivari of 1591.[64]

However, all the indications are that Tomkys (unlike White of Dorchester) failed to rally the whole town behind his zealous and forceful ministry. As we have seen, it was not in the nature of the town to be united, and Tomkys was certainly not the person to unite it. Rather his contribution may have been to add religious rancour to existing socio-economic and political animosities. In 1586 the stone font by the door of St Chad's church (a parish in which Tomkys is known to have poked his nose), a 'superstitious' object no doubt, was destroyed and replaced with a wooden font in the choir. But within a few months, a stone font reappeared in the 'olde and usuall place', 'for that the most parte of the parishioners did grudge against the removinge of the same'.[65] One senses a gathering storm, like that provoked in nineteenth-century Barchester by the Reverend Obadiah Slope. Like so many preachers of his ilk, and one thinks of Thomas Upcher in Colchester,[66] Tomkys represented an extra turn or two on the screw of intrusive, provocative godliness: a 'busy controller', the sixteenth century would have called him. However, like Upcher, we do not know that he was ever described or labelled as a puritan. There were other, less troublesome ministers in the town: particularly his under-curate at St Mary's, Evan Thomas, alias John Williams, a minister there for much longer than Tomkys, who was both a learned man and a staunch Calvinist, for the sixty books (fifty-four in folio) which he later bequeathed to the school library included sixteen volumes of scriptural commentaries by Calvin, as well as the *Institutes*, and such essential tools of an erudite clerical trade as the Tremellius Bible; but also such conformable English works as Whitgift's *Defence of the Answer to the Admonition* and Thomas Rogers's *English Creed*.[67]

When Tomkys died in 1592, our Shrewsbury chronicler wrote, not perhaps without irony: 'for whose deathe, of the perfect protestants, was great lamentation'.[68] These 'perfect protestants', not yet 'puritans' one notices, were to stick out like sore thumbs for two or three generations to come. Tomkys's successor but one as public preacher, William Bright, was the senior fellow of Emmanuel College at the time of his appointment, nominated by the master, Laurence Chaderton, and the brother of Timothy Bright, a famous physician and abridger of John Foxe.[69] Bright may have been acceptable to the perfect Protestants, although, if he adhered to the conformist line which Chaderton drew in the sand after the Hampton Court Conference, he was probably not above criticism from that quarter. Somewhat later, the Shrewsbury godly, led by a leading draper and brewer on a large scale, a notable figure in west Midlands godly circles, William Rowley, would rally around a lecturer of their own choice and persuasion, Julines Herring, of whom Archbishop Laud was to say: 'I will pickle up that *Herring* of *Shrewsbury*.' And now these people *were* called puritans, and worse, by the native-born minister of Caroline St Chad's, Peter Studley, who prided himself on being 'the knowne *Anti-puritane* of the County'.[70]

We are now in a position to compare the Reformation in Shrewsbury, as a cultural experience, with what was happening in some other places, between 1560 and the early 1600s. Elsewhere,[71] I have compiled from the raw materials gathered in many volumes of the great Toronto series, *Records of Early English Drama*, what may be called the ideal-typical situation. In the early Elizabethan decades, Protestant preaching, often a comparative novelty, coexisted with elements of a more traditional culture which it tended to appropriate rather than to suppress or supplant. In particular, a locally based and supported drama with roots in the old play cycles, the 'mysteries', and a particular association with the early summer festival of Corpus Christi, was still alive and well, if purged of specifically popish references. It was now appropriated to the new doctrine, with a prominent anti-Catholic polemical edge to it: vices in the costumes of priests and friars, mitres thrust towards the audience horizontally, making the jaws of a wolf.[72] This kind of Protestant culture was opposed to 'false', 'idolatrous' art, not to art as such. It was a model of urban Reformation compatible with the demonstrative, outdoors culture of the streets and common fields: in a word, still part of Merry England.

In many places, there was a kind of sea-change, or climacteric, towards 1580, intensifying in the last two Elizabethan decades. As the indigenous drama died out, which had happened almost everywhere by 1600, the notion of promoting religion by means of plays and pastimes became obnoxious; while the urban magistracy, from whatever motives (public health was one consideration, as well as 'religion' and morals), was increasingly unfriendly to the visits of professional itinerant players, even when these were backed, as such companies usually were, by the clout of some great patron. Typically, the actors were paid off and told to take themselves elsewhere, much as street singers in my London childhood would be bribed to sing 'in the next street'. In the Devon towns of Plymouth and Barnstable, the phrases used were 'to ridd the Towne of them', 'to ridd them out of Towne'.[73] At Chester, not far from Shrewsbury, citizens could even be fined for going out of the city to witness plays and bear-baiting in other places.[74]

In many towns, there was a more general repression of all aspects of traditional festivity and pastime, provoked in good measure by the fact that such activities were bound of necessity to take place on Sundays and other holidays, which, in the increasingly sabbatarian atmosphere of late Elizabethan England, were held to be desecrated by such 'idle' practices: the holier the day, the worse the deed. In early seventeenth-century Norwich, attempts were made to stamp out the pleasant habit of taking summer picnics on the river, as well as morris dancing and cudgel play on the streets.[75] At Chester and York, we can observe the substitution for old 'indecent' customs, such as naked boys dancing in nets, or devils tempting transvestites with beer cans, of a sterner, more martial celebration of militant Christian values, symbolised at Chester by a knight in shining armour.[76] Everywhere, traditional bonfires (but now perhaps without the customary fireworks, which may have been deemed 'unnecessary') were used to celebrate the triumphs and even more the deliverances of a nation inspired and protected by a jealous Protestant God.[77]

Usually, and understandably, what in modern Australia would be called 'wowser', in America 'blue', laws met with spirited resistance. In some communities, and much depended upon the vagaries of local politics, and on personalities, cultural conflict persisted over decades.[78] Elsewhere, the issue was resolved decisively, for or against enforced godliness; often, as, notoriously, at Banbury, in favour of godliness.[79] Since these provincial-urban *causes célèbres*, or even 'moral panics', were inevitably politicised, if not actually political in origin, they may be seen as manifestations either of 'faction', or of the full internalisation of the values of the Protestant Reformation. It depends which end of the telescope you choose to look down.

Shrewsbury conforms in large measure to this model, but with an interesting and inconclusive end to the story. This was not one of the decisive places. The 1560s in Shrewsbury provides a particularly brilliant example of first-generation Protestant festive culture, for this decade belonged to the schoolmaster Thomas Ashton, when the town became a mecca on account of his famous Whitsun plays, staged in the old dry quarry, an ex-monastic site beyond the walls; and subsidised by the corporation and the various 'occupations', utilising old ecclesiastical vestments as costumes. Ashton was a Johnian who seems to have transported to this provincial town the strongest dramatic tradition in Tudor Cambridge. In effect, this was to continue the 'mysteries' by other means, with schoolboys taking the place of artisan actors, but the tradespeople still footing the bill.[80] The imagination of the poet Thomas Churchyard, a native of Shrewsbury, transformed a modest quarry into a kind of neo-classical Theatre, 'both deepe and huge, in goodly auncient guise', seating hundreds, Churchyard said thousands, with evident hyperbole ten, twenty thousand spectators.[81] In 1569, we come across a London haberdasher who had 'none occasion to com to this towne savinge only to see the playes'.[82] Nothing of these evidently lavish productions survives beyond one or two titles, but one of these, 'The Passion of Christ', indicates their continuity with the past.[83] As in John Bale's Canterbury,[84] the schoolboy actors were at the sharp end of a Reformation without tears. But 1569 witnessed the last of Ashton's plays, for by Whitsun 1570 the great man was gone from Shrewsbury. Presently, the staging in the old quarry was dismantled and put to some other use.[85]

As we should expect, there was compensation for Shrewsbury playgoers in the regular visits of players and bearwards under noble sponsorship, which do not seem to have been discouraged.[86] Some of these performances were for paying customers only, even in the middle of the night.[87] But in July 1584 our chronicler records 'a notable stadge playe', performed in the High Street without charge, by the earl of Essex's men.[88] This was as much a part of the mid-Elizabethan cultural scene as Tomkys's sermon, preached before the earl of Leicester seven weeks earlier. According to the chronicler, Shrewsbury was very receptive to visiting entertainers of all kinds. In July 1583 there was an ambitious freak and wild beast show, which included among other attractions a coffin containing a dead child with two heads, a live eagle, a dead porpoise, a fierce wild lynx, and a wonderful kaleidoscope.[89] In July 1590, the entertainment was provided by a troupe of acrobats which included a Hungarian tightrope-walker ('the lick was never seene in Shrewsburie before');[90] in September 1591, as part of the 'fringe' at the assizes, by the soon-to-be-famous showman Banks, a Staffordshire man, and the first of his performing horses. This was a learned animal, who could tell with his hoof how many pieces of money were in his master's purse, and could identify and thank the friendly bailiff who had bade him and his master welcome.[91]

As we have already seen, Sunday for the younger generation was a day for archery and cudgel play; and for churchgoing too? In 1598, the town gaoler supplemented his income by staging 'a great cockfight' in his garden, to which came lords, knights and gentlemen, wagering great sums of money. It was the cocks of Cheshire and Lancashire versus the cocks of Shropshire and Wales, but the event attracted even some Londoners with their cocks. The men of Cheshire and Lancashire won, 'and wannt away with the gaynes'.[92] In 1619, there was morris dancing from street to street, parish to parish.[93] Evidence was heard in 1608–9 in a great law suit concerning disputed land in and around the old dry quarry that the ground was regularly used for 'bearebaytinges, bullbaitings, makinge butts and shooting, for stage plaies and common playes, silver games, wrestlings, Runnings, Leapeinge and other like activities of recreation'.[94] It begins to look as if reports of the death of Merry England in Jacobean Shrewsbury would have resembled those premature rumours of the demise of Mark Twain. However, dead porpoises and educated horses are not what is meant by Merry England. What was dead, or all but dead, was the old calendrical structure, what Ronald Hutton calls 'the ritual year'.[95]

Tomkys the preacher would not have been very happy about all the fun still enjoyed by the townspeople of Shrewsbury. (How ironical that his son should have become a playwright, just like Nathan Field, Ben Jonson's apprentice and the son of the radical puritan John Field!)[96] But Tomkys and his successors were evidently impotent. The sectarian story of Shrewsbury religion in the 1620s and 1630s, Herring's puritan conventicles versus Studley's studied anti-puritanism, can be seen as the end- product of that impotence: retreat from the vision of a city set on a hill into a holy huddle, which the likes of Studley deemed seditious. One reading of the Shearmen's Tree incident is that banning the maypole-like Tree was the one concession won by the preacher from a magistracy otherwise inclined to avoid trouble by tolerating the pastimes and pleasures of the young. As the mascot of the Shearmen it was a concession which the dominant Drapers Company may have been more than happy to make.[97]

It would be a mistake to suppose that all drapers to a man favoured Tomkys's austere reforms and nonconformist radicalism; or that all shearmen were fun-loving opponents of godliness. (But their disorderly Welsh apprentices mostly were.) Yet Tomkys lived with the Drapers Company in a kind of symbiosis. Like his predecessor and all his successors up to the Civil War, he made his home in their Guildhall (the most splendid of Shrewsbury's guildhalls), paid them much-needed rent from his well-lined pockets (corporately, the Drapers were strapped for cash), and addressed to them his bills for repairs and improvements, 'from my studie, colde in winter and melancholick in summer'.[98] Whether the Drapers used Tomkys as their tool, or whether Tomkys manipulated and managed the Drapers with the power of his pulpit utterance is reminiscent of an old difference of interpretation of the Fast Sermons preached before the Long Parliament in the early 1640s. Were the preachers merely mouthpieces and catspaws for their political masters, providing a religious rationale for what had already been decided on political grounds? Or were they pointing the revolutionary way forward, with genuine prophetic inspiration?[99] In Weberian terms, this is to ask: did Tomkys represent that mysterious substance, or factor, 'charisma'; or was he no more than the paid agent of something called 'social control'? I don't think that we shall ever be able to tell. And perhaps we should not even put the question.

13. Religious Satire in English Towns, 1570–1640

ADAM FOX

I

Towards the end of his life, the famous divine William Perkins preached a sermon at Stourbridge Fair, a couple of miles from Cambridge. In his audience were the tradesmen and merchants who had travelled from far and wide to buy and sell at this most famous entrepôt, being drawn 'from the most populous cities and townes of England'. In the congregation were said to be visitors from London and from the great provincial capitals at Norwich, Bristol, Newcastle, Coventry and York. There were representatives from the other ancient cathedral cities of Chester, Lincoln and Worcester, and from the university seats at Oxford and Cambridge. Some came from the expanding ports of Hull and King's Lynn; and others from important market towns such as Bath, Colchester, Derby, Ipswich, Kendal, Leicester, Manchester, Northampton and Nottingham. 'Contempt for religion', Perkins intoned, was the great sin of those days. Not only with 'the simplest fellow in a countrie towne' that 'knowes not one point of religion', but even among 'the better sort', religion was made 'a mocking stock and matter of reproach'. He enjoined his listeners to 'carry home this message to your great towns and cities where you dwell, for in these populous places are the great mockers'.[1]

To a great extent, Perkins was right. The towns were often the greatest centres of mockery, in derogation of religion as of other forms of authority. We need not now accept the customary hyperbole of a godly preacher, decrying the iniquities and infirmities of the reprobate majority, in order to recognise the prevalence of religious ridicule at this time among all social groups and of the importance of urban environments in facilitating it. For the century following the Reformation of the 1530s witnessed perhaps the highest point of polemical religious satire in England, and much of it was filtered through London and disseminated nationwide via the provincial towns.

There were around 600 market towns in England at this time, the majority of which were small in size and simple in structure. Some contained no more than 600 people and most had a population of less than 1,500, being distinguished only by their weekly markets and the fairs which they hosted once or twice a year. But there were among them perhaps 100 county towns or regional centres with populations of up to 7,000 in Elizabeth's reign and these contained, in addition to their more variegated economies and complex social structures, more of the communications infrastructure which facilitated the dissemination of information and ideas.[2] Together with London and the half-dozen provincial capitals at the apex of the urban hierarchy, it was in these larger towns that many of the polemical disputes over doctrinal issues in the period were most visibly played out. The religious complexion of a corporation and the lectureships which they supported helped to give many towns a particular identity in this respect, albeit one often disputed and contested.[3]

From the earliest days of the Reformation ballads and satirical prints began to flood from the London presses, while comic plays and interludes soon crowded the courtyards of urban inns throughout the land. 'The vernacular drama, like every other form of literary expression, was swept into the war of creeds', as E. K. Chambers put it.[4] The religious authorities, both Protestant and Catholic in their turn, sought to exploit these visual and mnemonic devices as the most effective forms of communication in a society where reading skills were still selectively dispersed. One of Thomas Cromwell's propagandists, the lawyer Richard Morison, extolled the value of plays for this purpose, for 'into the common people things sooner enter by the eyes than by the ears'. It was in the same spirit that the bishop of Winchester, John Ponet, wrote to John Bale in exile during Mary's reign: 'Ballads, rhymes and short toys that be not dear, and will easily be born away do much good at home among the rude people'.[5]

Soon after Henry VIII's move to dissolve the monasteries, deriding verses were circulating against the reformed religion which minstrels and travelling players did much to disseminate from town to town. Thus in the spring of 1537, John Hogon, a minstrel from Diss in Norfolk, was found spreading such seditious songs around East Anglia. A little later, and still in the wake of the Pilgrimage of Grace which was convulsing the northern counties, a Dominican friar from Yorkshire, John Pickering, was in trouble for composing a ballad against the new faith, said to be 'in every man's mouth about Bridlington and Ponte-fract'. He admitted to having made it 'rhyme by rhyme that the hearers might better bear it away', but denied that it 'had been sung abroad by minstrels', as was claimed. The following year in Wakefield a song of similar import was also being 'learned by heart by young boys and others'. At the end of June 1538 a minstrel on his travels from Lanca-shire, Alexander Stotson, 'was playing on his feddill and makyng mery' at William Willan's alehouse in Winster near Windermere, Westmor-land, when one of the patrons told him 'to sing a song he had sung at one Fayrbank's howsse in Crosthwaite in the said countye of Westmor-land in the tyme of the rebellion, which song was called "Cromwell"'.[6]

By the following decade, however, a Protestant response in like kind had become fully developed. At Worcester in 1546 a twelve-year-old boy, John Davis, wrote out an anti-Catholic 'ballet called "Come downe for all your shaven crown"'.[7] Two years later a rash of ballads called *Mistress Mass*, lampooning her and mocking her demise, were printed in London and circulated on the streets of the capital. They must also have been dispersed across the country over the following years for, as Margaret Spufford discovered, one version even cropped up at an alehouse in the remote Cambridgeshire village of Orwell in 1553 where a local man, Thomas Cundale, was offering to show a copy to the patrons.[8] By this time, the attempts to reverse the Reformation under Mary were helping to draw more such material to the attention of the authorities. In 1554, John Cornet, 'prentice with a minstrel at Colchester', was at a wedding outside the town and being asked 'to sing some songs of the Scripture, chanced to sing a song called "News out of London"', which tended against the mass and against the queen's mis-proceedings'.[9] In Norfolk, meanwhile, another minstrel, Robert Gold, had been playing his harp 'at the signe of the Wastell' in Wymondham and singing a ballad 'against the Mass and the godly proceedinges of the Catholike faythe of the churche'. James Wharton, a colleague from near King's Lynn who himself carried 'bookes of songes' containing scandalous material, borrowed this composition and two of his apprent-ices were caught singing it in Norwich.[10]

That drama of a similar tenor continued to circulate around the country at the same time is suggested by the visitation articles of Bishop Cuthbert Scott of Chester which, in the last years of Mary's reign, were inquiring after 'any assembles or conventicles wherein is redd previe lecturs, sermons or playes to thindrance or derysion of the Catholike faythe'. In due course, the accession of Elizabeth I in 1558 was said to have been greeted with a flood of 'squibs, lewd lampoons, or ballads' mocking the papacy and its supporters, while interludes and plays of like sort were reported to be 'usually performed in the hostels and taverns' of London. Among the latter were Wager's *The Longer Thou Livest*, written about 1559, Thomas Inglend's *The Disobedient Child*, probably written the following year, and the popular *Nice Wanton*, printed in 1560. The anti-Catholic ballads of the following decade reached a peak in 1570 with the appearance in print of William Elderton's *Northomberland Newes* and *Donstable Way* together with a series of ballads in the form of mock letters to and from the pope, set to the new tune of 'Row well ye Mariners'.[11]

By the late 1570s and 1580s, however, Protestant opinion began to turn against ballads and plays as a means of creating and dispersing anti-Catholic propaganda and humour. The infamous puritan attacks on the stage and profane amusements were paralleled by an increasing distaste, even among more orthodox churchmen, for the treatment of religious matters in this way. From this time, therefore, the evidence for such polemical satire in print becomes less plentiful: Protestant material was ever less liable to be written and Catholic productions were increasingly unlikely to evade the tightening laws of censorship.[12]

It is at this point, then, that it is instructive to direct attention towards the evidence, which becomes more available from the second half of Elizabeth's reign, for the tendency of people in the localities to compose their own rhymes, ballads and jigs in mockery of religion. This practice of inventing such 'libels' to be chanted or sung, and sometimes written out for dispersal, was a familiar feature of the period.[13] Furthermore, amateur verses of this sort seem often to have been found composed, or at least disseminated, in market towns. This tendency may be explained in part by the fact that it was in urban environments where literacy skills were greatest. In towns rhymers would most readily find someone to set down their work and meet with the highest concentration of those with the ability to read it.[14] Moreover, as William Perkins noted, these were the most 'populous places', those in which the opportunities for mass publicity were greatest. At their many taverns, inns and alehouses, in their streets, shops and market squares, and via their public announcements, communal gatherings and staged events, messages could be broadcast to the widest audiences and with the greatest effects.[15]

A typical illustration of this occurred in eastern Wiltshire in June 1611 when Stephen Hewes wanted to expose to general ridicule the name of Virgil Pleydell, a gentleman from the village of Sevenhampton. He took two friends off to the nearest market town, that of Highworth, where at an inn they railed openly in front of the patrons and wrote their message 'uppon the wall...with a peece of chalke playnlie and apparanntlie to be reade'. In addition they framed their scurrility into a rhyme which Hewes 'pasted and fixed' to the market cross. But one of his accomplices was not satisfied, 'sayeing it was not sett up publiquely enough and enquirde of some there present uppon which post of the crosse [the king's] proclamacons used to be sett and there caused the said Hewes to paste the said libell on that poste of the said crosse in open view of the towne'. They then stood in a shop doorway directing passers-by to their handiwork 'with great iollytie and laughter'. Such vehicles of communication – the written word, the inns, shops and other places of 'common resort', the market square with its cross, the density of population – were all available in towns as they were not in villages. Even in the late sixteenth and early seventeenth centuries, what may loosely be described as 'the public sphere' was an essentially urban construction.[16]

II

Much of the mockery of religion which William Perkins had in mind was probably of an age-old anti-clerical variety, disrespectful of the authority of the Church and its ministers. Many of the scandalous lampoons and songs which can be found pasted up and sung on the streets of English towns at this time were of this sort, scoffing at the offices of particular clergymen or simply deriding religion in general. Thus, on Twelfth Night 1623 a libel was afoot in Colchester which depicted several of the town's ministers taking tobacco with the devil. Some years before, John Penne, a husbandman of Bellbroughton in Worcestershire was said to have been 'a man given altogether to frequent alehouses and taverns on Sabbath daies in tyme of devine services' and a great depraver of 'godly preachers'. One of his many 'songs and rhymes', crude but effective, was composed in 1611 against his own vicar, Thomas Tristram, and began: 'If the parson were in hell/and another in his house to dwell/then it would doe well.' Penne would have found a kindred spirit in Sephen Lea of Stratford-upon-Avon who was in trouble in 1624 'for singing profane and filthie songs, scoffing and deriding on ministers and the profession of religion'.[17]

Other libels arose from the parochial squabbles over innumerable issues which seem often to have taken place between a clergyman and his flock. On one such occasion in September 1615 Richard Eaton, the vicar of Great Budworth in Cheshire, found himself the victim of a series of libels which contrived the charge that he 'had gott his benifyce by cosininge, symonie and falsehood' and these were 'fixed... upon diverse poasts in the open streete within the town of Great Budworth aforesaid to the open viewe of all [his] parishioners'. In 1631–2 rhymes were flying around north-west Leicestershire directed against Thomas Pestell, vicar of Packington and Coleorton and previously of that renowned centre of godliness at Ashby-de-la-Zouche. Under the title 'T.P.' or 'Thomas Pluralities', Francis Stacey of Coleorton invented a railing ballad which he touted around the alehouses until it allegedly became 'public and notorious within the said parish' and 'almost in every young man's mouth in Coleorton'.[18]

On occasion, attempts to mock local clergymen could develop into a full-blown charivari with such songs accompanied by musicians and the sound of rough music beaten on pots and pans together with the ritualised 'riding' of the victim backwards on a horse or astride a 'cowlstaff'. Such an act was orchestrated at Upper Mitton in Worcestershire by two local clothworkers, John Hucke and Thomas Hardman, together with William Hardman, a weaver from neighbouring Hartlebury.

> These three with divers other vppon Wensday 20 October 1613 betwixt ix and x of the clocke in the night, beinge gathered together at the house of Thomas Hucke in Mitton tooke Mr Thomas Smithe, curat of Mitton, and by violence putt him vppon a cowlestaffe and caried him vp and downe the towne and caused fidlers beinge then in company to playe by them, and one range vppon a fryinge panne, another blewe a horne and the rest followed makinge a great disorderly noise to the greate disturbance of all the neighbourbood there about.[19]

At other times, general anti-clericalism spilled on to the stage in the improvised interludes and jigs which people contrived on festive occasions. Thus, on the last Sunday in August 1601 at the end of the summer games at South Kyme near Horncastle in Lincolnshire, local yeoman John Cradock the elder got up on the stage and 'in frowne of religion, and the profession thereof, being attired in a minister's gowne and having a corner cap on his head, and a book in his hand opened, did ... in a pulpit made for that purpose, deliver and utter a prophane and irreligious praier' which ran 'The Marcie of Mustard seed and the blessinge of Bullbeefe and the Peace of Pottelucke be with you all. Amen'. He then proceeded to 'reade a text out of the book of Mabb' which was a ridiculous combination of local folklore and traditional tales. Similarly, one Saturday in October 1625 a group of youngsters from Kendal 'brought in a ... showe before a sommer rodd or Maypole, diuers beinge disguysed some in mens apparell and others in womens apparell'. Among them was Anthony Wilkinson who was said to have 'carried a booke in his hand' and to be dressed 'in the habite or shape of a devill' for the 'purpose to deprave and scoff att religion'.[20]

Sometimes anti-clerical libelling might touch even the highest churchmen, as was the case in an incident at Northampton in 1607. It was probably the culmination of a background animosity between Jerome Lowe, a gentleman of Yardly Park, and John Lambe of Northampton, vicar of Yardly Hastings and a proctor of the ecclesiastical court at Peterborough. Lowe, together with his son Francis, Robert Oliver his servant and many others, who had already been responsible for a libel in June of that year 'against the knightes and justices of the county', now published on 22 September, the very day of Archbishop Bancroft's visit to the town, a composition against the ecclesiastical officers of the diocese, accusing them of injustice and uncharity. It took the form of a dialogue in rhyme between a man and a woman and was to be found in the church of Allhallows, 'in the street, in inns and alehouses, in sadlers and smiths and other tradesmen's shops' in the town where it was read out, discussed, passed around and copied. Edmond Wheatley, a husbandman, found a copy in the church but being unable to read it took it to Alexander Hall who 'did reade it out at his request'. A sadler, Richard Trewman, got hold of another transcript and lent it to Thomas Burton 'twice in one daie, and Burton said he woulde give an angell for a coppie of it, and shewe it to his lord'. William Lucas, a smith, seems to have been very active in the dissemination. It was said that he 'reade the libell in an inne in Northampton and the chamberlain looked over his shoulder whilest he read the same'; when Edward Thorowgood, woollen-draper, came into his shop 'Lucas delivered him the libell to reade (sayinge it was a fine thing)'; Thorowgood borrowed a copy and, in turn, told others that 'he had the libel made against the spirituall courte and that he would sende it into Cambridgeshire to his friendes'. Copies were certainly sent up to Leicester and down to Dunstable in Bedfordshire.[21]

That some clergymen were not above giving back as good as they got, however, is illustrated by the behaviour of Thomas Taylor, vicar of Hemel Hempstead. He was, apparently, the author of a series of very salacious rhymes against various of his parishioners over the course of several years between 1617 and 1620. One he was said to have sung with gusto in the local alehouses and taverns 'with greate delight, felicitie and pleasure'; another was also to be 'found in the streets of the said towne of Hemstead'. When his alleged victims eventually took him before the Star Chamber in 1621 to answer for his work he denied all knowledge of it, claiming that they had made up the charges in a vendetta against him 'for pressing them into conformyty'.[22]

III

Beyond the generally anti-clerical, propaganda wars of a more doctrinal and sectional nature were also carried out through these media of song and drama. The attempts of Catholics to mock the Protestant faith and its professors through such means were among those most likely to concern the authorities, of course. In 1594, Thomas Hale, a convicted recusant and member of an old-established family of Catholic gentry from the town of Walthamstow, was indicted before the Essex assizes for having copied down, eight years before, a 'ballad or rhyme' lamenting the loss of the old religion and its replacement by 'a gospell full of heresies'.[23] The first six of its twenty verses ran:

> Weepe, weepe, and still I weepe,
> For who can chuse but weepe,
> To thyncke how England styll,
> In synne and heresey doth sleepe.

> The Christian faythe and Catholick,
> Is everywhere detested,
> In holy servyce, and such like,
> Of all degrees neglected.

The Sacramentes are taken awaye,
The holy order all,
Religious men do begg astraye,
To ground their howses fall.

The Byshoppes and our pastors gone,
Our Abbottes all be deade,
Deade (alas), alyve not one,
Nor other in their steede.

The Churches gaye defaced be,
Our alters are thrown downe,
The walles lefte bare, a greefe to see,
That once coste maney a Crowne.

The monumentes and lefe of Sayntes
Are Brent and torne by vyolence,
Some shedd the holye Sacramentes,
O Christe thy wondrous pacyence.

The polished quality of this piece suggests that Hale may have taken his copy from a printed broadside, or that it was intended to become such, and there is certainly evidence of similar material which seems to have evaded censorship. In October 1600, for example, a tailor's servant stumbled across 'a popishe ballett', sealed and left outside his master's shop in Hereford, about which stationer and book-binder, William Cowper, was examined. The following year, Nicholas Foster, a London schoolmaster, was found in possession of another 'scandalous ballad or libel in print between a Papist and a Protestant' which seems to have favoured the cause of the former. 'I am persuaded that there are many such Pamphlets', wrote John Rhodes in 1602, 'together with other like Romish wares, that are sent abroad amongst the common people, both Protestant and Papists in London and in the country'. He warned against 'certaine women Brokers and Peddlers (as of late in Staffordshire there was) who with baskets on their arms, shall come and offer you other wares under a colour, and so sell you these'.[24]

In the case of anti-Protestant plays, they too continued to be performed cryptically, only occasionally, it seems, being brought to the attention of the authorities. In December 1575, for example, the court of Aldermen in London was informed of the way in which 'one

Sebastain, that wyll not comvnycate with the Church of England, kepethe playes and resorte of the people, to great gaine and pyll of the corrupting of the chyldren with papistrie'.[25] Clearly an effective way of avoiding suspicion was to improvise illicit material into a licensed play. The evidence for what must have been a common practice is rarely so well illustrated as in one remarkable and well documented performance given by a troupe of travelling players, widely known in the north of England when Shakespeare was at the height of his powers.[26] Simpson's Company, otherwise known as Sir Richard Cholmeley's Players, were a band of at least fifteen in number, mostly shoemakers and cordwainers by profession, and Catholics by religion. They toured around Yorkshire in the first and second decades of the seventeenth century where they 'did vse to playe playes in the wynter tyme in townes and gentlmens houses'. The winter of 1609 was no different from any other, taking them across the north of the county through some of its major market towns. From Whitby on the east coast they journeyed down to Pickering and thence across to Helmesley, before travelling through Thirsk to Ripon and as far as Nidderdale in the West Riding. From there, they set off northward towards Richmond before turning for home again via Northallerton. It was at about Christmas time that they found themselves at the upper end of Nidderdale where they stopped at Gouthwaite Hall near Ramsgill, home to Sir John and Lady Julian Yorke, Catholic landowners in the area.[27]

In the great hall at Gouthwaite they offered Sir John a choice from the company's repertoire: either *The Travailes of the Three English Brothers* (1607) or another play, also printed but apparently unlicensed, called *Saint Christopher*. It was to see the latter that over a hundred of the local gentry and their tenants arrived that evening. They were met by Sir John's bailiff, Roger Harbergeon, who kept the door and turned away some sixty people, presumably on grounds of religious sympathy. At least nine members of the company took part in the play which featured Christopher and Robert Simpson in the leading roles, 'one in the likeness of an English or protestant minister and another in the likeness of a popish priest'. During the performance these two, apparently departing from the printed text, improvised a scene in which they did

> counterfeit a forme of disputation in points or matters of religion . . . whether the religion now professed and established by and of his Majestie in the Church of England or the doctrine of the Church of

Rome were the truer or the better. And whilest they thus disputed or seemed thus disputing . . . there was one who played the fooles part and did . . . then and there make words and other foolish and ridiculous gestures or laughed or scoffed or iested at him that played the English minister [and] he that played the fooles part, as aforesaid, sometimes stare[d] in the face of him that played the English or protestant minister and sometimes plucking him and clipping him on the shoulder.

What followed was later described by Sir Stephen Proctor from the neighbouring manor of Fountains, a Justice of the Peace and an enemy of the Yorkes, who had been in the audience. He remembered that

at the [end] of the said counterfeite disputation in the said play, that one of the players [had] in his armes a great yellowe coloured crosse from whence the divells still fled, and the English minister had under his arme or in his hand a booke like a Bible, and being asked what he could say or how he could defend his religion, he answered, 'By this book', and then offering to shew it foorth it was rejected and that after some flasheinges of fire the said English minister was carried away by the divell or divells.

Thus the symbol of the cross was represented as being more powerful than the mere word and it 'appear[ed] to the beholders (being many)' that the Protestant 'was put to sylence and could not tell how to maintain his religion' being carried on the back of a devil to hell. Interestingly, Sir Stephen Proctor related how the players could, like any professional travelling troupe no doubt, adapt their material as the persuasion of the audience and the nature of the occasion demanded. 'When they plaide the said play at any protestant house they . . . would leave out all that part of the said Acte which concerned the counterfeitinge of the said disputation [between the] popishe priest and English minister, and would and could neverthelesse when the owners of the house were popishelie affected, play and acte the same' so as to include these characters. Before travelling on their way, the company treated Sir John's household to a pair of less controversial performances. For they gave on successive nights renditions of two of the great successes on the London stage from the previous year, Shakespeare's *King Lear* (1608) and *Pericles* (1609).

Passing judgement on the perpetrators of *Saint Christopher* in the Star Chamber five years later, Sir Edward Coke summed up the change in official attitudes which had taken place since Thomas Cromwell's day. 'The very bringing of religion on stage', he pronounced, 'is libell.' As for the Yorkes, legal censure does not seem to have deterred them. In 1628 a certain Christopher Mallory was sentenced for having acted the part of the devil in a play at Gouthwaite: apparently he had carried the figure King James down to hell on his back, alleging that all Protestants were damned.[28]

IV

So far as libellous squibs or ballads are concerned, it is perhaps as examples of just such material circulating on the streets and in the alehouses of English towns, Patrick Collinson has suggested, that we should view the seven famous Martin Marprelate tracts, printed between October 1588 and June 1589. They carried a highly successful attack on the bishops and provoked in response a series of anti-Martinist, or anti-puritan, pamphlets in print soon afterwards. The first copies of Martin, it appears, were probably circulated in London in manuscript form before they were set in type, as was then common with many works, especially those of a polemical kind. The bishop of Exeter, John Woolton, wrote to Archbishop Whitgift early in 1588 on hearing of 'a slaunderous libell latelie cast abroad in London intituled Martin Mar Prelate' which had been dispersed in 'written pamphlets that he hath sent from hand to hand full of all malicious slaunders'. Like any other libel, therefore, they seem to have been passed around in handwritten copies and may well have been posted up in public to be read aloud or transcribed to be 'cast abroad'. They were untypical of such material only in that they found their way into print and it was this which helped to spread them so widely and to ensure their notoriety both then and since.[29]

As Collinson suggests, it may well have been Martin and anti-Martin which was responsible for crystallising the stereotypical image of the puritan both in satirical literature and on the stage, as well as in the popular mind. Many examples can be found in the subsequent decades of amateurish ballads and verses, plays and jigs satirising puritanism and its characteristic traits. More surprisingly, given the renowned puritan dislike of Martin Marprelate's methods and the use of humour in general as a polemic weapon, there are also a number of recorded instances of satirical material contrived by those branded as puritans and directed against their more conforming adversaries. In many towns across England, it would seem, rival factions played out their doctrinal and political quarrels through the medium of ridiculing derision in rhyme, song and drama.

In Nottingham, for example, there rumbled through the second decade of the seventeenth century a factional dispute over religious doctrine and practice which produced satirical libels and counter-libels worthy of Martin and anti-Martin polemic.[30] On the one side were members of a godly group within the town which included Anker Jackson, 'an ancient alderman' and several times mayor, and his son George together with Richard Caldwell, a clergyman and 'zealous preacher of the Word of God', George Cotes the parson of St Peter's Church, plus Francis and Christian Hall and Thomas and Margaret Willson, among others. It was alleged, by their enemies, that this group held secret conventicles at Jackson's house at which they 'prayed of their own heads together without the forme of prayer prescribed and catachised each other in the matter of religion after their own fashion'. On Sundays and at other times they would reject the services of the ministers 'in their proper parishes and traveled 5 or 6 myles distant to heare the sermons and exercises of other sectaries which were of their humorous faction'. They were said to believe that

> the signe of the crosse in Baptisme, the ringe in marriage and the cappe and surplisse commanded to be worne by ministers and other decent rights and ceremonies of the Church are superstitious and unlawful. That the Lord's supper must be taken by persons standinge or sittinge and not kneelinge, that the . . . booke of common praier prescribed by [the king's] authoritie is (for the most parte) taken out of the masse booke and therefore unlawful, that the churching of women accordinge to the said forme of the booke of common prayer is a kind of witchcraft. . . .

On the other side was an equally well connected group which included Thomas Nixe, another alderman and mayor of the town, Francis Withington, a clergyman, together with his brother William, plus William Hansby, also a cleric, and other important gentlemen of the country. The former faction charged the latter with popery and the latter returned with accusations of puritanism.

In 1614 Jackson's faction were responsible for a railing rhyme spread throughout the town against Michael Purfrey, claimed by his defenders to be 'a man of a Christian and civil life, of good credit in his countrey'. The libel called for his banishment from Nottingham, 'And then shall this towne be att peaceable rest / For beinge shutt of such a member yt wilbe happie and blest'. Forty copies were said to have been transcribed to be 'published, sunge, spread abroad and divulged' together with other 'such like ribauldry'. The following year another rhyme appeared, this time against William Withington, which suggests that he had already filed some kind of legal action against Jackson or his associates for it referred to 'A lying bill that was made by pursinge Will'. 'Oh then leave off the theevinge trade and spurr att home thy popishe jade', it concluded.

For this insult and ridicule Withington was to have his revenge in 1617. In that year two more songs were in circulation, this time levelled at the conventicling puritans of the town, the second of which was certainly written by him as, it seems likely, was the first. It began:

> My muse arise and truth then tell,
> of a Pure secte that sprang from hell,
> who are so vaine soe false and fickle,
> they leave the Church to Conventicle
> On huge Sct Anker they lay hould,
> who is an hipocrite most bould,
> he travells often to Jordaine,
> where in the lord he taketh gaine.

It was set to the popular tune of 'Bonny Nell' and was played and sung up and down the streets, in the cellar of Collishaw's tavern and in houses of gentlemen all over town. At an alehouse in Lenton, Thomas Nixe asked a piper to perform the song: he obliged only with a different one, at which the alderman stopped him, saying 'that's not the song, I mean the song of the Puritans of Nottingham'. When Nixe eventually heard what he wanted he was said to have laughed heartily at the sport.[31]

The libelling abilities of Anker Jackson and his co-religionists in Nottingham well demonstrate that those people whose Calvinism led them to want further reform of the Church of England, and who so often found themselves abused in this way, were perfectly capable of acting in like kind. This is further illustrated by examples of libels composed against the orthodox, both ministers and others, charging them with popery or with not being true Protestants. At the end of

1603, for instance, long-standing religious controversy in Colchester came to a head again when a libel began circulating in and around the town. The occasion was the feud between Richard Harris, the parson of Gestingthorpe and for ten years prior to this a public lecturer in Colchester, and Steven Newcomin, the minister of St Peter's in the town, said to be 'a particular congregation' of separatists. For a period of weeks before the appearance of the libel, Harris had been speaking out against 'certaine obstinate recusante Brownists' and had from the pulpit been 'disputinge with them sylogisticallie'. At the same time some Brownist sympathisers had lately been imprisoned in Colchester Castle from where they had denounced Archbishop Whitgift as 'the Antechristian Pope of Lambeth'. It was Thomas Dixon, a woolcomber, and Steven Parson, a weaver, aided by Newcomin and Thomas Knevett, another clergyman, together with four others, who were said to have composed, written and distributed the libel in December 1603 and throughout the first three months of the following year, with 'greate delighte and contentemente'. In twenty detailed verses supported by Biblical citations in the margin it combined particular attacks upon Harris with general abuse in Martinist style of episcopacy and the government of the established Church.[32] The fourteenth and fifteenth verses ran:

Rev: 9:3:7:	We are taughte in Scripture plaine that noe suche prelates as nowe there are,
Jeremy: 23:21:	Should be admitted to rule as Lords over theire brethren for lucre sake,
Sephn: 3:4:	Those locusts runne yet are not sente thus usurpe they dare,
	And to mainteine theire wickednes the Worde of God they both turne and racke.
Isay: 9:6:7:	They knowe our Saviour Christe hath soe an order for his Churche govermente,
Mat: 17:5:	And charged the same for to be kepte untill his cominge, nothinge thereto added or abated,
Eph: 1:21:22	
Luke: 22:25:26 et 28:20:	But whoe soe seeth howe muche it is abused with them they sore are discontente,
Mat: 18:15:16: 17:18:19:	To prevente the searchinge for that matter they avouche it not cannonicalle as in English it is translated.

This polemic was still flying around Colchester when Archbishop Whitgift died in March 1604. On the 27th of that month his body was paraded through Croydon and interred in the parish church there. But pinned to the hearse was discovered a libellous verse entitled 'The lamentation of Dickie for the Death of his brother Jockie', these being references to Whitgift and his successor as Archbishop, Richard Bancroft. The apparent author of this doggerel was Lewis Pickering, a puritan gentleman from Northamptonshire who had found favour at the court of the new king, James I. The verses contained familiar puritan complaints over the policy of the Church, deriding Whitgift as 'The prelates pope, the canonists hope', as the 'Reformers hinderer, trew pastors slanderer', and as 'The cermonyes procter' and 'non residens champion'. As Alastair Bellany has shown, this incident was to form the background against which Sir Edward Coke reformulated the law of seditious libel in 1605.[33]

That the authorities failed to prevent the proliferation of such satirical invective, however, is well attested in the politically charged climate of the 1630s, by which time Laudian policies were raising the temperature of religious controversy. The diary of the Suffolk clergyman John Rous, for instance, is littered with examples of the verses and squibs which came into his hands on visits to Bury St Edmunds, Downham Market, Ipswich, Norwich, Thetford and other market towns around East Anglia. In 1635 he brought home a typical jibe at the 'new churchman of the times' and his perceived leanings back towards popery. 'He hopes to be saved by prevision / Of Good workes, but will doe none / He will be no Protestant, but a Christian / And comes out Catholicke the next edition', ran one of six stanzas. 'Many of these rimes came out in these late times, about 1635 and 1636', noted Rous, 'on both sides, some against the orthodoxe, others against these "new churchmen", &c.' More verses attacking salvation by works and popish ceremonies circulated in the following years, including one composition directed at James 'Ceremonius' Buck, the vicar of Stradbrooke. Another flurry of 'railing rimes' on matters of doctrine and Church government appeared in 1640 and 1641 when Rous collected 'A Dialogue Between Two Zelots', 'A Dismall Summons to the Doctor's Commons', 'God Have Mercy, Good Scot', 'The Scholler's Complaint, to the Tune of Alloo, Alloo, Follow My Fancy', 'The Canterbury Bell' and 'The Masse-Priest's Lamentation / For the Strange Alteration begun in this Nation'. All of these and more he transcribed to 'keepe them for president of the times'.[34]

In the decades preceding Rous's collections, it was anti-puritan satire which had been the most common form of religious squib. Libels, taunts and jigs were often inspired by the arrival in a provincial town of a new Calvinist preacher who had radical designs, or so it was perceived, to create a godly commonwealth, a little Geneva in the English provinces. Many of those urban centres which experienced such Protestant evangelism in the early Elizabethan decades, witnessed satirical responses from some of those ill-disposed to be thus reformed. The habit, among many of the plain-spoken godly preachers of the second half of Elizabeth's reign, of using the pulpit to denounce by name notorious sinners in the community, seems to have been partly responsible for provoking a reaction in like kind. Soon after the arrival of the zealous Percival Wiburn in Northampton in 1570, a libellous ballad was circulating against him and actually found its way into print. From the 1560s, Colchester had experienced a wave of reforming zeal which saw magistracy and ministry in alliance to bring about moral regulation and godly discipline. This and the preaching of Thomas Upcher, the rector of St Leonard's, helped to inspire the spate of about fourteen separate anti-clerical libels which, as Mark Byford has shown, were flying around the town in the summer and early autumn of 1575. King's Lynn was another centre noted for its precocious reform at this time, due in no small part to the influence of William Saunderson, salaried town preacher there from the 1560s until 1590. In 1581 a certain John Pell, together with his son Jeffrey and 'diverse others light indeed persons' could be found spreading abroad 'slaunderous libelles, letters and rayling rymes' against, among others, 'Mr Saunderson and Mr Leedes ministers and prechers of God's holly woorde ... contynually resident in the said towne'.[35]

Much the same was to occur in Dorchester during the summer and autumn of 1606, as David Underdown has recently described so well. Soon after the arrival of the staunchly Calvinist minister John White early that year, libels were circulating against him and the doctrines of his supporters. Instrumental in their propagation was Matthew Chubb, bailiff and member of parliament for the town, who disliked White's preaching of predestinarian theology since it offended his own suspected belief 'that a man might be saved by his owne merytts'. One of these compositions which Chubb was said to have read aloud 'openly at a market crosse in one of the streets of the said town' on 4 August, was addressed 'To the execrable Companie of Puritans and the deepest desemblinge Anabaptistes of this tyme'. With fitting irony, it singled out William Perkins, inveigher against just this kind of mockery, who had died in 1602, calling him 'scismaticke dogge and ympe of the dyvell'. It also included the by now familiar jibes against puritan hypocrisy, divisiveness, lechery and pride.

> For noe ones soe symple that on you doth looke,
> But knowes that you live contrary to your booke.
> You carry your Bible, God's Word to expound,
> And yet in all knavery you dailie abound.
> For envies, hatred and mallice great store,
> In noe creatures lyveinge I thinke is more.
> As daily by experience amongst us we fynd,
> To mischeef and hatred none more enclyned.
> Yea, covetousnes, letchery and lyinge for gayne,
> Amongst you Puritans is not counted vayne.
> But first with pride if I should beginn,
> Because it is knowne for a principall synne.

Also involved in the libelling was Robert Adyn, a Catholic recusant of the town who claimed that these squibs 'are not properly to be termed or taken for libells but are rather pamphletts or invectives against malefactors and reported enemyes to the state such as Purytans or Brownists'. He admitted writing one of them himself in October, entitled 'To the Counterfeit Company and Packe of Puritans', after hearing one of White's sermons which had claimed that 'Christ was not the Savyor of the whole world, nor did dye for the synnes of the whole world, but for his elected and chosen people only'.[36]

In just the way that White's arrival in Dorchester immediately caused controversy and polemic within the town, so too did the introduction of Thomas Wilson to the people of Stratford-upon-Avon in March 1619. Within six months, four libels were in circulation deriding Wilson and his like. Two of them, 'A Satyre to the Cheife rulers in the Synagogue of Stratford', and, 'To any honest Puritant where you finde him', also made reference to the works of William Perkins.[37]

In Perkins's Cambridge, meanwhile, there was a tradition of anti-puritan satire centred on the dramatic performances in the colleges which stretched back at least to the first staging of the *Pilgrimage to Parnassus*, in St John's College around 1598. It featured the character of Stupido, a 'plodding puritane', who probably represented a thinly-veiled satire on the formidable William Gouge, then an undergraduate at King's College but already famed for his godly zeal.[38] The following year saw a performance of *Re Vera*, a play left in manuscript and probably written by George Ruggle for staging at Clare College. Although no copy survives, this was also very likely an anti-puritan comedy, commonly known by the title 'Verily' after the popular puritan cant word.[39] When two foreign ambassadors left Charles I in Newmarket early in March 1623 they were given hospitality at Trinity College and there invited to a performance of the new play by John Hacket and Edmund Stubbs, *Loiola* (1648): 'the argument of yt consisted chiefly of a Jesuite and a Puritan', as John Chamberlain wrote to Dudley Carleton.[40] Later that month a company from Queens' College went to Newmarket to stage a royal performance of *Fucus Histriomastix*, probably by Robert Ward. Henry Moll of King's College had obviously been in the audience for he composed some verses on the performance which made reference to the stereotypical puritan demeanour, dress and nasal whine:

> The Puritan surlely lookt very demurely
> With his little ruffe and hose
> Each word that he spoke was as long as his cloake
> And drawn quite through his nose.[41]

There was, however, always a danger of overstepping the mark when performing before the king. On 1 April 1632 the University Vice-Chancellor, Henry Butts, hanged himself in his room with a towel. A contributory factor, among many, to this desperate act seems to have been the offence which Charles I had taken to another performance by Queens' students, this time of Peter Hausted's *The Rivall Friends* (1632), said to have been 'full of scurrility against the gravest ministers of the Kingdome, whome they call Puritans'.[42] Clearly this failed to deter the Queens' men, however, for on 6 February 1637 'a most prophane Comedy' was performed in the College,

> (the compiler of it being a divine and two other of the actors men in orders) and this to the abuse of religion and religious men under the name of puritanisme and puritans. Three of the principall actors in this play were Ipswichus, Linna, [and] Magnecticus, in derision (as was generally supposed) of the townes of Ipswich and Lynn and of Mr Samuell Ward, preacher in Ipswich who had a little before printed a book de Magnete.[43]

That the unpopularity of puritans was taken for granted is revealed by the gratuitous figures which appeared in a mocking play enacted in the precinct of Kendal Castle in July 1621. This was another amateur performance, written by Jasper Garnett, a schoolmaster with local connections, and 'drawn into fower large bookes', in which about twenty local people took a role. Its purpose was to make a polemical point on behalf of the copyholders of the area who were in dispute with their landlords over the local custom of tenant-right. Beneath the stage was an area representing hell and during the action 'there was a jeast betweene Thomas Duckett and Henry Warde who acted the parts of towe clownes' in which they inquired of a boy looking into hell what he saw. He replied that he 'did see Landlords and puritanes and Sheriffs bailiffs and other sorts of people'. This reference to puritans may have been a particular joke for the benefit of the members of the local Catholic gentry who were in the audience, among them Lady Marian Duckett whose household had been partly responsible for providing the costumes for the performance. How many of these Catholic gentry, it is tempting to speculate, had been over the moors in Nidderdale at Christmas time a dozen years before?[44]

V

The struggles for the religious sympathies of the English people which endured, often in the most polemical, virulent and satirical ways, for over a century after the break with Rome were in many ways won and lost on the streets and in the hostelries of the nation's towns. In the rhymes hooted by schoolboys and the ballads sung in market squares, in the jigs improvised at the end of plays and in the interludes staged in tavern courtyards, points were scored and victories won. In a piece of well-drawn caricature or in a good jest, through a witty catch-phrase or memorable tune, messages were easily 'born away' by people and the better impressed upon their minds. Despite the later attempts of the Church to stem the tide of religious satire, it could never entirely control what it had itself started. If William Perkins was able to look out over the towns and cities of England and see only mockery, there was a sense in which he had only the first generation of reformers to blame.

Notes

1. J. S. Morrill, *The Revolt of The Provinces: Conservatives and Radicals in the English Civil War, 1630–1650* (London, 1976; rev. edn, London, 1980).

2. See, for example, M. Coate, *Cornwall in the Great Civil War and Interregnum* (Oxford, 1933); A. C. Wood, *Nottinghamshire in the Civil War* (Oxford, 1937).

3. For a corrective to excessive 'localism', see Clive Holmes, 'The County Community in Stuart Historiography', *Journal of British Studies*, xix (1980), and Ann Hughes, *Politics, Society and Civil War in Warwickshire, 1620–1660* (Cambridge, 1987); for the more recent master narrative, Brendan Bradshaw and John Morrill (eds), *The British Problem*, c. *1534–1707: State Formation in the Atlantic Archipelago* (Basingstoke, 1996), a trend critically appraised by, amongst others, Peter Lake, 'Retrospective: Wentworth's Political World in Revisionist and Post-Revisionist Perspective', in J. F. Merritt (ed.), *The Political World of Thomas Wentworth, Earl of Strafford, 1621–1641* (Cambridge, 1996), pp. 252–83.

4. A revised and updated version appeared in 1989. See also A. G. Dickens, *Reformation Studies* (London, 1982) and further essays and studies in *Late Monasticism and the Reformation* (London and Rio Grande, 1994). On English Reformation studies before and after 1964, see Rosemary O'Day, *The Debate on the English Reformation* (London and New York, 1986), and, more recently, Patrick Collinson, 'The English Reformation, 1945–1995', in Michael Bentley (ed.), *The Writing of History: A Companion to Historiography* (London, 1997).

5. See especially the studies collected in *Lollards and Protestants in the Diocese of York, 1509–1558* (Oxford, 1959; pbk. repr., London, 1982).

6. See some of the papers first read in these colloquia in Rosemary O'Day and Felicity Heal (eds), *Continuity and Change: Personnel and Administration of the Church in England, 1500–1642* (Leicester, 1976), Felicity Heal and Rosemary O'Day (eds), *Church and Society in England Henry VIII to James I* (London and Basingstoke, 1977), Rosemary O'Day and Felicity Heal (eds), *Princes and Paupers in the English Church, 1500–1800* (Totowa, New Jersey, 1981).

7. Christopher Haigh, 'The Recent Historiography of the English Reformation', in Haigh (ed.), *The English Reformation Revised* (Cambridge, 1987), pp. 19–33; Christopher Haigh, 'The English Reformation: a Premature Birth, a Difficult Labour and a Sickly Child', *Historical Journal*, xxxiii (1990), 449–59; Christopher Haigh, *English Reformations: Religion, Politics and Society under the Tudors* (Oxford, 1993). See also J. J. Scarisbrick, *The Reformation and the English People* (Oxford, 1984).

8. See the self-explanatory Preface to Haigh's *English Reformations*. Professor Scarisbrick's credentials as a Roman Catholic historian are not, of course, in doubt; nor those of Eamon Duffy, author of the most influential of revisionist accounts of what happened in the sixteenth century, *The Stripping of the Altars: Traditional Religion in England c. 1400–c. 1580* (New Haven and London, 1992).

But whereas Dr Duffy can only regret the Reformation, he appears resigned, as Dr Haigh is not, to its eventual success.

9. Peter Clark and Paul Slack (eds), *Crisis and Order in English Towns, 1500–1700: Essays in Urban History* (London, 1972); P. Clark and P. Slack (eds), *English Towns in Transition, 1500–1700* (Oxford, 1976); Alan Everitt (ed.), *Perspectives in English Urban History* (London and Basingstoke, 1973). Many of the more important articles inspired by this vogue are reprinted in Jonathan Barry (ed.), *The Tudor and Stuart Town: A Reader in English Urban History, 1530–1688*, in the series 'Readers in Urban History' (London, 1990).

10. Charles Phythian-Adams, *Desolation of a City: Coventry and the Urban Crisis of the Late Middle Ages* (Cambridge, 1979).

11. Alan Dyer, *Decline and Growth in English Towns, 1400–1640* (Cambridge, 1991) reviews the recent state of the question. An important contribution to the debate was the article by R. B. Dobson, 'Urban Decline in Late Medieval England', *Transactions of the Royal Historical Society*, 5th ser. xxvii (1977).

12. Peter Borsay, *The English Urban Renaissance: Culture and Society in the Provincial Town, 1660–1770* (Oxford, 1989). Borsay posits 'a new wave of prosperity' from which 'cultural refinement and prestige' derived (p. viii). See also the essays collected in Peter Clark (ed.), *The Transformation of English Provincial Towns* (London, 1984).

13. Peter Clark, ' "The Ramoth-Gilead of the Good": Urban Change and Political Radicalism at Gloucester, 1540–1640', in Peter Clark, Alan G. R. Smith and Nicholas Tyacke (eds), *The English Commonwealth, 1547–1640* (Leicester, 1979), pp. 167–87; repr. in Barry (ed.), *The Tudor and Stuart Town*.

14. Bernd Moeller, *Imperial Cities and the Reformation: Three Essays*, trans. H. C. E. Midelfort and M. U. Edwards (Philadelphia, 1972); Steven E. Ozment, *The Reformation in the Cities: The Appeal of Protestantism to Sixteenth-Century Germany and Switzerland* (New Haven and London, 1975). To be fair, Moeller and his school did not write a one-eyed religious account of the Reformation in the cities but linked the reception and appeal of Protestantism to the idea of community, or communal identity, in the late medieval city. But 'community' is evidently a 'religious' idea, if not a synonym for religion itself.

15. R. W. Scribner, 'Civic Unity and the Reformation in Erfurt', *Past & Present*, lxvi (1975), 29–60, repr. in Scribner, *Popular Culture and Popular Movements in Reformation Germany* (London, 1987), pp. 185–216, together with 'Why Was There no Reformation in Cologne?', pp. 217–41, originally published in *Bulletin of the Institute of Historical Research*, xlviii (1975), 217–41. See also R. W. Scribner, 'Is There a Social History of the Reformation?', *Social History*, iv (1977), 483–505, and his 'Communalism: Universal Category or Ideological Construct? A Debate in the Historiography of Early Modern Germany and Switzerland', *Historical Journal*, xxxvii (1994), 199–207. Note the acknowledged debt to Scribner in A. G. Dickens, *The German Nation and Martin Luther* (London, 1974), especially in Chapters 7–9, on the cities. The issue is further problematised by the introduction of gender in Lyndal Roper, *The Holy Household, Women and Morals in Reformation Augsburg* (Oxford, 1989), and her ' "The Common Man", "The Common Good", "Common Women": Gender and Meaning in the German Commune', *Social History*, xii (1987), 13–18. And see, most recently, P. J. Broadhead, 'Guildsmen, Religious Reform and the

Search for the Common Good: The Role of the Guilds in the Early Reformation in Augsburg', *Historical Journal*, xxxix (1996), 577–97.

16. Debora Shuger, *Habits of Thought in the English Renaissance: Religion, Politics and the Dominant Culture* (Berkeley, 1990), pp. 5–6. The second assertion is quoted from Frederic Jameson, 'Religion and Ideology: A Political Reading of *Paradise Lost*', in *Literature, Politics and Theory*, ed. Francis Barker *et al.* (London, 1986), p. 39.

17. Beat Kümin, *The Shaping of a Community: The Rise and Reformation of the English Parish* c. *1400–1560* (Aldershot and Brockford, VT, 1996); John Craig, 'Co-operation and Initiatives: Elizabethan Churchwardens and the Parish Accounts of Mildenhall', *Social History*, xviii (1993), 357–80; Eric Carlson, 'The Origins, Functions and Status of the Office of Churchwarden with Particular Reference to the Diocese of Ely', in M. Spufford (ed.), *The World of Rural Dissenters, 1520–1725* (Cambridge, 1995), pp. 164–207; Henry French, 'Chief Inhabitants and their Areas of Influence: Local Ruling Groups in Essex and Suffolk Parishes, 1630–1720', Cambridge PhD thesis, 1993.

18. Phythian-Adams, *Desolation of a City*, pp. 74–9, 158–79; David Harris Sacks, 'The Demise of the Martyrs: The Feasts of St Clement and St Katherine in Bristol, 1400–1600', *Social History*, xi (1986), 141–69; David Harris Sacks, *The Widening Gate: Bristol and the Atlantic Economy, 1450–1700* (Berkeley, 1981), pp. 1–15.

19. Of particular interest for our purposes are the volumes devoted to Chester, Coventry, Norwich and York. See the 'Suggestions for Further Reading' appended to Patrick Collinson's essay in this volume.

20. Harold C. Gardiner, *Mysteries' End: An Investigation of the Last Days of the Medieval Religious Stage* (New Haven, 1946); Patrick Collinson, 'The Protestant Town' and 'Protestant Culture and the Cultural Revolution', in his *The Birth-pangs of Protestant England: Religious and Cultural Change in the Sixteenth and Seventeenth Centuries* (Basingstoke, 1988), pp. 28–59, 94–126; Patrick Collinson, 'Elizabethan and Jacobean Puritanism as Forms of Popular Religious Culture', in C. Durston and J. Eales (eds), *The Culture of English Puritanism, 1560–1700* (Basingstoke, 1996), pp. 32–57.

21. D. M. Palliser, *Tudor York* (Oxford, 1979), esp. Ch. 9, 'Religion and the Reformation'.

22. Patrick Carter's essay, ch. 8 in this volume.

23. Wallace T. MacCaffrey, *Exeter, 1540–1640* (1958; Open University Set Book, Cambridge, MA, and London, 1975), pp. 196–7.

24. See Robert Tittler, *The Reformation and the Towns in England* (forthcoming). See also Victor Morgan, 'The Elizabethan Shirehouse at Norwich', with references to the literature on the Norwich Guildhall, in Carole Rawcliffe, Roger Virgoe and Richard Wilson (eds), *Counties and Communities: Essays on East Anglian History Presented to Hassell Smith* (Norwich, 1996), pp. 149–60; and a forthcoming essay by Dr Morgan on 'Civic Fame in Renaissance Norwich'.

25. See the short essay 'Anticlericalism, Catholic and Protestant', added by Dickens to the 1989 edn of his *English Reformation*, summarising his 'The Shape of Anticlericalism and the English Reformation', in *Late Monasticism and the Reformation*, pp. 151–75. For the opposed views of Christopher Haigh, see his 'Anticlericalism and the English Reformation', in *The English*

Reformation Revised, pp. 56–74. The question is placed on firmly empirical ground in Peter Marshall, *The Catholic Priesthood and the English Reformation* (Oxford, 1994).

26. That the term, however anachronistic to late medieval and Reformation studies, is here to stay is suggested by a massive Europe-wide collection of studies, Peter A. Dykema and Heiko Oberman (eds), *Anticlericalism in Late Medieval and Early Modern Europe* (Leiden, 1993).

27. And see, for a more extensive and fully documented account of these parishes, Kümin, *The Shaping of a Community*.

28. Christopher Hill, *Society and Puritanism in Pre-Revolutionary England* (London, 1964), especially Ch. 14, 'Individuals and Communities'.

29. *A Survey of London by John Stow*, 2 vols, ed. C. L. Kingsford (Oxford, 1908); Ian Archer, 'John Stow's *Survey of London*: the Nostalgia of John Stow', in David L. Smith, Richard Strier and David Bevington (eds), *The Theatrical City: Culture, Theatre and Politics in London, 1576–1649* (Cambridge, 1995), pp. 17–34.

30. Sacks, *The Widening Gate*, title of ch. 5.

31. We owe this suggestion to the biblical scholar, the late Professor Hedley Sparks.

32. Quoted, Collinson, *Birthpangs of Protestant England*, p. 29; and see ibid., pp. 28–31 for a more extensive treatment of the 'city set on an hill' theme.

33. *Geneva Bible* (1560) sig. AAi; David Underdown, *Fire from Heaven: Life in an English Town in the Seventeenth Century* (London, 1992); *The Woefull and Lamentable wast and spoile done by a suddaine fire in S. Edmonds-bury in Suffolke* (London, 1608).

34. *Sermons by Hugh Latimer*, ed. G. E. Corrie, Parker Society (Cambridge, 1844), pp. 196–7.

35. Collinson, *Birthpangs*, p. 31.

36. Patrick Collinson, 'Biblical Rhetoric: the English Nation and National Sentiment in the Prophetic Mode', in Claire McEachern and Debora Shuger (eds), *Religion and Culture in Renaissance England* (Cambridge, 1997); Collinson, 'The Protestant Nation', in *Birthpangs*, pp. 1–27. A much fuller account of 'Paul's Cross Prophecy' will be found in Alexandra Walsham's Cambridge PhD thesis, 'Aspects of Providentialism in Early Modern England' (1995), forthcoming from the Oxford University Press in published form.

37. British Library, MS. Add. 48064, fol. 47^r.

38. Patrick Collinson, *The Religion of Protestants: The Church in English Society, 1559–1625* (Oxford, 1982), pp. 170–7; Patrick Collinson, 'Episcopacy and Pseudo-Episcopacy in the Elizabethan Church', *Collogue de Strasbourg, Septembre 1983 sur L'Institution et Les Pouvoirs dans les Eglises de L'Antiquité a nos Jours*, ed. Bernard Vogler, *Miscellanea Historiae Ecclesiasticae*, VIII, *Bibliotheque de la Revue D'Histoire Ecclésiastique*, 72 (Louvain, 1987), pp. 229–38.

39. Norfolk Record Office, King's Lynn, Kings Lynn Hall Books KL/C7/7, fols 253^v, 149, 362^v.

40. Collinson, *Religion of Protestants*, pp. 176–8.

41. Thetford Borough Records T/C1/1, p. 74 (entry for 23 February 1578(9)).

42. William Burton, *Seven Dialogues both Pithie and Profitable* (1606), sig. A2.

43. British Library, MS. Harl. 7517, fols 35^r, 36^r.

44. Patrick Collinson, 'Lectures by Combination: Structures and Characteristics of Church Life in 17th-Century England', in Collinson, *Godly People: Essays on English Protestantism and Puritanism* (London, 1983), pp. 467–98.

45. On education, see John Morgan, *Godly Learning, Puritan Attitudes towards Reason, Learning and Education, 1560–1640* (Cambridge, 1986); on Sabbatarianism, Patrick Collinson, 'The Beginnings of English Sabbatarianism', in *Godly People*, pp. 429–33, Kenneth Parker, *The English Sabbath* (Cambridge, 1988).

46. John Craig, 'Reformation, Politics and Polemics in Sixteenth-Century East Anglian Market Towns', Cambridge PhD thesis, 1992, ch. 3; *HMC Report, Various Collections*, VII, 266, 86, 83. Cf. the orders passed in Leicester, enforcing attendance at the weekly sermons on Wednesdays and Fridays and instruction in the catechism for all children over the age of eight. (Mary Bateson (ed.), *Records of the Borough of Leicester, 1509–1603*, 3 vols (Cambridge, 1905), vol. 3. 101, 118, 162, 183.)

47. L. J. Redstone and E. Stokes (eds), 'Calendar of the Muniments of the Borough of Sudbury', *Proceedings of the Suffolk Institute of Archaeology and History*, XIII (1909), 280. Examples of the Colchester placards are preserved in the Essex Record Office in Colchester: Book of Tumbril Signs, Acc. C.l.

48. PRO, S. P. 12/78/38; Patrick Collinson, *The Elizabethan Puritan Movement* (London, 1967; paperback edn, Oxford, 1990), pp. 141–3.

49. B. Mackerell, *The History and Antiquities of the Flourishing Corporation of King's Lynn* (London, 1738), p. 231.

50. Thetford Borough Records, T/Cl/2, p. 90 (25 December 1582).

51. Ibid. (28 December 1582).

52. Ibid., p. 91 (25 February 1583).

53. Palliser, *Tudor York*; MacCaffrey, *Exeter, 1540–1640*; Graham Mayhew, *Tudor Rye* (Falmer, 1987). See also Claire Cross, 'Parochial Structures and the Dissemination of Protestantism in Sixteenth Century England: a Tale of Two Cities', in Derek Baker (ed.), *The Church in Town and Countryside: Studies in Church History*, XVI (Oxford, 1979), 269–78, and 'Wills as Evidence of Popular Piety in the Reformation Period: Leeds and Hull 1520–1640', in David Loades (ed.), *The End of Strife: Reconciliation and Repression in Christian Spirituality* (London, 1984), pp. 44–57; Elaine Sheppard, 'The Reformation and the Citizens of Norwich', *Norfolk Archaeology*, XXXVIII (1983), 84–95; Muriel McClendon, ' "Against God's Word": Government, Religion and the Crisis of Authority in Early Reformation Norwich', *Sixteenth Century Journal*, XXV (1994), 353–69, and 'Religious Toleration and the Reformation: the Case of Norwich in the Sixteenth Century', in Nicholas Tyacke (ed.), *The Long Reformation* (forthcoming). See also a recent account of the Reformation in Shrewsbury: Barbara Coulton, 'The Establishment of Protestantism in a Provincial Town: a Study of Shrewsbury in the Sixteenth Century', *Sixteenth Century Journal*, XVII (1996), 307–35.

54. Sacks, *The Widening Gate*; Martha C. Skeeters, *Community and Clergy: Bristol and the Reformation c. 1530–c. 1570* (Oxford, 1993).

55. MacCaffrey, *Exeter, 1540–1640*; Underdown, *Fire from Heaven*; Peter Clark, 'Reformation and Radicalism in Kentish Towns c.1500–1553', in W. Mommsen *et al.*, *Stadtbürgertum und Adel in der Reformation* [*The Urban Classes, the Nobility and the Reformation: Studies on the Social History of the Reformation in England and*

Germany] (Stuttgart, 1979) (and see also his *English Provincial Society from the Reformation to the Revolution: Religion, Politics and Society in Kent, 1500–1640*, Hassocks, 1977); David Marcombe, *English Small Town Life: Retford, 1520–1642* (Nottingham, 1993).

56. Lucy Hutchinson, *Memoirs of Colonel Hutchinson*, ed. Julius Hutchinson (Everyman edn, 1908, repr. 1965), p. 92.

57. As we have explained in the Preface, John Craig's essay on the reformation in Hadleigh, originally intended for this volume, will appear elsewhere.

58. Scarisbrick, *The Reformation and the English People*, p. 1.

59. See especially his essays, 'The Early Expansion of Protestantism in England, 1520–58', and 'Early Protestantism and the Church in Northamptonshire', in *Late Monasticism and the Reformation*, pp. 101–49.

60. John Bruce (ed.), *The Correspondence of Matthew Parker*, Parker Society (Cambridge, 1853), p. 105.

61. F. M. Powicke, *The Reformation in England* (Oxford, 1941), p. 1.

62. R. Po-Chia Hsia (ed.), *The German People and the Reformation* (Ithaca and London, 1988); P. Broadhead, 'Popular Pressure for Reform in Augsburg, 1524–1534', in Mommsen, Alter and Scribner (eds), *Stadtbürgertum und Adel*, pp. 80–7; Broadhead, 'Guildsmen, Religious Reform and the Search for the Common Good'.

63. Haigh, *English Reformations*.

64. Neale Lecture and Colloquium in British History (University College London, 1996): 'The Long Reformation: Catholicism, Protestantism and the Multitude in England, *c.* 1500–1800'. The Neale Lecture, under that title, was given by Dr Eamon Duffy. It will be published, with supporting papers, in a volume edited by Nicholas Tyacke (UCL Press, 1997).

65. See the debate arising from Eamon Duffy's *Stripping of the Altars*: and, in particular, David Aers, 'Altars of Power', *Literature and History*, 3rd ser. III (1994), 90–105, and Duffy's response in the same journal, IV (1995), 86–9.

66. J. S. Morrill, *The Nature of the English Revolution* (London, 1993), Part I, 'England's Wars of Religion', pp. 31–175. Ann Hughes, 'Religion and Society in Stratford upon Avon, 1619–1638', *Midland History*, XIX (1994), 58–84; David Harris Sacks, 'Bristol's "Wars of Religion"', in R. C. Richardson (ed.), *Town and Countryside in the English Revolution* (Manchester, 1992), pp. 100–129.

67. Collinson, *Birthpangs of Protestant England*, Chapter 5, 'Wars of Religion'; Patrick Collinson, 'The Cohabitation of the Faithfull with the Unfaithful', in O. Grell, J. Israel and N. Tyacke (eds), *From Persecution to Toleration* (Oxford, 1991), pp. 51–76; Peter Lake, '"A Charitable Christian Hatred": the Godly and their Enemies in the 1630s', in Durston and Eales (eds), *The Culture of English Puritanism*, pp. 145–83.

68. Albert Peel (ed.), *A Seconde Parte of a Register*, 2 vols (Cambridge, 1915), I, 238–41.

69. Collinson, *Elizabethan Puritan Movement*, p. 142.

70. PRO, S. P. 12/150/97. Saunderson had powerful enemies in the town as early as *c.*1574 (*Seconde Parte of a Register*, I, 98–9).

1. THE BIRTH OF A PROTESTANT TOWN   *Mark Byford*

1. J. G. Nichols (ed.), 'Narratives of the Days of the Reformation', *Camden Society*, LXXVII (1859), 212.

2. See, *inter alia*, C. Haigh, *English Reformations* (1993), pp. 197–8; A. G. Dickens, *The English Reformation* (2nd edn, 1989), pp. 303–4; P. Collinson, *Archbishop Grindal*, (1979), pp. 114–15. An honourable exception is the article by Jennifer Ward, 'The Reformation in Colchester, 1528–1558', *Essex Archaeology & History*, 15 (1983).

3. For an excellent summary, of these factors, see C. Haigh, 'The Recent Historiography of the English Reformation', in his (ed.), *The English Reformation Revised* (1987), pp. 19–29.

4. Ward, 'Reformation in Colchester', 84.

5. *Victoria History of the County of Essex*, IX (1994), pp. 64–5, 331.

6. W. G. Benham, *The Red Paper Book of Colchester* (1902), p. 92; Haigh, *English Reformations*, p. 119; *Letters and Papers, Foreign and Domestic, of the Reign of Henry VIII*, VII, no. 406; G. R. Elton, *Policy and Police* (1972), pp. 176–82, 209; Foxe, IV, p. 585 and V, p. 34.

7. B. Usher, 'Colchester and Diocesan Administration, 1539–1604': Essex Record Office (ERO) T/Z 440/1, passim; ERO D/ACR 4, fol. 82; D/ABW 33/126; Ward, 'Reformation in Colchester', 86, 89; *VCH Essex*, IX, p. 320.

8. Usher, 'Colchester and Diocesan Administration', pp. 6, 10, 31, 33; *VCH Essex*, IX, p. 325; E. P. Dickin, 'The Embezzled Church Goods of Essex', *Essex Archaeological Society Transactions*, XIII, 165.

9. *VCH Essex*, IX, pp. 303–8.

10. Ward, 'Reformation in Colchester', 87–9; E. Duffy, *The Stripping of the Altars* (1992), pp. 513ff. The foundation of chantries in Essex had ceased by this date, in contrast to some other areas, such as the north and west of England: cf. R. Whiting, 'Local Responses to the Henrician Reformation', in D. MacCulloch (ed.), *The Reign of Henry VIII: Politics, Policy and Piety* (1995), pp. 213–15.

11. *Letters and Papers, Foreign and Domestic, of the Reign of Henry VIII*, XIV (1), pp. 462–3; ERO D/B 5 CR104 rot. 3.

12. Ward, 'Reformation in Colchester', 86–7, 90; *Letters and Papers, Foreign and Domestic, of the Reign of Henry VIII*, XVIII (2), p. 331; XXI, pp. 417, 550–1, 586, 648; *Acts of the Privy Council of England*, ed. J. R. Dasent (32 vols, London, 1890–1907; hereafter *APC*), vol. I, pp. 418, 464, 485–6; C. Wriothesley, 'A Chronicle of England during the Reigns of the Tudors', *Camden Society*, 11 (1875), 90; J. E. Oxley, *The Reformation in Essex to the Death of Mary* (1965), pp. 147–8.

13. ERO D/ACA 1, fo 90v; M. S. Byford, 'The Price of Protestantism: Assessing the Impact of Religious Change on Elizabethan Essex: the Cases of Heydon and Colchester, 1558–1594' (University of Oxford DPhil thesis, 1988), pp. 150–1. These factors were apparently unknown to R. Houlbrooke in his *Church Courts and the People during the English Reformation* (1979) p. 240; and to Whiting, 'Local Responses to the Henrician Reformation', p. 213, who incorrectly extends the evidence from St Giles' to the whole of Colchester. I am grateful to Dr Janet Cooper for help on the number of parishioners in St Giles' parish.

14. The estimate for the Lollards is based on the detections arising from John Hacker's confessions, on which see Haigh, *English Reformations*, pp. 63–4, and

Ward, 'Reformation in Colchester', 84–5. For Colchester's population cf. *VCH Essex*, IX, p. 67.

15. Haigh, *English Reformations*, pp. 168–83; Ward, 'Reformation in Colchester', 87–9.

16. E. Cardwell, *Documentary Annals* (1844), I, pp. 93–6.

17. Usher, 'Colchester and Diocesan Administration', passim.

18. British Library (BL) MSS Stowe 829, fo. 30r; Usher, 'Colchester and Diocesan Administration', p. 10. Colchester's livings were similarly placed to those in Ipswich following the Dissolution, on which see D. MacCulloch and J. Blatchly, 'Pastoral Provision in the Parishes of Tudor Ipswich', *Sixteenth Century Journal*, XXII, no. 3 (1991), 458–62.

19. ERO D/Y 2/7, p. 13; see P. Collinson, *The Religion of Protestants* (1982), pp. 171–7. MacCulloch and Blatchly are wrong to imply that there were any amalgamations of parishes or demolitions of churches in Colchester in the sixteenth century: cf. *idem*, 'Pastoral Provision', 462.

20. P. Hughes, *The Reformation in England* (1953), II, 141; *The Acts and Monuments of John Foxe*, ed. G. Townsend and S. R. Cattley (8 vols, London, 1837–41; hereafter Foxe), VIII, p. 393; Byford, 'Price of Protestantism', pp. 113–14, 227–31.

21. Ibid., pp. 113, 181; Oxley, *Reformation in Essex*, pp. 166–7; J. Fines, *A Biographical Register of Early English Protestants*, typescript deposited in Bodleian Library, sn. Putto; ERO D/B 5 Cr122, rot. 4d; Putto's presentment is printed in W. G. Benham, 'Twelve Colchester Persons Indicated as Heresy in 1566 [*sic*]', *Essex Review*, 50 (1941), 157–62. Much of this article is inaccurate. For Mile End, cf. *VCH Essex*, IX, pp. 402–7.

22. Foxe, VIII, p. 139.

23. On the difficulties of the Marian authorities in filling poor urban parishes, see the example of Ipswich in MacCulloch and Blatchly, 'Pastoral Provision', 463–5; Usher, 'Colchester and Diocesan Administration', passim; ERO T/A 105, fos 57v, 62r & v, 72r, 77v; Foxe, VIII, p. 304.

24. *APC*, V (1892), p. 395; Byford, 'Price of Protestantism', pp. 112–13; Foxe, VIII, p. 384; J. G. Nichols (ed.), 'The Diary of Henry Machyn', *Camden Society*, XLII (1848), 6, 13; Fines, *Biographical Register*, sn. Whitehead. See also Dickens, *English Reformation*, pp. 274–5, and Haigh, *English Reformations*, p. 228. I am grateful to Mr B. Usher for help on the identity of William, a Scot.

25. See J. W. Martin, *Religious Radicals in Tudor England* (1989), pp. 128–33; Foxe, VII, p. 738.

26. Ibid., VIII, pp. 382–3.

27. Haigh, *English Reformations*, pp. 223–30; ERO D/B 5 Cr122, rot. 4d; Foxe, VIII, appendix VI.

28. Ibid., VI, p. 740; *APC*, 5, pp. 134, 137. See also ibid., pp. 141, 153 viz. the Council's concern about the management of the burnings; ERO D/B 5 Cr (1553–8).

29. Foxe, VIII, pp. 414, 382–3, 384 n.5, 390; *VCH Essex*, IX, pp. 108–9; Nichols, 'Narratives', 212; Byford, 'Price of Protestantism', pp. 118–19, 158–62. Allerton's argument echoes Peter Martyr's view, expressed in his *Treatise of the Cohabitation of the Faithful with the Unfaithful* (1555), that no company was to be kept with incorrigible unbelievers: cf. P. Collinson, 'The Cohabitation of the Faithful

with the Unfaithful', in O. Grell, J. Israel and N. Tyacke (eds), *From Persecution to Toleration* (1991), pp. 64–5. I am grateful to Ian Archer for this reference. See also A. Walsham, *Church Papists* (1993), pp. 37–8, 109–10.

30. Byford, 'Price of Protestantism', p. 117; Canterbury witnessed more burnings, but it cannot be shown that any of the victims were natives of the town: cf. P. Collinson, N. Ramsay and M. Sparks (eds), *A History of Canterbury Cathedral* (1995), pp. 164–5.

31. Foxe, viii, pp. 387, 389–90, 422–3.

32. Byford, 'Price of Protestantism', p. 116; Foxe, viii, pp. 392, 421.

33. Bonner is quoted in G. Alexander, 'Bonner and the Marian Persecutions', in Haigh, *Reformation Revised*, p. 160; Margaret Aston, *Faith and Fire: Popular and Unpopular Religion, 1350–1600* (1993), p. 300. Moral offenders in Colchester were usually sentenced to walk the length of the market place, and then stand for an hour in front of the Moot Hall door proclaiming their offence, cf. W. J. Pressey, 'Penance in Essex', *Essex Review*, L, no. 200 (1941), p. 215. For other examples of ecclesiastical penance cf. Byford, 'Price of Protestantism', pp. 319–20, 400; on the subject of heretics' burnings as spectacle see D. Nicholls, 'The Theatre of Martyrdom in the French Reformation', *Past & Present*, 121 (1988), passim.

34. BL MSS Harleian 425, fo. 119v; Foxe, viii, pp. 383, 392, 305.

35. D. Loades, *The Reign of Mary Tudor* (2nd edn 1991), p. 384; BL MSS Harleian 416, fos 74r, 75r; Nicholls describes a similar failure of the 'theatre of martyrdom' in the French Reformation. In his view, in order to work such policies required a complete lack of sympathy for heretics' views in their local community, conditions which did not apply once the Reformation had begun to take hold: see Nicholls, 'Theatre of Martyrdom', 71–3.

36. Alexander, 'Bonner and the Marian Persecutions', in Haigh, *Reformation Revised*, p. 165; see also Haigh, *English Reformations*, pp. 231–3.

37. BL MSS Harleian 416, fo. 74v; Byford, 'Price of Protestantism', pp. 117–26; Foxe, viii, pp. 138–40, 304–7, 382–4; J. Foxe, *Acts and Monuments* (1563), p. 1610 (margin); Elizabeth Pepper claimed that she 'was apprehended by two constables *and an alderman* [my italics] for that she would not come to church': ibid., p. 1524.

38. ERO D/B 5 Cr (1553–8), passim; ERO D/B 5 Cr122, rot. 4d; D. M. Loades, 'The Essex Inquisitions of 1556', *Bulletin of the Institute of Historical Research*, 35 (1962); Foxe, viii, pp. 139–40.

39. Ibid., viii, p. 140; Nichols, 'Narratives', 211–12; J. Webb, 'Peter Moone of Ipswich (d. 1601): A Tudor Tailor, Poet and Gospeller and his Circle', *Proceedings of the Suffolk Institute of Archaeology and History*, 38 (1993), 39–41.

40. Byford, 'Price of Protestantism', pp. 117–22; on the social composition of the Marian martyrs cf. M. Spufford, 'Puritanism and Social Control?', in A. J. Fletcher and J. Stevenson (eds), *Order & Disorder in Early Modern England* (1985), p. 46; see also Alexander, 'Bonner and the Marian Persecutions', in Haigh, *Reformation Revised*, pp. 165–6; Nichols, 'Narratives', 211–12; Foxe, viii, p. 388.

41. Quoted in Foxe, v, p. 131.

42. W. Wilkinson, *A Confutation of certaine articles delivered unto the familye of love* (1579), preface; Byford, 'Price of Protestantism', p. 117. The reference is to Matthew v: 14–15.

43. Wilkinson, *Confutation*, preface. This account is extensively discussed by C. W. Marsh, *The Family of Love in English Society, 1550–1630* (1994), pp. 54–64.

Marsh suggests that Orinel may in fact have been a Familist himself by the time he recounted the episode. It is also discussed by M. Spufford, *Contrasting Communities* (1974), pp. 246–8, and Martin, *Religious Radicals*, pp. 130–1, 206–7.

44. Foxe, VIII, pp. 303–10; Martin, *Religious Radicals*, p. 132; ERO D/B 5 Cr122, rot. 4d; Byford, 'Price of Protestantism', p. 120; P. Collinson, *Elizabethan Essays* (1994), pp. 166–68.

45. Haigh, *English Reformations*, pp. 62–4; W. Hunt, *The Puritan Moment* (1983), pp. 87–8.

46. DNB, *sn.* Pullain; H. J. Cowell, 'The Sixteenth-Century English-Speaking Refugee Churches at Geneva and Frankfurt', *Proceedings of the Huguenot Society of London*, XVI, no.2 (1937–41), 222; Anon., *A Brieff Discours off the troubles begonne at Franckford . . .* (Heidelberg, 1574), p. 188; *APC,* VII, p. 71; Byford, 'Price of Protestantism', p.184 n.58.

47. *APC*, VII, p. 87; J. Strype, *Annals of the Reformation* (1824) I, i, p. 229; P. L. Hughes and J. F. Larkin, *Tudor Royal Proclamations* (1969) II, p. 102–3; F. A. Youngs, *The Proclamations of the Tudor Queens* (1976), pp. 188–9; C. Haigh, *Elizabeth I* (1988), pp. 31–3.

48. *The Seconde Parte of a Register*, ed. A. Peel (1915) II, pp. 49–56, 58–9; Byford, 'Price of Protestantism', pp. 131, 185 n.61.

49. ERO D/B 5 Cr125, rot 1d; *VCH Essex*, IX, p. 111; *Letters and Papers, Foreign and Domestic, of the Reign of Henry VIII*, XIV (1), pp. 462–3; GL MS 9535/1, fos 89v, 91v; ERO D/Y 2/2, p. 65.

50. In 1556, Bonner's commissary suggested that church attendance might be improved if 'the householders might be compelled to bring every man his own wife to her own seat in the church in time of divine service': Foxe, VIII, p. 306.

51. Byford, 'Price of Protestantism', pp. 135–6; ERO D/B 5 Cr126.

52. In this respect, Pulleyne's status in Colchester was not unlike Grindal's in London: cf. Collinson, *Grindal*, pp. 91, 115.

53. Usher, 'Colchester and Diocesan Administration', passim; Corpus Christi College Cambridge MS 122, fos 50–3; W. Pressey, 'The State of the Church in Essex in 1563', *Essex Review*, XLVI (1937), no. 182, p. 154.

54. Benjamin Clere's answer to chancery petition: PRO C. 3/132/67; GL MS.9537, vol. 2 (1561–2), fos 57r–65r; ERO D/B 5 Sr6, rot. 13; Usher, 'Colchester and Diocesan Administration', pp. 18, 21, 34; ERO D/B 5 Sb 2/2, fo. 49v.

55. Corpus Christi College Cambridge MS 122, fos 50–3; Collinson, *Grindal*, pp. 114, 172; Byford, 'Price of Protestantism', pp. 137, 139, 186 n.77. The archdeaconry was usually held in plurality by a non-resident, cf. Oxley, *Reformation in Essex*, pp. 274–8. Pulleyne was rector of Copford from March 1560, but was listed as non-resident there in the 1561 visitation: Guildhall Library MS 9537, vol. 2, fo. 67v. I am grateful to Mr Brett Usher for this reference.

56. In August 1557, the bailiffs of Colchester had 'received letters from the council for the attachment of certain persons, and especially of one priest, whose name is Pulleyne': Foxe, VIII, p. 305.

57. ERO D/B 5 R5, fo. 45v.

58. Ibid., fos 83r, 86r & v; BL MSS Stowe 829, fo. 84r; on Pykas cf. Haigh, *English Reformations*, pp. 63–4.

59. ERO D/Y 2/2, pp. 115, 117; P. Collinson, *The Elizabethan Puritan Movement* (1967), p. 50; Byford, 'Price of Protestantism', pp. 247, 250–2; ERO D/B 5 Sb 2/2, fo. 49v; R. H. Tawney and E. Power, *Tudor Economic Documents* (1924) I, p. 310.

60. Byford, 'Price of Protestantism', pp. 143–7, 187; ERO D/B 5 R5, fos 12v–13r.

61. Byford, 'Price of Protestantism', pp. 147, 187 n.88; ERO D/B 5 R5, fos 49r, 130v; ERO D/Y 2/2 p. 117. Pulleyne's 'gynaecological' sermons may have expounded the need for sexual abstinence between husband and wife during menstruation and the lochia (post-childbirth bleeding), subject-matter which was still distasteful to the auditory of the preacher at Banbury, William Whately, some sixty years later. See William Whately, *A Bride-Bush: Or a Direction for Married Persons* (London, 1619), pp. 21–4. I am grateful to Dr John Craig for this reference.

62. Byford, 'Price of Protestantism', pp. 158–62; ERO D/B 5 Cr 125; ERO D/B 5 R5, fos 33r, 34v; on recusancy see Haigh, *English Reformations*, pp. 258–61.

63. On the unsettledness of the 1560s cf. N. Jones, *The Birth of the Elizabethan Age* (1993), esp. pp. 25–35; Byford, 'Price of Protestantism', pp. 162–4; ERO D/B 5 Cr 129, rot. 1d; C. Garrett, *The Marian Exiles* (1938), p. 123; Corpus Christi College Oxford MS 316, fos 67r–68r.

64. Byford, 'Price of Protestantism', ch. 4; ERO D/Y 2/9, p. 373; D/Y 2/6, pp. 82, 134; P. Collinson, *Godly People: Essays on English Protestantism and Puritanism* (1983), pp. 8, 480; idem, *Religion of Protestants*, pp. 129–30, 172–4; idem, *Elizabethan Puritan Movement*, pp. 246, 256–7.

65. ERO D/B 5 R5, fo. 94v.

66. ERO D/B 5 R6, fos 214v–215v; D/B 5 R7, fo. 152r; Byford, 'Price of Protestantism', pp. 377–8, 385–7, 391–2; ERO D/B 5 Gb 1, fos 10r & v, 17r.

67. J. S. Craig, 'The Bury Stirs Revisited: an Analysis of the Townsmen', *Proceedings of the Suffolk Institute of Archaeology and History*, XXXVII, Part 3 (1991), 208–23.

68. *VCH Essex*, IX, p. 81; Byford, 'Price of Protestantism', pp. 156–7.

69. Byford, 'Price of Protestantism', ch. 3, esp. pp. 225–32, 249–57; on the marriage of Clere's daughter, Sarah, to Nicholas Challenor, cf. ibid., pp. 199, 271–2; ERO D/B 5 Sb 2/2, fo. 84v; PRO STAC 5 C.81/23; STAC 5 C.70/2, answer of Christopher Johnson.

70. Byford, 'Price of Protestantism', pp. 263–8, 308–15; PRO PROB 11/84, fos 8r–11r.

71. E. Cameron, *The European Reformation* (1991), pp. 135, 311–13, 417–22. For an example, see L. J. Abray, 'The Laity's Religion: Lutheranism in Sixteenth-Century Strasbourg', in R. Po-Chia Hsia (ed.), *The German People and the Reformation* (1988), pp. 216–21. I am grateful to Dr Ian Archer for this reference.

72. This militates against the theory that magistrates adopted Protestantism as a means of enforcing 'social control', on which see Byford, 'Price of Protestantism', pp. 275–84. On the thirty-five years or more needed to internalise Protestant ideas in Strasbourg, cf. Abray, 'The Laity's Religion', p. 221.

2. RELIGION IN DONCASTER   *Claire Cross*

1. L. Toulmin Smith (ed.), *The Itinerary of John Leland*, I (London, 1964), pp. 34–5. The spelling has been modernised in this and all subsequent quotations.

2. D. Hey, *Yorkshire from AD 1000* (London, 1986), pp. 42, 136–7; D. Hey, *The Making of South Yorkshire* (London, 1979), pp. 51–4; P. J. P. Goldberg, 'From Conquest to Corporation', in G. H. Martin, E. A. Danbury, P. J. P. Goldberg, B. J. Barber and M. W. Beresford, *Doncaster: A Borough and its Charters* (Doncaster, 1994), pp. 47–65; W. Page (ed.), *The Certificates of the Commissioners Appointed to Survey the Chantries, Guilds and Hospitals, etc. in the County of York*, I, Surtees Society, XCI (1894), p. 175.

3. D[oncaster] A[rchives] O[ffice] St George's Marriage Register P1/1/B1 ff. 35r–36v; Courtiers Book AB 2/1/1 f. 177r; J. Hunter, *South Yorkshire: The History and Topography of the Deanery of Doncaster*, I (London, 1828), p. 1; J. E. Jackson, *History and Description of St George's Church at Doncaster Destroyed by Fire February 28, 1853* (London, 1855), appendix pp. lii–iii, lix.

4. This study is largely based on an analysis of some 560 Doncaster wills made between 1520 and 1650 (51 in 1520–47; 11 in 1547–53; 42 in 1553–8; 212 in 1558–1603; 108 in 1602–25; 138 in 1625–50) now in the Borthwick Institute at York (subsequently cited as BI); BI Prob. Reg. 9 ff. 70r (Turton), 109v–109r (Halton), 317r (Lyndsay); Prob. Reg. 11 f. 80r–v (Marshall); Jackson, *St George's Church at Doncaster*, app. pp. x–xv; Hunter, *South Yorkshire*, I, p. 39; Page (ed.), *Chantry Certificates*, I, pp. 181–2.

5. Toulmin Smith (ed.), *Itinerary of John Leland*, I, pp. 34–5; *Eighth Report of the Deputy Keeper of the Public Records* (London, 1847), appendix II, p. 19.

6. C. Cross, *Urban Magistrates and Ministers: Religion in Hull and Leeds from the Reformation to the Civil War*, Borthwick Paper no. 67 (York, 1985), pp. 3–4; BI Abp. Reg. 27 f. 163r–v (Robynson); Prob. Reg. 10 ff. 99r–100r (Denton); Prob. Reg. 11 f. 35r (Drynkall).

7. BI Prob. Reg. 9 ff. 108v–109r (Halton), 256r (Lynsey), 271v (Firth), 317r (Lyndsay), 441r (Smyth); Prob. Reg. 11 ff. 41v (Parsonsone), 80r–v (Marshall), 376r (Bulloke), 552v (Johnson).

8. BI Prob. Reg. 10 ff. 15r–16r (Strey).

9. BI Abp. Reg. 27 ff. 163r–v (Robynson); Prob. Reg. 10 ff. 99r–100r (Denton); Hunter, *South Yorkshire*, I, p. 30.

10. J. and J. A. Venn, *Alumni Cantabrigienses* (Cambridge, 1922–7), I, vol. II, pp. 75, 163, 382; A. B. Emden, *Biographical Register of the University of Oxford, 1501–1540* (Oxford, 1974), pp. 336, 352.

11. *Letters and Papers of Henry VIII*, IX, no. 230; A. G. Dickens, *Lollards and Protestants in the Diocese of York* (London, 1959), pp. 140–5.

12. *L. P. Hen. VIII*, XII, pt I, no. 854; pt II, no. 181; XV, no. 498 (l. 57); XVI, no. 220 (7); G. Baskerville, *English Monks and the Suppression of the Monasteries* (London, 1937), p. 165.

13. Toulmin Smith (ed.), *Itinerary of John Leland*, I, pp. 34–5; Dickens, *Lollards and Protestants*, p. 141; L. M. Goldthorpe, 'The Franciscans and Dominicans in Yorkshire', *Yorkshire Archaeological Journal*, XXXII (1936), 264–320; W. Page (ed.), *The Certificates of the Commissioners Appointed to Survey the Chantries, Guilds, Hospitals, etc. in the County of York*, Part II, Surtees Society XCII (1895), pp. 307, 400, 415.

14. BI Prob. Reg. 11 ff. 373v–374r (Milnay), 746v–747r (Wirrall); Prob. Reg. 13 ff. 166v–167r (Butterfelde), 287v (Personson).

15. BI Prob. Reg. 13 ff. 466v–467r (Midlefeilde), 601v (Pawmer), 655v (West), 757v (Browne), 767v–768r (Worrall), 982r (Lylyman); Prob. Reg. 14 ff. 75r (Scrommyn), 308r (Gryme).

16. Venn, *Alumni Cantabrigienses*, I, vol. I, p. 163; Page (ed.), *Chantry Certificates*, II, pp. 390–3.

17. BI Prob. Reg. 15 pt I f. 83r–v (Alland); pt II f. 196v (Personson).

18. A. G. Dickens, *The Marian Reaction in the Diocese of York*; Part I: *The Clergy*, Borthwick Paper no. 11 (York, 1957), pp. 12–13.

19. BI Prob. Reg. 15 pt I f. 83r–v (Alland); pt II ff. 92v–93r (Copley), 227v (Blenkynshopp); pt III ff. 25r, 48v (Philippe), 49r–v (Shaw), 141r–v (Petet), 144v (Smithe).

20. Venn, *Alumni Cantabrigienses*, I, vol. I, p. 163; Jackson, *St George's Church, Doncaster*, app. pp. xxix–xxx; BI Prob. Reg. 17 f. 137v (Dickynson).

21. Jackson, *St George's Church, Doncaster*, app. pp. xv–xx; E. Miller, *History and Antiquities of Doncaster* (Doncaster, 1804), p. 81; Hunter, *South Yorkshire*, I, p. 49; BI Prob. Reg. 17 ff. 133r–134v (Ellis).

22. BI Prob. Reg. 15 pt III f. 328r–v (Fang); Prob. Reg. 16 f. 46r–v (Symkinson); 19 ff. 123v–124v (Simpkinsonne).

23. W. J. Hardy, *Calendar to the Records of the Borough of Doncaster*, III (Doncaster, 1902) pp. iv, 6; DAO AB 2/1/1 ff. 32v, 40r, 74v, 80r.

24. BI V 1582 CB f. 254v; V 1604 CB 1 f. 55r; J. C. H. Aveling, *Catholic Recusancy in the City of York, 1558–1791* (London, 1970), p. 172; Venn, *Alumni Cantabrigienses*, I, vol. 3, p. 205; Jackson, *St George's Church, Doncaster*, app. p. xxx.

25. Venn, *Alumni Cantabrigienses*, I, vol. 3, p. 12; DAO St George's Baptisms Register P1/1/Cl f. 1; BI V 1586 CB f. 203v; V 1595/6 CB 1 f. 204v; V 1604 CB 1 f. 55r; Abp. Reg. 31 ff. 176v–177v (Kay), 190r–v (Postlethwaite); B[ritish] L[ibrary] Add. Ms 4293 f. 41r–v; R. A. Marchant, *The Puritans and the Church Courts in the Diocese of York, 1560–1642* (London, 1960), pp. 27–8, 258, 281–2.

26. BI Prob. Reg. 22 f. 697r–v (Lupton); Prob. Reg. 23 f. 121r–v (Skargill); Prob. Reg 27 ff. 259v–260r (Moore); Prob. Reg. 30 ff. 646r–647r (Bradforth); Prob. Reg. 34 f. 697r–v (Deareman); Prob. Reg. 35 f. 555r (Trosse).

27. DAO AB 2/1/1 f. 65r.

28. J. Foster, *Alumni Oxonienses, 1500–1714*, vol. 2 (Oxford 1891), p. 794; Jackson, *St George's Church, Doncaster*, app. p. xlv; BI Prob. Reg. 35 f. 95r–v (Levett).

29. Jackson, *St George's Church, Doncaster*, app. p. lxxiii; DAO AB 6/1/4/1; Marchant, *Puritans and Church Courts*, pp. 275–6, 293; BI Abp. Reg. 32 ff. 56r–57r (Winter).

30. BI Chanc. AB 26 f. 243v; Marchant, *Puritans and Church Courts*, pp. 55–7.

31. J. Tomlinson, *Doncaster from the Roman Occupation to the Present Time* (Doncaster, 1887), pp. 43–4; Hunter, *South Yorkshire*, I, p. 37; BI Orig. Wills Ap. 1640 (Armitage), Orig. Wills Oct. 1644 (Fayram).

32. BI Orig. Wills Mar. 1641/2 (Carver); Venn, *Alumni Cantabrigienses*, I, vol. II, pp. 324, 455.

33. BI Prob. Reg. 17 ff. 38v–39r (Brokesbanke), 375v (Hall); Prob. Reg. 41 ff. 172r–173r (Fang), 380v–381v (Barwike); Tomlinson, *Doncaster from the Roman*

Occupation to the Present Time, pp. 138–9; Cross, *Urban Magistrates and Ministers*, pp. 24–6.

34. BI V 1575 CB 1 f. 78r; V 1594 CB 1 f. 78r; V 1600 CB 1 pt 2 f. 194r; V 1619 CB 1 f. 144v; V 1636 CB 1 pt I f. 193r; HC CP 1597/1; CP H 118; CP H 2245; BL Add. Ms. 4293 ff. 41r–v.

3. POLITICS AND RELIGION IN EARLY MODERN BEVERLEY   *David Lamburn*

1. P. Collinson, ' "De Republica Anglorum": Or, History with the Politics Put Back', in his *Elizabethan Essays* (London, 1994), p. 8.

2. P. Collinson, *The Birthpangs of Protestant England: Religious and Cultural Change in the Sixteenth and Seventeenth Centuries* (London, 1988), pp. 28–59; P. Collinson, *The Religion of Protestants: The Church in English Society, 1559–1625* (Oxford, 1982), pp. 141–88; D. Underdown, *Revel, Riot, and Rebellion: Popular Politics and Culture in England, 1603–1660* (Oxford, 1987), pp. 44–72, 106–12.

3. C. Haigh (ed.), *The English Reformation Revised* (Cambridge, 1987), pp. 209–15; C. Haigh, *English Reformations* (Oxford, 1993), pp. 278–84; P. Clark, *English Provincial Society from the Reformation to the Revolution: Religion, Politics and Society in Kent, 1500–1640* (Hassocks, 1977), pp. 323, 340–1; Borthwick Institute of Historical Research, York (BIHR), HC. CP. 1563/4.

4. Collinson, *Birthpangs*, pp. 56–9; P. Slack, 'Religious Protest and Urban Authority: the Case of Henry Sherfield, Iconoclast, 1633', in D. Baker (ed.), *Schism, Heresy and Religious Protest, Studies in Church History*, IX (Cambridge, 1972), pp. 295–302.

5. F. Hill, *Tudor and Stuart Lincoln* (Stamford, 1991), pp. 101–8, 227–32; J. S. Craig, 'The "Godly" and the "Froward": Protestant Polemics in the Town of Thetford, 1560–1590', *Norfolk Archaeology*, vol. XLI (1992), 279–93.

6. P. Clark, ' "The Ramoth-Gilead of the Good": Urban Change and Political Radicalism at Gloucester 1540–1640', in P. Clark, A. G. R. Smith and N. Tyacke (eds), *The English Commonwealth, 1547–1640* (Leicester, 1979), pp. 167–88; P. Clark, 'The Civic Leaders of Gloucester, 1580–1800', in P. Clark (ed.), *The Transformation of English Provincial Towns, 1600–1800* (London, 1984), pp. 311–45.

7. M. Spufford, 'Puritanism and Social Control?', in A. J. Fletcher and J. Stevenson (eds), *Order and Disorder in Early Modern England* (Cambridge, 1985), pp. 41–57.

8. J. Barry, 'Bourgeois Collectivism? Urban Association and the Middling Sort', in J. Barry and C. Brooks (eds), *The Middling Sort of People: Culture, Society and Politics in England, 1550–1800* (London, 1994), p. 94; P. Clark, 'Reformation and Radicalism in Kentish Towns c. 1500–1533', in W. J. Mommsen (ed.), *Stadtbür-gertum und Adel in der Reformation: The Urban Classes, the Nobility and the Reformation* (London, 1979), pp. 107–27; P. Lake, *Anglicans and Puritans?* (London, 1988), pp. 34–7, 53–66, 114–29.

9. Full references and details are in my 'Politics and Religion in Sixteenth-Century Beverley' (unpublished University of York DPhil dissertation, 1991), chs 3 and 4, upon which many of the arguments advanced here are based.

10. K. J. Allison (ed.), *A History of the County of York East Riding*, volume VI: *The Borough and Liberties of Beverley*, (hereafter *VCH Beverley*) (Oxford, 1989), pp. 76–80, 89–90; W. Page (ed.), *The Certificates of the Commissioners Appointed to Survey the Chantries, Guilds, Hospitals, etc. in the County of York*, vol. II (Surtees Society, vol. XCII, 1895), pp. 529, 537–8, 542, 552.

11. BIHR Ch. A. B. 6 fols 37v, 38r–38v, 18v, 26; A. G. Dickens, *Lollards and Protestants in the Diocese of York, 1509–1558* (London, 1982), pp. 191–2, 223–4, 227–30; BIHR Ord. 1554/1/10 and 11; Humberside Record Office (HRO) BC/II/6/22. The two governors were Thomas Settrington and Arkinwald Shepherd and the common councillors were John Jennison and Thomas Booth; HRO BC/II/7/2 ff. 2, 15, 25; *VCH Beverley*, p. 201.

12. R. Whiting, *The Blind Devotion of the People: Popular Religion and the English Reformation* (Cambridge, 1991), p. 268; BIHR V1615. CB. ff. 212v–213, V1615 Visitation Papers (D/C York); R. A. Marchant, *The Puritans and the Church Courts in the Diocese of York, 1560–1642* (London, 1960), pp. 37–8, 48, 271–2.

13. C. Cross, *Urban Magistrates and Ministers: Religion in Hull and Leeds from the Reformation to the Civil War* (Borthwick papers no. 67, 1985), p. 23; P. J. Wallis, *William Crashawe, the Sheffield Puritan* (Transactions of the Hunter Archaeological Society, vol. 8, pts 2–5, 1960–3); *VCH Beverley*, p. 79; HRO PE 1/51.

14. HRO BC/I/74; ibid. BC/II/6/36–53; ibid. BC/II/7/4/1 fols 6, 24.

15. HRO BC/II/3 fols 44, 35, 77v; ibid. BC/II/6/22; ibid. BC/II/4 fol. 18; ibid. BC/II/7/2 fol. 85v; K. L. Parker, *The English Sabbath* (Cambridge, 1988); BIHR V. 1594 fol. 167; BIHR CP.G. 1334 and 2456; HRO BC/II/7/2 fol. 75v.

16. *VCH Beverley*, pp. 65–70; Lamburn, 'Politics and Religion', pp. 29–106, 175–271; HRO BC/I/70; ibid. DDBC/2/12.

17. BIHR Reg. 25, fols 52, 60; ibid. Reg. 28 fol. 30; J. Lister (ed.), *Yorkshire Star Chamber Proceedings*, vol. 4 (Yorkshire Archaeological Society, Record Series, vol. LXX, 1927), pp. 80–4; BIHR HC.CP. 1594/4; HRO BC/II/7/2 fols, 77v, 25v, 70v.

18. BIHR V1615 Visitation Papers (D/C York); BIHR V1615, CB. fols 212v–213; Marchant, *Puritans and the Church Courts*, pp. 37–8; K. D. Murray, 'Puritanism and Civic Life in York, Newcastle, Hull, Beverley and Leeds, 1590–1640', unpublished University of Durham PhD thesis (1990), pp. 257–9.

19. Nicholas Ardron, *The Ploughman's Vindication: or a Confutation of some Passages Preached in Divers Sermons by Sherland Adams* (London, 1646), pp. 28–9.

20. Marchant, *Puritans and the Church Courts*, chs 2–4; R. C. Richardson, *Puritanism in North-west England* (Manchester, 1972), chs 2 and 3; Collinson, *Religion of Protestants*, pp. 237–8, 129–30, 248–9, 264–7.

21. BIHR V. 1595–6, CB 1 fol. 119v.

22. BIHR Prob. Reg. 36, fols 667v–668v; Marchant, *Puritans and the Church Courts*, p. 248; BIHR V 1615 Visitation Papers (D/C York); N. Tyacke, *Anti-Calvinists: The Rise of English Arminianism c. 1590–1640* (Oxford, 1987), pp. 17–18; R. Thoresby, *Vicaria Leodiensis; or, The History of the Church of Leedes, Yorkshire* (1724), pp. 65, 162–3.

23. K. Wrightson and D. Levine, *Poverty and Piety in an English Village: Terling, 1525–1700* (London, 1979), ch. 6; Collinson, *Religion of Protestants*, pp. 239–41.

24. HRO BC/1/74; ibid. BC/II/6/49–54.

25. The seven were: Marmaduke Attmar, Robert Horsley, Alexander Spalding, Richard Brigham, Robert Harrison, Richard Pickering and John Thornabie. HRO BC/II/7/4/1 fol. 47v names 16 men, the remainder are named in the account rolls, HRO BC/II/6/50 and 51. See also HRO BC/II/7/4/1 fols 28 and 29v.

26. Full details and analysis are in Lamburn, 'Politics and Religion', esp. pp. 203–71; HRO BC/II/7/4/1 fols 13v, 16, 28, 29v, 47; ibid. BC/II/5/1 (second part), fol. 3; ibid. BC/II/5/1 (first part), fol. 1; BIHR HC. CP. 1594/4 and HC.AB.12, 1591–5/6 fols 202, 207, 218, 220, 232, 241, 247, 257, 258v; J. Dennett (ed.), *Beverley Borough Records, 1575–1821* (Yorkshire Archaeological Society, vol. LXXXIV, 1933), pp. 36–47, 94–101.

27. BIHR V1615.CB. fols 212v–213; occupational information from prosopographical work, using mainly wills in BIHR Probate Registers, account rolls and minute books in HRO.

28. BIHR HC.CP. 1594/4. The opposing factions were headed by John Truslove and Peter Harpham. Clark, 'Ramoth- Gilead', pp. 176–81.

29. Lamburn, 'Politics and Religion', pp. 214–71, 449–50; HRO BC/II/5/1 (second part) f. 6; J. T. Evans, *Seventeenth-Century Norwich* (Oxford, 1979), p. 6; G. Mayhew, *Tudor Rye* (Falmer, 1987), pp. 112–13; D. H. Sacks, *The Open Gate: Trade, Society and Politics in Bristol, 1500–1640* (New York, 1985), ch. 14; D. MacCulloch, *Suffolk and the Tudors: Politics and Religion in an English County, 1500–1600* (Oxford, 1986), ch. 11; Clark, *English Provincial Society*, p. 252; PRO STAC 8/267/18 and STAC 8/233/1; Clark, 'Civic Leaders of Gloucester', pp. 321–2.

30. BIHR Prob. Reg. 29B fol. 611; ibid. Prob. Reg. 31 f. 228; ibid. V. 1586/ CB fols 130–5; J. C. H. Aveling, *Post Reformation Catholicism in East Yorkshire, 1558–1790* (East Yorkshire Local History Series, 11, 1960), p. 631; Lamburn, 'Politics and Religion', pp. 375–8.

31. W. Crashaw, *The Parable of Poyson in Five Sermons of Spiritual Poyson* (London, 1618), p. 7.

32. HRO BC/II/6/37; Wallis, *Crashawe*, pp. 11, 21–3, 29, 56; see Crashaw's dedication to Gee of W. Perkins, *A Faithful and Plaine Exposition upon the First Two Verses of the Second Chapter of Zephaniah* (London, 1605); HRO BC/II/7/4/1 fol. 6.

33. W. Crashaw, *The Sermon Preached at the Crosse, February xiiii 1607 Justified by the Author* (London, 1609), p. 168.

34. BIHR V. 1586. CB–V. 1619. CB; HRO BC/II/7/4/1/fols 55–55v. The Arminian candidate was William Bland.

35. BIHR HC.CP. 1594/4; HRO PE 1/51; ibid. BC/II/6/38–43; BIHR Bp. C and P XVIII/7; HRO PE/1/47; P. and J. Clark, *The Boston Assembly Minutes, 1545–1575* (Lincoln Record Society, vol. 77, 1987), p. xv; HRO BC/II/7/4/1 fol. 46v; R. Pricke, *The Doctrine of Superiority and Subjection* (London, 1609), sig. C5.

36. G. de la Perriere, *The Mirrour of Policie* (London, 1599), sig. Ki–L.

37. HRO BC/II/7/4/1 fol. 45.

38. HRO BC/II/3; ibid. BC/II/5/1 (second part), fols 3–4, 6–8, (first part), fols 1–4; Crashaw, *Parable of Poyson*, p. 7.

39. HRO BC/II/7/4/1 fol. 31; ibid. BC/II/5/1 (first part), fols 15–16, 46–7.

40. J. King, *Lectures upon Jonas Delivered at Yorke 1594* (London, 1618), pp. 86, 89–90; Crashaw, *Sermon Preached at the Crosse*; Crashaw, *Parable of Poyson*.

41. Collinson, ' "De Republica Anglorum": or, History with the Politics Put Back', p. 18.

4. PROTESTANTISM IN ELIZABETHAN TEWKESBURY
Caroline Litzenberger

1. Gloucestershire Record Office (hereafter GRO), Tewkesbury Borough Records (hereafter TBR) B2/1, 1.

2. GRO, P329 CW 2/1, passim; printed in C. Litzenberger (ed.), *Tewkesbury Churchwardens' Accounts. 1563–1624* (1994). (Hereafter all references to the Tewkesbury Churchwardens' Accounts will cite the printed edition.)

3. *The Testament of Master Wylliam Tracie esquier / expounded both by William Tyndale and Jhon Frith* (Antwerp, 1535), STC 24167. Cf. J. Craig and C. Litzenberger, 'Wills as Religious Propaganda: the Testament of William Tracy', *Journal of Ecclesiastical History*, 44 (July 1993), 415–31.

4. Hereford and Worcester Record Office 802 BA 2764, 107–72, passim. (I would like to thank Susan Wabuda for this reference.)

5. Susan R. Wabuda, 'The Provision of Preaching during the Early English Reformation: with Special Reference to Itineration, *c.* 1530 to 1547' (University of Cambridge PhD, 1991), 112–14.

6. C. R. Elrington (ed.), *The History of the County of Gloucester*, vol. 8 (1968), 147.

7. Gloucester City Library, Hockaday Abstracts, vol. 369, 1548 (unpaginated).

8. PRO Req. 2/19/17; Dr Williams's Library, Morice MS 31.L/3, 28.

9. GRO Gloucestershire Wills 1557/91, 1557/163, 1557/338.

10. PRO, PROB 11/40, fols. 284v–287v.

11. E. Cardwell (ed.), *Documentary Annals of the Reformed Church of England*, vol. 1 (1839), 193.

12. GRO Gloucester Diocesan Records (hereafter GDR) 50, Tewxburie 1582 (unpaginated).

13. GRO GDR 40, 47; C. Litzenberger (ed.), *Tewkesbury*, 35–6, 40, 57; E. Grindal, 'Articles to be enquired of within the Province of Canterbury [1576]', in *The Remains of Edmund Grindal*, ed. W. Nicholson (Cambridge, 1843), 159.

14. C. Litzenberger (ed.), *Tewkesbury*, 84.

15. GRO P154/14 CW 1/13, 1/25, P197 CW 2/1, 4–5.

16. C. Litzenberger (ed.), *Tewkesbury*, 1–2.

17. C. Litzenberger, 'Richard Cheyney, Bishop of Gloucester: an Infidel in Religion?', *Sixteenth-Century Journal*, 25 (Fall 1994), 567–84.

18. C. Litzenberger (ed.), *Tewkesbury*, 24–5.

19. C. Litzenberger (ed.), *Tewkesbury*, 38; M. Aston, *England's Iconoclasts*, vol. 1: *Laws against Images* (Oxford, 1988), 260 n, 346–74, passim.

20. C. Litzenberger (ed.), *Tewkesbury*, 38.

21. GRO TBR D1/1, 17.

22. GRO TBR A 1/1, fol. 9v.

23. Theodore Hannam-Clark, *Drama in Gloucestershire* (1928), 21.

24. C. Litzenberger (ed.), *Tewkesbury*, 33, 40, 58. Cf. *Records of Early English Drama: Cumberland, Westmorland, Gloucestershire*, ed. A. Douglas and P. Greenfield (Toronto, 1986), 255–6, 268, 335–8.

25. C. Litzenberger (ed.), *Tewkesbury*, 93–4; GRO TBR A 1/1, fols 15, 24.

26. C. Litzenberger (ed.), *Tewkesbury*, 65, 74, 78, 79, 112, 113.

27. GRO GDR 43, fol. 41v; C. Litzenberger, 'Richard Cheyney', 567–84; F. D. Price, 'Bishop Bullingham and Chancellor Blackleech: a Diocese Divided', *Transactions of the Bristol and Gloucestershire Archaeological Society*, 91 (1973), 175–98.

28. GRO TBR A 1/1, fols 11, 12v, 20–22v, 24.

29. GRO GDR 24, 723; GDR 31, 81–7; GDR 35, 27–71, passim.

30. GRO GDR 28, 3.

31. GRO Gloucestershire Wills 1553/80; C. Litzenberger (ed.), *Tewkesbury*, 29, 35.

32. PRO PROB 11/73, fols 211–211v, PROB 11/80, fols 207–9.

33. GRO TBR B2/1, passim; GRO P329 IN 1/1 passim.

34. A. Heales, *The History and Law of Church Seats or Pews, Book I – History* (London, 1872), 84–109, passim.

35. C. Litzenberger (ed.), *Tewkesbury*, 36–7.

36. F. R. Raines (ed.), 'A Description of the State, Civil and Ecclesiastical of the County of Lancashire about the Year 1590', in *Chetham Miscellanies* (1875), vol. 5, 3.

37. C. Litzenberger (ed.), *Tewkesbury*, 5, 10, 20.

38. C. Litzenberger (ed.), *Tewkesbury*, 26, 32, 37.

39. Margaret Aston, 'Segregation in Church', in *Women in the Church*, ed. W. J. Sheils and D. Wood (1989), 237–94.

5. WORCESTER: A CATHEDRAL CITY IN THE REFORMATION *Diarmaid MacCulloch*

I must acknowledge with gratitude the helpful comments made on earlier drafts of this chapter on the occasions when it was delivered as a paper in the Church History seminar of the Divinity Faculty, Cambridge, the early modern Church History seminar of the Institute of Historical Research, London, and the early modern seminar on the British Isles, Oxford.

1. Hereford and Worcester Record Office, St Helen's Worcester (hereafter HWRO) 009:1/BA 2636 parcel 11 (no. 43701), fos 155–9. I am very grateful to Dr Hughes for drawing my attention to her important discovery; our edition of the whole document with commentary is published in the *Antiquaries Journal*, 74 (1995): 'A Bailiffs' List and Chronicle from Worcester'. I also acknowledge with gratitude the permission of the authorities in the diocese of Worcester to quote from the text of the Chronicle.

2. For the detailed discussion backing these identifications, see MacCulloch and Hughes, 'A Bailiffs' List and Chronicle from Worcester'.

3. S. T. Bindoff (ed.), *The History of Parliament: the House of Commons, 1509–1558* (London: Secker and Warburg, 3 vols, 1982), vol. 3, pp. 683–4.

4. *Narratives of the Reformation*, ed. J. G. Nichols (Camden Society [hereafter CS] 1st ser. 77, 1859, hereafter *Narratives of the Reformation*), p. 66; *The Acts and Monuments of John Foxe*, ed. G. Townsend and S. R. Cattley (8 vols, London, 1837–41; hereafter Foxe), vol. 8, pp. 554–5 has a shorter version of Davis's story.

5. HWRO, 496.5 BA 9360: A 19 f. 19; A 10 (first city account book, early pages, for 1540s), A 23/4. I am grateful to Dr Hughes for these references.

6. On Yowle's school benefaction, A. D. Dyer, *The City of Worcester in the Sixteenth Century* (Leicester University Press, 1973, hereafter Dyer, *Worcester*), p, 245. Yowle's will is at PRO, Prerogative Court of Canterbury 29 Loftes.

7. A. F. Leach, *Early Education in Worcester* (Worcestershire Historical Society [hereafter WHS], 1913), pp. 197, 199.

8. HWRO, 705: 318 BA 1857/1; Probate Records 1622/61c; Robert Steynor's will, 1622. County Hall: St Nicholas Worcester parish register: this has records of six children of the Steynors baptised. Robert and John were born before the current register began in 1564. I am grateful to Dr Hughes for these details.

9. HWRO, Shelsey Beauchamp parish register, 1582: '29 day of April were married together John Steynor of Worcester and Anne Parton of the same city' (ex inf. Dr Hughes). Recusancy: Dyer, *Worcester*, p. 238.

10. HWRO, 989.9:191 BA 1811.

11. Dyer, *Worcester*, p. 238. He was admitted to Lincoln's Inn in 1579.

12. Some of the documents borrowed and copied by John Steynor have been traced: cf. Worcester Cathedral Library A 3, *Liber Pensionum* (see also F. D. Price (ed.), *Liber Pensionum Prioratus Wigorn*, WHS, 1925); Worcester Cathedral Library A XII, volume of miscellaneous collections (part quoted in E. S. Fegan (ed.), *The Journal of Prior More*, WHS, 1914). One MS which he borrowed from Parry (Bishop 1610–16) was HWRO, 009:1 BA 2636/179 92519: compotus rolls for Bishop Pate, 1554–5.

13. HWRO, 009:1 BA 2636/11: final pages.

14. HWRO, 009:1 BA 2636/11.

15. Dyer, *Worcester*, p. 145.

16. S. E. Lehmberg, *The Reformation of Cathedrals: Cathedrals in English Society, 1485–1603* (Princeton University Press, 1988; hereafter Lehmberg, *Reformation of Cathedrals*), p. 273.

17. Dyer, *Worcester*, pp. 195, 232–5, 239, and cf. the regulations of 1583 about access to the cathedral: Lehmberg, *Reformation of Cathedrals*, pp. 271–2. On Laud, cf. ibid., p. 275.

18. Dyer, *Worcester*, pp. 26–7.

19. Dyer, *Worcester*, pp. 51, 59, 70–1.

20. *Leland's Itinerary in England and Wales*, ed. L. Toulmin Smith (London: G. Bell and Sons, 5 vols 1907–8), vol. 2, p. 91; and see Dyer, *Worcester*, pp. 81–2, 84, 93–4.

21. Dyer, *Worcester*, p. 106.

22. Dyer, *Worcester*, p. 50.

23. Dyer, *Worcester*, p. 251; on the Prayer Book, see *A Short Title Catalogue of Books printed in England, Scotland, and Ireland and of English Books Printed Abroad*, ed. A. W. Pollard and G. R. Redgrave, rev. W. A. Jackson and F. S. Ferguson and completed by K. F. Pantzer (London: Bibliographical Society, 3 vols, 1976–91),

nos 16271, 16276. Oswen seems to have continued printing here up to the beginning of Mary's reign.

24. The version of this entry reproduced in Nash, Appx., is misdated to 1522, and hence has misled Margaret Aston: M. Aston, *England's Iconoclasts I. Laws against Images* (Oxford: Clarendon Press, 1988, hereafter Aston, *England's Iconoclasts*), p. 212.

25. Kent: cf. P. Clark, *English Provincial Society from the Reformation to the Revolution: Religion, Politics and Society in Kent, 1500–1640* (Hassocks: Harvester, 1977), pp. 37 and 416 n.10, and Corpus Christi College Cambridge MS 301, pp. 210–11. Suffolk: D. MacCulloch, *Suffolk and the Tudors: Politics and Religion in an English County, 1500–1600* (Oxford: Clarendon Press, 1986), pp. 154–5. General pardon: S. E. Lehmberg, *The Reformation Parliament, 1529–1536* (Cambridge University Press, 1970), p. 91.

26. *Sermons and Remains of Hugh Latimer*, ed. G. E. Corrie (Parker Society, 1845; hereafter *Latimer's Remains*), p. 55.

27. *Letters and Papers . . . Henry VIII*, 12 pt ii, no. 587; Aston, *England's Iconoclasts*, p. 173.

28. R. E. Hutton, 'The Local Impact of the Tudor Reformations', in C. Haigh (ed.), *The English Reformation Revised* (Cambridge University Press, 1987), pp. 114–37 (hereafter Hutton, 'Local Impact'), p. 118. *Tudor Royal Proclamations*, ed. P. L. Hughes and J. F. Larkin (New Haven and London: Yale University Press, 3 vols, 1964, 1969; hereafter Hughes and Larkin), vol. 1, no. 200.

29. Hughes and Larkin, vol. 1, no. 203.

30. P. Tudor-Craig, 'Henry VIII and King David', in D. Williams (ed.), *Early Tudor England* (Woodbridge: Boydell and Brewer, 1989), pp. 196, 202–5, particularly Henry's comments on Psalms 96 (97), 105 (106).

31. Province of York: Bodleian Library, Oxford, MS Jesus 74 fo. 257r. Southern Province: *Works of Archbishop Cranmer*, ed. J. E. Cox (2 vols, Parker Society, 1844 [in two paginations], 1846; hereafter Cranmer, *Works*), vol. 2, p. 490. St Paul's and Westminster Abbey: 'A London Chronicle during the Reigns of Henry the Seventh and Henry the Eighth', ed. C. Hopper, *Camden Miscellany*, 4 (CS Old Series 73, 1859, hereafter Hopper, 'London Chronicle'), 16.

32. See 'Robert Parkyn's Narrative of the Reformation', ed. A. G. Dickens, *English Historical Review*, 62 (1947), 58–83, also repr. in A. G. Dickens, *Reformation Studies* (London, Hambledon Press, 1982), pp. 287–312; hereafter 'Parkyn'.

33. Hughes and Larkin, vol 1, no. 287; Cranmer, *Works*, 2, p. 499.

34. London: *Chronicle of the Grey Friars of London*, ed. J. Gough Nichols (CS Old Series 53, 1852, hereafter *Grey Friars Chronicle*), p. 54. Privy Council to Aucher: *Acts of the Privy Council of England*, ed. J. R. Dasent (32 vols, London, 1890–1907; hereafter *APC*), vol. 2, p. 539. Council order, 21 February 1548: Cranmer, *Works*, vol. 2, pp. 509–11.

35. For government liturgical orders, see Cranmer, *Works*, vol. 2, p. 417; Hughes and Larkin, vol. 1, no. 299; 'Parkyn', 66–7; Winchester: Foxe 6, p. 222.

36. P. Heylyn, ed. J. C. Robertson, *Ecclesia Restaurata; or, the History of the Reformation of the Church of England* (2 vols, Cambridge: Ecclesiastical History Society, 1859), vol. 1, p. 114. On the order of 20 February 1548 to the Archbishop of York, see [N. Pocock], 'Preparations for the First Prayer Book of Edward VI', *Church Quarterly Review*, 35 (1892–3), 41.

37. F. B. Bond (ed.), *Certain Sermons or Homilies (1547) and a Homily against Disobedience and Wilful Rebellion (1570): a Critical Edition* (University of Toronto Press, 1987), p. 112.

38. I am indebted to Dr Ronald Hutton for this information.

39. On the Holy Week ceremonies, see Duffy, *Stripping of the Altars*, pp. 22–31, 461. Cf. J. Amphlett (ed.), *The Churchwardens' Accounts of St Michael in Bedwardine, 1539–1603* (WHS, 1896; hereafter *St Michael in Bedwardine*), pp. 18, 30.

40. Foxe 6, p. 65.

41. Cranmer, *Works*, vol. 2, pp. 154–9; cf. Duffy, *Stripping of the Altars*, p. 461.

42. *Grey Friars Chronicle*, p. 58.

43. Privy Council order, 25 December 1549: cf. Foxe 6, pp. 3–4, Hughes and Larkin, vol. 1, no. 353. 'Parkyn', 72. Heath and Council: *APC* 2, p. 388. On the antiphoner, see Lehmberg, *Reformation of Cathedrals*, pp. 114–15.

44. Privy Council letters sent to all bishops to demolish all altars on 19 November 1550: W. K. Jordan (ed.), *The Chronicle and Private Papers of Edward VI* (London: George Allen and Unwin, 1966), p. 49, and cf. the text of the letter to Bishop Ridley of London, 24 November 1550: Cranmer, *Works*, vol. 2, p. 524. Cf. *St Michael in Bedwardine*, p. 24.

45. MacCulloch, *Suffolk and the Tudors*, p. 170.

46. Hutton, 'Local Impact', pp. 121–2, and private communication extending the number of his overall sample.

47. *Early Writings of John Hooper*, ed. S. Carr (Parker Society, 1853), p. 492.

48. *Later Writings of Bishop Hooper*, ed. C. Nevinson (Parker Society, 1852; hereafter *Later Writings of Hooper*), p. 135.

49. *St Michael in Bedwardine*, p. 32.

50. 'Parkyn', 76.

51. *The Reformation of the Ecclesiastical Laws as Attempted in the Reigns of King Henry VIII, King Edward VI, and Queen Elizabeth*, ed. E. Cardwell (Oxford, 1850), pp. 32, 105.

52. E. W. Hunt, *The Life and Times of John Hooper (c.1500–1555) Bishop of Gloucester* (Lewiston/Queenston/Lampeter: Edwin Mellen Press, 1992), p. 283.

53. P. Collinson, *The Religion of Protestants* (Oxford, 1982), pp. 51–2.

54. 'Parkyn', pp. 74–5 and n.; *Grey Friars Chronicle*, p. 75.

55. On Johnson and Joliffe, cf. *Narratives of the Reformation*, pp. 61, 67.

56. Hooper to Cecil, 25 October 1552: cf. *Later Writings of Hooper*, p. xx, or J. Strype, ed. P. E. Barnes, *Memorials . . . of . . . Thomas Cranmer . . .* (London: George Routledge and Co., 2 vols, 1853; hereafter Strype, *Cranmer*), vol. 2, no. 48, pp. 381–2. *APC*, 4, pp. 162, 197–8 (6 November, 28 December 1552). For the reply of the canons and of Gardiner, cf. *Later Writings of Hooper*, p. xxn.

57. The date of about 1557 suggested for this letter by Lehmberg, *Reformation of Cathedrals*, p. 117 n., is probably a little too late.

58. *The Travels and Life of Sir Thomas Hoby . . .*, ed. E. Powell, *Camden Miscellany*, 10 (CS 3rd ser. 4, 1902), p. 126.

59. Lehmberg, *Reformation of Cathedrals*, p. 278.

60. N. Pevsner and A. Wedgwood, *The Buildings of England: Warwickshire* (London: Pelican, 1966), p. 425.

61. *The Sermons of Edwin Sandys . . .*, ed. J. Ayre (Parker Society, 1841), p. 250. Hutton, 'Local Impact', p. 134, seems to suggest that this sermon was preached

when Sandys was a royal commissioner in the north in 1559, rather than later during his time as Archbishop of York. This hypothesis has its attractions, but Sandys does seem to be considering the destruction of roodlofts as a *fait accompli*, which would be more appropriate after the royal order against roodlofts in 1561.

62. On Thomas Arderne, see A. B. Emden, *A Biographical Register of the University of Oxford AD 1501 to 1540* (Oxford: Clarendon Press, 1974), p. 12: he was a former fellow of Lincoln College and Christ Church Oxford, and rector of the episcopal living of Hartlebury from 1554.

63. *Correspondence of Matthew Parker*, ed. J. Bruce (Parker Society, 1853), pp. 124–7. When a full-scale feud developed between Sandys and the ultra-Catholic Worcestershire magnate Sir John Bourne in 1563, Bourne again made Arderne's and Norfolk's deprivation one of his complaints to the Privy Council: PRO, S.P. 12/28/38, 39.

64. PRO, S.P. 12/28/35 f. 125r. On Bourne's feud with Sandys, see L. M. Hill, 'The Marian "Experience of Defeat": the case of Sir John Bourne', *Sixteenth-Century Journal*, 25 (1994), 531–50. Cf. further notes of the early Elizabethan destruction at Worcester, Lehmberg, *Reformation of Cathedrals*, pp. 151, 176–7.

65. 'A Collection of Original Letters from the Bishops to the Privy Council, 1564', ed. M. Bateson, in *Camden Miscellany*, 9 (Camden Soc. 2nd ser. 53, 1895), 1–8.

66. On Martin, see D. Dymond and C. Paine, *The Spoil of Melford Church: The Reformation in a Suffolk Parish* (Ipswich, 1989), especially Martin's account of Melford church, ibid., pp. 1–9.

67. *Latimer's Remains*, p. 403.

68. *Narratives of the Reformation*, pp. 60–8.

69. Dyer, *Worcester*, p. 251.

70. Dyer, *Worcester*, pp. 214–16.

71. One should note that despite the city's bitter clashes in the 1620s and 1630s with the cathedral clergy, it became a royalist stronghold in the Civil War. Dyer, *Worcester*, pp. 233, 239, 255.

72. Dyer, *Worcester*, p. 74.

73. Hutton, 'Local Impact'; and cf. Hutton, *The Rise and Fall of Merry England* (Oxford: Clarendon Press, 1994), pp. 49–50, 61–2, 69–70, 176, 263–93.

6. LEADERSHIP AND PRIORITIES IN READING   *Jeanette Martin*

1. In the Domesday Survey, Reading is specifically called a borough and the town and manor are separately surveyed (*Victoria County History: Berkshire*, III, 342). Alan R. H. Baker, 'Changes in the Later Middle Ages', in H. C. Darby (ed.), *A New Historical Geography of England before 1600* (Cambridge, 1976; 1980 repr.), p. 243; Brian R. Kemp, *Reading Abbey: An Introduction to the History of the Abbey* (Reading Museum and Art Gallery, 1968), pp. 7, 9–11, Ch. 3, pp. 49–52; *Reading Records: Diary of the Corporation*, 4 vols, ed. J. M. Guilding (London and Oxford, 1892–6), vol. I, p. 119.

2. For important visitors, including Henry VIII, see below; Edward VI and Queen Mary only visited Reading once (*Corporation Diary*, vol. I, pp. 228, 240). Prelates included bishops of Salisbury, in whose diocese Reading lay: Edmund Audley visited in 1522–3 and John Salcot, alias Capon, in 1540–1 (Churchwardens' Accounts of St Giles', Reading: Berks RO D/P 96.5/1, 2nd MS p. of each above-dated account). J. E. Paul, 'The Last Abbots of Reading and Colchester', *BIHR*, XXXIII, no. 87 (May 1960) and app. I and II. The priests were John Eynon, who had resigned as vicar of St Giles' to become the abbot's chief counsellor, but maintained an interest in the parish (see below), and John Rugge, a former prebendary of Chichester (Paul, 'Last Abbots', p. 116; PRO KB 9/548 fos 5, 6; *LP*, XIV, ii, no. 613). Jeanette Martin, 'The People of Reading and the Reformation, 1520–1570: Leadership and Priorities in Borough and Parishes', University of Reading PhD, 1987, pp. 282–90, 336–56. Problems affecting the benefices and parishes are the subject of forthcoming articles.

3. J. H. Bettey, *Wessex from AD 1000* (Harlow and New York, 1986), pp. 116–17, 122, 129, 150, 195; Alan G. R. Smith, *The Emergence of a Nation State: The Commonwealth of England, 1529–1660* (Harlow and New York, 1984), Ch. 6; *LP*, VIII, no. 989.

4. Kemp, *Reading Abbey*, p. 31, Ch. 7; *VCH Berks*, II, 63, 64; A. Aspinall et al., *Parliament through Seven Centuries: Reading and its MPs* (1962), pp. 1–2. Henry VIII seems sometimes to have visited Reading more than once in a year during the period 1520–40, this latter year apparently being the last occasion, when he was attended by the Privy Council (*LP*, XV, no. 996). Martin 'People of Reading', pp. 259–63.

5. J. Sumption, *Pilgrimage: An Image of Mediaeval Religion* (1975), p. 116; Brian R. Kemp, 'The Miracles of the Hand of St James', *Berkshire Archaeological Journal*, 65 (1970), 1–19, especially pp. 3, 4, 5.

6. *LP*, III, ii, p. 1542; BL Cott. MS, Cleop. E iv, fo. 267r (*LP*, XIII, ii, no. 367). The Duke of Richmond died in July 1536 and his soul masses were completed by April 1537 (*LP*, XII, i, no. 947). *VCH Berks*, II, 89–90.

7. The annual fairs began on the vigil of the feast of SS. Philip and James (1 May) and on the feast of St James (25 July) (PRO, LR 2/187, fo. 343r). *VCH Berks*, III, 343; *LP*, XII, ii, no. 1256: 2, iii; *VCH Berks*, I, 387, 390, and ibid., III, 344; *Itinerary of John Leland*, 5 vols, ed. L. T. Smith (1907–10), Part II, 111; John Stow, *Survey of London*, ed. H. Morley (London, no date), p. 115.

8. *VCH Berks*, III, 342, 344–5, 346, 347, 348 and note 28; *Corporation Diary*, I, 280–2; C. Coates, *The History and Antiquities of Reading* (1802), p. 52, and appendix V (no pagination). In 1492 the abbot for some reason refused to elect a mayor and there ensued years of ill-feeling and dispute over urban elections between townsmen and abbot. In 1498 the burgesses threatened to expel any Guild member who accepted urban office by appointment of the abbot (*Corporation Diary*, I, 89, 90, 91, 94–5, 97–8; *VCH Berks*, III, 352–3).

9. Complaint was made to the Lord Privy Seal and the Lord Chamberlain (*Corporation Diary*, I, 105–8). Communicants could have included children (Certificates of Colleges and Chantries, 1548, PRO E301/3; Keith Thomas, *Religion and the Decline of Magic: Studies in Popular Beliefs in Sixteenth- and Seventeenth-Century England* (1971: paperback edn, Harmondsworth, 1973), pp. 41–2, 64–5).

Burgess lists were used retrospectively and notes such as *mortuus* would be inserted beside a name at a later date (*Corporation Diary*, I, 110, 119–20, 130, 133–4, 141, 152–3, 171). Aspinall et al., *Parliament through Seven Centuries*, pp. 3–5. For trade regulation, see *Reading Charters, Acts and Orders, 1253–1911*, ed. C. F. Pritchard (Reading and London, no date; preface dated 1913), p. 4; *VCH Berks*, III, 350; Coates, *Reading*, for a transcription of the *Puncta Gildae*, in the Supplement (published 1810) at the back of the book. For the wharf and beams, see *Corporation Diary*, I, 122, 123 et passim; for burgess dues, ibid., pp. 111, 115 et passim.

10. PRO E301/3. St Laurence's vicar received his meals daily at the abbot's table, bread, wine and wax for his cure for the whole year, and the use of a horse from the abbot's stable to ride to visitations; he also received predial 'and other smaller tithes' from 75 acres, while about another 132 acres (63.7%) were tithe-free (PRO E337/5, m. 2d–m. 3r). For St Mary's, see Coates, *Reading*, p. 74; and *VCH Berks*, III, 364–6 for the hamlets. For St Giles', see Coates, *Reading*, pp. 389–90. Incumbents of perpetual vicarages usually received the small tithes and other minor revenues. The wealth and importance of St Laurence's is indicated by the fact that between 1520 and 1570, 18 out of 25 mayors came from this parish, 5 came from St Mary's and 2 from St Giles' (Martin, 'People of Reading', Appendix C).

11. For Justice, see Wilts RO D1/2/14, fo. 7r and A. B. Emden, *A Biographical Register of the University of Oxford to AD 1500* (Oxford, 1957–9), sub Justyce, Thos. Two men of this name, probably cousins, were both priests in Reading at this time; it is therefore not surprising that Emden and Kerry (below, this note) should have confused them. Thomas Justice I, with whom we are concerned, was vicar of St Laurence's from 1502 to 1518, when he was succeeded by Bedow (see note 12); he died on 12 January 1536 (C. Kerry, *A History of the Municipal Church of St Lawrence, Reading* (Reading and Little Eaton, Derby, 1883), pp. 46, 161, 178–9; PRO PCC will, PROB 11/25,31). Thos. Justice I was the son of Henry Justice (*LP*, I, i, no. 438 (3) m. 11; Berks RO, D/P 97.5/2, p. 138; *Corporation Diary*, I, 65, 69, 119; Berks RO, R/Box 13, D 169; PRO PCC will of Richard Smyth PROB 11/18/22). Thos. Justice II was the son of William Justice senior of St Mary's parish (PRO PCC will PROB 11/20, 6). For Richard Herberd and William Pache, see Wilts RO D1/2/14, fos 23v, 38r and D1/19 fo. 64v; Emden, *Oxford Register to AD 1500*, sub nom. Emden was not able to trace Pache after 1516.

12. Wilts RO D1/2/14 fo. 76r and D1/2/15 fo. 51v. Emden, in error, describes Bedow as rector (*Oxford Register to AD 1500*, sub nom). Bedow was the nephew of Sir John ap Rice and his will reveals his connections and continuing interest in Wales (PRO PCC will PROB 11/25 22 proved 21 Jan. 1534/5; Kerry, *St Lawrence*, pp. 175–7). Admitted rector of Gladestry, Radnorshire, in 1514, he held the vicarage of Lewknor, Oxfordshire, concurrently with that of St Laurence's until his death (Emden, op. cit.). Lewknor was in the presentation of All Souls', Oxford.

13. Wilts RO D1/2/14 fo. 80r (surname spelled Enon) and D1/2/15 fo. 42v; A. B. Emden, *A Biographical Register of the University of Oxford A D 1501–1540* (Oxford, 1974), sub nom. Although Eynon did not proceed beyond B.C.L., he was usually addressed as 'master', probably because of his former position as principal of St Edward Hall (see below, note 15). He came from St David's

diocese and was a contemporary of Bedow at Oxford, who may well have had a beneficial influence on his presentation to St Giles' (PRO SP 1/112 fos 110v, 111r (*LP*, xi, no. 1231); see above, note 2). For a period of nearly nine years out of the thirteen during which he was vicar of St Giles', Eynon also held in succession two Northamptonshire rectories, Thenford and Slapton (Emden, op. cit.). He relinquished his incumbencies at Slapton (after only six months) and at Reading in order to become the abbot's chief counsellor.

14. Wilts RO D1/2/13 fo. 10v; Berks RO D/A 1/1 fo. 33v, will of Julian Bye, widow, proved 21 April 1520; PRO PCC will of Nicholas Nicholas, PROB 11/18, 1 proved 7 Nov. 1514.

15. Wilts RO D1/2/15 fos 42v–43r. 'Sir' (*Dominus*) was a title accorded both to non-graduate priests (of which Snow appears to be one), and to those with a bachelor's degree; the title 'Master' (*Magister*) was a distinction reserved for those with a Master of Arts degree (M. Bowker, *The Secular Clergy in the Diocese of Lincoln, 1495–1520* (Cambridge, 1968), p. 45). For an exception see above, note 13. Eynon was evidently assisting Snow in a priestly capacity at this time by saying mattins and mass (PRO SP 1/112 fos 110v–111r; Martin, 'People of Reading', pp. 105–6).

16. Wilts RO D1/2/15 fo. 51v; Berks RO D/A 1/1, fo. 134, will of John Brygat, dated 1 April 1521, and D/A 1/1, fos 177v–178r, will of Chris. Butteler, dated 28 Dec. 1531.

17. A new priest, Sir John More, was instituted to St Giles' on 14 Nov. 1550 after Snow's death (Wilts RO D1/2/16, fo. 43v). Mayneforth died *c.* late summer 1550 (Berks RO D/A 1/5 fo. 113r, for his will dated 16 Aug. 1550, proved 10 Oct. 1550).

18. Wilts RO D1/19 fo. 64v; Berks RO 2/c 152, p. 166. Whetham was buried in St Mary's on 25 Nov. 1569 (*The Registers of the Parish of St Mary, Reading, Berks, 1538–1812*, 2 vols, transcribed by G. P. Crawfurd (Reading, 1891–2), vol. ii, p. 94). Corpus Christi College, Cambridge MS 97 (Parker Certificates), fo. 197.

19. J. A. F. Thomson, *The Later Lollards, 1414–1520* (Oxford, 1965), Ch. 3, especially pp. 56, 57, 74, 80 ff; Wilts RO D1/2/13 fos 70r–72r. The Lollards were John and Alice Bisshopp, and John Roye of St Laurence's; Thomas and Agnes (Annes) Scochyn, John Stanway, Cecyly Letcomb and Agnes (Annes) Redhood of St Giles'. The Bisshopps and Thos. Scochyn confessed to receiving the Holy Sacrament purely out of fear (ibid., fo. 70r).

20. Scochyn was admitted a burgess on 22 Feb. 1498 (*Corporation Diary*, vol. i, pp. 95, 100, 110, 115). *Mortuus* is retrospectively set beside his name on the burgess list of 1510, since another such list was not made out until 1514 (ibid., pp. 119, 130). Wilts RO D1/2/13 fo. 70r; Martin, 'People of Reading', pp. 22–32.

21. Berks RO D/P 97.5/2, pp. 6, 33, 35, 74. Her husband hired a pair of fuller's shears from St Laurence's in 1507–8 (ibid., p. 33). For John Roye, whose name is alternatively spelled Rey, Raye, Roy, see (ibid.), pp. 30, 74, 80, 85, 90.

22. Wilts RO D1/2/14 fo. 148; John Foxe, *Acts and Monuments of the English Martyrs*, 8 vols, ed. Josiah Pratt (1853–70), vol. iv, pp. 174, 207–8; Martin, 'People of Reading', pp. 32–6; Thomson, *Later Lollards*, pp. 88–9; S. Brigden, *London and the Reformation* (Oxford, 1989; pb pp. 1991), pp. 87–8, 90, 93, 94.

23. *LP*, IV, ii, no. 4004; Foxe, *Acts and Monuments*, V, Appendix, 'State Paper Office, Wolsey Papers, vol. 7, no. 122'; A. G. Dickens, *The English Reformation* (1964; 2nd edn, 1989), pp. 99–100, 202.

24. Foxe, *Acts and Monuments*, V, 5–6; Appendix, p. 801; Emden, *Oxford, 1501–40*, sub Frith, John; G. R. Elton, *Reform and Reformation: England, 1509–1558* (1977), p. 128. Frith did meet Prior Shirbourne before he was executed; they were fellow prisoners in the Tower. The prior was released and Cromwell put pressure on Abbot Hugh to re-install him (*LP*, V, no. 1467; *LP*, VI, no. 943). Cox was master of the abbey school by 1530 (Emden, *Oxford, 1501–40, sub nom*). By supplying definite dates, Emden corrects the formerlyheld view that Cox visited the universities of Paris, Wittenberg, Prague and Cracow *c*.1546 (cf., Coates, *Reading*, p. 327 and *DNB, sub nom*). Cox achieved eminence as a grammarian, rhetorician and poet and was an enlightened educationalist, publishing in 1524 the first book in English on rhetoric, which he dedicated to Abbot Hugh as the chief maintainer and nourisher of his study (Coates, *Reading*, pp. 322–6, for the dedication published in the 1532 edition; for Cox's other works see Emden, op. cit., where the date of the above book on rhetoric is misprinted as 1542). PRO SP 10/2, no. 34.

25. Foxe, *Acts and Monuments*, V, Appendix, p. 801. One of the abbot's last acts before the monastery was dissolved in early September 1539 was to issue a patent formally instituting Cox as schoolmaster; this was an attempt not only to protect Cox's position but also the future of the school (Wilts RO D1/19 fo. 32, dated 12 Aug. 1539). This proved successful, for in Feb. 1541 Henry VIII, who now controlled patronage of the school, granted Cox for life the mastership, a dwelling, the schoolhouse and a stipend of £10 p.a., backdated to Michaelmas 1539. As the king was now pursuing a conservative religious policy, he must have had satisfactory reports about Cox (*LP* XVI, no. 580 (51); *VCH Berks*, II, 251). *LP*, VII, no. 659; 'The Paraphrase of Erasmus Roterdame upon ye Epistle of saint Paule vnto his discyple Titus', in E. J. Devereux, *A Checklist of English Translations of Erasmus to 1700* (Oxford Bibliographical Society Occasional Publications, no. 3, 1968), p. 22. Cox revised his English translation of the epistle to *Titus* for inclusion in Miles Coverdale's edition of the second volume of Erasmus's *Paraphrases* of the New Testament, published in August 1549. The Edwardian injunctions issued in July 1547 show that the government intended to use such English translations as an instrument in its programme of religious reform; copies were to be placed in every church for parishioners' convenience (Devereux, op. cit., p. 25; *Tudor Royal Proclamations*, 3 vols, ed. P. L. Hughes and J. F. Larkin (Newhaven and London, 1964–9), vol. I, no. 287, p. 395).

26. Abbot Hugh seems always to have been on good terms with the king, who even spoke of him as 'his own abbot'; they also exchanged gifts (*LP*, III, i, no. 1003; *LP*, V, no. 686, pp. 327, 329; *LP*, VI, no. 32; *LP* XIV, ii, no. 613). In November 1537 the king greatly favoured Abbot Hugh at the time of Queen Jane Seymour's funeral, choosing him to celebrate mass and conduct the service on Sunday, the most honourable of the four consecutive days over which the rites extended (*LP*, XII, ii, no. 1060). For Cromwell's support of Prior Shirbourne, see above, note 24. The abbot was also involved in a bitter dispute with another subordinate, his prior of Leominster, whose house was controlled by Reading Abbey. The prior sought Cromwell's intervention and also enjoyed the

support of Bishop Rowland Lee of Coventry and Lichfield (*LP*, vii, no. 1678; *LP*, viii, no. 593; *LP*, ix, no. 856 (copied as *LP*, vii, no. 1449); *LP*, xiii, ii, no. 1263; *LP*, xiv, i, no. 1020; *LP*, xiv, ii, no. 620; Martin, 'People of Reading', pp. 80–2). *LP*, vii, no. 1544; *LP*, xiv, i, no. 190 (13); *LP*, xiv, ii, no. 782, pp. 318, 321–2, 324, 325, 326, 328; Wilts RO D1/19 fos 30–1.

27. *LP*, xi, nos 313 and 324; Brigden, *London*, pp. 240–1.

28. The mayor was chosen by the abbot or his deputy in the week after Michaelmas (*Corporation Diary*, vol. i, p. 106). On 13 Sept. 1538 the Reading Grey Friars surrendered; 14 Sept. the church was defaced; 18 Sept. dismantling of the Caversham shrine was completed and the abbey relics were confiscated (*LP*, xiii, ii, nos 340, 346, 367, 377). The royal Injunctions of 1538 are dated 30 Sept. but were not issued with a mandate for publication until 11 Oct. (*Visitation Articles and Injunctions of the Period of the Reformation*, ed: W. H. Frere and W. P. M. Kennedy (Alcuin Club Collections, xiv–xvi, 1910), ii, 34, 37, 38, 39). The early assault on the relics at Reading and Caversham indicates that in the government's view these were among the more important and wealthiest shrines in the country (D. Knowles, *The Religious Orders in England: The Tudor Age*, 3 vols, (Cambridge, 1959; pbk 1979), vol. iii, pp. 352–3; J. Youings, *The Dissolution of the Monasteries* (1971), pp. 76–7). Reading Abbey was in royal possession by 12 Sept. 1539 (*LP*, xiv, ii, no. 202).

29. Berks RO D/P 97.5/2, pp. 163, 167; *Corporation Diary*, vol. i, p. 164; *LP*, iv, iii, no. 5330 and ibid. (v).

30. Berks RO D/P 97.5/2, pp. 203, 208. In his will, Cawood bequeaths his soul to the mercy of Almighty God, 'having full confidence . . . to be saved by the merits of the Passion of His most glorious Son our Saviour Jesus Christ who suffered pains and shed his blood for my redemption and all mankind's. . . .' It was witnessed by Mr Ambrose Barker and Mr Leonard Barker, citizens and merchants of London, and by Mr Anthony Barker, their brother, vicar of Sonning near Reading, who made a Protestant declaration in his will. Cawood desired burial within St Martin's, Ironmonger Lane, London, a church favoured by radical Protestants (PRO PCC will PROB 11/29,18, proved 10 April 1543; Foxe, *Acts and Monuments*, v, 447; Addenda, 855; *Acts of the Privy Council of England*, 32 vols, ed. J. R. Dasent (1890–1907), vol. ii, pp. 25–6; Brigden, *London*, pp. 384, 399, 424). PRO PCC will of Anthony Barker PROB 11/36,14 dated 4 Aug. 1551, proved 20 June 1553. Thomas Everard died on 10 June 1535 during his fourth mayoralty (*Corporation Diary*, vol. i, pp. 143, 148, 153, 161, 162; PRO PCC will PROB 11/29, 4).

31. An altar was situated by the mayor's seat in St Laurence's church and was probably the one used for the daily mass which he and his entourage were expected to attend (Berks RO D/P 97.5/2, p. 85; C. Phythian-Adams, 'Ceremony and the Citizen: the Communal Year at Coventry, 1450–1550', in *Crisis and Order in English Towns*, ed. P. Clark and P. Slack (1972), p. 61). At St Mary's in 1567–8, 3*s.* 6*d.* was spent on 'dressing' the mayor's seat (*The Churchwardens' Accounts of the Parish of St Mary, Reading, Berks, 1550–1662*, transcribed by F. N. Garry and A. G. Garry (Reading, 1893), p. 46).

32. St Laurence's church itself possessed a few relics, e.g. part of the Holy Cross contained in a silver and gilt cross, and a gridiron of silver and gilt containing a bone of St Laurence (Berks RO D/P 97.5/2, inventory of St Laurence's church goods, 1517, p. 48). For the corrody vicarage, see above, note 10.

33. BL Add. Charter 1965, Compotus of Father Walter Preston; *LP*, xi, no. 1270; *LP*, viii, no. 767; *Corporation Diary*, vol. i, pp. 202–3; S. T. Bindoff, *The History of Parliament: The House of Commons, 1509–1558* (History of Parliament Trust, 1982), sub Grey, William II; E. W. Dormer, *Gray of Reading: A Sixteenth-Century Controversialist and Ballad Writer* (Reading, 1923); Brigden, *London*, p. 323; *LP*, xx, i, no. 282 (34); *LP*, xx, ii, 707 (50). Among Gray's mayoral tenants were John White, already mentioned, Richard Turner, Richard Justice, William Edmundes, John Bourne and William Buryton; for these see text below. The monarch held the lordship of Reading from the Dissolution onwards, apart from two brief periods when it was held by the Duke of Somerset: (a) he was granted the manors of Reading and Whitley with Whitley park in July 1548 but was deprived of them when deposed as Protector in Jan. 1550; (b) these lands with the site of the abbey were restored to him in June 1550 but reverted to the Crown after his execution by act of Parliament passed in April 1552 (*Cal. Pat. Rolls, Edward VI*, ii, 27–9 and iii, 430–2). As one of Somerset's principal advisers, Gray was arrested and imprisoned in the Tower when the Duke fell from power; he seems to have been released some time after Feb. 1550 (*Acts of the Privy Council*, ii, 343, 398, 400, 402). Martin, 'People of Reading', pp. 376–82.

34. *LP*, xx, i, no. 1081 (52); *Cal. Pat. Rolls, Philip and Mary*, i, 173–4. The vicar was Sir John More (Wilts RO D1/2/16, fo. 43v). He seems to have vacated the living some time between 13 May 1560, when he witnessed the will of Thomas Clere and 6 Feb. 1561 when the will of Agnes Wilder of Whitley in St Giles' parish was witnessed by the vicar of St Mary's (Berks RO D/A 1/8 fos 183, 204r, proved 19 April 1961; ibid., fo. 202r). More, who almost certainly left his parish as the result of deprivation, was succeeded by John Walton BA, a licensed preacher who compounded for his first fruits and tenths on 14 Aug. 1561 (Corpus Christi College, Cambridge, MS 97, fo. 197; PRO E 344/7, fo. 129v). Reading's clergy are the subject of a forthcoming article.

35. *Corporation Diary*, vol. i, pp. 145, 150, 157, 162, 169, 175, 176; Berks RO D/P 97.5/2, pp. 78, 83, 134, 139; BL Cott. MS, Cleop. E iv, fos 264r, 267 (*LP*, xiii, ii, nos 367, 377); *Reading Charters*, pp. 8–9. Turner bequeathed his soul to 'Almighty God, my Maker and Redeemer and to all the blessed company of heaven', left money to St Laurence's two fraternities of Jesus and Our Lady, and made provision for masses at his month's mind, year's mind and on the anniversary for 20 years thereafter (PRO PCC will PROB 11/31, 47 dated 11 Sept. 1546, proved 31 Oct. 1547).

36. Mirth was admitted a burgess in 1519 (*Corporation Diary*, vol. i, pp. 139, 170). *LP*, x, no. 709 (name spelled Merzyth); *LP*, xiv, i, no. 67. Like Turner, though not to the same extent, Mirth also revealed himself to be conservative in religious matters, commending his soul to 'Almighty God and all the holy company of heaven'; he bequeathed money to St Laurence's fraternity of Jesus together with arrears 'that I am behind for my brotherhood', and also made a bequest to the fraternity of Our Lady. Mirth was the proud possessor of a silver-and-gilt cup and cover weighing more than $46\frac{1}{2}$ oz., given him by Henry VIII (PRO PCC will PROB 11/28,30 dated 28 March 1541, proved 10 June 1541). The charter of incorporation was granted on 24 April 1542 (*Reading Charters*, p. 14).

37. Paul, 'Last Abbots of Reading and Colchester', Appendix 11, pp. 119–20 (Mirth is spelled as Myrche, Cawood as Cawde, Buryton as Beryngton – a form generally used in respect of his three sons, e.g. *Corporation Diary*, vol. 1, pp. 247, 287). Buryton made his will on 1 Aug. 1553, two days before Mary made her triumphant entry into London as Queen (Brigden, *London*, p. 526 ff). Probably for reasons of caution, he simply commended his soul to Almighty God and made no conservative religious reference. However, although he bequeathed money to the vicar of his parish of St Laurence for tithes forgotten, the chief witness to his will was Sir John More, Sir Francis Englefield's presentee to the vicarage of St Giles'. Another witness was John Bourne, currently mayor of Reading and also a religious conservative (Berks RO D/A 1/7, fo. 1, proved 7 Oct. 1553; *Corporation Diary*, vol. 1, p. 229). In 1550 both Buryton and Bourne had been witnesses to the will of Sir John Mayneforth, Abbot Hugh's vicar of St Laurence's (Berks RO D/A 1/5, fo. 113r). For Bourne see below, note 46.

38. Paul, 'Last Abbots of Reading and Colchester', Appendix 1, p. 119; *Corporation Diary*, vol. 1, pp. 146, 154, 155, 158, 159, 160, 161, 162, 165, 171. Pastler was churchwarden of St Laurence's 1525–7, serving with John White 1526–7, and was churchwarden again 1534–5 (Berks RO D/P 97.5/2, pp. 159, 163, 195).

39. *Corporation Diary*, vol. 1, p. 172; see notes 28, 34.

40. *Corporation Diary*, vol. 1, p. 253 and below, note 43, for William Edmundes. For John Bourne, *Corporation Diary*, vol. 1, p. 257, and below, note 46. *Reading Charters*, pp. 5–14; *Corporation Diary*, vol. 1, pp. 176–7, 183–4, (and e.g.) 217, 252, 253, 256, 258.

41. *Corporation Diary*, vol. 1, p. 176. This other ally of Cromwell was Thomas Vachell of Coley in St Mary's parish, a member of the Berkshire gentry and a Reading MP during the Reformation Parliament (*VCH Berks*, vol. 111, p. 364; Bindoff, *House of Commons*, sub Vachell, Thomas I; Martin, 'People of Reading', pp. 85–7). Conflict between Vachell and the top townsmen began immediately the abbey was dissolved in Sept. 1539 at the time of the mayoral election. There seemed every danger that Vachell, Cromwell's under-steward and evidently acting as bailiff of the liberty, would establish some permanent ascendancy over them, thereby dashing their hopes of achieving incorporation (*Corporation Diary*, vol. 1, p. 172; *LP*, xiv, ii, no. 811; Martin, 'People of Reading', pp. 113–20, 124 n. 34, 125–8).

42. *Corporation Diary*, vol. 1, pp. 112, 117, 119, 164. Justice attended Henry VIII's coronation as a Groom of the Wardrobe of Robes to Queen Catherine of Aragon, and later was receiver and bailiff of various lands in Berkshire for Queen Anne Boleyn (*LP*, 1, i, no. 82, p. 41; vii, no. 352). He succeeded his stepfather, the royal servant Richard Smyth, as king's bailiff of Caversham manor 1515–43 (*LP*, 1, i, no. 519 (56); 11, i, 962; xviii, ii, no. 449 (2)). He also enjoyed a royal grant of tenements in St Michael Bassishaw parish, London, from 1516 to 1545 (*LP*, 11, i, no. 1751; xx, i, no. 465 (73)). PRO PCC will of Richard Smyth PROB 11/18, 22 proved 15 Aug. 1516, and see note 11 for Thomas Justice. Richard Justice was the first mayor elected after the dissolution of the abbey (*Corporation Diary*, vol. 1, p. 172; see above, note 41). Justice was conservative in religion; in his will, dated 1 Feb. 1542 (*sic*) he bequeathed his soul to 'God, Our Blessed Lady and to all the holy company of heaven' and clearly believed in purgatory. He survived until at

least 5 Sept. 1548 (PRO PCC will PROB 11/32,22, proved 12 Jan. 1548/9. *Corporation Diary*, vol. i, p. 211).

43. Richard Justice had just become mayor (*Corporation Diary*, vol. i, pp. 172–3). For Edmundes' profession and career, see PRO PCC will of Robert Brill PROB 11/21,4 dated 2 May 1519; retrospective entry on 1510 burgess list and predecessor's name in *Corporation Diary*, vol. i, p. 120, and e.g. Berks RO R/Box 430 deeds dated 11 Dec. 1512 and 31 Jan. 1513; Wilts RO D1/19, fo. 27v; *Corporation Diary*, vol. i, pp. 145, 178; *The Clerks of the Counties, 1360–1960*, compiled by L. E. Stephens (1961), p. 54; Berks RO D/P 97.5/2, pp. 123, 128. Abbot Hugh's respect for Edmundes and his wife was such that he entrusted them with the personal care of Lady Lisle's young son during his education (*LP*, vii, nos 1451, 1452, 1453). Sir William Penizon succeeded Cromwell as high steward in Nov. 1540 and restored Edmundes to the under-stewardship, originally granted him for life by Abbot Hugh (*LP*, xvi, no. 305 (54)). At this time Edmundes seems to have received royal confirmation of his conventual patent (e.g. PRO LR6/96 pt 1, no. 1, m. 25d) and remained as under-steward, irrespective of change of high steward (Martin, 'People of Reading', p. 127, n. 43). Edmundes wrote his own will, committing his soul to God's mercy, 'believing without any doubt or mistrust that by His grace and the merits of Jesus Christ and by virtue of His Passion I have and shall have remission of my sins' (Berks RO D/A 1/65 16a, dated 9 April 1555, proved 15 Nov. 1557).

44. *Corporation Diary*, vo. i, pp. 172, 174, 175, 176, 185.

45. *Corporation Diary*, vol. i, pp. 178, 179, 198; Berks RO D/P 97.5/2, St Laurence's CW Accounts for 1542–3 and 1543–4, pp. 228, 231. The end of the account for 1542–3 is missing along with the preamble to the account for 1543–4, but by tracing payment of deficits and quit rents, for example, the date of the latter account can be determined (Martin, 'People of Reading', Appendix A, note 1). See above, note 37.

46. While in his will dated 24 Nov. 1558, John Bourne (then mayor) trusted to be saved only by the merits of Christ's blessed Passion and Resurrection, he was otherwise clearly very conservative in his religious beliefs, e.g. desiring a traditional burial, his knell tolled in all three Reading churches, a trental of masses at his burial and month's mind with money for the poor, priests and clerks at these times, as well as at his year's mind. Whetham, St Mary's Catholic vicar, was chief witness to the will (see text above and note 18; PRO PCC will PROB 11/42a, 19 proved 29 Dec. 1558; *Corporation Diary*, vol. i, pp. 152, 154, 155, 158, 162, 174, 178, 187, 229, 231, 242, 256, 257). Bourne's relatives as churchwardens were *c.*1550–1 and in 1553 brother-in-law William Kynfytt (Kynfeld), and son-in-law John Hethe, both burgesses (*Corporation Diary*, vol. i, pp. 179, 195; Garry, *St Mary's CW Accounts*, p. 1). Other relatives as churchwardens were 1556–7 son-in-law Edward Kemys, 1557–8 son-in-law Robert Style, 1558–9 brother-in-law Henry Morwey, all urban office-holders but not burgesses (*Corporation Diary*, vol. i, pp. 158, 165, 178, 188, 194, 202, 204, 221, 230, 235, 241, 251; Garry, *St Mary's CW Accounts*, pp. 27, 30, 33).

47. *Corporation Diary*, vol. i, pp. 178, 179; PRO LR6/96 pt 1, no. 1, m. 3, m. 4, m. 63d. In his will Nicholas Nicholas Niclas commended his soul to the living Christ, trusting only through His merits and Passion to receive the kingdom of heaven. He made bequests to Mr Grey (almost certainly William Gray), to

Mr Anthony Barker, and to Mr Edmondes (William Edmundes) (above, notes 30, 33, 43; PRO PCC will of Nicholas Nyclas PROB 11/34, 1 dated 28 Aug. 1549, proved 17 Jan. 1550/1). He was elected to serve as one of St Laurence's two churchwardens in 1548–9 but the preamble to this account which would have been made up at the year's end asserts that John Poyntz served alone. However, as Niclas's will mentions nothing about his being ill, it is possible he had served for some part of the year (Berks RO D/P 97.5/2, pp. 254, 255). His father, Nicholas Nicholas the elder, a beer brewer, bequeathed £40 to St Giles'. for an image of the Visitation of Our Lady, and his grandfather Cristin Nicholas £20 for a silver-gilt cross (PRO PCC wills PROB 11/18,1 proved 7 Nov. 1514 and PROB 11/16,12 proved 16 Mar. 1508/9; *Corporation Diary*, vol. 1, p. 115). Cristin Nicholas was elected mayor 1491, 1497, 1499, and in 1507 when the decree was obtained, and became MP in 1504 (*Corporation Diary*, vol. i, pp. 89, 95, 98–9, 101, 104, 105; see above, note 9).

48. *Reading Charters*, pp. 6–14; R. Tittler, 'The Emergence of Urban Policy, 1536–1558' in *The Mid-Tudor Polity*, c.*1540–1560*, ed. J. Loach and R. Tittler (London and Basingstoke, 1980), 74–93, especially p. 88; R. Tittler, 'The Incorporation of Boroughs, 1540–1558', *History*, 62, no. 204 (Feb. 1977), pp. 24–42, esp. p. 33; D. M. Palliser, *The Age of Elizabeth: England under the later Tudors, 1547–1603* (Harlow 1983; 2nd edn, 1992), pp. 256–8, 260–1.

49. *Reading Charters*, pp. 15–53. The Tudor monarchs had not only neglected the site and premises of the abbey, said to be ruinous in 1563, but by 1560 Reading's 19 bridges were without exception also acknowledged to be 'very ruinous, falling, and in great decay for default of repairs so that no passage can be made over [them] without great danger' to men and animals alike (ibid., pp. 34–5, clause 51; *Calendar of Patent Rolls, Elizabeth*, vol. ii, p. 490). This state of affairs had been noted by Sept. 1552 when the Seven Bridges were already described as being '*in magna ruina*' (PRO LR 2/187, fo. 345v). As a result the 'resort and access' of townsmen and travellers was 'greatly diminished', causing great poverty to Reading's inhabitants as well as the 'decay and ruin' of property. In her charter, Queen Elizabeth granted timber and, among other materials, 200 loads of stone from the abbey site to assist with repairs (*Reading Charters*, p. 35).

50. John Strype, *Annals of the Reformation and Establishment of Religion . . . during Queen Elizabeth's Happy Reign* (Oxford, 1824), vol. i, ii, p. 132. At St Laurence's, Michaelmas 1526, it was 'enacted by the assent and consent of all the worshipfuls of this parish' that the churchwardens should present their accounts on the feast of St Matthew; they could fine any churchwarden failing to meet this obligation (Berks RO D/P 97.5/2, p. 162). In Feb. 1564/5 William Milles of Whitley, then aged about 50, who had twice been a churchwarden of St Giles', remembered as a boy of 11, *c.*1526, 'the elders of the parish . . . going in procession' (Berks RO D/A 2/c. 153 fo. 23; Berks RO D/P 96.5/1, MS p. 1 of each account for 1546–7, 1547–8, 1561–2, 1562–3). Martin, 'People of Reading', p. 184 and note 49.

51. The question of parochial membership lacked precise legal definition. Both law and custom assumed that parish membership was comprised of 'inhabitants' considered to 'belong' to their parish. However, Sir Edward Coke, the great Elizabethan lawyer, considered the word 'inhabitants' was

'needful to be explained, being the largest word of this kind'. Referring to the statute 22 Henry VIII, c. 5, he stated that 'inhabitants' meant householders who, whether resident or non-resident, had lands and tenements within their own possession and manurance in the area of liability. It did not include servants and other such persons who had nothing upon which distraint could be made (*The Second Part of the Institutes of the Laws of England* (3rd edn, 1669), pp. 702–3; C. Drew, *Early Parochial Organisation in England: The Origins of the Office of Churchwarden* (St Anthony's Hall Publications, no. 7, York, 1954), pp. 11–12). At St Laurence's in 1551–2 it was decreed that 'every inhabitant of the parish shall pay every Sunday in the year 5*d.* for every tenement as of old time the holy loaf was used to be paid' (Berks RO D/P 97.5.2, p. 267). At St Mary's in 1599–1600 it was agreed that 'every householder shall pay unto the churchwardens ... according to the old custom 2*d.* for their house for the holy loaf every year' (Garry, *St Mary's CW Accounts*, p. 85). For the assent of 'the parish' on financial matters, e.g. cost of a cope, altar cloths, and fees for bell-tolling, see Berks RO D/P 97.5/2, pp. 34, 97, 108; on forgiveness of debt, see Berks RO D/P 96.5/1, 3rd MS pp. 1540–1 acct; 2nd MS pp. 1551–2 acct. Bills had to be 'showed and examined' and the churchwardens had to 'pray to be allowed' certain debts or expenditure (ibid., passim; Garry, *St Mary's CW Accounts*, passim).

52. PRO E 301/3; M. K. McIntosh, *A Community Transformed: The Manor and Liberty of Havering, 1500–1620* (Cambridge, 1991), pp. 34–42 where the information about households is analysed from a list of communicants. On the matter of children as communicants, see Thomas, *Religion and the Decline of Magic*, above, note 9.

53. Strype, *Annals*, vol. I, ii, p. 132.

54. Beat Kümin, *The Shaping of a Community: The Rise and Reformation of the English Parish c. 1400–1560* (St Andrew's Studies in Reformation History, Aldershot, 1996), Ch. 2; Martin, 'People of Reading', pp. 190–8; J. S. Craig, 'Co-operation and Initiatives: Elizabethan Churchwardens and the Parish Accounts of Mildenhall', *Social History*, 18 (1993), 359, 362–80.

55. Berks RO D/P 97.5/2, pp. 85, 108, 244; Garry, *St Mary's CW Accounts*, p. 46.

56. Berks RO D/P 97.5/2, p. 32.

57. Berks RO D/P 97.5/2, p. 244. The mayor was William Buryton, the two former mayors were Richard Justice and William Edmundes (*Corporation Diary*, vol. I, pp. 172, 174, 185, 193, 198). The churchwardens were John Sawnders, a burgess, and Edward Butler, who became a burgess in December 1549 (ibid., pp. 194–5, 213). The other dignitaries were Alderman Nicholas Niclas, Alderman John Bell, Robert Blake, John Bukland, Thomas Sayntmore, Raphe Gladwyn and Gilbert Johnson (ibid., for the aldermen, pp. 178, 199; for the burgesses, pp. 133, 163, 165, 179).

58. Mayneforth was a notary. See text above and notes 11, 12, 13.

59. The ancient custom whereby a substantial parishioner took custody into his own home of valuable church goods was disliked by the Church which frequently prohibited the practice, but it was still prevalent in the sixteenth century. However, churchwardens did not, as Drew believed, gain 'complete control over the custody, acquisition and disposal of church goods' (*Origins of the Office of Churchwarden*, pp. 9, 10; see text below). Mayoral custody of charters, goblets, etc., continued into the era of the new corporation and probably

thereafter, even though not mentioned in their minutes (*Corporation Diary*, vol. I, pp. 142–94, passim (1520–45).

60. Berks RO D/P 97.5/2, p. 190. Mrs Hyde was the widow of a mayor, Nicholas Hyde (PRO PCC will PROB 11/22,35 proved 3 July 1528; *Corporation Diary*, vol. I, p. 144). The current mayor was John Rede, alias Skynner, and the three former mayors were Thomas Everard, Richard Turner and John Vausby (or Fawsby, usually transcribed Vansby) (ibid., pp. 143, 145, 148, 150, 151, 153, 157). Rede, alias Skynner, was churchwarden 1510–12; Everard 1517–19; Turner 1509–11, 1520–2; Vausby 1516–18 (Berks RO D/P 97.5/2, pp. 78, 83, 88, 109, 113, 118, 123, 134, 139). The two dignitaries were John White, who up to this point had been a churchwarden 1526–8 and admitted a burgess in 1529, and Walter Barton, the wealthy relative of William Buryton (Beryngton). Barton was a mercer and member of the Middle Temple (ibid., pp. 163, 167; *Corporation Diary*, vol. I, p. 154; PRO PCC will PROB 11/27,17 proved 16 May 1538; *Minutes of Parliament of the Middle Temple, 1501–1603*, 3 vols, ed. C. H. Hopwood (1904), vol. I, p. 46).

61. William Lambard, *Eirenarcha*: the fourth book, *The Dueties of Constables, Borsholders, Tythingmen, and such other lowe and lay Ministers of the Peace* (1606 edn), pp. 58–9; Berks RO D/P 97.5/2, p. 61. In 1544–5, St Laurence's churchwardens paid 6*d.* for horse hire to go to Newbury 'for the indicting of William Paytser that stole the chalice' (ibid., p. 238). At St Giles', some time before Easter 1518, a silver cruet was lost by Master Beke and Thomas Wilson who between them had to repay the value of it by instalments to the parish (Berks RO D/P 96.5/1, 7th MS p. of 1518–19 acct., 1st and 6th MS pp. of 1519–20 acct.).

62. Lambard, *Eirenarcha Dueties of Constables, etc.*, pp. 58–60.

63. Ibid. This provided legal justification for sales of church goods in Edward's reign. In Reading, proceeds of genuine sales of church goods were used for making necessary religious changes and for public works within the parishes, e.g. making a highway, street-paving, repair of church housing property, and it is likely that the rebuilding of St Mary's church was another such project for which official sanction for sale of church plate was obtained. Other transactions were token sales of church goods, e.g. vestments and bells sold to local dignitaries for custody purposes on the understanding these could be redeemed at will by the parish (Martin, 'People of Reading', p. 462 ff. and my forthcoming article; W. K. Jordan, *Edward VI: The Threshold of Power* (1970), pp. 388 ff.).

64. See above, note 33, for the two brief periods of the Duke of Somerset's lordship.

65. *Narratives of the Days of the Reformation*, ed. J. G. Nichols (Camden Society, O.S., LXXVII, 1859), p. 126; PRO PCC will of John Bourne PROB 11/42a,19, proved 29 Dec. 1558.

7. TEXTILES AND REFORM: HALIFAX AND ITS
HINTERLAND   *William and Sarah Sheils*

1. The classic statement is in C. Hill, 'From Lollards to Levellers', printed in his collected essays, vol. 2: *Religion and Politics in Seventeenth-Century England*

(Brighton, 1986), pp. 89–116; see also J. F. Davis, 'Lollard Survival and the Textile Industry in the South-east of England', *Studies in Church History*, 3 (1966), 191–201; M. Spufford (ed.), *The World of Rural Dissenters, 1520–1725* (Cambridge, 1995), pp. 45, 51, 135.

2. A. Everitt, 'Non-Conformity in Country Parishes', in J. Thirsk (ed.), *Land, Church and People* (Reading, 1970), pp. 188–9; this is the approach adopted in Spufford, *Rural Dissenters*, but see the critical comments by P. Collinson at pp. 393–6.

3. More detailed studies of Halifax in this period are found in S. A. Sheils, 'Aspects of the History of Halifax 1480–1547' (MA dissertation, University of York, 1981), and M. E. Francois, 'The Social and Economic Development of Halifax, 1558–1640', *Proceedings of the Leeds Philosophical and Literary Society* (1966), vol. 11, pt VIII, pp. 217–80.

4. R. A. Marchant, *The Puritans and the Church Courts in the Diocese of York, 1560–1642* (1960), pp. 30–1, 107, 113; B. Manning, *The English People and the English Revolution* (1976), pp. 210–15. For Cranbrook, see P. Collinson, 'Cranbrook and the Fletchers: Popular and Unpopular Religion in the Kentish Weald' in his *Godly People*, (1983), pp. 399–428.

5. W. Nicholson (ed.), *The Remains of Edmund Grindal* (Parker Society, 1843), p. 380; P. Collinson, *Archbishop Grindal 1519–1583: The Struggle for a Reformed Church* (1979), pp. 206–10; A. G. Dickens, *Lollards and Protestants in the Diocese of York, 1509–1558* (Oxford, 1959), p. 149.

6. J. Craig and C. Litzenberger, 'Wills as Religious Propaganda: the Testament of William Tracy', *Journal of Ecclesiastical History*, 44 (1993), 415–31, esp. 427–8, 430.

7. W. Page (ed.), *Yorkshire Chantry Surveys*, I (Surtees Society, no. 92, 1895), p. 421; R. B. Smith, *Land and Politics in the England of Henry VIII: The West Riding of Yorkshire, 1530–1546* (Oxford, 1970), pp. 112–13, discusses the comparative wealth of Halifax farmers; J. Lister, 'Shibden Hall, South Owram', *Transactions of the Halifax Antiquarian Society* (1907), 159–90.

8. Page, *Yorks. Chantries*, II, p. 423.

9. Ibid., pp. 421–4.

10. J. Lister, 'The Life of Dr Robert Haldesworth, part i', *Trans. Halifax Antiq. Soc.* (1902), unpaginated; Smith, *Land and Politics*, pp. 148–9; R. and M. Dodds, *The Exeter Conspiracy and the Pilgrimage of Grace* (1915), I, pp. 257–9.

11. J. W. Clay and E. W. Crossley, *Halifax Wills 1450–1559* (2 vols, privately printed, n.d.), passim.

12. Francois, *Halifax*, p. 231; Lister, 'Haldesworth'; Clay, *Halifax Wills*, I, no. 40, and no. 176 for bequests to friars.

13. R. K. Morris, *Churches in the Landscape* (1989), pp. 350–76: E. Duffy, *The Stripping of the Altars: Traditional Religion in England 1400–1580* (New Haven and London, 1992), pp. 131–2.

14. J. Lister, 'The Old Free Chapels in the Parish of Halifax', *Trans. Halifax Antiq. Soc.* (1909), 29.

15. Ibid., 31–6, 48–51; Clay, *Halifax Wills*, I, nos 127, 182, 210, 217.

16. Lister, 'Old Free Chapels', 37–9, 44, 46–7; Clay, *Halifax Wills*, I, nos 79, 114, 117, 133, 134, 176.

17. E. W. Crossley, 'Notes on some Chantry Endowments in the Parish of Halifax', *Trans. Halifax Antiq. Soc.* (1909), 58–74, esp. p. 68; Clay, *Halifax Wills*, I, no. 180; II, no. 172.

18. D. M. Palliser, *Tudor York* (Oxford, 1979), pp. 226–31, 234–8; J. C. Ward, 'The Reformation in Colchester 1528–1558', *Essex Archaeology and History*, 15 (1983), 84–95.

19. Dickens, *Lollards and Protestants*, pp. 148, 200.

20. Clay, *Halifax Wills*, I, nos 76, 186, 238.

21. C. Burgess, ' "By Quick and by Dead": Wills and Pious Provision in Late Medieval Bristol', *English Historical Review*, 102 (1987), 837–58; G. Rosser, 'Parochial Conformity and Voluntary Religion in Late Medieval England', *Transactions of the Royal Historical Society*, 6 series, 1 (1991), 173–89, esp. 188; E. Duffy, *Stripping of the Altars*, ch. 5: 'The Saints', pp. 155–205, is particularly strong in delineating these devotions.

22. Thirty of the 42 charitable wills in table 1 refer to roads and bridges solely.

23. The most recent pessimistic assessment of this source is J. D. Alsop, 'Religious Preambles in Early Modern English Wills as Formulae', *Journal of Ecclesiastical History*, 40 (1989), 19–27; more optimistic views are in C. Marsh, 'In the Name of God? Will-making and Faith in Early Modern England'; G. H. Martin and P. Spufford (eds), *The Records of the Nation* (Woodbridge, 1990), pp. 215–49. For a recent study based on wills see C. J. Litzenberger, 'Local Responses to Changes in Religious Policy Based on Evidence from Gloucestershire Wills, 1540–1580', *Continuity and Change*, 8 (1993), 417–39.

24. Borthwick Institute of Historical Research, York, Pro. Reg. 9, fols 349, 363; Prob. Reg. 11, fol. 355; Clay, *Halifax Wills*, I, no. 152.

25. Borthwick, Prob. Reg. 11, fol. 333.

26. These are at ibid., fols 342, 252, 379–v, 387v, 439–v, 445v. The traditional will was at fol. 267v; Duffy, *Stripping of the Altars*, pp. 515–21.

27. Borthwick, Prob. Reg. 11, fols 328–v, 373, 386, 400; Dickens, *Lollards and Protestants*, pp. 200, 248.

28. Borthwick, Prob. Reg. 11, fols 697v, 755, 774v; Dickens, *Lollards and Protestants*, pp. 225–6; E. W. Crossley, ed., *Halifax Parish Registers*, II (Yorkshire Parish Register Society, 1914), pp. ii–iv identifies members of the Best, Maude and Hargreaves families acting as curates in the parish during the mid-16th century.

29. Borthwick, Prob. Reg. 11, fols 379v, 439–v, 713, 774v; Prob. Reg. 13, fol. 181.

30. Marsh, 'In the Name of God?', p. 248.

31. C. Burgess and B. Kümin, 'Penitential Bequests and Parish Regimes in Late Medieval England', *Journal of Ecclesiastical History*, 44 (1993), pp. 610–30. The absence of churchwardens' or chapel accounts in Halifax means that support from the living, which was significant in many of the parishes studied by Burgess and Kümin, and also by Duffy, is lost, and may leave the historian with a restricted understanding of the devotional range within the parish. Similar disruption was noted in the extensive Essex parish of Havering: M. McIntosh, *A Community Transformed: The Manor and Liberty of Havering, 1500–1620* (Cambridge, 1991), pp. 219–23.

32. See the wills printed in Clay, *Halifax Wills*, II, for the reigns of Edward and Mary.

33. Crossley, *Halifax Parish Register*, I (1910), p. 58.

34. J. A. Hoeppner Moran, *The Growth of English Schooling, 1340–1548* (Princeton, NJ, 1985), pp. 119–20; Dickens, *Lollards and Protestants*, p. 198.

35. Smith, *Land and Politics*, p. 37; M. Drake, 'An Elementary Exercise in Parish Register Demography', *Economic History Review*, 2 series, 14 (1961–2), 434.

36. See Collinson, *Archbishop Grindal*, pp. 233–49 for the context of the letter.

37. Borthwick, York, V. 1578-9/CB 1, fol. 147; Marchant, *Puritans and Church Courts*, pp. 29–31, 246; M. C. Cross, *The Puritan Earl* (1966), p. 256; Francois, *Halifax*, pp. 272–5.

38. W. K. Jordan, *The Charities of Rural England, 1480–1660*, (1961), pp. 323–6; J. Walker, *The History of Halifax* (1775), pp. 421, 426, 433–6, 442, 447, 451.

39. Marchant, *Puritans and Church Courts*, pp. 227, 231.

40. D. Underdown, *Fire from Heaven: Life in an English Town in the Seventeenth Century* (New Haven and London, 1992), pp. 109–29. Again the absence of evidence for the charitable activity of the living diminishes our knowledge of the extent of charitable giving in Halifax at this time. From the evidence of wills between 1480 and 1660 the parishioners gave the largest sum to charitable uses of any place in Yorkshire, except for the cities of York and Hull: Jordan, *Rural Charities*, tables at pp. 446–51.

8. ECONOMIC PROBLEMS OF PROVINCIAL URBAN CLERGY   *Patrick Carter*

1. Public Record Office (hereafter PRO), E 347/17/1.

2. L. T. Smith (ed.), *The Itinerary of John Leland* (London, 1907–10), vol. II, p. 108; and C. Phythian-Adams, *Desolation of a City: Coventry and the Urban Crisis of the Late Middle Ages* (Cambridge, 1979).

3. For two contrasting views of the subject, see R. B. Dobson, 'Urban Decline in Late Medieval England', *Transactions of the Royal Historical Society*, 5th ser. XXVII (1977), 1–22; and A. R. Bridbury, 'English Provincial Towns in the Later Middle Ages', *Economic History Review*, 2nd ser. XXXIV (1981), 1–24.

4. 6 Henry VIII, c.5 (*Statutes of the Realm*, vol. III, p. 127).

5. Smith (ed.), *Itinerary*, vol. I, pp. 7–8, 29–30; vol. II, p. 107.

6. J. J. Scarisbrick, *The Reformation and the English People* (Oxford, 1984), p. 33; Dobson, 'Urban Decline', p. 10.

7. H. E. Salter, *A Subsidy Collected in the Diocese of Lincoln in 1526* (Oxford, 1909), pp. 60–1.

8. For Boston, see S. H. Rigby, ' "Sore Decay" and "Fair Dwellings": Boston and Urban Decline in the Later Middle Ages', *Midland History*, X (1985), 47–61.

9. Canterbury, Coventry, Dover, Exeter, Gloucester, Ipswich, Leicester, Lincoln, Northampton, Norwich, Shrewsbury, Southampton, Stamford, Winchester and Worcester.

10. *Valor Ecclesiasticus* (London, 6 vols, 1810–26), vol. III, pp. 231–7.

11. Ibid., vol. II, pp. 316–17; W. T. MacCaffrey, *Exeter, 1540–1640* (Cambridge MA, 1958), pp. 177–9.

12. C. Cross, 'The Incomes of Provincial Urban Clergy, 1520–1645', in R. O'Day and F. Heal (eds), *Princes and Paupers in the English Church, 1500–1800* (Leicester, 1981), pp. 68–9; A. G. Little, 'Personal Tithes', *English Historical Review*, LX (1945), 67–88; and S. Brigden, 'Tithe Controversy in Reformation London', *Journal of Ecclesiastical History*, XXXII (1981), 287.

13. *Valor Ecclesiasticus*, vol. II, pp. 13, 19, 316, 327; vol. IV, p. 144.

14. Ibid., vol. I, pp. 27, 39; vol. III, p. 231; vol. IV, p. 144.

15. M. C. Skeeters, *Community and Clergy: Bristol and the Reformation c.1530–c.1570* (Oxford, 1993), pp. 159–60; PRO, C 1/861/24.

16. C. Cross (ed.), *York Clergy Wills, 1520–1600*, vol. II: *City Clergy* (York, 1989), pp. 4–5, 16–17.

17. Scarisbrick, *Reformation*, p. 44; and D. M. Owen, *Church and Society in Medieval Lincolnshire* (Lincoln, 1971), pp. 127–9.

18. Skeeters, *Community and Clergy*, p. 22; Cross (ed.), *York Clergy Wills*, pp. 39–40; *Northants. Clergy*, vol. VII, p. 25; PRO, E 334/3 fo. 15.

19. E. Roberts and K. Parker (eds), *Southampton Probate Inventories 1447–1575*, vol. I (Southampton, Southampton Rec. Soc. XXXIV, 1992), pp. 22, 79–80, 223–4.

20. Cross (ed.), *York Clergy Wills*, pp. 42–3, 50–3. It was not clear whether the £5 6s. 8d. which Thomas Worrall, a priest of St Michael Spurriergate at York, left 'remainyng in the handes of mistres Savaige' had been lodged for safekeeping or as credit on account, or if this represented a loan or investment with a moneylender? (Cross (ed.), *York Clergy Wills*, pp. 53–5).

21. Roberts and Parker (eds), *Southampton Probate*, vol. I, pp. 23–86. On Newton's associates Maurizio and Niccolo de Marini, see A. A. Ruddock, *Italian Merchants and Shipping in Southampton, 1270–1600* (Southampton, 1950), pp. 241–54.

22. 26 Henry VIII, c.3. For clerical taxation, see F. Heal, 'Clerical Tax Collection under the Tudors: the Influence of the Reformation', in R. O'Day and F. Heal (eds), *Continuity and Change: Personnel and Administration of the Church of England, 1500–1642* (Leicester, 1976), pp. 97–122; and P. R. N. Carter 'Royal Taxation of the English Parish Clergy, 1535–58' (Cambridge, unpubl. PhD dissertation, 1994).

23. R. O'Day and J. Berlatsky (eds), *The Letter-Book of Thomas Bentham, Bishop of Coventry and Lichfield, 1560–1561* (London, Camden Soc. Miscellany XXVII, 1979), p. 225.

24. M. Aston, *England's Iconoclasts: Laws against Images* (Oxford, 1988), pp. 226–8; E. Duffy, *The Stripping of the Altars* (New Haven, 1992), pp. 155–63.

25. PRO, E 347/17/1.

26. R. M. Serjeantson, *A History of the Church of All Saints, Northampton* (Northampton, 1901), pp. 86–8.

27. *Valor Ecclesiasticus*, vol. IV, p. 88; R. A. McKinley (ed.), *Victoria County History of Leicester*, vol. IV (Oxford, 1958), pp. 358, 366; *An Inventory of Historical Monuments: The Town of Stamford* (London, Royal Commission on Historical Monuments, 1977), pp. xlix, 23, 37, 42, 46.

28. British Library, Add. Charter 24, 705.

29. Skeeters, *Community and Clergy*, p. 117.

30. Ibid., p. 109; B. A. Kümin, 'The Late Medieval English Parish, *c.* 1400–1560' (Cambridge, unpubl. PhD dissertation, 1992), p. 98.

31. PRO, E 347/17/1.

32. N. M. Herbert (ed.), *The Victoria County History of the County of Gloucester*, vol. IV (Oxford, 1988), p. 295.

33. *Calendar of Patent Rolls, Philip and Mary*, vol. II, pp. 153–5; C. Cross, 'Communal Piety in Sixteenth-Century Boston', *Lincolnshire History and Archaeology*, XXV (1990), 37.

34. 37 Henry VIII, c.21 (*Statutes of the Realm*, vol. III, pp. 1013–14).

35. 1 Edward VI, c.9 (*Statutes of the Realm*, vol. IV, pt. I, pp. 14–15).

36. 2 and 3 Edward VI, c.48 (Lincoln) and c.50 (Stamford). The text of the Lincoln statute is printed in W. de Gray Birch, *The Royal Charters of the City of Lincoln, Henry II to William III* (Cambridge, 1911), pp. 188–9. A third private act of the same Parliament united two Rochester parishes (2 and 3 Edward VI, c.56).

37. D. M. Palliser, 'The Union of Parishes at York, 1547–1586', *Yorkshire Archaeological Journal*, LXVI (1974), 87–102; J. W. F. Hill, *Tudor and Stuart Lincoln* (Cambridge, 1956), pp. 20–2, 56–8; Smith (ed.), *Itinerary*, vol. I, p. 30; D. A. Stocker, 'The Archaeology of the Reformation in Lincoln: a Case Study in the Redistribution of Building Materials in the Mid Sixteenth Century', *Lincolnshire History and Archaeology*, XXV (1990), 18–32; J. Thirsk, 'Stamford in the Sixteenth and Seventeenth Centuries', in *idem, The Rural Economy of England* (London, 1984), pp. 310–11.

38. W. J. Sheils, 'Religion in Provincial Towns: Innovation and Tradition', in R. O'Day and F. Heal (eds), *Church and Society in England: Henry VIII to James I* (London, 1977), p. 160; PRO, SP 12/21/7; Palliser, 'Union of Parishes', p. 91.

39. P. Collinson, *The Elizabethan Puritan Movement* (Oxford, repr. 1990), pp. 50–1; *idem, The Birthpangs of Protestant England: Religious and Cultural Change in the Sixteenth and Seventeenth Centuries* (London, 1988), p. 42; Sheils, 'Religion in Provincial Towns', p. 163.

40. H. Robinson (ed.), *The Zurich Letters*, vol. I (Oxford, 1842), pp. 86–7.

9. THE DISSOLUTION OF THE CHANTRIES *Peter Cunich*

1. The Act dissolving the chantries (1 Edward VI, cap. 14, An Act for Chantries Collegiate, see *Statutes of the Realm*, vol. IV (i), p. 24) carries the superscription *Le roi remerciesez loyalles subiectez accepte leur benevolence et ainsi le veult*, words which were normally reserved for subsidy bills; see also Alan Kreider, *English Chantries: The Road to Dissolution* (Cambridge, MA, 1979), p. 190. The commission for the sale of chantry lands is in *Acts of the Privy Council*, vol. II, p. 184.

2. For the passage of the Act see Kreider, pp. 189–200.

3. For the opposition of the burgesses of King's Lynn and Coventry see *APC*, vol. II, pp. 193–4.

4. J. J. Scarisbrick, *The Reformation and the English People* (Oxford, 1984), p. 39.

5. Eamon Duffy, *The Stripping of the Altars: Traditional Religion in England, 1400–1580* (New Haven and London, 1992), pp. 131–41.

6. Kreider, pp. 5–8, describes types of intercessory institutions.

7. For the Winchester chantries see John Vaughan, *The Mediaeval Chantries of Winchester* (Winchester, 1977); for the Spring family chantry at Lavenham see B. McClenaghan, *The Springs of Lavenham* (London, 1924).

8. *VCH, Yorkshire*, 3, pp. 353–9 (Beverley), pp. 372–4 (Rotherham); *Nottinghamshire*, 2, pp. 152–9 (Southwell).

9. Gervase Rosser, 'Going to the Fraternity Feast: Commensality and Social Relations in Late Medieval England', *Journal of British Studies*, 33 (1994), 431.

10. Scarisbrick, pp. 19–22.

11. Henry Hillen, *History of the Borough of King's Lynn* (Norwich, 1907), p. 265.

12. E. L. Holland (ed.), *The Canterbury Chantries and Hospitals*, Kent Records, 12 (1934), pp. 19–20.

13. Emanuel Green, *The Survey and Rentals of the Chantries, Colleges and Free Chapels, Guilds, Fraternities, Lamps, Lights and Obits in the County of Somerset* (Bath, 1888), pp. 114–15, 301–2.

14. Arthur Leach, *English Schools at the Reformation, 1546–8* (1896), pp. 34, 42–5.

15. Susan Brigden, *London and the Reformation* (Oxford, 1989), pp. 385–9.

16. For the view that the dissolution of the chantries was a disaster for education in the towns, see Leach, pp. 1–6, 78–9.

17. For chantries see Kreider, pp. 9–14; for the fraternities see Scarisbrick, pp. 28–9 and Rosser, p. 431.

18. PRO, LR6/61/2–6; Brigden, pp. 389–91; Scarisbrick, p. 36.

19. Leach, pp. 116–18.

20. Dickens, pp. 240–2; Duffy, p. 454.

21. Dickens, p. 240.

22. For London, see PRO, LR6/61/2–6; for Coventry, SC6/EDVI/465–6, 714–15.

23. Duffy, p. 494.

24. Rosser, pp. 433–7.

25. Ibid., p. 446.

26. Ibid., pp. 441–6.

27. For Coventry, York and Boston, see Scarisbrick, pp. 34–5; for Northampton, p. 28.

28. Rosser, p. 441.

29. Hillen, pp. 265, 275.

30. For Abingdon, see Rosser, p. 445; for Birmingham and Ashburton, see Scarisbrick, pp. 21–2.

31. Duffy, pp. 478–503.

32. Green, pp. xv–xvi, 3.

33. Ibid., p. xvii.

34. Scarisbrick, pp. 32–3.

35. For examples of this see Scarisbrick, pp. 101–3, and Duffy, pp. 490–1.

36. These figures are taken from the receivers' accounts for 1547–8 and 1548–9, PRO, LR6/96/1, 61/2–3, 138/7–8, 104/2, 121/7, 122/1, 56/2–3, 113/1; SC6/EDVI/685–6, 692, 697–8, 707, 714–15, 723.

37. In 1548, there were 2,806 ex-religious still living who received pensions valued at approximately £23,250 per annum.

38. For Lybbe, see SC6/EDVI/692, m.58b; for Wheler, see LR6/104/2, m.46; for Silvester and Bentley, LR6/121/7, mm. 34b and 35b; and for Chamber, LR6/61/3, m.53b.

39. Peter Heath, *The English Parish Clergy on the Eve of the Reformation* (1969), pp. 22, 185. A surprising number of the chantry priests who appear in the chantry certificates were over sixty years of age.

40. Joan Simon, *Education and Society in Tudor England* (Cambridge, 1966), especially chs 8 and 9; Scarisbrick, pp. 112–13.

41. These figures are based on an analysis of all the Receivers' Accounts of the Court of Augmentations in the period 1547–53. The figures for land sales are based on the Treasurer's Accounts.

42. For London, see Brigden, pp. 389–90; Coventry, PRO, C66/847, mm. 16–21; King's Lynn, C66/812, mm. 22–3; York, E323/5, m. 19; Chichester E323/5, m. 13; Colchester, E323/6, m. 14b: Derby, E323/8, m. 25b; Leominster, E323/8, m. 26.

43. Scarisbrick, p. 39.

10. VOLUNTARY RELIGION AND REFORMATION CHANGE IN EIGHT URBAN PARISHES   *Beat Kümin*

The author is grateful for comments and suggestions made at the 28th International Congress on Medieval Studies at Kalamazoo 1993, the 'Religious History of Britain' seminar at London's Institute of Historical Research in January 1994, and by the editors of this volume.

1. C. Haigh, *English Reformations* (Oxford, 1993); E. Duffy, *The Stripping of the Altars: Traditional Religion in England, 1400–1580* (New Haven and London, 1992), subtitle and p. 479; cf. R. O'Day, *The Debate on the English Reformation* (London and New York, 1986), esp. ch. 6.

2. The three quotations from P. Collinson, *The Religion of Protestants* (Oxford, 1982), p. 247; C. Hill, *Society and Puritanism in Pre-Revolutionary England* (London, 1964), p. 484; C. Cross, *Church and People 1450–1660: the Triumph of the Laity in the English Church* (Hassocks, 1976).

3. Cross, *Church and People*, esp. pp. 31–52 (the limited room for lay initiatives in the pre-Reformation period); A. G. Dickens, *The English Reformation*, 2nd edn (London, 1989), p. 55 (quote).

4. See the works by Burgess, Duffy, Rosser and Scarisbrick quoted in the bibliography; J. Bossy, 'Blood and Baptism: Kinship, Community and Christianity in Western Europe', in D. Baker (ed.), *Sanctity and Secularity* (Oxford, 1973), pp. 129–43; and for a general evaluation D. Palliser, 'Introduction: the Parish in Perspective', in S. Wright (ed.), *Parish, Church & People* (London etc., 1988), esp. p. 17. The options offered by Lollardy (production and reading of vernacular religious texts; gatherings in 'known' houses etc.) have attracted much scholarly attention and will not be recapitulated here; cf. A. Hudson, *The Premature Reformation* (Oxford, 1988).

5. W. J. Sheils and D. Wood (eds), *Voluntary Religion* (Oxford, 1986).

6. G. Rosser, 'Parochial Conformity and Voluntary Religion in Late Medieval England', *TRHS*, 6th ser. 1 (1991), 176, emphasises the 'extensive voluntarism which shaped the parish itself'.

7. This is broadly in line with the definition given in Sheils and Wood (eds), *Voluntary Religion*, pp. viii and xii, which limited the scope of the inquiry to 'societies and associations which brought together groups of like-minded individuals for a religious purpose either within or without the life of the broader church', yet 'at no time *claimed* to be churches, but professed to perform a role . . . understood to be complementary to that of the Church or churches, providing additional emotional satisfaction, social support and fellowship'.

8. P. Collinson, 'Introduction', ibid., p. xii.

9. Examples in K. Wood-Legh (ed.), *The Account Book of Munden's Chantry* (Manchester, 1956), p. xi (rector of Bridport presents), or London, Guildhall Library [hereafter: GL], MS 9531/6, f. 25: Register of Robert Gilbert, Bishop of London (rector of St Ethelburga within Bishopsgate presents to St Mary chantry).

10. A concise summary of parochial development and duties in C. Drew, *Early Parochial Organisation in England* (London, 1954). For the continuity in official requirements cf. Duffy, *Stripping of the Altars*, ch. 2, and P. Collinson, 'The Elizabethan Church and the New Religion', in C. Haigh (ed.), *The Reign of Elizabeth I* (Basingstoke, 1984), pp. 173–8.

11. R. Swanson, 'Standards of Livings', in C. Harper-Bill (ed.), *Religious Beliefs and Ecclesiastical Careers in Late Medieval England* (Woodbridge, 1991), p. 167.

12. P. Heath (ed.), *Medieval Clerical Accounts* (York, 1964), pp. 43, 36.

13. P. Seaver, *The Puritan Lectureships* (Stanford, 1970), pp. 42–3. For a survey of post-Reformation 'voluntary religion' see Collinson, *Religion of Protestants*, ch. 6.

14. From the 1560s, new officers and records emerged (primarily as a result of official local government duties), and longer-term comparison would call for a radically different approach. The shadows of compulsion in terms of poor relief, for instance, intensified between 1552 and 1563: M. McIntosh, 'Local Responses to the Poor in Late Medieval and Tudor England', *Continuity and Change*, 3 (1988), 235.

15. All references to these churchwardens' accounts (hereafter: CWA) are based on GL, MS 1279/1–2: Andrew Hubbard CWA; ibid., MS 1454, rolls 1–65: Botolph Aldersgate CWA; Bristol Record Office, P/AS/ChW/1 and 3: All Saints CWA; B. R. Masters and E. Ralph (eds), *The Church Book of St Ewen's, Bristol, 1454–1584* (Bristol, 1967); A. Hanham (ed.), *The CWA of Ashburton 1479–1580* (Torquay, 1970); F. Somers (ed.), *Halesowen CWA 1487–1582* (London, 1952–7); W. T. Mellows (ed.), *Peterborough Local Administration: CWA 1467–1573* (Kettering, 1939); F. A. Bailey (ed.), *The CWA of Prescot, Lancashire 1523–1607* (Preston, 1953).

16. For a more detailed discussion of the reliability and potential of CWA see my *The Shaping of a Community: The Rise and Reformation of the English Parish* c. *1400–1560* (Aldershot and Brookfield, VT, 1995).

17. Canonical and legal requirements are discussed in Drew, *Early Parochial Organisation*; the full list of categories in Kümin, *The Shaping of a Community*, app. 2.

18. All quotes from the respective CWA.

19. Hanham (ed.), *CWA Ashburton*, p. 192.

20. J. Oxley, *The Reformation in Essex to the Death of Mary* (Manchester, 1965), p. 68; Bailey (ed.), *CWA Prescot*, pp. 153 ff.

21. Duffy, *Stripping of the Altars*, p. 148.

22. Ibid., p. 180 and plate 73.

23. An example of a majority decision in J. Binney (ed.), *Accounts of the Wardens of Morebath* (Exeter, 1904), p. 83; see also B. Kümin, ' "By all the hole Body of the Paryssh" ' (forthcoming).

24. Bristol Record Office, P/AS/C/1: Halleway Chantry accounts, 1530–1 ff.

25. The decision at Andrew Hubbard was taken on the parish's audit day (17 January 1547): CWA 1545–7; Mellows (ed.), *CWA Peterborough*, p. 158.

26. P. Basing (ed.), *Parish Fraternity Register* (London, 1982), no. 91, and pp. 84–5.

27. GL, MS 5141; Botolph CWA 1548–9 (formal purchase in CWA 1560–1 for £45).

28. Expenses amounted to over £1 in CWA 1519–20. The phenomenon is discussed in C. Burgess, 'The Benefactions of Mortality', in D. Smith (ed.), *Studies in Clergy and Ministry in Medieval England* (York, 1991), pp. 65–86.

29. Detailed examples in B. Kümin, 'Parish Finance and the early Tudor Clergy', in A. Pettegree (ed.), *The Reformation of the Parishes* (Manchester, 1993), pp. 43–62.

30. J. Thomson, 'Piety and Charity in Late Medieval London', *Journal of Ecclesiastical History*, 16 (1965), 180.

31. C. Pearson (ed.), 'The CWA of St Michael, Bath', *Somersetshire Archaeological and Natural History Society Proceedings*, 23 (1877), pp. 1–2.

32. The gradual acquisition of property by parish feoffees is best documented in R. Worth (ed.), *Calendar of Tavistock Parish Records* (Plymouth, 1887).

33. Mellows (ed.), *CWA Peterborough*, pp. xxxii f (1482); CWA St Botolph, 1516–7.

34. Hanham (ed.), *CWA Ashburton*, p. xii.

35. A good example is the *REED* volume for Devon, where the Ashburton CWA feature prominently: J. M. Wasson (ed.), *Devon* (Toronto, 1986), pp. 17–30; see also A. Johnston, 'Parish Entertainments in Berkshire', in J. Raftis (ed.), *Pathways to Medieval Peasants* (Toronto, 1981), pp. 335–8.

36. W. Ault, 'Manor Court and Parish Church in Fifteenth-Century England', *Speculum*, 42 (1967), 64; K. Wood-Legh (ed.), *Kentish Visitations of Archbishop Warham, 1511–12* (Maidstone, 1984), p. 159.

37. W. Simpson (ed.), 'Visitations of Churches Belonging to St Paul's', *Camden Miscellany*, 9 (1895), p. 12.

38. Thomson, 'Piety and Charity', 188; C. Burgess, 'Practical Piety: London Bridge in the Fifteenth and Sixteenth Centuries' (Paper to the 28th International Medieval Congress, Kalamazoo, 1993).

39. Examples in Duffy, *Stripping of the Altars*, pp. 367–8.

40. If possible, an equal number of years has been scrutinised for each of the four periods in any given case-study. Due to the unequal survival of evidence, however, 'first CWA' (for starting-dates see table 1) and 'last pre-Reformation CWA' (normally the early to mid-1540s) may cover different years in different parishes.

41. The 'various' category includes (unspecified or illegible) items which cannot be safely placed in one of the others.

42. 'It would be wrong to assume that...the Protestant Reformation, at any rate in its first phase, made possible an enlarged scope for self-determination on the part of the laity' (Rosser, 'Parochial Conformity', 189).

43. For an insight into the density of regulation see W. Frere and W. Kennedy (eds), *Visitation Articles and Injunctions of the Reformation Period*, 3 vols (London, 1910), passim; the correspondence with Swiss reformers in H. Robinson (ed.), *The Zurich Letters, 1558–79* (2 ser., Cambridge, 1842–5); see Duffy, *Stripping of the Altars*, ch. 14, and Kümin, *Shaping of a Community*, ch. 6, for detailed accounts of the Reformation impact on parish religion.

44. Duffy, *Stripping of the Altars*, p. 485. At Halesowen, Crown-related payments accounted for over a quarter of churchwarden expenditure in this period.

45. A few parishes witnessed anti-clerical outbreaks and iconoclasm already in the early 1530s (Cross, *Church and People*, p. 78), while others like Halesowen were slow to give up the paschal candle or the ringing for the dead on the feast of All Saints (R. Hutton, *The Rise and Fall of Merry England* (Oxford, 1994), pp. 84–5); for a detailed account of Morebath, see Duffy, *Stripping of the Altars*, pp. 497–502, and his forthcoming monograph on the same parish.

46. 'The visitations had clearly been the principal force behind the changes', which 'left local people with no other choice than acquiescence or armed resistance' (Hutton, *Merry England*, p. 87).

47. Legal costs in the (slightly larger) sample used for Kümin, *The Shaping of a Community*, rose from just over 1 per cent in the immediate pre-Reformation period to nearly 6 per cent under Edward. From the late 1530s, expenditure at visitations and in ecclesiastical courts started to dominate the category and was at its highest level ever in seven out of ten case-studies. In a poor parish like Prescot (which may have also needed a lot of convincing), this could average almost 10s. after 1550.

48. With the Reformation, 'religion became more dogmatic, it laid more emphasis on uniformity – on everyone in a kingdom or diocese or parish believing and doing the same, and it reduced variety' (N. Orme, *Unity and Variety: a History of the Church in Devon and Cornwall* (Exeter, 1991), p. 70); Duffy, *Stripping of the Altars*, p. 497.

49. The classic study of the parishes' role in early modern local government remains S. and B. Webb's *The Parish and the County* (London, 1906).

50. Somerset Record Office: D/P/yat/4/1/1–3; P. Northeast (ed.), *Boxford CWA 1530–61* (Woodbridge, 1982), where the high proportion of poor relief payments led to a further – yet misleading – increase in the 'voluntary' proportion during Edward VI's reign.

51. M. Rubin, 'Religious Culture in Town and Country: Reflections on a Great Divide', in D. Abulafia et al. (eds), *Church and City, 1000–1500* (Cambridge, 1992), pp. 3–22, provides examples for similarities in both orthodox and dissenting religious culture.

52. Kümin, *The Shaping of a Community*, table 3.4 (parish incomes); for ales as a predominantly rural fundraiser, see Hutton, *Merry England*, p. 28, and C. Burgess and B. Kümin, 'Penitential Bequests and Parish Regimes in Late Medieval England', *Journal of Ecclesiastical History*, 44 (1993), 610–30.

53. H. Baillie, 'A London Church in Early Tudor Times', *Music & Letters*, 36 (1955), 55–64; F. Harrison, 'The Repertory of an English Parish in the Early

Sixteenth Century', in J. Robijns (ed.), *Renaissance-Muziek 1400–1600* (Louvain, 1969), pp. 143–7 (All Saints).

54. C. Marsh, *The Family of Love in English Society, 1550–1630* (Cambridge, 1994), p. 30. This is of course not to deny the many fundamental differences.

55. P. Collinson, *The Elizabethan Puritan Movement* (London, 1990), p. 222.

56. The classic study of a religiously and socially polarised local community is K. Wrightson and D. Levine, *Poverty and Piety in an English Village: Terling 1525–1700* (New York, 1979; 2nd edn, 1995). For an insight into the heterogeneous nature of post-Reformation parish congregations, see A. Walsham, *Church Papists: Catholicism, Conformity and Confessional Polemic in Early Modern England* (Woodbridge, 1993), p. 111.

57. Seaver, *Puritan Lectureships*, pp. 81–3, identifies two main types of lectureships: those endowed by urban corporations (outside the capital) and those under the control of the parish (in London).

58. C. Barron, 'The Parish Fraternities of Medieval London', in Barron and C. Harper-Bill (eds), *The Church in Pre-Reformation Society* (Woodbridge, 1985), pp. 34–5.

59. Collinson, 'The Elizabethan Church', p. 175; for renewed investment in building, see A. Foster's contribution to K. French, G. Gibbs and B. Kümin (eds), *The Parish in English Life c. 1400–1600* (Manchester, forthcoming).

11. REFORMATION, RESOURCES AND AUTHORITY IN ENGLISH TOWNS   *Robert Tittler*

I would like to thank the Social Sciences and Humanities Research Council of Canada for the funding which supported the research for this paper, and Professor Paul Seaver for his helpful critique of an earlier version, delivered at the North American Conference on British Studies, Vancouver, British Columbia, in October 1994.

1. Especially in *Crisis and Order in English Towns, 1500–1700* (London, 1972), and *English Towns in Transition* (Oxford, 1976).

2. Patrick Collinson, *The Birthpangs of Protestant England: Religious and Cultural Change in the Sixteenth and Seventeenth Centuries*, the Third Anstey Memorial Lectures in the University of Kent at Canterbury, 12–15 May 1986 (Basingstoke, 1988).

3. Collinson, *Birthpangs*, p. 49.

4. One thinks particularly of David Underdown's *Fire from Heaven: Life in an English Town in the Seventeenth Century* (New Haven and London, 1992).

5. See the development of this theme in Tittler, 'The Incorporation of Boroughs, 1540–1558', *History*, 62, no. 204 (Feb. 1977), 24–42.

6. Clark and Slack, *Crisis and Order*, pp. 21–2.

7. My book manuscript, tentatively entitled 'The Reformation and the Towns in England', has been completed and is shortly (as of this writing) to be submitted for publication.

8. E.g., Dom David Knowles, *The Religious Orders in England* (3 vols, London, 1950–9), esp. vol. iii; Philip Hughes, *The Reformation in England* (2 vols, London, 1950–3), J. J. Scarisbrick, *The Reformation and the English People* (Oxford, 1984);

J. H. Bettey, *Suppression of the Monasteries in the West Country* (Gloucester, 1989); Eamon Duffy, *The Stripping of the Altars: Traditional Religion in England, 1400–1580* (London and New Haven, 1992).

9. Clark and Slack, for example, saw net losses brought about by the cessation of the lucrative pilgrim trade and by what they saw as the outflow of rents which once went to urban treasuries. *Crisis and Order*, p. 12.

10. E.g., J. J. Scarisbrick, *Henry VIII* (London, 1968), pp. 511–25.

11. In remarks delivered at the North American Conference on British Studies (Vancouver, British Columbia, 14 October, 1994) on an earlier version of the present essay, Professor Paul Seaver has usefully and provocatively compared the economic aftermath of dissolution to the economic crisis wreaked by the closure of many military bases in the State of California.

12. Exceptions include Joyce Youings, 'The City of Exeter and the Property of the Dissolved Monasteries', *Transactions of the Devonshire Association*, 84 (1952), 122–41; Janis C. Housez, 'The Property Market in Bury St Edmunds, 1540–1600' (MA Original Essay, Concordia University, 1988).

13. A point made by C. J. Kitching, 'The Disposal of Monastic and Chantry Lands', in F. Heal and R. O'Day (eds), *Church and Society in England: Henry VIII to James I* (Basingstoke, 1977), pp. 128–33. As indicated in the title of the work cited in note 12, even Youings, for example, restricted her study of dissolved lands in Exeter to monastic lands and, though working much more recently, J. H. Bettey, for one, has followed suit; Youings, 'The City of Exeter and the Property of the Dissolved Monasteries'; Bettey, *The Suppression of the Monasteries*.

14. Kitching repeats the commonly accepted figures of 90 colleges, 2,374 chantries and 110 hospitals derived from the *Valor*, but emphasises as well the 'considerable underestimate' represented by those figures. Kitching, 'Disposal of Monastic and Chantry Lands', p. 129.

15. Michael Zell, 'The Mid-Tudor Land Market in Crown Lands in Kent', *Archeologia Cantiana*, 97 (1982), 66.

16. 27 Henry VIII, c. 16 (1535–6). The timing cannot be coincidental. It came at the very start of the great sales of confiscated lands, apparently emanating from the conceptual mindset which produced the *Valor Ecclesiasticus* in the same year. It shows both the Crown's consciousness of the need to keep track of subsequent purchases and its awareness of the difficulties which could accrue in tracing title at such times.

17. This has often been noted, but see: W. G. Hoskins, 'English Provincial Towns in the Early Sixteenth Century', *Transactions of the Royal Historical Society*, 5th ser., vol. 6 (1956), 10–11; A. F. Butcher, 'Rent and the Urban Economy: Oxford and Canterbury in the Late Middle Ages', *Southern History* I (1979), 14; S. R. R. Jones, 'Property, Tenure and Rents: Some Aspects of the Topography and Economy of Medieval York' (PhD thesis, University of York, 1987), pp. 277–8, 300; J. Cornwall, *Wealth and Society in Early Sixteenth-Century England* (London, 1988), p. 244.

18. This is well exemplified in York, say, which still suffered from the economic decay of preceding decades. It confiscated what it could before dissolution and bought extensively when its finances rebounded later in the century. D. M. Palliser, *The Reformation in York, 1534–1553* (Borthwick Papers, no. 40, 1971), pp. 17–25.

19. B. Dobson, 'Cathedral Chapters and Cathedral Cities, York, Durham and Carlisle in the Fifteenth Century', *Northern History*, xix (1983), 35–6; Jones, 'Property, Tenure and Rents', pp. 289–90.

20. R. Tittler, 'For the "Re-edification of Townes": the Rebuilding Statutes of Henry VIII', *Albion* 22, no. 4 (Winter, 1990), 591–605. This study notes that, although the acts were passed in the reign of Henry, their sanctions tended not to be applied until later in the century (603–4).

21. The best general discussion is still Alan Kreider, *English Chantries: The Road to Dissolution* (Cambridge, MA, 1979), ch. 6.

22. Colin Platt, *The English Medieval Town* (1976), pp. 180–1.

23. Carried out with government permission, this was not, strictly speaking, a pre-emption quite like the others. It included, *inter alia*, Haxey's Chantry, one of the biggest in the city, various chantries which had been left to the jurisdiction of the Bridgemasters, and the lucrative endowments of the Fraternity of York Mercers, 27 Henry VIII; A. G. Dickens, 'A Municipal Dissolution of Chantries at York, 1536', *Yorkshire Archeological Society Journal*, 38 (1944–7), 164–73. See also Palliser, *The Reformation at York*.

24. L. P. Wernham, 'The Chantries . . . of Richmond', *Yorkshire Archeological Society Journal*, 38, 210.

25. Robert Whiting, *The Blind Devotion of the People: Popular Religion and the English Reformation* (Cambridge, 1989), pp. 67, 180. Whiting also notes the continued confiscation of church property after the dissolutions, as in Exeter in both 1552 and 1559. Ibid., p. 216.

26. Whiting, *Blind Devotion*, p. 31.

27. Peter Clark, 'Reformation and Radicalism in Kentish Towns', in W. J. Mommsen, P. Alter and R. Scribner (eds), *Urban Classes, the Nobility and the Reformation* (Publications of the German Historical Institute, v, 1979), p. 119; and *English Provincial Society from the Reformation to the Revolution: Religion, Politics and Society in Kent, 1500–1640* (Hassocks, Sussex, 1977), p. 44. Chantry property was also confiscated in Sandwich; Clark, 'Reformation and Radicalism', p. 124.

28. This is despite the fact that the town's petition for grants in the Augmentations indicates lands worth but £65; PRO, E.318/5/143. But see details of further acquisitions in *Letters and Papers of Henry VIII* (1545), grants no. 648 and 51, and C.66/771/m. 32, Patent Roll entry of Boston's charter indicating these properties. A discussion of the purchase, which was contested by some local interests, may be found in PRO, STAC 3/Bundle 5/11, petition of John Brown of Boston.

29. An impression confirmed in David Thomas, 'The Elizabethan Crown Lands: their Purposes and Problems', in Richard Hoyle, *The Estates of the English Crown, 1558–1640* (Cambridge, 1992), p. 69.

30. Clark and Slack not only missed this point, but rather casually assumed that most often ' . . . rents [which had] once [been] transferred to urban treasuries were lost to the coffers of the Crown and country gentry' (*Crisis and Order*, p. 12).

31. Rosemary Horrox (ed.), *Selected Rentals and Accounts of Medieval Hull, 1293–1528* (Yorkshire Archeological Society Record Series, 141 (1983 for 1981)), p. 17.

32. PRO, E.133/1/61.

33. Margaret Statham, *Jankyn Smith and the Guildhall Feoffees* (Bury St Edmunds, 1981), p. 7.

34. *Victoria History of the County of Hampshire* (hereafter *VCH*), IV (1911), p. 356.

35. *VCH Bedfordshire*, III (1912), p. 24.

36. The lands were successfully concealed until incorporation in 1588, when they were confirmed in the borough's possession. Adrienne Rosen, 'Economic and Social Aspects of the History of Winchester, 1520–1670' (Oxford University DPhil thesis, 1975), pp. 66, 79–80. See also *CPR, Eliz.*, II, p. 155.

37. *VCH Yorkshire, E. Riding*, VI, p. 69. As was often the case when such lands were discovered, the Crown compounded with the borough, allowing it to retain the properties for a fair consideration.

38. Catalogued in the PRO as E.318.

39. Chichester petitioned for purchase of lands worth but £3 3s. 7d. per annum (PRO, E.318/26/1496); Dorchester for lands worth £8 7s. 2d. (PRO, E.318/28/1583); and Faversham for lands worth £8 (PRO, 318/10/433).

40. Bristol purchased lands worth £72 12s. 10d. and then lands worth £105 2s. 6 1/2d. (PRO, E.318/5/172 and 173); Coventry bought lands worth £68 18s. 6d. in 1547, and £196 9s. 3d. in 1552 (E.318/8/321 and E.318/27/1548); Ludlow made purchases of lands formerly held by the Palmer's Guild for £121 3s. 11 1/2d. in 1551 (E.318/31/1766); Norwich purchased lands worth £142 19s. 2 1/2d. (E.318/32/1827); and Warwick purchased lands worth £58 14s. 4d. (E.318/22/1187).

41. E.g. Michael Zell, 'The Mid-Tudor Market in Crown Lands in Kent', *Archeologia Cantiana*, 97 (1982), 66.

42. Noted by many, including G. H. Woodward, 'The Dissolution of the Chantries in the County of Somerset' (MLitt thesis, University of Bristol, 1980), pp. 138–40.

43. *VCH Gloucestershire*, IV (1988), pp. 26–9, 82; deeds to individual properties may be found in the Gloucester Borough Records, as, e.g. GBR/D3269/ 3 and 11; J 1/24, J 1/64–5, J 1/1243, J 1/1254, J 1/1253–5, J 1/1781, J 1/1943A and 1277, J 1/1946B; G12/1, etc. See also grant of the Hospital of St Katherine (1564), *CPR, 6 Eliz.*, pp. 71–2. Acquisition of the Manor of Abbots Barton alone around the first year of Elizabeth's reign brought in an additional £52 per year, raising the city's assize rent income by more than a third thereafter. As a result of this and some other, smaller increases, the total income of the city went from an average of about £125 in the last two years of Mary's reign to nearly £240 two years later. Gloucester Stewards and Chamberlains' Accounts, Gloucester Borough Records MS. GBR F4/3, 4 and 5 Philip and Mary to 2 and 3 Elizabeth.

44. Well summarised in Adrienne Rosen, 'Economic and Social Aspects of the City of Winchester', pp. 59–66, 74–5, 97, though, significantly, she was unable to locate any grant formally conveying the hospital lands, suggesting a concealment and/or informal appropriation. The revenues, none the less, are accounted for in the City Treasurers' accounts.

45. Alan Dyer, *The City of Worcester in the Sixteenth Century* (Leicester, 1973), pp. 217–18.

46. PRO, E.318/28/1602; no value is assigned to the property.

47. Described in detail in Wallace MacCaffrey, *Exeter, 1540–1640* (Cambridge, MA, and London, 1975), pp. 184–5. Some of the lands had in the end

to be sold off again so as to raise funds to complete the purchase, but a substantial number of these rent-bearing properties remained in the hands of the feoffees of the corporation.

48. R. C. Latham (ed.), *Bristol Charters, 1509–1899* (Bristol Record Society, xii (1946)), pp. 26–7.

49. Abingdon, Berkshire Record Office MSS. D/EP7/36 pp. 2–4, 6–7; Bridgwater, *Calendar of Patent Rolls, Mary*, i, p. 192; *VCH Somerset*, vi (1992), p. 224; Chichester, *VCH Sussex*, iii (1935), pp. 92–3; Chipping Sodbury, F. F. Fox, 'On the Gilds of Sodbury and Dyrham', *Trans. Bristol and Gloucestershire Archeol. Soc.*, 13 (1889), 6–9; High Wycombe, *CPR, 4 Eliz.* (1562), p. 259; Ipswich, *CPR, 14 Eliz I* (16 May 1572), p. 443; Leominster, Hereford County Record Office MS. B 56/12, fol. 47r; Ludlow, noted in Penry Williams, 'Government and Politics in Ludlow, 1590–1642', *Transactions of the Shropshire Archeological Society*, 56, pt 3 (1960), 282; Maidstone, *CPR, Edward VI (1548–49)*, pp. 174–6; Marlborough, *VCH Wiltshire*, xii (1985), p. 206; *CPR, Edward VI* (vol. iv, 1551), p. 128; Reading, summarised in *VCH Berkshire*, iii (1923), pp. 354–5; Romsey, *VCH Hampshire*, iv (1911), p. 452; Stratford, PRO, C.66/863/m. 2; Wisbech, *CPR, Edw. VI*, vol. iii (1549), pp. 339–40; Woodstock, *VCH Oxfordshire*, xii (1990), p. 328.

50. Gloucester Borough Records, Gloucestershire Record Office, MS. GBR G 12/1: a copy of Pate's bequest to the city of Gloucester, and GBR F4/3; A. L. Browne, 'Richard Pates, [*sic*] M.P. for Gloucester', *Transactions of the Bristol and Gloucestershire Archeological Society*, 56 (1935 for 1934), 201–25.

51. Bristol, for example, used revenue from former monastic lands to replace tolls which had been abandoned in the effort to increase trade. David Harris Sacks, *The Widening Gate: Bristol and the Atlantic Economy, 1450–1700* (Berkeley and London, 1991), p. 78.

52. The control of such leases also sparked allegations of favouritism and patronage in their award. Williams, 'Government and Politics in Ludlow, 1590–1642', p. 282; Faraday, *Ludlow*, pp. 35–6.

53. See note 8 above.

12. THE SHEARMEN'S TREE AND THE PREACHER: THE STRANGE DEATH OF MERRY ENGLAND IN SHREWSBURY AND BEYOND
Patrick Collinson

I have been assisted in the preparation of this essay by Mr James Lawson, Archivist of Shrewsbury School, who has supplied much information and detected not a few egregious blunders. He cannot be held responsible for any errors which persist. I am grateful to Mr W. A. Champion for further corrections and advice. My essay was to all intents and purposes complete when Barbara Coulton shared with me her article 'The Establishment of Protestantism in a Provincial Town: a Study of Shrewsbury in the Sixteenth Century', which has now appeared in the *Sixteenth Century Journal*, xvii (1996), 307–35. I have subsequently benefited from her critical comments on this essay.

1. Shrewsbury was governed by two bailiffs selected from a council of twelve aldermen and twenty-four common councillors until, in 1638, a mayor replaced

the bailiffs. This account of the Lacon case is based on evidence collected in Shropshire Records and Research (here after SRR), MS 3365/2209, C/3–11; and on the reports in a contemporary Shrewsbury chronicle, known, since the eighteenth century, when it was deposited in Shrewsbury School Library (MS.Mus.X.31), as 'Dr Taylor's MS'. (Dr John Taylor, an old Salopian, was Librarian of Cambridge University.) The contents relating to Shrewsbury are extracted by W. A. Leighton in 'Early Chronicles of Shrewsbury, 1372–1603', *Transactions of the Shropshire Archaeological and Natural History Society*, III (1880), 239–352 (here after 'Early Chronicles'). I am grateful to Mr Lawson for facilitating a visit to the school to inspect this and other MSS. Formally and generically, 'Dr Taylor's MS' may be compared with Diarmaid MacCulloch's Worcester chronicle (see ch. 5 above). To date, the Shrewsbury Anonymous remains unidentified. The Lacon murder documents are copied, in part, in *Records of Early English Drama, Shropshire*, ed. Alan B. Somerset (Toronto, 1994), vol. I, pp. 281–3. This essay could not have been completed in the time available but for the work undertaken at the coalface in the Shropshire *REED*.

2. On the morning before the 1583 election, a proclamation was made 'that no schollers, boyes nor prentises shulld that nyght goe a broade to disquyett the towne wth unreasonable noyses feyghtings and dysorders wch were woontt usually to proceede as that nyght.' The order was prompted by a particular act of misrule perpetrated the night before the order was made: an act of unauthorised iconoclasm in the destruction of a stone cross in the churchyard of St Julian's parish ('Early Chronicles', 295).

3. Ibid., 331–2.

4. Ibid., 336, 337, 339. But after this holocaust, the Shrewsbury hangman enjoyed some respite. There were apparently only six executions in the last five years of Elizabeth's reign (ibid., 340–51).

5. Peter Lake, 'Puritanism, Arminianism and a Shropshire Axe-Murder', *Midland History*, XV (1990), 37–63. Professor Lake's essay on religion in early modern Northamptonshire also begins with a murder (' "A Charitable Christian Hatred": The Godly and their Enemies in the 1630s', in *The Culture of English Puritanism, 1560–1700*, ed. Christopher Durston and Jacqueline Eales (Basingstoke, 1996), pp. 145–83). This thick-descriptional convention, which I adhere to in this essay, is not so much operatic as anthropological.

6. Evidence of street talk given by Roger Wootton, servant to Richard Beaton, tailor (SRR MS 3365/2209/C/9).

7. Testimony of Richard ap Griffith, servant to William Morris, shearman (ibid.).

8. Testimony of Richard Chirwell, draper, and of Robert Stephens, draper (ibid.).

9. 'Early Chronicles', 332.

10. SRR, MS 3365/2209/C/3–11, passim.

11. Testimony of Richard Purchas, shearman, Alan Downynge, servant to Mr William Jones, draper, and Richard Chirwell (ibid., 5, 6, 11). According to *REED, Shropshire*, vol. II, 680, Hughes was a draper. Not so, James Lawson tells me. He was the son of a Welsh (Montgomeryshire) butcher, and was identified as a shearman when sworn a burgess in 1560 and made bailiff in 1593. This incident occurred on 24 June, Midsummer Day, so the tree may have been

intended to mark that occasion rather than the Shearmen's festival, which happened on 2 June. I owe this point to Mr Bill Champion.

12. SRR, MS 3365/2209/C/9. Wootton's testimony.

13. 'Early Chronicles', 315.

14. *REED*, *Shropshire*, vol. I, pp. 260–3, 266–71.

15. Ibid.

16. Ibid., p. 252. It was this prohibition which led to the *cause célèbre* of the Shearmen's Tree, with copious documentation preserved in its integrity by the Shrewsbury magistrates (SRR, MS 3365/1113). This material is printed in something like its entirety and extensively discussed in *REED*, *Shropshire*.

17. *REED*, *Shropshire*, vol. I. pp. 252–9, 263–5.

18. Ibid., p. 271.

19. Ibid., p. 254.

20. Patrick Collinson, *The Religion of Protestants: the Church in English Society 1559–1625* (Oxford, 1982), pp. 158–9; Elliott Rose, *Cases of Conscience: Alternatives Open to Recusants and Puritans Under Elizabeth I and James I* (Cambridge, 1975), pp. 158–68; Patrick Collinson, 'Ben Jonson's *Bartholomew Fair*: the Theatre Constructs Puritanism', in *The Theatrical City: Culture, Theatre and Politics in London, 1576–1649*, ed. David L. Smith, Richard Strier and David Bevington (Cambridge, 1995), pp. 157–69. One of the most informative accounts of overreaching godly magistracy will now be found in Margaret Aston's essay 'Puritans and Iconoclasm, 1560–1660', in *The Culture of English Puritanism*, pp. 92–121.

21. Collinson, *The Religion of Protestants*, p. 145.

22. *REED*, *Shropshire*, vol. I, pp. 266–71; vol. II, pp. 615–17.

23. Ibid., vol. II, p. 680.

24. Ibid., vol. I, p. 260; vol. II, pp. 675–6.

25. Ibid., vol. I, pp. 265–6; vol. II, p. 617. Warwick in itself was an odd circumstance, since Shropshire and Warwickshire were not on the same assizes circuit. However, there is no doubt that the case was taken to Warwick.

26. *REED*, *Shropshire*, vol. I, p. 274; vol. II, p. 678; 'Early Chronicles', 322.

27. Coulton, 'The Establishment of Protestantism'; *REED*, *Shropshire*, vol. II, p. 676.

28. Ibid., vol. I, p. 312.

29. T. C. Mendenhall, *The Shrewsbury Drapers and the Welsh Wool Trade in the XVI and XVII Centuries* (Oxford, 1953).

30. Ibid., p. 39.

31. On the social meanings of civil ceremony, see Charles Phythian-Adams, 'Ceremony and the Citizen: the Communal Year at Coventry 1450–1550', in *Crisis and Order in English Towns 1500–1700: Essays in Urban History*, ed. Peter Clark and Paul Slack (London, 1972), pp. 57–85.

32. I am reliant here on the advice of James Lawson.

33. *REED*, *Shropshire*, vol. I, p. 269.

34. H. Owen and J. B. Blakeway, *A History of Shrewsbury* (1825), vol. I, p. 376 n.2.

35. Ibid., vol. II, p. 212. Barbara Coulton ('The Establishment of Protestantism') supplies further details of Hawkhurst's preaching ministry; and more generally provides a full account of the beginnings of Protestantism in Shrewsbury.

36. J. Basil Oldham, *A History of Shrewsbury School, 1552–1952* (Oxford, 1952), pp. 5–12; J. B. Oldham, *Headmasters of Shrewsbury School, 1552–1908* (Shrewsbury,

1937), pp. 9–13. Oldham corrects the *DNB* and Venn's *Alumni*, which identify Ashton with a Trinity man who matriculated in 1555. Ashton was a fellow of St John's from 1524 until some time in the 1540s, and several times bursar. He was already an oldish man when he settled in Shrewsbury. His whereabouts before that are unknown. Barbara Coulton thinks it likely that Thomas Lever, some-time master of his college and a famous preacher in the west Midlands, may have introduced Ashton to Shrewsbury. He is known to have been in the service of Walter Devereux, earl of Essex, in his later years, and to have been tutor to the future favourite of Queen Elizabeth. His Shrewsbury pupils included Andrew Downes, a native of Shrewsbury and a famous regius professor of Greek at Cambridge.

37. Patrick Collinson, *The Elizabethan Puritan Movement* (London, and Berkeley, 1967), pp. 173, 174, 176; 'Early Chronicles', 273. In 1574, two shillings and sixpence was spent 'upon the mynisters at their exercise this yere', doubtless for wine (Owen and Blakeway, *History of Shrewsbury*, vol. I, p. 360).

38. Early Chronicles', 273, 296, 315.

39. Ibid., 288. In 1584, on the occasion of a visitation by the ecclesiastical commissioners, consent was given by the commissioners for the pulling down of the crosses in the churchyards of St Chad's and St Alkmund's. The work disclosed a wax candle placed before one of the images on the St Chad's cross, which the chronicler supposed to have been offered by some superstitious person (ibid., 296).

40. Oldham, *History of Shrewsbury School*, pp. 7, 17. Sir Henry Sidney's famous letter to his son Philip 'at schoole at the towne of Shrowesbury with one M. *Astone*' was printed in 1591 as *A very godly letter* (J. B. Oldham, 'Shrewsbury School Library', *The Library*, 5th ser. XIV (1959), 81–99).

41. 'Early Chronicles', 286–7.

42. Ibid., 307.

43. Ibid., 309.

44. These are James Lawson's reflections on the situation in Tomkys's time and under Ashton's successors. For a somewhat different view, see Coulton, 'The Establishment of Protestantism'.

45. Alexander Rodger, 'Roger Ward's Shrewsbury Stock: an Inventory of 1585', *The Library*, 5th ser. XIII (1958), 247–68. Ward's Shrewsbury shop had for sale more than 500 titles, a good proportion of them religious, including, besides a fair range of Calvin, 42 copies of a sermon by the Essex puritan Arthur Dent (which Ward had pirated), and a good stock of the catechisms of Eusebius Paget and Edward Dering/John More. There were four copies of John Field's attack on Robert Parsons, *A Caveat for Parsons Howlet*. The Shrewsbury chronicle ('Dr Taylor's MS') is packed with evidence of close cultural contact with London, especially in the form of transcribed ballad texts, hot from the press, which have been used extensively by Dr Alexandra Walsham in her Cambridge PhD thesis, 'Aspects of Providentialism in Early Modern England' (1995).

46. 'The Letter-Book of Thomas Bentham, Bishop of Coventry and Lich-field', ed. Rosemary O'Day and Joel Berlatsky, *Camden Miscellany*, XXVII, Camden 4th ser. XXII (1979), 113–238. Note especially a letter to Archbishop Parker of 11 April 1561, in which Bentham refers to 'one Mr Aston a godlye preacher within thes parties of my dioces' (210).

47. 'Early Chronicles', 280; Public Record Office, S. P. 12/81/52. The advanced nonconformity of the minister at Moreton Corbet, William Axton, who was brought in by a kind of 'presbyterian' procedure, is documented in *The Seconde Parte of a Register*, ed. Albert Peel (Cambridge, 1915), vol. i, pp. 68–74. (However, it was Robert Corbet, not his father Sir Andrew (as often stated), who appointed Axton, and Axton's interview with the bishop is now known to have been conducted not by Bentham but by Bentham's successor, William Overton.) The Corbets may have been the taproot not only of Shrewsbury's Reformation but of the godliness of the Harleys of Brampton Bryan, Herefordshire. See Jacqueline Eales, *Puritans and Roundheads: The Harleys of Brampton Bryan and the Outbreak of the English Civil War* (Cambridge, 1990), pp. 17, 35, 40–1.

48. Simon Adams, '"Because I am of That Countrye & Mynde to Plant Myself There": Robert Dudley, Earl of Leicester and the West Midlands', *Midland History*, xx (1995), 21–74. Leicester's 1584 itinerary, the occasion of his only visit to Shrewsbury (and to Chester), which I owe to Dr Adams, took him from Kenilworth to Shrewsbury (26 May), Denbigh (28 May), Hawarden (1 June), Chester (3–6 June) and Buxton (14 June). Dr Adams tells me that Leicester's Shropshire connections have yet to be fully explored. I cannot claim that he enjoyed the close links with Shrewsbury which he had with Warwick: only that the Dudley clientage seems to have loosely embraced much of the provincial political society in which Shrewsbury was set. Barbara Coulton, an authority on the Corbets with whom there were marriage links, sheds further light on these connections.

49. 'Early Chronicles', 285–8, 296–7, 302.

50. On 19 July 1580, Shrewsbury's governers considered the bequest of Thomas Blackwell of £200 for 'the maintenaunce of a preacher within the parishe of St Chadd'. The plan to use the money to redeem a portion of the tithes of St Chad's was probably abortive. (Barbara Coulton has explained to me the complex story of the competing interests of the town and the school in the tithes of St Chad's.) On 3 August 1582 there was 'some conference had concerning a publicke precher for this towne and mayntenance for the same'. It was decided to rate the inhabitants in order to raise a stock of £200 to maintain a preacher, provided Sir George Bromley, recorder of the town, approved of the scheme. On 9 September 1582, Bromley's nomination of Tomkys was discussed. It was agreed that he should receive the same wages as Dr Bulkeley, that this should no longer be dependent upon voluntary contributions, and that the bailiffs should have the power to levy the sum of £300 by various means. These decisions were ratified by a special assembly of the 'commonalty' of the town, but whether the rate was ever levied is perhaps doubtful (SRR, Assembly Minutes 1554–83, MS 3365/76, fols 348ᵛ, 364, 365; Coulton, 'The Establishment of Protestantism').

51. For Colchester, see Mark Byford's chapter in this book; for Ipswich, Collinson, *The Religion of Protestants*, pp. 170–7, and Diarmaid MacCulloch and John Blatchly, 'Pastoral Provision in the Parishes of Tudor Ipswich', *Sixteenth Century Journal*, xxiii (1991), 457–74.

52. Patrick Collinson, 'Episcopacy and Pseudo-Episcopacy in England in the Elizabethan Church', *Colloque de Strasbourg, Septembre 1983 sur L'Institution et les*

Pouvoirs dans les Église et L'Antiquité à Nos Jours, ed. Bernard Vogler, Miscellanea Historiae Ecclesiasticae, VIII, *Bibliothèque de la Revue D'Histoire Ecclésiastique*, Fasc. 72 (Louvain, 1987), pp. 229–38. When the skimmington took place in 1591, Tomkys was returning from a sick visit in St Chad's, not his parish (*REED, Shropshire*, vol. I, p. 269).

53. 'Early Chronicles', 285. Barbara Coulton ('The Establishment of Protestantism') provides further examples of Bulkeley acting as the town's conscience and taking an active part in civic affairs.

54. SRR, MS 3365/76, fol. 365; Coulton, 'The Establishment of Protestantism'. Bulkeley enjoyed prebends at Chester, Westminster and Lichfield, in addition to the living of Odell in Bedfordshire, to which he went from Shrewsbury. He was the author of a number of polemical, anti-Catholic works, and the editor of the 1610 edition of John Foxe's *Acts and Monuments*. While his 'godly' credentials appear impeccable, he was perhaps a more comfortable and even complacent figure than Tomkys.

55. Shrewsbury School Library, Hotchkiss MS 1, p. 72. This was an unusual and unwarranted title. Tomkys was the employee of the town and even leased his peculiar ecclesiastical jurisdiction from the school. Hotchkiss (an eighteenth-century antiquary) cites his reference as p. 161 of the act book (now lost) of Tomkys's consistory court at St Mary's. This is perhaps evidence of Tomkys's *folie de grandeur*.

56. SRR, MS 3365/76, fol. 365^r.

57. Heinrich Bullinger, trans. John Tomkys, *A most godly and learned discourse of the woorthynesse, authoritie and self-sufficiencie of the holy scriptures* (1579), sig. A5^r. Tomkys came from a good family in Bilston and married a rich, pious and literate wife. The Pipes were neighbours. In his will, Tomkys left books by Edward Dering and James Pilkington to the sons of the lord mayor, Humfrey and Samuel Pipe (G. P. Mander, *The Wolverhampton Antiquary*, vol. I (Wolverhampton, 1933), pp. 69–83). I owe this reference to James Lawson.

58. Heinrich Bullinger, trans. John Tomkys, *A most excellent sermon of the lordes supper* (1577), Epistle.

59. John Tomkys, *A sermon preached the 26. day of May. 1584 in S. Maries church in Shrewsbury. Before the right honorable the earle of Leicester* (1584). This is the only sermon preached before Leicester to have been printed. Note this statement: 'I did twise serve at his spiritual table, once in the Countie of Stafford where I was borne, and once in Shrewsburie, where I have my charge....' Tomkys's dedication is quoted in Eleanor Rosenberg, *Leicester Patron of Letters* (New York, 1955), pp. 225–6. Shortly before his arrival in Shrewsbury, Tomkys dedicated his *The summe of the foure evangelists* (another translation from Bullinger) to William Overton, Bentham's newly installed successor as bishop of Coventry and Lichfield, and one of Leicester's bishops (Patrick Collinson, *Godly People: Essays on English Protestantism and Puritanism* (1983), pp. 64, 77, 79). Tomkys flattered Overton, welcoming him 'into our countrey'. Evidently he was no Presbyterian. But Overton was a semi-Presbyterian bishop.

60. John Tomkys, *A briefe exposition of the Lordes Prayer* (1584), which followed his order of catechising 'for the Evening prayer exercise', and was intended for

children. Cf. Thomas Settle's *A catechisme, briefly opening the misterie of our redemption* (1587), dedicated, in somewhat divisive terms, to his people at Mildenhall, Suffolk (Collinson, *The Elizabethan Puritan Movement*, pp. 378–9).

61. SRR, MS 3365/76, fol. 353^r.

62. James Lawson, 'The Plague of 1593 at Bishop's Castle: a Postscript', *South West Shropshire Historical and Archaeological Society Journal*, no. 6, Spring 1995. For the exportable charity of puritan Dorchester, see David Underdown, *Fire from Heaven: the Life of an English Town in the Seventeenth Century* (London, 1992); and Collinson, *The Religion of Protestants*, p. 262. In 1625, when Jordan was the only magistrate to remain in plague-stricken Exeter, Dorchester sent £40 collected at a fast.

63. Shrewsbury School Library, Hotchkiss MS 1, p. 71. For the famous act of unauthorised iconoclasm by Henry Sherfield, the recorder of Salisbury, see most recently Aston, 'Puritans and Iconoclasm', pp. 107–9.

64. 'Articles to be enquired of in the visitation of the reverend Mr John Tomkys, ... public preacher of God's word in the town of Salop', partly printed by Owen and Blakeway, *History of Shrewsbury*, vol. i, p. 333; vol. ii, p. 362, from a copy in the churchwardens' accounts of St Mary's, SRO, P 257/B/3/1, fols 92–7 (a reference I owe to Mr Bill Champion). All that survives from the act book of Tomkys's court are a few items extracted by Hotchkiss. Cf. the act book of the peculiar consistory court of Stratford-upon-Avon for the same period, E. R. C. Brinkworth, *Shakespeare and the Bawdy Court of Stratford* (London, 1972).

65. 'Early Chronicles', 310, 312. It is not suggested that Tomkys was wholly responsible for introducing religious controversy into the town. In 1578, we hear of 'scoffers of there neybors and the serchers of Godes worde' (*REED, Shropshire*, vol. i, pp. 223–4).

66. See Byford's essay, ch. 1 above; and his unpublished Oxford DPhil thesis, 'The Price of Protestantism: Assessing the Impact of Religious Change on Elizabethan Essex: the Cases of Heydon and Colchester, 1558–1594' (1988).

67. Shrewsbury School Library, MS Benefactors' Book, *c.*1634, fols 17–19. The Library still contains some of the books of the Welsh-speaking and learned Thomas Price (or ap Reese), minister of St Chad's from *c.* 1577 until 1620 (Owen and Blakeway, *History of Shrewsbury*, vol. ii, p. 212), whose motto was 'Christus mihi sola salus'. It would be good to know more about Price, and about his relations with Tomkys. But we do know that his two sons, Daniel and Sampson, became prominent Jacobean churchmen and prolific publishers of godly and robustly anti-Catholic sermons. Daniel, who was chaplain in turn to Prince Henry and Prince Charles, became dean of Hereford. Sampson was another of Charles's chaplains. (I owe this information to P. E. McCullough, *The Sermon at the Elizabethan and Jacobean Courts, 1558–1625: Preaching, Religion and Politics* (forthcoming).)

68. 'Early Chronicles', 324. Tomkys had buried his wife in St Mary's in August 1584. In his will, he asked to be buried beside her, but not for any 'superstitious' reason; but if he were to die in Wolverhampton, near to 'the blue marble stone under which my father Richard Tomkys and others of my ancestors are buried.' 'My will is that there be no superstition used in my funeral, either in ringing, or alms giving, or in entertaining of friends.' (*Wolverhampton Antiquary*, vol. i, pp. 69–83.)

69. J. S. Ibish, 'Emmanuel College: the Founding Generation, With a Biographical Register of Members of the College 1584–1604', unpublished Harvard PhD thesis, 1985, p. 369.

70. Lake, 'Puritanism, Arminianism and a Shropshire Axe-Murder'; and two of Lake's principal sources, Peter Studley, *The looking-glasse of schisme* (1634), and the life of Herring in Samuel Clarke, *Lives of Thirty-Two English Divines* (1677), pp. 160–8. See also Jacqueline Eales, 'Thomas Pierson and the Transmission of the Moderate Puritan Tradition', *Midland History*, xx (1995), 75–102. However, Studley was not the first of Shrewsbury's 'Anti- puritans'. He was preceded by Humphrey Leech, vicar of St Alkmund's, who was accused of preaching 'many points of popery' and later converted to Catholicism. (Coulton, 'The Establishment of Protestantism'.)

71. Patrick Collinson, *From Iconoclasm to Iconophobia: The Cultural Impact of the Second English Reformation* (the Stenton Lecture 1985) (Reading, 1986); Patrick Collinson, *The Birthpangs of Protestant England: Religious and Cultural Change in the Sixteenth and Seventeenth Centuries* (Basingstoke, 1988); Patrick Collinson, 'Elizabethan and Jacobean Puritanism as Forms of Popular Religious Culture', in *The Culture of English Puritanism*, pp. 32–57. Some of the worst excesses in Collinson's 1986–8 argument are corrected in Tessa Watt, *Cheap Print and Popular Piety, 1550–1640* (Cambridge, 1991); and in Walsham, 'Aspects of Providentialism'.

72. Paul Whitfield White, *Theatre and Reformation: Protestantism, Patronage and Playing in Tudor England* (Cambridge, 1993).

73. *REED, Devon*, ed. John M. Wasson (Toronto, 1986), pp. 51–2, 265.

74. *REED, Chester*, ed. Lawrence M. Clopper (Toronto, 1979), p. 184.

75. *REED, Norwich 1540–1642*, ed. David Galloway (Toronto, 1984), pp. 198–9.

76. *REED, Chester*, pp. 198, 234–5, 251–3, 354, 434–5, 526; *REED, York*, ed. Alexandra F. Johnston and Margaret Rogerson (Toronto, 1979), vol. i, pp. 407, 434–5, 441, 445, 452–3, 458–9, 468–9.

77. David Cressy, *Bonfires and Bells: National Memory and the Protestant Calendar in Elizabethan and Stuart England* (Berkeley and Los Angeles, 1989).

78. David Underdown, *Revel, Riot and Rebellion: Popular Politics and Culture in England 1603–1660* (Oxford, 1985); Ronald Hutton, *The Rise and Fall of Merry England: The Ritual Year, 1400–1700* (Oxford, 1994); Ann Hughes, 'Religion and Society in Stratford upon Avon, 1619–1638', *Midland History*, xix (1994), 58–84.

79. Collinson, *Religion of Protestants*, p. 145; Collinson, 'Ben Jonson's *Bartholomew Fair*'.

80. *REED, Shropshire*, vol. i, pp. 205–15; vol. ii, p. 663. J. B. Oldham (*History of Shrewsbury School*, pp. 22–3) thought it a reasonable assumption that the schoolboys acted in Ashton's plays, although the fact is not documented. Ashton's ordinances required the highest form to declaim a play and one act of a comedy once a week (ibid., p. 12).

81. *REED, Shropshire*, vol. i, p. 243.

82. Ibid., vol. i, p. 212.

83. We owe the title to a somewhat dubious source, 'The Eschutcheons of the Bailiffs' (ibid., vol. i, p. 207).

84. Collinson, *Birthpangs*, pp. 103–4; Patrick Collinson, 'The Protestant Cathedral', in *A History of Canterbury Cathedral*, ed. Patrick Collinson, Margaret Sparks and Nigel Ramsay (Oxford, 1995), pp. 170–1.

85. *REED, Shropshire*, vol. 1, p. 220.

86. See a typical entry in the accounts for 1574–5: 'Item players of noble men and others and berwardes of noble men and minstrells of noble men this yere' (£4 10s. 8d.). (Ibid., vol. 1, p. 220. See also a note on 382.) The fact that such visits were not, for the most part, recorded by the Shrewsbury chronicler probably indicates that they were too commonplace to deserve notice.

87. *REED, Shropshire*, vol. 1, p. 382.

88. 'Early Chronicles', 298.

89. Ibid., 294.

90. Ibid., 318. The Hungarian visited Norwich in the same year (*REED, Norwich*, p. 96).

91. 'Early Chronicles', 322–3. This was the first recorded appearance of Banks. The horse which performed at Shrewsbury was white, and was soon replaced by the famous bay horse 'Morocco', with which Banks toured the British Isles and Europe, visiting London, Frankfurt, Orleans, Paris and even, it was said, Rome. The pair were the subject of printed ballads and are referred to by Shakespeare in *Love's Labour's Lost*, as well as by Thomas Nashe, Ben Jonson, Thomas Dekker, Isaac Casaubon, and others (Sidney H. Atkins, 'Mr Banks and His Horse', *Notes & Queries*, 21 July 1934, 39–44). I owe this reference to Arnold Hunt.

92. 'Early Chronicles', 338. John Stow described the cock-fights of late Elizabethan London: 'Also Cockes of the game are yet cherished by diverse men for their pleasures, much money being laide on their heades, when they fight in pits whereof some be costly made for that purpose' (*A Survey of London By John Stow*, ed. C. L. Kingsford (Oxford, 1908), 1. 93).

93. *REED, Shropshire*, vol. 1, pp. 311–12.

94. Ibid., vol. 1, p. 295. 'Silver games' are discussed in my 'Elizabethan and Jacobean Puritanism as Forms of Popular Religious Culture', p. 35 and note.

95. Hutton, *The Rise and Fall of Merry England*.

96. Thomas Tomkis's comedy *Albumazar*, performed before James I at Cambridge (where Tomkis had been a scholar at Trinity College) appeared in nine editions between the first in 1615 and 1634. There is a modern edition by Hugh C. Dick (Berkeley and Los Angeles, 1944). I owe this reference to James Lawson.

97. Lake, 'Puritanism, Arminianism and a Shropshire Axe-Murder'. At Coventry, the suppression of the traditional drama was blamed on the preachers, 'men very commendable for their behaviour and learning, and sweet in their sermons, but somewhat too sour in preaching away their pastimes' (Collinson, *Birthpangs*, p. 100).

98. Tomkys to the warden and others of the Shrewsbury Company of Drapers, 22 September 1586; SRR, 1831, uncatalogued. There is also extant a bill of charges for repairs and improvements, addressed: 'May it please your worships...' (ibid.). James Lawson has helped me with details of Tomkys's tenancy. The entry fine was £31 10s. and the annual rent, £3.

99. H. R. Trevor-Roper, 'The Fast Sermons of the Long Parliament', in Trevor-Roper, *Religion the Reformation and Social Change* (1967), pp. 294–344;

John F. Wilson, *Pulpit in Parliament: Puritanism during the English Civil Wars, 1640–1648* (Princeton, 1969).

13. RELIGIOUS SATIRE IN ENGLISH TOWNS, 1570–1640
Adam Fox

1. William Perkins, *A Faithfull and Plaine Exposition upon the Two First Verses of the Second Chapter of Zephaniah* (London, 1606), p. 15, cited in Patrick Collinson, *The Religion of Protestants: The Church in English Society, 1559–1625* (Oxford, 1982), p. 146.

2. For convenient summaries of the number and the size of market towns in this period, see D. M. Palliser, *The Age of Elizabeth: England under the Later Tudors, 1547–1603* (2nd edn, London, 1992), pp. 236–8, 253–6; C. G. A. Clay, *Economic Expansion and Social Change: England, 1500–1700*, 2 vols, (Cambridge, 1984), vol. I, pp. 165–73; E. A. Wrigley, 'Urban Growth and Agricultural Change: England and the Continent in the Early Modern Period', *Journal of Interdisciplinary History*, XV, 4 (1985), reprinted in Peter Borsay (ed.), *The Eighteenth Century Town* (London, 1990), pp. 41–51; Alan Dyer, *Decline and Growth in English Towns, 1400–1640* (Cambridge, 1991), pp. 51–7, 66–9. For the best general survey of the topic, see Peter Clark and Paul Slack, *English Towns in Transition, 1500–1700* (Oxford, 1976). Alan Everitt estimated the rather higher figure for English market towns of 760: 'The Marketing of Agricultural Produce', in Joan Thirsk (ed.), *The Agrarian History of England and Wales*, vol. IV: *1500–1640* (Cambridge, 1967), p. 467.

3. On the impact of the urban environment with its market day lectures and corporation lectureships on the dissemination and disputation of religious ideas, see W. J. Sheils, 'Religion in Provincial Towns: Innovation and Tradition', in Felicity Heal and Rosemary O'Day (eds), *Church and Society in England: Henry VIII to James I* (London, 1977), pp. 156–76; Patrick Collinson, 'Lectures by Combination: Structures and Characteristics of Church Life in 17th-Century England', in his *Godly People: Essays on English Protestantism and Puritanism* (London, 1983), pp. 467–98, and see p. 563 for a list of 85 towns in which combination lectures are known to have been established; Patrick Collinson, 'The Protestant Town', in his *The Birthpangs of Protestant England: Religious and Cultural Change in the Sixteenth and Seventeenth Centuries* (Basingstoke, 1988), ch. 2. The progress of the Reformation in particular towns can be traced in Wallace T. MacCaffrey, *Exeter, 1540–1640: The Growth of an English County Town* (2nd edn, Cambridge, MA, 1975), ch. 8; Alan D. Dyer, *The City of Worcester in the Sixteenth Century* (Leicester, 1973), ch. 18; Mervyn James, *Family, Lineage, and Civil Society: A Study of Society, Politics, and Mentality in the Durham Region, 1500–1640* (Oxford, 1974), chs 3, 5; D. M. Palliser, *Tudor York* (Oxford, 1979), ch. 9; Claire Cross, *Urban Magistrates and Ministers: Religion in Hull and Leeds, from the Reformation to the Civil War* (Borthwick Papers, 67, York, 1985); Susan Brigden, *London and the Reformation* (Oxford, 1989).

4. E. K. Chambers, *The Medieval Stage*, 2 vols (Oxford, 1903), vol. II, p. 219.

5. Richard Morison quoted in G. R. Elton, *Policy and Police: The Enforcement of the Reformation in the Age of Thomas Cromwell* (Cambridge, 1972), p. 185; John Ponet quoted in Collinson, *Birthpangs of Protestant England*, p. 103.

6. J. S. Brewer and James Gardiner (eds), *Letters and Papers, Foreign and Domestic, of the Reign of Henry VIII*, 21 vols, (London, 1862–1910), vol. xii, pt I, pp. 206, 461–4; vol. xiii, pt I, pp. 387–8, 501.

7. David N. Klausner (ed.), *Records of Early English Drama: Herefordshire, Worcestershire* (Toronto, 1990), p. 419.

8. J. N. King, *English Reformation Literature: The Tudor Origins of the Protestant Tradition* (Princeton, 1982), pp. 287–9; Brigden, *London and the Reformation*, pp. 436–8; Margaret Spufford, *Contrasting Communities: English Villagers in the Sixteenth and Seventeenth Centuries* (Cambridge, 1974), pp. 208, 245.

9. John Foxe, *Acts and Monuments*, ed. S. R. Cattley, 8 vols (London, 1837–41), vol. viii, p. 578.

10. Walter Rye (ed.), *Depositions taken before the Mayor and Aldermen of Norwich, 1547–1567* (Norfolk and Norwich Archaeological Society, ii, Norwich, 1905), p. 55; and see David Galloway (ed.), *Records of Early English Drama: Norwich, 1540–1642* (Toronto, 1984), pp. 34–5.

11. David George (ed.), *Records of Early English Drama: Lancashire* (Toronto, 1991), p. 213; C. R. Baskervill, *The Elizabethan Jig and Related Song Drama* (Chicago, 1929), p. 45; Chambers, *Medieval Stage*, vol. ii, pp. 219–23; Collinson, *Birthpangs of Protestant England*, pp. 105, 109; Tessa Watt, *Cheap Print and Popular Piety, 1550–1640* (Cambridge, 1991), p. 88.

12. Collinson, *Birthpangs of Protestant England*, pp. 110–15.

13. C. J. Sisson, *The Lost Plays of Shakespeare's Age* (Cambridge, 1936), chs 3–5; Martin Ingram, 'Ridings, Rough Music and Mocking Rhymes in Early Modern England', in Barry Reay (ed.), *Popular Culture in Seventeenth-Century England* (London, 1985), pp. 166–97; Adam Fox, 'Ballads, Libels and Popular Ridicule in Jacobean England', *Past and Present*, 145 (1994), pp. 47–83.

14. The greater levels of literacy in urban environments are suggested by the evidence of signatures: David Cressy, *Literacy and the Social Order: Reading and Writing in Tudor and Stuart England* (Cambridge, 1980), pp. 72–5, 128–35; Clark and Slack, *English Towns in Transition*, pp. 73, 153; D. M. Palliser, 'Civic Mentality and the Environment in Tudor York', *Northern History*, 18 (1982), 101–2. For examples of anecdotal evidence to the same effect, see Nicholas Breton, *The Court and Country* (1618), in W. C. Hazlitt (ed.), *Inedited Tracts: Illustrating the Manners, Opinions and Occupations of Englishmen during the Sixteenth and Seventeenth Centuries* (London, 1868), pp. 191–2, 198; R. F. Young (ed.), *Comenius in England* (London, 1932), p. 65.

15. On the role of inns, alehouses and market squares in the publicising of news and information, see respectively, Alan Everitt, 'The English Urban Inn, 1560–1760', in Everitt (ed.), *Perspectives in English Urban History* (London, 1973), pp. 110–13; Peter Clark, *The English Alehouse: A Social History, 1200–1830* (London, 1983), pp. 13–14; Jonathan Barry, 'Popular Culture in Seventeenth-Century Bristol', in Reay (ed.), *Popular Culture in Seventeenth-Century England*, p. 69. Further evidence of the importance of towns and their centres of sociability in this respect is given in Adam Fox, 'Rumour, News and Popular Political Opinion in Elizabethan and Early Stuart England', *Historical Journal*, 40 (1997), 597–620.

16. Public Record Office, London (hereafter PRO), STAC 8/240/26. Highworth was one of 23 market towns in Wiltshire at this time: Everitt, 'The

Marketing of Agricultural Produce', in Thirsk (ed.), *The Agrarian History of England and Wales*, pp. 471–2. Urban environments play a central part in Jurgen Habermas's analysis of the development of the 'public sphere' in Britain, although he does not date its emergence until the eighteenth century: *The Structural Transformation of the Public Sphere: an Inquiry into a Category of Bourgeois Society*, trans. Thomas Burger (1962; Cambridge, MA, 1989), e.g. pp. 15–16.

17. J. A. Sharpe, *Defamation and Sexual Slander in Early Modern England: the Church Courts at York* (Borthwick Papers, 58, York, 1980), p. 5; PRO, STAC 8/281/13, m. 2; E. R. C. Brinkworth, *Shakespeare and the Bawdy Court of Stratford* (London, 1972), p. 164.

18. PRO, STAC 8/129/2, m. 2; Huntington Library, San Marino, California, Hastings MSS., Legal Box 5 (9), fols 50–1, 55v–56r, 72, 83v, 86r, 106v–107r (I am grateful to Patrick Collinson for this reference).

19. Klausner (ed.), *Records of Early English Drama: Herefordshire, Worcestershire*, p. 392. On charivaris, see E. P. Thompson, ' "Rough Music": Le Charivari Anglais', *Annales*, 27 (1972), pp. 285–312; Martin Ingram, 'Ridings, Rough Music and the Reform of Popular Culture in Early Modern England', *Past and Present*, 105 (1984), pp. 79–113; Ingram, 'Ridings, Rough Music and Mocking Rhymes', pp. 166–78.

20. N. J. O'Conor, *Godes Peace and the Queenes: Vicissitudes of a House, 1539–1615* (London, 1934), pp. 118–20; Audrey Douglas and Peter Greenfield (eds), *Records of Early English Drama: Cumberland, Westmorland, Gloucestershire* (Toronto, 1986), p. 201. On various occasions in the 1620s Richard Romsbothom employed 'one Robert Wood, a ballett munger, or one that vseth to sell ballettes, a wandringe fellowe', to stand in the pulpit of the parish church at Holcombe in Lancashire and 'to preach or to make some ridiculous or prophaned sermon therein to the great dishonor of Almightie God and the prophanacion of his Saboth': George (ed.), *Records of Early English Drama: Lancashire*, pp. 26–7.

21. PRO, STAC 8/205/19; STAC 8/205/20; Huntington Library, Ellesmere MS. 5956.

22. PRO, STAC 8/53/7, mm. 1–2.

23. F. G. Emmison, *Elizabethan Life: Disorder* (Chelmsford, 1970), pp. 59–61.

24. W. D. Macray (ed.), 'The Manuscripts of the Corporation of Hereford', *Historical Manuscripts Commission, 13th Report, Appendix 4* (London, 1892), p. 338; J. C. Jeaffreson (ed.), *Middlesex County Records*, 4 vols (Middlesex County Record Society, London, 1886–92), vol. I, p. 272; John Rhodes quoted in Margaret Spufford, *Small Books and Pleasant Histories: Popular Fiction and its Readership in Seventeenth-Century England* (London, 1981), p. 11. For typical injunctions against the singing of popish ballads, see J. S. Purvis (ed.), *Tudor Parish Documents of the Diocese of York* (Cambridge, 1948), p. 15; George (ed.), *Records of Early English Drama: Lancashire*, p. 234.

25. E. K. Chambers (ed.), 'Dramatic Records of the City of London: the Repertories, Journals and Letter Books', in *Collections, Volume II, Part III* (Malone Society, Oxford, 1931), p. 309. 'Sebastain' was Sebastian Westcott, master of the Choristers at St Paul's. See Trevor Lennam, *Sebastian Westcott, the Children of Paul's and 'The Marriage of Wit and Science'* (Toronto and Buffalo, 1975).

26. The following is based on PRO, STAC 8/19/10; and see the discussion in Christopher Howard, *Sir John Yorke of Nidderdale, 1565–1634* (London, 1939),

pp. 20–6; C. J. Sisson, 'Shakespeare Quartos as Prompt-Copies: with some Account of Cholmeley's Players and a New Shakespeare Allusion', *Review of English Studies*, XVIII (1942), pp. 135–43.

27. On Simpson's Company, see E. K. Chambers, *The Elizabethan Stage*, 4 vols (Oxford, 1923), vol. I, pp. 304–5n, II, p. 339; J. C. Atkinson (ed.), *Quarter Sessions Records*, 8 vols (North Riding Record Society, London, 1884–90), vol. I, 154, 204, 206, 260; vol. II, 110, 119, 197.

28. J. S. Burn, *The Star Chamber* (London, 1870), p. 119; Chambers, *Elizabethan Stage*, vol. I, p. 328 n.

29. Patrick Collinson, 'Ecclesiastical Vitriol: Religious Satire in the 1590s and the Invention of Puritanism', in John Guy (ed.), *The Reign of Elizabeth I: Court and Culture in the Last Decade* (Cambridge, 1995), pp. 162–4; and Patrick Collinson, 'Ben Jonson's *Bartholomew Fair*: the Theatre Constructs Puritanism', in David L. Smith, Richard Strier and David Bevington (eds), *The Theatrical City: Culture, Theatre and Politics in London, 1576–1649* (Cambridge, 1995), pp. 164–6.

30. The following details are based upon PRO, STAC 8/303/8 and PRO, STAC 8/27/7; and see the discussion of the second of these cases in Sisson, *Lost Plays of Shakespeare's Age*, pp. 196–203.

31. For similar examples of factional rivalry in other towns at this time, see Paul Slack, 'Poverty and Politics in Salisbury, 1597–1666', in Peter Clark and Paul Slack (eds), *Crisis and Order in English Towns, 1500–1700* (London, 1972), pp. 164–203; Peter Clark, ' "The Ramoth-Gilead of the Good": Urban Change and Political Radicalism in Gloucester, 1540–1640', in Peter Clark, A. G. R. Smith and Nicholas Tyacke (eds), *The English Commonwealth, 1547–1640* (Leicester, 1979), pp. 167–87; David Underdown, *Revel, Riot and Rebellion: Popular Politics and Culture in England, 1603–1660* (Oxford, 1985), pp. 54–8; Collinson, *Birthpangs of Protestant England*, pp. 137–9; J. S. Craig, 'The "Godly" and the "Froward": Protestant Polemics in the Town of Thetford, 1560–1590', *Norfolk Archaeology*, XLI (1992), pp. 279–93; J. A. B. Somerset (ed.), *Records of Early English Drama: Shropshire* (Toronto, 1994), pp. 251–74, 398–400.

32. PRO, STAC 8/177/5, m 9.

33. Alastair Bellany, 'A Poem on the Archbishop's Hearse: Puritanism, Libel, and Sedition after the Hampton Court Conference', *Journal of British Studies*, 34 (1995), 137–64.

34. Mary Anne Everett Green (ed.), *Diary of John Rous, Incumbent of Santon Downham, Suffolk, from 1625 to 1642* (Camden Society, 1st ser., LXVI, London, 1856), pp. xi, 78–9, 80, 83–4, 101–3, 109–11, 115–19.

35. Patrick Collinson, *The Elizabethan Puritan Movement* (London, 1967), pp. 141–2; M. S. Byford, 'The Price of Protestantism: Assessing the Impact of Religious Change on Elizabethan Essex: the Cases of Heydon and Colchester, 1558–1594' (unpublished Oxford University DPhil thesis, 1988), pp. 219–20; PRO, SP 12/150/201 (I am grateful to John Craig for this reference). On William Saunderson, see Collinson, *Religion of Protestants*, p. 174.

36. PRO, STAC 8/94/17; David Underdown, *Fire From Heaven: Life in an English Town in the Seventeenth Century* (London, 1992), pp. 27–32.

37. PRO, STAC 8/26/10; and discussed in Sisson, *Lost Plays of Shakespeare's Age*, pp. 188–96; E. I. Fripp, *Shakespeare: Man and Artist* (Oxford, 1938), pp. 838–45;

Ann Hughes, 'Religion and Society in Stratford upon Avon, 1619–1638', *Midland History*, XIX (1994), pp. 58–84.

38. J. B. Leishman (ed.), *The Three Parnassus Plays (1598–1601)* (London, 1949), pp. 68–71, 112–16, 117. Stupido refers to the Marprelate Tracts, pp. 113–14: 'buye a good Martin, and twoo or three hundreth of catechismes of Ieneuas printe, and I warrant you will haue learning enoughe'; Alan H. Nelson (ed.), *Records of Early English Drama: Cambridge* (Toronto, 1989), pp. 912–14, 974. On Gouge, see William Haller, *The Rise of Puritanism* (New York, 1938), pp. 67–9.

39. Nelson, *Records of Early English Drama: Cambridge*, pp. 860, 931–2.

40. John Hacket (and Edmund Stubbs), *Loiola* (London, 1648); Nelson (ed.), *Records of Early English Drama: Cambridge*, pp. 588, 908–9, 957.

41. G. C. Moore Smith (ed.), *Fucus Histriomastix: A Comedy Probably Written by Robert Ward and Acted at Queens' College, Cambridge in Lent 1623* (Cambridge, 1909); Nelson (ed.), *Records of Early English Drama Cambridge*, pp. 878–80, 897, 956–7. For these stereotypical characteristics of the stage-puritan, see William P. Holden, *Anti-Puritan Satire, 1572–1642* (New Haven, 1954), pp. 101–21.

42. Peter Hausted, *The Rivall Friends: A Comoedie* (London, 1632); Nelson (ed.), *Records of Early English Drama: Cambridge*, pp. 641–2, 920, 960–1; *William Whiteway of Dorchester: His Diary 1618 to 1635* (Dorset Record Society, 12, Dorchester, 1991), p. 122.

43. Nelson (ed.), *Records of Early English Drama: Cambridge*, p. 682. Samuel Ward, 'the glory of Ipswich', was town preacher there from 1605 until his death in 1638: see Collinson, *Religion of Protestants*, pp. 175–7. As early as 1585, the corporation had been concerned about 'libels of sedition within this towne against the government and preacher at the same, being lately scattered abroad': Nathaniell Bacon, *Annalls of Ipswiche*, ed. W. H. Richardson (Ipswich, 1884), p. 341.

44. PRO, STAC 8/34/4; Douglas and Greenfield (eds), *Records of Early English Drama: Cumberland, Westmorland, Gloucester*, pp. 188–94, 195–8, 235–8; Mildred Campbell, *The English Yeoman under Elizabeth and the Early Stuarts* (London, 1960), p. 152.

Bibliography

1. BIRTH OF A PROTESTANT TOWN   *Mark Byford*

The best general survey of Colchester is Janet Cooper (ed.), *Victoria History of the County of Essex* (Oxford: OUP, 1994) IX. Vol. II of the *VCH* also contains some useful material. Another important work is P. Morant, *The History and Antiquities of the most ancient Town and Borough of Colchester in the County of Essex*, 2nd edn (London, 1768): republished as part of *The History and Antiquities of the County of Essex* (Wakefield: EP Publishing, 1978), vol. I.

The most important printed source on the Reformation in Colchester up to Elizabeth's accession is S. Cattley (ed.), *John Foxe's Acts and Monuments* (London, 1839), vol. VI, p. 740; vol. VII, pp. 139–42; vol. VIII, pp. 138–41, 303–10, 380–97, 420–3, 466–9, 535, 578, apps. VI, VIII. This period is also described in: J. C. Ward, 'The Reformation in Colchester, 1528–1558', *Essex Archaeology & History*, 15 (1983), 84–95; and as part of J. E. Oxley, *The Reformation in Essex to the Death of Mary* (Manchester: Manchester University Press, 1965), and of W. Hunt, *The Puritan Moment* (Harvard & London: Harvard University Press, 1983), chs 4–6. There is also an unpublished thesis: L. M. A. Higgs, 'Lay Piety in the Borough of Colchester, 1485–1558', University of Michigan PhD, 1983. There is no detailed survey of Elizabethan Colchester in print, although P. Collinson, *The Elizabethan Puritan Movement* (London: Jonathan Cape, 1967; reprinted London & New York: Methuen, 1982; Oxford: Clarendon Press, 1991); *Archbishop Grindal, 1519–1583: The Struggle for a Reformed Church* (London: Jonathan Cape, 1979); and 'The Godly: Aspects of Popular Protestantism' in his *Godly People* (London: Hambledon Press, 1983) all include important discussions of Protestant activity in north-eastern Essex. Religion in Elizabethan Colchester is extensively discussed in an unpublished thesis: M. Byford, 'The Price of Protestantism: Assessing the Impact of Religious Change on Elizabethan Essex: the Cases of Heydon and Colchester, 1558–1594', University of Oxford DPhil, 1988.

Comparative material from other English towns can be found in: C. Phythian-Adams, *Desolation of a City: Coventry and the Urban Crisis of the Late Middle Ages* (Cambridge: CUP, 1979); W. MacCaffrey, *Exeter, 1540–1640* (Cambridge, MA: Harvard University Press, 1958); for Ipswich see P. Collinson, *The Religion of Protestants* (Oxford: OUP, 1982), paperback edn (Oxford: OUP, 1984), pp. 170–7, J. Webb, 'Peter Moone of Ipswich (d. 1601). A Tudor Tailor, Poet and Gospeller and his Circle', *Proceedings of the Suffolk Institute of Archaeology and History*, 38 (1993), and D. MacCulloch and J. Blatchly, 'Pastoral Provision in the Parishes of Tudor Ipswich', *Sixteenth Century Journal* XXII, no. 3 (1991); P. Clark, 'Reformation and Radicalism in Kentish Towns, *c.* 1500–1553', in W. J. Mommsen (ed.), *Stadtbürgertum und Adel in der Reformation* (Stuttgart: Klett-Cotta, 1979); P. Clark, ' "The Ramoth-Gilead of the Good": Urban Change and Political Radicalism at Gloucester, 1540–1640', in J. Hurstfield (ed.), *The English Commonwealth, 1547–1640* (Leicester: LUP, 1979); 'The City of Leicester', in

Victoria History of the County of Leicestershire (London: OUP, 1958) IV; J. W. F. Hill, *Tudor and Stuart Lincoln* (Cambridge: CUP, 1956); A. Crossley (ed.), 'The City of Oxford', in *Victoria History of the County of Oxfordshire* (Oxford: OUP, 1979) IV; G. Mayhew, *Tudor Rye* (Falmer, Sussex: Centre for Continuing Education, 1987).

The best general surveys of the English Protestant town are to be found in P. Collinson, *The Birthpangs of Protestant England* (Basingstoke: Macmillan, 1988) ch. 2; and *The Religion of Protestants*, ch. 4. On the growth of Protestantism in English towns under Henry, see A. G. Dickens, *The English Reformation*, 2nd edn (London: Batsford, 1989), brief summaries in C. Haigh, *English Reformations* (Oxford: OUP, 1993), and S. Brigden, *London and the Reformation* (Oxford: OUP, 1989): paperback edn (Oxford: OUP, 1991). On Protestants in England under Mary, see Dickens, op. cit., and the relevant essays in J. W. Martin, *Religious Radicals in Tudor England* (London: Hambledon Press, 1989), esp. ch. 7, 'The Protestant Underground Congregations of Mary's Reign'. The best general work on the Marian burnings (despite its title) is still D. Loades, *The Oxford Martyrs* (London: Batsford, 1970): 2nd paperback edn (Bangor: Headstart History, 1992). See also: G. Alexander, 'Bonner and the Marian Persecutions', in C. Haigh (ed.), *The English Reformation Revised* (Cambridge and New York: CUP, 1987). On the post of the common preacher, see the important discussion in Collinson, *The Religion of Protestants*, pp. 173–6. Different aspects of Protestant moral regulation are discussed in: Collinson, 'The Beginnings of English Sabbatarianism', in his *Godly People*, also in *Birthpangs*, and *The Religion of Protestants*; M. Ingram, *Church Courts, Sex and Marriage in England, 1570–1640* (Cambridge: CUP, 1987); R. Hutton, *The Rise and Fall of Merry England* (Oxford: OUP, 1994), ch. 4, 'Reformation of Manners'.

2. RELIGION IN DONCASTER   *Claire Cross*

P. Clark and P. Slack (eds), *Crisis and Order in English Towns, 1500–1700* (London, 1972) provides an excellent starting point for the study of English towns in general, and in addition supplies a very full bibliography for urban history in the early modern period. Contributions to other volumes of essays, F. Heal and R. O'Day (eds), *Church and Society in England Henry VIII to James I* (London, 1977) and S. Wright (ed.), *Parish, Church and People: Local Studies in Lay Religion, 1350–1750* (London, 1988), concentrate more specifically on urban religion. Two classic histories of English towns, W. MacCaffrey, *Exeter, 1540–1650* (Cambridge, MA, 1958) and R. Howell, *Newcastle-upon-Tyne and the Puritan Revolution* (Oxford, 1967) include detailed discussions of civic religion, as does P. Clark, *English Provincial Society from the Reformation to the Revolution: Religion, Politics and Society in Kent, 1500–1640* (Hassocks, Sussex, 1977).

D. Hey, *Yorkshire from AD 1000* (London, 1986) and the more specialised D. Hey, *The Making of South Yorkshire* (London, 1979) furnish a helpful background to Yorkshire history. In the last four decades a succession of historians has considered in depth aspects of the religious history of the county in the sixteenth and seventeenth centuries. These include A. G. Dickens, *Lollards and*

Protestants in the Diocese of York (London, 1959), and R. A. Marchant, *The Puritans and the Church Courts in the Diocese of York, 1560–1642* (London, 1960). Since the publication of the *Victoria County History* for the city of York (P. M. Tillott (ed.), *A History of Yorkshire: the City of York*, London, 1961) York in particular has attracted the attention of historians of religion; D. M. Palliser, *The Reformation in York, 1534–1553*, Borthwick Paper no. 40 (York, 1971), pioneered the use of will preambles. The influence of former monks, friars and chantry priests upon the city is discussed in C. Cross, 'Priests into Ministers: the Establishment of Protestant Practice in the City of York 1530–1630', P. N. Brooks (ed.), *Reformation Principle and Practice: Essays in Honour of A. G. Dickens* (London, 1980). York recusancy has been treated in scholarly detail by J. C. H. Aveling, *Catholic Recusancy in the City of York, 1558–1791* (London, 1970). In contrast not a great deal has yet been published on the religious history of other Yorkshire towns, though C. Cross in *Urban Magistrates and Ministers: Religion in Hull and Leeds from the Reformation to the Civil War*, Borthwick Paper no. 67 (York, 1985) has made a brief attempt to investigate the religious climate of Leeds and Hull.

The Victoria County History volume for Doncaster has still to be written and, apart from a collection of essays celebrating the eight hundredth anniversary of its first charter, G. H. Martin, E. A. Danbury, P. J. P. Goldberg, D. J. Barber and M. W. Beresford, *Doncaster: A Borough and its Charters* (Doncaster, 1994), the town has failed to capture the interest of historians in the twentieth century. This makes all the more valuable the work of nineteenth-century antiquarians and topographers, of which the most important is J. Hunter, *South Yorkshire: The History and Topography of the Deanery of Doncaster*, 1 (London, 1828). E. Miller, *History and Antiquities of Doncaster* (Doncaster, 1804); J. E. Jackson, *History and Description of St George's Church at Doncaster destroyed by Fire February 28, 1853* (London, 1855); and J. Tomlinson, *Doncaster from the Roman Occupation to the Present Time* (Doncaster, 1887) also contain much useful material.

3. POLITICS AND RELIGION IN EARLY MODERN BEVERLEY   *David Lamburn*

Although there is no overall synthesis dealing with the interaction of politics and religion in urban society, many of the themes relevant to this essay are raised and discussed in P. Collinson, *The Religion of Protestants: The Church in English Society, 1559–1625* (Oxford: Clarendon Press, 1982), and his *The Birthpangs of Protestant England: Religious and Cultural Change in the Sixteenth and Seventeenth Centuries* (Basingstoke: Macmillan, 1988).

The political development of towns has also suffered from the absence of a detailed recent study; the standard interpretation remains that set out in P. Clark and P. Slack, *English Towns in Transition, 1500–1700* (London, 1976), and there is still a temptation to assume that politics was the concern only of the urban elite. For a contrasting view, see D. Underdown, *Revel, Riot and Rebellion: Popular Politics and Culture in England, 1603–1660* (Oxford, 1987), and his *Fire from Heaven: Life in an English Town in the Seventeenth Century* (London: HarperCollins, 1992). J. Barry and C. Brooks (eds), *The Middling Sort of People: Culture, Society and*

Politics in England, 1550–1800 (Basingstoke: Macmillan, 1994), tackles the relatively neglected middling sector and offers valuable insights.

Generally, studies of the religious and political development of towns have been dealt with in urban monographs and in regional studies. See, for example, D. M. Palliser, *Tudor York* (Oxford, 1979); J. T. Evans, *Seventeenth-Century Norwich* (Oxford, 1979); G. Mayhew, *Tudor Rye* (Falmer: University of Sussex, 1987); M. K. McIntosh, *A Community Transformed: The Manor and Liberty of Havering, 1500–1620* (Cambridge, 1991); R. C. Richardson, *Puritanism in North-West England: A Regional Study of the Diocese of Chester to 1642* (Manchester, 1972); W. J. Sheils, *The Puritans in the Diocese of Peterborough, 1558–1610* (Northants Record Society, xxx, 1979). Among useful studies of the interaction of politics and religion are R. Howell, 'Newcastle and the Nation: the Seventeenth-Century Experience', *Archaeologia Aeliana*, 8 (1980), and his *Newcastle upon Tyne and the Puritan Revolution* (Oxford: Clarendon Press, 1967), and R. Cust, 'Anti-Puritanism and Urban Politics: Charles I and Great Yarmouth', *Historical Journal*, 35 (1992). For London, S. Brigden, *London and the Reformation* (Oxford: Clarendon Press, 1989) is invaluable; I. Archer, *The Pursuit of Stability: Social Relations in Elizabethan London* (Cambridge, 1991), stresses the importance of elite solidarity, undisturbed by religious conflict, in enabling popular unrest to be restrained. The stress of civil war revealed previous political fractures in urban society, for which see the first six contributions to R. C. Richardson, *Town and Countryside in the English Revolution* (Manchester, 1992).

As yet there is no adequate published study of early modern Beverley, though there is useful background information in B. A. English and D. Neave (eds), *Tudor Beverley* (Beverley, 1973), and in K. J. Allison, *A History of the County of York East Riding: The Borough and Liberties of Beverley* (Oxford, 1989). Useful collections of printed primary sources are in J. Dennett (ed.), *Beverley Borough Records, 1575–1821* (Yorkshire Archaeological Society Record Series, vol. lxxxiv, 1933), and A. F. Leach (ed.), *Beverley Town Documents* (Selden Society, vol. xiv, 1900).

4. THE COMING OF PROTESTANTISM TO ELIZABETHAN
TEWKESBURY   *Caroline Litzenberger*

There are a number of works which focus on the particular issues raised by the effects of religious change on sixteenth-century Tewkesbury, specifically the effects on religious drama and church seating. For further discussion of the effects of Protestantism on drama see E. K. Chambers, *The Elizabethan Stage*, 4 vols (Oxford, 1923); and H. C. Gardiner, *Mysteries' End: An Investigation of the Last Days of the Medieval Religious Stage* (New Haven, CT, 1946). Both were published some time ago, but they still provide a thorough discussion of the topic. However, the most comprehensive treatment of the subject may be found in the volumes of the Records of Early English Drama being published by the University of Toronto. The volume which discusses Gloucestershire and Tewkesbury is *Records of Early English Drama: Cumberland, Westmorland, Gloucestershire*, ed. A. Douglas and P. Greenfield (Toronto, Buffalo and London, 1986). The *REED* volume includes selected excerpts from civic and parish records pertaining to drama. Another printed primary source which relates specifically to the Reformation in Gloucestershire is *The Commission for Ecclesiastical Causes within the Dioceses of Bristol and Gloucester*, ed. F. D. Price (Gateshead, 1973). For other perspectives on issues of church seating in sixteenth-century English parishes see A. Heales, *The History and Law of Church Seats or Pews, Book I – History* (London, 1872); M. Aston, 'Segregation in Church', in *Women in the Church*, ed. W. J. Sheils and D. Wood (1989), 237–94; and R. Tittler, 'Seats of Honor, Seats of Power: the Symbolism of Public Seating in the English Urban Community, *c.* 1560–1620', *Albion*, 24 (1992). Heales still provides the most comprehensive discussion of the relevant legal issues despite its publication date, while Aston and Tittler provide insights into ways in which issues of gender and status are reflected in where people sat in church.

Additionally, the Gloucestershire context for religious developments in Tewkesbury during the Reformation can be found in C. Litzenberger, *The English Reformation and the Laity: Gloucestershire, 1540–1580* (Cambridge, forthcoming). Further discussion of the use of wills as evidence of lay piety is provided in C. Marsh, 'In the name of God? Will-making and Faith in Early Modern England', in *The Records of the Nation*, ed. G. H. Martin and P. Spufford (Woodbridge, 1990), 215–49; and C. Litzenberger, 'Local Responses to Changes in Religious Policy based on Evidence from Gloucestershire Wills (1540–1580)', *Continuity and Change*, 8 (1993), 417–39.

5.   WORCESTER: A CATHEDRAL CITY IN THE REFORMATION
Diarmaid MacCulloch

Essential background reading is the survey by S. E. Lehmberg, *The Reformation of Cathedrals: Cathedrals in English Society, 1485–1603* (Princeton University Press, 1988). For two different perspectives on the iconoclasm which is one of the essay's themes, see M. Aston, *England's Iconoclasts, vol. 1; Laws against Images* (Oxford: Clarendon Press, 1988) and E. Duffy, *The Stripping of the Altars: Traditional Religion in England 1400–1580* (London and New Haven: Yale University Press, 1992). A very useful account of Tudor Worcester, which however concentrates on its economic rather than its spiritual life, is A. D. Dyer, *The City of Worcester in the Sixteenth Century* (Leicester University Press, 1973). We are fortunate in having one informative set of churchwardens' accounts for the city, albeit (as is not infrequent with urban parishes) for a church which no longer exists: J. Amphlett (ed.), *The Churchwardens' Accounts of St Michael in Bedwardine, 1539–1603* (Worcestershire Historical Society, 1896): for the general context here, see the brilliant summary essay by R. E. Hutton, 'The Local Impact of the Tudor Reformations', in C. Haigh (ed.), *The English Reformation Revised* (Cambridge University Press, 1987). The whole text of the document which is the backbone of this essay is edited with additional commentary in D. MacCulloch and P. Hughes (eds), 'A Bailiffs' List and Chronicle from Worcester', *Antiquaries Journal*, 74 (1995). Earlier imperfect transcripts can be found in T. R. Nash, *Collections for Worcestershire* (London, 1799), a classic county history with all the virtues and defects of that genre. Two of Worcester's bishops in the crucial years were fortunately loquacious in the evangelical cause: see *Sermons and Remains of Hugh Latimer...*, ed. G. E. Corrie (Parker Society, 1845) and *Later Writings of Bishop Hooper...*, ed. C. Nevinson (Parker Society, 1852). The latter's episcopate is also illuminated by F. D. Price, 'Gloucester Diocese under Bishop Hooper, 1551–3', *Transactions of the Bristol and Gloucester Archaeological Society*, 60 (1938), 51–151, who also quotes some extracts from the Steynor chronicle via another source. No such treasury of sources or comment survives from their religious opponents.

6.   LEADERSHIP AND PRIORITIES IN READING DURING THE
REFORMATION   *Jeanette Martin*

General

For understanding the nature of secular authority, daily governance, the legal system, offices, status and the interaction of the local community with the centre in this earlier period, see A. L. Brown, *The Governance of Late Medieval England, 1272–1461* (London: Edward Arnold, 1989); also important for understanding the complexities and variations in urban government is Susan Reynolds's *An Introduction to the History of English Medieval Towns* (Oxford: Clarendon Press, 1977; corrected paperback reprint 1982, with glossary). For ecclesiastical and religious life, see R. N. Swanson, *Church and Society in Late Medieval England* (Oxford: Blackwell, 1989; paperback edn, 1993, with glossary); J. A. F. Thomson, *The Early Tudor Church and Society, 1485–1529* (Harlow: Longman, 1993, with glossary). For late medieval religion, its practice, and eventual destruction, see E. Duffy, *The Stripping of the Altars: Traditional Religion in England c. 1400–1580* (New Haven and London: Yale University Press, 1992); J. J. Scarisbrick, *The Reformation and the English People* (Oxford: Blackwell, 1984). For the 'revisionist' view, see C. Haigh, *English Reformations: Religion, Politics, and Society under the Tudors* (Oxford: Clarendon Press, 1993). For the seasonal rituals, customs and festivities in the parishes and the impact of reform, see R. Hutton, *The Rise and Fall of Merry England: The Ritual Year, 1400–1700* (Oxford: Oxford University Press, 1994). For works on iconoclasm and enforcement of reform, see M. Aston, *England's Iconoclasts: Laws Against Images*, vol. I (Oxford: Clarendon Press, 1988), and G. R. Elton, *Policy and Police: The Enforcement of the Reformation in the Age of Thomas Cromwell* (Cambridge: Cambridge University Press, 1972; first paperback edn, 1985). For analytical accounts taking note of recent research on the English Reformation, see R. Rex, *Henry VIII and the English Reformation* (Basingstoke: Macmillan, 1993); D. MacCulloch, *The Later Reformation in England, 1547–1603* (Basingstoke: Macmillan, 1990) and for stimulating insights into the eventual religious and cultural changes, see P. Collinson, *The Birthpangs of Protestant England* (Basingstoke: Macmillan, 1988; paperback reprint 1991).

Sample Works for Comparative Purposes

S. Brigden, *London and the Reformation* (Oxford: Oxford University Press, 1989; corrected paperback edn, 1991). I. W. Archer, *The Pursuit of Stability: Social*

Relations in Elizabethan London (Cambridge: Cambridge University Press, 1991). A. G. Dickens, *Lollards and Protestants in the Diocese of York, 1509–1558* (Oxford: Oxford University Press, 1959; 2nd edn, London: Hambledon, 1982, paperback). D. M. Palliser, *Tudor York* (Oxford: Oxford University Press, 1979). C. Haigh, *Reformation and Resistance in Tudor Lancashire* (Cambridge: Cambridge University Press, 1975). P. Clark, *English Provincial Society from the Reformation to the Revolution, 1500–1640* (Hassocks: Harvester, 1977). G. Mayhew, *Tudor Rye* (Falmer: Centre for Continuing Education, University of Sussex, 1987). B. L. Beer, *Rebellion and Riot: Popular Disorder in England during the Reign of Edward VI* (Kent State University Press, USA, 1982). R. Whiting, *The Blind Devotion of the People: Popular Religion and the English Reformation* (Cambridge: Cambridge University Press, 1989).

7. TEXTILES AND REFORM: HALIFAX AND ITS HINTERLAND
William and Sarah Sheils

The role of towns in furthering the English Reformation was recognised by Thomas Cromwell, and their impact is noted in all general histories, up to and including Patrick Collinson's *The Birthpangs of Protestant England* (1988), which has a chapter entitled 'The Protestant Town'. Urban historians have also reflected on the relationship in general books such as P. Clark and P. Slack, *English Towns in Transition, 1500–1700* (Oxford, 1976), and also in studies of particular towns, most of which are referred to elsewhere in this volume. The relationship between textile communities and the Reformation also has a long pedigree, going back to W. H. Summers, *The Lollards of the Chiltern Hills: Glimpses of English Dissent in the Middle Ages* (London, 1906), and was given its most eloquent modern airing in C. Hill, 'From Lollards to Levellers', first published in 1978 and now available in his *Collected Essays*, vol. 2: *Religion and Politics in Seventeenth-Century England* (Hassocks, 1986). The most recent discussion of the relationship between economic and social life and religious affiliation is in M. Spufford (ed.), *The World of Rural Dissenters, 1520–1725* (Cambridge, 1995), and the essays it contains will certainly influence work on towns also. For a later period the relationship is discussed in Pat Hudson (ed.), *Regions and Industries: A Perspective on the Industrial Revolution in Britain* (Cambridge, 1989). The modern historiography of the Reformation in Yorkshire begins with A. G. Dickens, *Lollards and Protestants in the Diocese of York, 1509–1558* (Oxford, 1959), and the later phases are treated in a rather institutional fashion in R. A. Marchant, *The Puritans and the Church Courts in the Diocese of York, 1560–1642* (1960). Studies of the urban Reformation in the county are in D. M. Palliser, *Tudor York* (Oxford, 1979), and M. C. Cross, *Urban Magistrates and Ministers: Religion in Hull and Leeds from the Reformation to the Civil War* (Borthwick Papers, 67, 1985). More general background on Halifax is in S. A. Sheils, 'Aspects of the History of Halifax, 1480–1547' (MA dissertation, University of York, 1981) and M. E. Francois, 'The Social and Economic Development of Halifax, 1558–1640', *Proceedings of the Leeds Philosophical and Literary Society* (1966), pp. 217–80. More general background on the West Riding can be found in J. T. Cliffe, *The Yorkshire Gentry from the Reformation to the Civil War* (1969). For the history of the Reformation in the similar upland and urbanising area of south-west Lancashire see C. Haigh, *Reformation and Reaction in Tudor Lancashire* (Cambridge, 1975) and R. C. Richardson, *Puritanism in North-West England* (Manchester, 1972). Continuity of form, if not of content, is also noted in more developed urban communities by W. J. Sheils, 'Religion in Provincial Towns: Innovation and Tradition', in F. Heal and R. O'Day (eds), *Church and Society in England: Henry VIII to James I* (London and Basingstoke, 1977).

8. ECONOMIC PROBLEMS OF PROVINCIAL URBAN CLERGY DURING
       THE REFORMATION   *Patrick Carter*

For an examination of the economic circumstances of the parish clergy during the early sixteenth century, see P. Heath, *The English Parish Clergy on the Eve of the Reformation* (London, 1969), pp. 135–74; and more recently J. A. F. Thomson, *The Early Tudor Church and Society, 1485–1529* (London, 1993). These studies may be supplemented by the excellent survey of the economic activities of the late medieval English Church in R. N. Swanson, *Church and Society in Late Medieval England* (Oxford, 1989), pp. 191–251. Although based solely upon printed sources and now somewhat dated in interpretation, C. Hill, *Economic Problems of the Church from Archbishop Whitgift to the Long Parliament* (Oxford, 1956), remains useful if employed with caution. Local Reformation studies devote varying attention to the economic plight of clergy; three of the most valuable are S. Brigden, *London and the Reformation* (Oxford, 1989); M. Bowker, *The Henrician Reformation: The Diocese of Lincoln under John Longland, 1521–1547* (Cambridge, 1981); and especially M. C. Skeeters, *Community and Clergy: Bristol and the Reformation c. 1530–c.1570* (Oxford, 1993). For local efforts to address the economic problems facing urban clergy, see D. M. Palliser, 'The Union of Parishes at York, 1547–1586', *Yorkshire Archaeological Journal*, XLVI (1974), 87–102; and D. MacCulloch and J. Blatchly, 'Pastoral Provision in the Parishes of Tudor Ipswich', *Sixteenth Century Journal*, XXIII (1991), 457–74. C. Cross (ed.), *York Clergy Wills, 1520–1600*, vol. II: *City Clergy* (York, 1989) is a useful collection of urban clerical wills and inventories, together with a helpful editorial introduction, supplemented by C. Cross, 'The Incomes of Provincial Urban Clergy, 1520–1645', in R. O'Day and F. Heal (eds), *Princes and Paupers in the English Church, 1500–1800* (Leicester, 1981), pp. 65–89. Michael Zell devotes particular attention to the position of unbeneficed clergy in his 'Economic Problems of the Parochial Clergy in the Sixteenth Century', in O'Day and Heal (eds), *Princes and Paupers*, pp. 19–43. On the vexed question of urban tithes, see A. G. Little, 'Personal Tithes', *English Historical Review*, LX (1945), 67–88; and S. Brigden, 'Tithe Controversy in Reformation London', *Journal of Ecclesiastical History*, XXXII (1981), 285–301. For the impact of increased clerical taxation, the standard published work remains F. Heal, 'Clerical Tax Collection under the Tudors: the Influence of the Reformation', in R. O'Day and F. Heal (eds), *Continuity and Change: Personnel and Administration of the Church of England, 1500–1642* (Leicester, 1976), pp. 97–122.

There is no really comprehensive account of the dissolution of the chantries. The closest is Alan Kreider, *English Chantries: The Road to Dissolution* (Cambridge, MA, 1979), but this volume has little to say about the actual process of the suppression and its impact upon religious life in England. These issues are dealt with by W. K. Jordan, *Edward VI: The Threshold of Power* (Cambridge, MA, 1970), but some of his conclusions regarding the economic impact are rather suspect. The subject is treated in more general terms as part of the larger Reformation movement by A. G. Dickens, *The English Reformation* (2nd edn, 1989); Christopher Haigh, *English Reformations: Religion, Politics, and Society under the Tudors* (Oxford, 1993); J. J. Scarisbrick, *The Reformation and the English People* (Oxford, 1984); and Eamon Duffy, *The Stripping of the Altars: Traditional Religion in England, 1400–1580* (New Haven and London, 1992).

The purpose of the chantries is discussed in Kreider (1979) and K. L. Wood-Legh, *Perpetual Chantries in Britain* (Cambridge, 1965). There are numerous works which deal with individual chantry foundations and many of these are mentioned in Kreider's bibliography, while the architectural wonders of the chantry chapels are explored in G. H. Cook, *Mediaeval Chantries and Chantry Chapels* (London, 1963). Several authors of monographs about particular towns have made reference to the chantries, especially Susan Brigden, *London and the Reformation* (Oxford, 1989), and D. M. Palliser, *Tudor York* (Oxford, 1979). Many cathedrals and parish churches have guidebooks which make some mention of the pre-Reformation chantries which existed within their walls. Some of the collegiate churches have been treated in detail in monographs, while the *Victoria County History* gives excellent summaries of most of the collegiate foundations and the more important chantry foundations in the churches of the larger towns. G. H. Cook, *English Collegiate Churches of the Middle Ages* (London, 1959), and A. Hamilton Thompson, *English Colleges of Chantry Priests* (London, 1945), are good general introductions to the subject.

For the Henrician suppression of selected secular colleges see J. J. Scarisbrick, 'Henry VIII and the Dissolution of the Secular Colleges', in *Law and Government under the Tudors*, ed. Claire Cross, David Loades and J. J. Scarisbrick (Cambridge, 1988). For the guilds and lay fraternities the only monograph available is H. F. Westlake, *Parish Gilds of Medieval England* (London, 1919), but Gervase Rosser is presently working on a more up-to-date assessment, *Medieval English Guilds 900–1600*. For a more limited but thought-provoking treatment of these institutions see chapter 2 of Scarisbrick, *The Reformation and the English People*; and for the social role of the fraternity in the local community see Gervase Rosser, 'Going to the Fraternity Feast: Commensality and Social Relations in Late Medieval England', *Journal of British Studies*, 33 (1994), 430–46. Very little has been written about the obits, lamps and lights which were confiscated at the same time as the larger intercessory institutions. Information about the individual institutions suppressed in 1548 may be found in the returns of the Chantry Commissioners in the Public Record Office (E301). Many of these so-called 'chantry certificates' have been published by local and county record societies, and the majority of these are mentioned in Kreider's bibliography.

There has been relatively little detailed research into the impact of the dissolution of the chantries on parish and community life in the English towns, but some suggestions are made by W. J. Sheils, 'Religion in Provincial Towns: Innovation and Tradition', in *Church and Society in England: Henry VIII to James I*, ed. Felicity Heal and Rosemary O'Day (London, 1977). For the impact on education, the earlier assessment of A. F. Leach, *English Schools at the Reformation, 1546–8* (London, 1896), has now been superseded by the work of Joan Simon, *Education and Society in Tudor England* (Cambridge, 1966), and N. Orme, *English Schools in the Middle Ages* (London, 1973). The effect of the dissolution on the unbeneficed clergy of Tudor England has been largely neglected, but for some general comments about the chantry priests before the dissolution see Peter Heath, *The English Parish Clergy on the Eve of the Reformation* (London, 1969). The fate of the chantry lands is examined in numerous local studies, but a good general introduction (which asks more questions than it answers) is Christopher Kitching, 'The Disposal of the Monastic and Chantry Lands', in *Church and Society in England*. On the more general question of the social and religious impact of the dissolution on parish life, Scarisbrick (1984), Dickens (1989) and Duffy (1992) all have much to say in passing.

10. VOLUNTARY RELIGION AND REFORMATION CHANGE IN EIGHT URBAN PARISHES   *Beat Kümin*

The only long-term approach to this topic is a collection of papers read at two conferences held by the Ecclesiastical History Society and published as vol. 23 of 'Studies in Church History': W. J. Sheils and D. Wood (eds), *Voluntary Religion* (Oxford: Basil Blackwell, 1986). The first post-Reformation century, of course, has always been seen as a heyday for 'voluntary religion' and no short bibliography can hope to do justice to the massive amount of existing literature. Good starting-points are P. Collinson, *The Religion of Protestants: The Church in English Society, 1559–1625* (Oxford: Clarendon Press, 1982), esp. ch. 6; C. Hill, *Society and Puritanism in Pre-Revolutionary England* (London: Panther, 1964); and A. Dures, *English Catholicism, 1558–1642* (Harlow: Longman, 1983). Complementary accounts of the importance of preaching will be found in P. Seaver, *The Puritan Lectureships: The Politics of Religious Dissent, 1560–1662* (Stanford University Press, 1970), and P. Collinson, 'Lectures by Combination: Structures and Characteristics of Church Life in Seventeenth-Century England', in his *Godly People* (London: Hambledon Press, 1983), pp. 467–98. An original recent account of an unorthodox movement is C. W. Marsh, *The Family of Love in English Society, 1550–1630* (Cambridge University Press, 1994), and R. J. Acheson, *Radical Puritans in England, 1550–1660* (London and New York: Longman, 1990), provides a brief introduction to the separatist wing of radical Protestantism.

The reassessment of the chronology and extent of 'voluntary religion' proposed in this essay owes much to the recent expansion of work on the pre-Reformation period, culminating in Eamon Duffy's broad panorama of late medieval Catholicism in *The Stripping of the Altars: Traditional Religion in England, 1400–1580* (New Haven and London: Yale University Press, 1992). In addition, there are now a number of specialised studies on the two most prominent medieval voluntary institutions. K. L. Wood-Leigh, *Perpetual Chantries in Britain* (Cambridge University Press, 1965), A. Kreider, *English Chantries: The Road to Dissolution* (Cambridge MA and London: Harvard University Press, 1979) and a series of essays by Clive Burgess, starting with ' "For the Increase of Divine Service": Chantries in the Parish in Late Medieval Bristol', *Journal of Ecclesiastical History*, 36 (1985), 46–65, are among the most notable contributions to the history of perpetual and temporary mass foundations, while J. J. Scarisbrick, *The Reformation and the English People* (Oxford: Basil Blackwell, 1984), ch. 2, and G. Rosser, 'Communities of Parish and Guild in the Late Middle Ages', in S. Wright (ed.), *Parish, Church & People* (London: Hutchinson, 1988), pp. 29–55, have reminded us of the importance of lay fraternities in pre-Reformation England. Monographs on the long-term development of English guilds (by G. Rosser) and the fraternities of Cambridgeshire (V. Bainbridge, *Gilds in the Medieval Countryside*) are about to be published. Ann Hudson, *The Premature Reformation* (Oxford: Clarendon Press, 1988), and Margaret Aston, *Lollards and Reformers* (London: Hambledon Press, 1984), to name but two of a number of recent works on Lollardy, exemplify the unorthodox dimension of late medieval voluntary religion.

The various compulsory and voluntary aspects of religious activities within the parish community itself are discussed in D. Palliser, 'Introduction: the Parish in Perspective', in Wright, *Parish, Church & People*, pp. 5–28, G. Rosser, 'Parochial Conformity and Voluntary Religion in Late Medieval England', *Transactions of the Royal Historical Society*, 6th Ser. 1 (1991), 173–89 (with a particular emphasis on chapels), B. Kümin, *The Shaping of a Community: The Rise and Reformation of the English Parish c. 1400–1560* (Aldershot and Brookfield, VT: Scolar Press, 1995), esp. ch. 3.4, and – from the clergy's point of view – R. Swanson, 'Standards of Livings: Parochial Revenues in Pre-Reformation England', in C. Harper-Bill (ed.), *Religious Beliefs and Ecclesiastical Careers in Late Medieval England* (Woodbridge: Boydell Press, 1991), pp. 151–96.

Moving to the sources, a very full list and bibliography of churchwardens' accounts will be found in the appendix to R. Hutton, *The Rise and Fall of Merry England: The Ritual Year, 1400–1700* (Oxford University Press, 1994). Those for Ashburton (edited by A. Hanham, 1970) and All Saints, Bristol (C. Burgess, forthcoming; including the accounts of the Halleway chantry) are among the case-studies used here. P. Heath (ed.), *Medieval Clerical Accounts* (York: St Anthony's Hall Publications, 1964) allows occasional glimpses of voluntary religion in the records of parish priests, while P. Basing (ed.), *Parish Fraternity Register* (London: London Record Society, 1982) yields detailed information about membership and activities of a fraternity at Botolph Aldersgate in London. Lollard beliefs are illustrated in N. Tanner (ed.), *Heresy Trials in the Diocese of Norwich, 1428–31* (London: Royal Historical Society, 1977). An idea of the commissioning of additional preaching in the Elizabethan period can be gathered from parochial records printed in E. M. Tomlinson, *A History of the Minories, London* (London: Smith, Elder & Co., 1907), esp. pp. 212ff, and the life of a separatist congregation is documented in E. Underhill (ed.), *The Records of the Church of Christ meeting in Broadmead, Bristol* (London: Hanserd Knollys Society, 1847).

11. REFORMATION, RESOURCES AND AUTHORITY IN ENGLISH TOWNS:
    AN OVERVIEW   *Robert Tittler*

As the argument tries to connect two bodies of writing which have hitherto
remained discrete, it will do to begin with key works on both urban history and
the Reformation in the urban context. Peter Clark and Paul Slack's *Crisis and
Order in English Towns, 1500–1700* (London: Routledge, 1972), and to a lesser
extent *English Towns in Transition, 1500–1700* (Oxford: Oxford University Press,
1976), are the places to begin the first line of enquiry, though Wallace
T. MacCaffrey's *Exeter, 1540–1640: The Growth of an English County Town* (Cambridge, MA and London: Harvard University Press, Open University, 1958 and
1976) was a forerunner of considerable and continued value. Amongst the
many other useful studies of provincial urban communities at this time are
Alan Dyer, *The City of Worcester in the Sixteenth Century* (Leicester: Leicester
University Press, 1973), David Palliser, *Tudor York* (Oxford: Oxford University
Press, 1979), and Charles Phythian-Adams, *Desolation of a City: Coventry and the
Urban Crisis of the Late Middle Ages* (Cambridge: Cambridge University Press,
1979). Studies working toward the connection of Reformation and urban
change, but still essentially from an urban perspective, include Palliser's brief
The Reformation in York, 1534–1553 (Borthwick Papers no. 40, 1971 and 1979),
and David Underdown's brilliant and delightful *Fire from Heaven: Life in an
English Town in the Seventeenth Century* (New Haven and London: Yale University
Press, 1992).

On the Reformation side of the equation required reading begins with
Patrick Collinson's *The Birthpangs of Protestant England: Religious and Cultural Change
in the Sixteenth and Seventeenth Centuries* (Basingstoke: Macmillan, 1988), especially
ch. 2, and *The Religion of Protestants: The Church in English Society, 1559–1625*
(Oxford: Oxford University Press, 1982) especially ch. 4. More general works
emphasising the deleterious effects of the Reformation and especially the Dissolutions include Dom David Knowles, *The Religious Orders in England*, 3 vols
(Cambridge: Cambridge University Press, 1950–9) esp. vol. III; J. J. Scarisbrick, *The Reformation and the English People* (Oxford: Blackwell, 1984) and Eamon
Duffy, *The Stripping of the Altars: Traditional Religion in England, 1400–1580* (London and New Haven: Yale University Press, 1992).

Amongst a number of useful treatments of the disposition of urban property
prior to Dissolution are Rosemary Horrox's edition of the *Selected Rentals and
Accounts of Medieval Hull, 1293–1528* (Yorkshire Archeological Society Record
Series, 141 (1983 for 1981); Alan Kreider, *English Chantries: The Road to Dissolution* (Cambridge, MA: Harvard University Press, 1979), and S. R. R. Jones,
'Property, Tenure and Rents: Some Aspects of the Topography and Economy
of Medieval York' (PhD thesis, York University, 1987). Work on the disposition
of dissolved property which takes in the chantries as well as the monasteries is
far thinner on the ground, but monastic properties alone are well treated in
Joyce Youings, 'The City of Exeter and the Property of the Dissolved Monasteries', *Transactions of the Devonshire Association*, 84 (1952), 122–41. C. J. Kitching, 'The Disposal of Monastic and Chantry Lands', in F. Heal and R. O'Day
(eds), *Church and Society in England: Henry VIII to James I* (Basingstoke: Macmillan,
1977), pp. 128–33; and Adrienne Rosen, 'Economic and Social Aspects of the

History of Winchester, 1520–1670' (Oxford University DPhil thesis, 1975),
passim, deal with both waves of dissolution, but the former is brief and the
latter not easily accessible. For the most part, alas, information on the distribution of Henrician and Edwardian dissolutions is best traced only by the
laborious examination of the history of individual towns, a task happily facilitated in at least some cases by the volumes of the *Victoria County History* series and
the *Calendar of Patent Rolls*.

12.   THE SHEARMEN'S TREE AND THE PREACHER
Patrick Collinson

The fullest history of Shrewsbury is H. Owen and J. B. Blakeway, *A History
of Shrewsbury*, published in 2 volumes in 1825. See also J. Basil Oldham, *A History
of Shrewsbury School, 1552–1952* (Oxford, 1952). T. C. Mendenhall, *The Shrewsbury Drapers and the Welsh Wool Trade in the XVI and XVII Centuries* (Oxford, 1953),
is of fundamental importance. James Lawson has in hand an edition of the
Shrewsbury chronicle known (since the eighteenth century) as 'Dr Taylor's MS'.
Most entries relating to Shrewsbury are printed, but without conveying any
sense of their original integument in a larger whole, by W. A. Leighton, 'Early
Chronicles of Shrewsbury 1372–1603', *Transactions of the Shropshire Archaeological
and Natural History Society*, III (1880), 239–352. The story of Protestantisation in
Shrewsbury is told by Barbara Coulton, 'The Establishment of Protestantism in
a Provincial Town: a Study of Shrewsbury in the Sixteenth Century', *Sixteenth
Century Journal*, XVII (1996), 307–35.

Much of the source material for this essay is collected in the *Shropshire*
volumes of *Records of Early English Drama*, ed. Alan B. Somerset (Toronto,
1994). Anyone wishing to explore the impact of the Reformation on the
cultural life of some of England's major provincial centres should consult the
REED volumes for *Chester*, ed. Lawrence M. Clopper (Toronto, 1979), *York*, ed.
Alexandra F. Johnston and Margaret Rogerson (Toronto, 1979), *Coventry*, ed.
R. H. Ingram (Toronto, 1981), *Norwich 1540–1642*, ed. David Galloway (Toronto, 1984) and *Cambridge*, ed. Alan H. Nelson (Toronto, 1989). These materials
are the basis of discussion in Patrick Collinson, *From Iconoclasm to Iconophobia: The
Cultural Impact of the Second English Reformation* (Reading, 1986); and in his *The
Birthpangs of Protestants England: Religious and Cultural Change in the Sixteenth and
Seventeenth Centuries* (Basingstoke, 1988), which contains chapters on 'The Pro-
testant Town' and 'Protestant Culture and the Cultural Revolution'. See also
his essay 'Elizabethan and Jacobean Puritanism as Forms of Popular Religious
Culture', in *The Culture of English Puritanism, 1560–1700*, ed. C. Durston and J.
Eales (Basingstoke, 1996).

The themes of this essay may be further pursued in David Cressy, *Bonfires and
Bells: National Memory and the Protestant Calendar in Elizabethan and Stuart England*
(Berkeley and Los Angeles, 1989); David Underdown, *Revel, Riot and Rebellion:
Popular Politics and Culture in England, 1603–1660* (Oxford, 1985); and, especially,
Ronald Hutton, *The Rise and Fall of Merry England: The Ritual Year, 1400–1700*
(Oxford, 1994). For the traditional, nostalgic perspective on the decline and fall

of the pre-Reformation drama, see Harold C. Gardiner, *Mysteries' End: An Investigation of the Last Days of the Medieval Religious Stage* (New Haven, 1946); and for a balancing account of the Protestant appropriation of old dramatic genres and conventions, especially by John Bale, see Paul Whitfield White, *Theatre and Reformation: Protestantism, Patronage and Playing in Tudor England* (Cambridge, 1993).

13. RELIGIOUS SATIRE IN ENGLISH TOWNS, 1570–1640
Adam Fox

The impact of the Reformation on the social and cultural environment in English towns is most succinctly discussed in Patrick Collinson's essay 'The Protestant Town' which forms chapter 2 of his *The Birthpangs of Protestant England: Religious and Cultural Change in the Sixteenth and Seventeenth Centuries* (Basingstoke, 1988). Chapters 4 and 5 in the same volume, 'Protestant Culture and the Cultural Revolution' and 'Wars of Religion', are also invaluable for the present purpose. The former, which examines the influence of religious change in this period on attitudes towards both drama and song, may also be found with fuller references as *From Iconoclasm to Iconophobia: the Cultural Impact of the Second English Reformation* (Stenton Lecture, Reading, 1986).

A great deal of valuable material relating to the songs and plays performed in towns is being edited and published in the *Records of Early English Drama* series by the University of Toronto Press. The first twelve volumes to appear are: *York*, ed. Alexandra F. Johnston and Margaret Rogerson, 2 vols (1979); *Chester*, ed. Lawrence M. Clopper (1979); *Coventry*, ed. R. W. Ingram (1981); *Newcastle upon Tyne*, ed. J. J. Anderson (1982); *Norwich 1540–1624*, ed. David Galloway (1984); *Cumberland, Westmorland, Gloucestershire*, ed. Audrey Douglas and Peter Greenfield (1986); *Devon*, ed. John Wasson (1986); *Cambridge*, ed. Alan H. Nelson, 2 vols (1988); *Herefordshire, Worcestershire*, ed. David N. Klausner (1990); *Lancashire*, ed. David George (1991); *Shropshire*, ed. J. A. B. Somerset, 2 vols (1994); and *Somerset*, ed. James Stokes, 2 vols (1996).

The best reference works on the popular drama of this period are still those of E. K. Chambers, in particular *The Medieval Stage*, 2 vols (Oxford, 1903), and *The Elizabethan Stage*, 4 vols (Oxford, 1923). C. R. Baskervill, *The Elizabethan Jig and Related Song Drama* (Chicago, 1929), remains the essential guide to contemporary dramatic satire and balladry. Broadside ballads, particularly those of a religious nature, have been subject to detailed analysis more recently in Tessa Watt's excellent *Cheap Print and Popular Piety, 1550–1640* (Cambridge, 1991).

The study of libellous verses and plays was pioneered by C. J. Sisson in *The Lost Plays of Shakespeare's Age* (Cambridge, 1936). More detailed studies of the mocking rhymes and ballads composed in local communities at this time are provided by Martin Ingram, 'Ridings, Rough Music and Mocking Rhymes in Early Modern England', in Barry Reay (ed.), *Popular Culture in Seventeenth-Century England* (London, 1985), pp. 166–97, and Adam Fox, 'Ballads, Libels and Popular Ridicule in Jacobean England', *Past and Present*, 145 (1994), 47–83. It is in the light of this practice of 'ballading' that Patrick Collinson discusses the

Martin Marprelate tracts and their impact on subsequent religious polemic in 'Ecclesiastical Vitriol: Religious Satire in the 1590s and the Invention of Puritanism', in John Guy (ed.), *The Reign of Elizabeth I: Court and Culture in the Last Decade* (Cambridge, 1995), pp. 150–70. The genre is further explored in Alastair Bellany, 'A Poem on the Archbishop's Hearse: Puritanism, Libel, and Sedition after the Hampton Court Conference', *Journal of British Studies*, 34 (1995), 137–64.

Three scandalous dramatic performances, which involved the mockery of religion in some form, are particularly well documented and have been discussed in detail. One of these was a jig appended to the May games at South Kyme, Lincolnshire, in August 1601 and is described in N. J. O'Conor, *Godes Peace and the Queenes: Vicissitudes of a House, 1539–1615* (London, 1934), pp. 108–26. Another was an anti-Protestant interlude improvised during the performance of a play called *Saint Christopher*, staged around Christmas 1609 at Gowlthwaite Hall, the home of Sir John Yorke in Nidderdale, West Riding. On this incident, see Chambers, *The Elizabethan Stage*, vol. I, p. 328n; Christopher Howard, *Sir John Yorke of Nidderdale, 1565–1634* (London, 1939), pp. 20–6; and C. J. Sisson, 'Shakespeare Quartos as Prompt-Copies: with some Account of Cholmeley's Players and a New Shakespeare Allusion', *Review of English Studies*, XVIII (1942), 129–43. (The players involved here were known as Simpson's Company and they were also responsible for the equally well recorded libellous song-drama performed at Osmotherly at Christmas eight years before, as discussed in Sisson, *Lost Plays of Shakespeare's Age*, pp. 129–40). The third example involved references in a play produced at Kendal Castle in April 1621, occasioned by a dispute between local people and their landlords over the border custom of tenant-right. Legal records detailing the affair are printed in *Records of Early English Drama: Cumberland, Westmorland, Gloucestershire*, ed. Douglas and Greenfield, pp. 188–94, 195–8, 235–8, and there is a brief discussion in Mildred Campbell, *The English Yeoman under Elizabeth and the Early Stuarts* (London, 1960), p. 152. All of the above cases occasioned suits in the court of Star Chamber at Westminster, the records of which are preserved in the Public Record Office, London.

Two fully documented examples, also from the Star Chamber records, of libellous verses composed and sung on the arrival of a puritan minister in a town, are those involving John White at Dorchester in 1607 and Thomas Wilson at Stratford-upon-Avon in 1619. On the former, see David Underdown, *Fire from Heaven: Life in an English Town in the Seventeenth Century* (London, 1992), pp. 27–32. Among a number of discussions of the latter, see Sisson, *Lost Plays of Shakespeare's Age*, pp. 188–96; E. I. Fripp, *Shakespeare: Man and Artist* (Oxford, 1938), pp. 838–45; and Ann Hughes, 'Religion and Society in Stratford upon Avon, 1619–1638', *Midland History*, XIX (1994), 58–84.

Notes on the Contributors

Mark Byford is a manager in the London office of the Boston Consulting Group. He studied at New College, Oxford, where he was the Salvesen Junior Fellow from 1985 to 1988. He completed a DPhil thesis on the Reformation in Elizabethan Essex under the direction of Dr Penry Williams.

Patrick Carter recently completed a PhD at Cambridge University on royal taxation of the English clergy during the Reformation, and after holding a SSHRCC research fellowship at McMaster University in Hamilton, Canada, is now lecturing at St Andrews University. He is undertaking a study of the economic consequences of the Reformation for English parish clergy.

Patrick Collinson retired from the regius chair of Modern History at Cambridge, which he held from 1988, in September 1996. He previously held chairs in Sydney, Kent at Canterbury, and Sheffield. He is a Commander of the British Empire and a Fellow of the British Academy. He is a co-editor and contributor to *A History of Canterbury Cathedral* (Oxford, 1995), author of 'The Medieval Church and its Reformation', in *The Oxford Illustrated History of Christianity*, ed. J. McManners (Oxford, 1989) and of many books and articles on Elizabethan and Jacobean Protestantism and puritanism, including *The Birthpangs of Protestant England: Religious and Cultural Change in the Sixteenth and Seventeenth Centuries* (Basingstoke, 1988).

John Craig is an Assistant Professor in the Department of History at Simon Fraser University in British Columbia. He is currently working on a study entitled *English Parishioners, 1500–1700*.

Claire Cross is Professor of History at the University of York and the author of many articles and books on the English Reformation, including *Church and People, 1450–1660*.

Peter Cunich is a Lecturer in History at the University of Hong Kong. He is one of the authors of *A History of Magdalene College, Cambridge, 1428–1988*, and has edited Albert the Great's *De adhaerendo Deo*. He is now working on a financial history of the Court of Augmentations and is co-ordinating a research project which aims to produce a biographical register of the ex-religious in England and Wales *c.* 1530–1603.

Adam Fox is a lecturer in the Department of Economic and Social History at the University of Edinburgh. He is currently working on a book which examines the relationship between oral and literate forms of culture in early modern England.

Beat Kümin was a Research Fellow at Magdalene College, Cambridge, before taking up a research appointment in Berne. He is currently engaged in a comparative study of European local communities supported by the Swiss National Science Foundation. He studied at Berne and Cambridge Universities and has published a number of articles on the late medieval and early modern parish. He is the author of *The Shaping of a Community: The Rise and Reformation of the English Parish, 1400–1560* (Aldershot and Brookfield, VT: Scolar Press, 1995), and editor of two collections of essays on the impact of the Reformation in Europe.

David Lamburn is a Lecturer in Local and Regional History at the University of Leeds. He studied at York University where he completed a dissertation on 'Politics and Religion in Sixteenth-Century Beverley'.

Caroline Litzenberger is an Assistant Professor of History at West Virginia University. She studied history at Portland State University (in Portland, Oregon) and at the University of Cambridge where she received her PhD in 1993. Her dissertation on responses of the Gloucestershire laity to official religious policies is being published by Cambridge University Press as *The English Reformation and the Laity: Gloucestershire, 1540–1580*.

Diarmaid MacCulloch is Professor in the Faculty of Theology of Oxford University, and is a Fellow of St Cross College. His books include *Suffolk and the Tudors: Politics and Religion in an English County, 1500–1600* (Oxford: Clarendon Press, 1986, which won the Whitfield Prize of the Royal Historical Society in1986), and *The Later Reformation in England, 1547–1603* (Basingstoke: Macmillan, 1990). His *Thomas Cranmer: A Life* (London: Yale University Press, 1996) won the Whitford Biography of the Year award in 1996.

Jeanette Martin, educated at Henley-on-Thames, was a journalist for some years, then travelled worldwide before taking her BA (Hons) and PhD degrees at the University of Reading.

William Sheils is Senior Lecturer in Economic and Social History at the University of York. He has written books on Midland puritanism and on the English Reformation, and several articles on the religious and social history of the period. He was editor, latterly co-editor, of Studies in Church History from 1981 to 1990.

Sarah Sheils is Director of Curriculum at the Mount School, York, where she also teaches history. She took an interdisciplinary MA at the Centre for Medieval Studies at York, the dissertation for which provided the basis for this contribution.

Robert Tittler is Professor of History at Concordia University in Montreal. He is the author of many articles and books including *The Reign of Mary I* and *Architecture and Power, the Town Hall and the English Urban Community, 1500–1640*.

Index